'This a wonderful compilation of clinically ric
would appeal to both accomplished therapists ai
— **Jeffery Yo**

G000160369

'The editors have assembled a great line up (
years of experience of Schema Therapy approac
to the name on the cover — introducing many ~~~~~~ ~~~~~~~, ~~~~~~~~~ ~~~~~
using imagery interventions, that can be adopted and implemented in a range of
settings. This book highlights again that therapists can show flexibility with the
techniques we use if we are true to the underlying principles and conceptual
model.

This is a book both for experienced practitioners and those new to the ideas;
for those providing 'true' Schema Therapy and also for those who wish to use
these ideas to inform their CBT. This is an intensely practical book and I predict
you'll be using it and recommending it for years to come'.

— **Nick Grey,** Lead Consultant Clinical Psychologist,
Sussex Partnership NHS Foundation Trust, UK

'I am so pleased to endorse this extraordinary body of work offered by Gillian
Heath and Helen Startup, *Creative Methods in Schema Therapy: Advances and Innovation in Clinical Practice.* It is an important contribution to psychotherapists worldwide, a comprehensive collection of talented colleagues from the Schema
Therapy global community. This instrumental book, informed by the work of
Dr. Jeffrey Young (founder of the model), offers chapters that delve into both
the theory and application of the Schema Therapy approach. Gillian and Helen
are highly experienced and talented Schema Therapy practitioners and educators,
who have put forth a rigorous effort in bringing this edited book to fruition,
resulting in a thoughtful and relevant guide for addressing some of the most challenging treatment populations in the most effective ways. This evidence-based
model is beautifully represented throughout the book with clearly articulated
illustrations of robust Schema Therapy conceptualization, assessment tools, and
treatment strategies for meeting unmet emotional needs and healing lifelong maladaptive patterns of behavior.

I am deeply grateful for Gillian and Helen's invitation to participate in this
remarkable book, and confidently recommend it to the professional community
as a valuable resource for your clinical library'.

— **Wendy Behary**, Past-President,
International Society of Schema Therapy (ISST)

'This book lives up to the promise of its title and is a welcome addition to the
resources available to clinicians practising Schema Therapy, whether just beginning or already experienced. Psychotherapy is a craft and within the integrative
framework of the Schema Therapy model for conceptualising cases, there is considerable room for the creativity and artistry of the therapist in responding to the
challenges we inevitably meet when responding to the unique features of the

individuals we work with. Extensively illustrated with accessible clinical examples, the chapters of the book provide clear and helpful perspectives on assessment, case conceptualisation, and the application of a wide range of specific interventions (including imagery, chair work, relational work with reparenting and standard CBT methods). These are applied to a range of clinical problems including, but not limited to, depression, anxiety, trauma and complex trauma, eating disorders, forensic populations and working with couples. There are contributions from a diverse range of authors who reflect the originality, diversity, creativity, and clinical acumen that increasingly characterise our Schema Therapy community. I look forward to recommending this book to my colleagues and supervisees'.

– David Edwards, Professor Emeritus, Department of Psychology,
Rhodes University, South Africa; President,
International Society of Schema Therapy

'*Creative Methods* is the first overview of the current state and new developments in Schema Therapy (ST) since ... [a] handbook in 2012. In addition to hands-on descriptions of established techniques such as imagery and chair work, it adds some new topics to the table including body awareness, treating complex PTSD and schema informed brief CBT. Everything in the book has a strong focus on practical and clinical applications, especially of new creative techniques. This is unique! Besides some renowned authors it also brings a large number of new writers "on stage", especially from the Anglo-Australian sphere, reflecting the growth of ST worldwide. The contributions are profound and provide depth to the reader's understanding of the model. Therapists new to ST, wanting a broad overview, as well as experienced schema therapists looking for more depth and detailed guidance, will find what they are looking for! Among the increasing number of Schema Therapy publications, this book is surely one of the most valuable and a *must have* for a comprehensive library on Schema Therapy. I am sure this book will be a success story'.

– Eckhard Roediger, Past-President,
International Society of Schema Therapy (ISST);
Director of Schema Therapy Institute, Germany

Creative Methods in Schema Therapy

Creative Methods in Schema Therapy captures current trends and developments in Schema Therapy in rich clinical detail, with a vividness that inspires and equips the reader to integrate these new ways of working directly into their practice.

It begins with creative adaptations to assessment and formulation, including the integration of body methods to promote engagement and to bring about early emotional change. Other chapters introduce innovative methods to lift a formulation off the page and it goes on to bring to life new developments across all aspects of the ST change repertoire, including limited reparenting, imagery, trauma processing, chair work, the therapy relationship, empathic confrontation and endings. For the specialist, there are chapters on working with forensic modes, eating disorders and couples work. Finally, the book includes chapters on the integration of key principles and techniques from Cognitive Behavioural Therapy, Emotion Focused Therapy and Compassionate Mind work into a core schema model.

The book will appeal not only to fully fledged schema therapists, but also to junior therapists and therapists from other modalities who are willing to enhance their ways of working.

Gillian Heath is a Clinical Psychologist and Co-Director of the Schema Therapy Associates Training Programme. She has co-authored a number of highly regarded Schema Therapy resources, including the Schema Therapy Toolkit, an online video training tool demonstrating core and advanced Schema Therapy techniques.

Helen Startup is a Consultant Clinical Psychologist and joint Head of Psychology for the Sussex Partnership NHS Eating Disorders Service. She is also an honorary Senior Lecturer with Sussex University and Co-Directs Schema Therapy School, UK.

Creative Methods in Schema Therapy

Advances and Innovation in
Clinical Practice

**Edited by Gillian Heath and
Helen Startup**

LONDON AND NEW YORK

First published 2020
by Routledge
2 Park Square, Milton Park, Abingdon, Oxon OX14 4RN

and by Routledge
52 Vanderbilt Avenue, New York, NY 10017

Routledge is an imprint of the Taylor & Francis Group, an informa business

British Library Cataloguing-in-Publication Data
A catalogue record for this book is available from the British Library

Library of Congress Cataloging-in-Publication Data
Names: Heath, Gillian, editor.
Title: Creative methods in schema therapy : advances and innovation in clinical practice / edited by Gillian Heath and Helen Startup.
Description: Milton Park, Abingdon, Oxon ; New York : Routledge, 2020. | Includes bibliographical references and index. |
Identifiers: LCCN 2020014143 (print) | LCCN 2020014144 (ebook) | ISBN 9780815398776 (hardback) | ISBN 9780815398820 (paperback) | ISBN 9781351171847 (ebook)
Subjects: LCSH: Schema-focused cognitive therapy.
Classification: LCC RC489.S34 C74 2020 (print) | LCC RC489.S34 (ebook) | DDC 616.89/1425–dc23
LC record available at https://lccn.loc.gov/2020014143
LC ebook record available at https://lccn.loc.gov/2020014144

ISBN: 978-0-815-39877-6 (hbk)
ISBN: 978-0-815-39882-0 (pbk)
ISBN: 978-1-351-17184-7 (ebk)

Typeset in Bembo
by Swales & Willis, Exeter, Devon, UK

MIX
Paper from
responsible sources
FSC   FSC® C013056
www.fsc.org

Printed and bound in Great Britain by
TJ Books Limited, Padstow, Cornwall

To Simon, Lauren and Luke, my lovely family, who bring so much happiness, humour and learning at so many levels. Also, to Will Swift, who has taught me more about being a good therapist than I can quantify.

Gillian Heath

To my husband, Simon, and to my three children, Maisie, Charlie and Rosalie. You continue to teach me so much about love, friendship and healthy attachment. I love you all dearly.

Helen Startup

Contents

Foreword

Schema Therapy (ST) is an increasingly popular approach for treating chronic conditions related to characterological factors. There are several primary reasons for its popularity: first, the premise that chronic frustration of early core developmental needs is at the heart of adult psychopathology (especially when manifesting at the most severe end of the spectrum) makes intuitive sense to both therapists and patients alike. It also provides a normalising and compassionate frame for naming the contextual and relational origins of psychological distress. Moreover, the integrative nature of the treatment (offering experiential, as well as cognitive and behavioural ways of working) is highly attractive, as it affords multiple potential routes into clinical change. Specifically, the integration of experiential techniques into ST has shown itself to be a powerful contributor to treatment effectiveness, and comes into its own when we consider how best to support patients who have endured early and prolonged trauma. Furthermore, the central tenet of limited reparenting allows therapists to attune to their patient's core unmet needs and to provide emotionally corrective, schema healing experiences. This relational component is welcomed by patients as, sometimes, their very first experience of attuned, safe relating. Therapists report having previously felt constrained by an emphasis on 'head level' logic among traditions such as cognitive–behavioural and psychoanalytic approaches, with too little in the way of a felt relational connection or 'heart level' change in the patient's belief and attachment systems.

The concept of schema modes, which can be used to formulate via a 'schema mode map', acts as a shared account of an individual's full 'self' rather than merely a summary of their symptoms. As therapy progresses it provides a 'road map' for talking about the unfolding process of therapy and of planning and tracking therapy goals. Indeed, qualitative studies with patient groups suggests that the schema mode model is believed to be one of the most powerful components of therapy. Last, but not least, the positive results shown by treatment studies further raises the profile of ST – the treatment model has now been successfully tested across almost all personality disorder presentations, demonstrating high acceptability and good treatment effectiveness. Adaptations have also been developed for treating chronic depression, complex eating disorders and dissociative identity disorder, with outcome studies complete or in process.

Another interesting observation is the recent surge in integration of ST techniques within other treatment modalities, such as cognitive–behaviour therapy, couples therapy, and child/youth therapy, and the use of such techniques as 'stand-alone' treatments for targeting core symptoms for some specific clinical problems. The evidence base for one of the core techniques, imagery rescripting, is rapidly expanding, with clinical trials documenting its effectiveness over a range of disorders, including (complex) PTSD, social anxiety disorder, body dysmorphic disorder, depression, and others.

There are currently several books available that offer introductions to ST or discuss specific applications of the model. Typically, these books describe the basic applications of core methods. However, these core ways of working have evolved to better meet the needs of our patients, to improve outcomes for more complex patients and to do so across a broader range of settings. Such variations and advancements are necessary for the evolution of ST and for it to reach its potential. Although clinicians might occasionally be exposed to these creative initiatives in specialised workshops or trainings, as yet, there is no single text offering a rich summary of these innovations to date. This book offers exactly this and provides a comprehensive and exciting overview of developments across a wide range of methods, including case conceptualisation, limited reparenting, imagery, chair work and using the therapy relationship for change. Each innovation is brought to life by key principles and clinical example, and, as such, meets a need for those who want to further deepen their clinical skills and better get alongside their patients to promote clinical change and well-being. With the chapters written by leading schema therapists, this book provides a comprehensive and high quality overview of the latest developments in ST.

Arnoud Arntz
Professor of Clinical Psychology at the
University of Amsterdam

Contributors

Arnoud Arntz is Professor of Clinical Psychology at the University of Amsterdam in the Netherlands. He is one of the founders and innovators of Schema Therapy and has published extensively on the application of Schema Therapy for complex presentations.

Travis Atkinson is the Director of the Schema Therapy Training Center of New York (STTC). He helped establish the Schema Therapy Institute of New York, and worked as a staff member of the Cognitive Therapy Center of New York with Dr Jeff Young for many years. Travis is a Certified Advanced Individual and Couples' schema therapist, supervisor, and trainer. He was awarded his certification as a Gottman Method Couples Therapist at the Gottman Institute in Seattle in 2006. Travis was supervised and trained by Sue Johnson, the founder of Emotionally Focused Couple Therapy, and was awarded certification as an emotionally focused couples therapist and supervisor in 2010. Since 2014, Travis has served on the Executive Board as Public Affairs Coordinator for the International Society of Schema Therapy (ISST), and is the chair of the Schema Couples Therapy Workgroup and Committee. He has trained therapists internationally for more than 15 years, and is the author of 'Healing partners in a relationship' in the *Handbook of Schema Therapy* (Wiley: 2012).

Anna Balfour, a UK Chartered Psychologist, has been working with Schema Therapy since 1997, training in the first UK cohort with Jeffrey Young; she is an Advanced Level schema therapist trainer-supervisor. After working in Liberia with war trauma survivors, Anna moved to the USA in 2006 and is a Licensed State Counselor. She taught as an Adjunct Professor in the Graduate Psychology programme at Eastern University and built her private practice. Anna established 'Schema Therapy Pennsylvania', a growing group of schema therapists who meet for peer supervision and training. She enjoys integrating 'Improvisation' into Schema Therapy and ran a skills workshop on 'Bridges to Imagery' at the 2018 ISST conference in Amsterdam. Anna now lives in NW Florida, where she supervises and works with therapists on personal development and practice building.

More recently, Anna has pursued her interest in re-envisioning what it means to be fully human, incorporating ecological and soul-orientated understandings of the psyche, and strengths-based positive psychology, with Schema Therapy.

Wendy Behary is the founder and director of the Cognitive Therapy Center of New Jersey and co-director (with Dr Jeffrey Young) of the Schema Therapy Institutes of NJ–NYC. She has been treating clients, training professionals and supervising psychotherapists for more than 25 years. Wendy was on the faculty of the Cognitive Therapy Center and Schema Therapy Institute of New York (until merging in 2012 with the NJ Institute), where she trained and worked with Dr Jeffrey Young since 1989. She is a Founding Fellow and consulting supervisor for the Academy of Cognitive Therapy (Aaron T. Beck Institute). Wendy served as the President of the Executive Board of the International Society of Schema Therapy (ISST) from 2010–2014 and is currently the chairperson for the Schema Therapy Development Programs Committee. Wendy Behary has co-authored several chapters and articles on Schema Therapy. She is the author of *Disarming the Narcissist* (New Harbinger, 2013), which has been translated into 12 languages.

David Bernstein is a Clinical Psychologist (PhD, New York University, 1990) and Associate Professor of Psychology at Maastricht University in the Netherlands, where he has served as Professor of Forensic Psychotherapy (endowed Chair, 2010–2018), and Chair of the Section on Forensic Psychology (2010–2015). He is a former President of the Association for Research on Personality Disorders (2001–2005) and Vice President of the International Society for the Study of Personality Disorders (2003–2007). He was also Vice President of the International Society of Schema Therapy (2010–2012) and is an Advanced Level schema therapist and Schema Therapy supervisor. He is the author or co-author of more than 120 publications on psychotherapy, personality disorders, forensic psychology, childhood trauma, and addictions, and the co-author, with Eshkol Rafaeli and Jeffrey Young, of *Schema Therapy: Distinctive Features* and the DVD series, *Schema Therapy: Working with Modes*, with Remco van der Wijngaart. He is also the author of the *Childhood Trauma Questionnaire*, a reliable and valid self-report questionnaire for child abuse and neglect, used worldwide. He is the creator of the *iModes*, a cartoon-based system for working with schema modes, and the founder of SafePath Solutions, a team-based programme for adults and youth with personality disorders, aggression, and addiction. He was the Principal Investigator on a recently completed randomised clinical trial of Schema Therapy for forensic patients with personality disorders in the Netherlands.

Benjamin Boecking received his PhD and DClinPsy from the Institute of Psychiatry, Psychology & Neuroscience (IoPPN), London. He is a Principal Clinical Psychologist and qualified schema therapist with several years' post-qualification experience in the assessment and treatment of psychological difficulties and in conducting research. He currently works at the Tinnituscentre at Charité Universitätsmedizin Berlin, Germany, where he conceptualises, implements, conducts and evaluates effective psychological treatment provision and supervises other clinicians in delivering this work. His research interest lies in developing the evidence base for therapeutic approaches to alleviate tinnitus-related distress and other somatoform conditions, and he is currently evaluating the application of schema-focused interventions in this area. Previous research investigated psycho-biological mechanisms of effective psychological treatment for social anxiety disorder as well as cognitive processes underlying interpersonal stress generation in depression. Across a variety of settings, Dr Boecking is actively involved in training students and clinicians on a variety of topics, including personality disorders, clinical interviewing and principles of cognitive–behavioural therapy.

Katrina Boterhoven de Haan is a Clinical Psychologist and a PhD candidate with research interests in the area of trauma and complex PTSD. Her work experience across both government and not-for-profit sectors has predominately been in the treatment of trauma, in particular complex presentations, with children, young people and adults. She has trained in Schema Therapy and published research investigating different treatment processes of Schema Therapy, CBT and Psychodynamic Therapy, and how Schema Therapy can be used to treat PTSD.

Janis Briedis is a Principal Practitioner Psychologist working in private practice in London, having worked in a complex case service in the National Health Service (NHS) for many years. He is an accredited Advanced Level schema therapist, supervisor and trainer and has been involved with Schema Therapy for over a decade. Janis is a co-director of Schema Therapy School and runs courses in the UK and overseas. He is also a visiting lecturer at a number of universities in the UK and teaches Schema Therapy, Cognitive-Behavioural Therapy and trauma-focused approaches to psychology students. Janis has completed training in sensorimotor psychotherapy and has an interest in the integration of therapeutic modalities to aid clients with complex presentations.

Suzanne Byrne is the Joint Course Director of the IoPPN's Postgraduate Diploma in CBT (IAPT Programmes) Kings College London. She has extensive experience of successfully delivering CBT training and of working with complex presentations of anxiety disorders and depression. She has trained in Schema Therapy and has an interest in using schema informed therapy in time limited settings in the NHS.

Tara Cutland Green is a Consultant Clinical Psychologist based primarily in London. She was trained by Jeffrey Young at the New York Institute of

Schema Therapy, becoming a certified Advanced Level schema therapist and trainer-supervisor. She has delivered Schema Therapy training in the UK, Poland and Bulgaria and is co-director, with Dr Gillian Heath, of Schema Therapy Associates Training. Together; she and Gillian created *Schema Therapy Toolkit*, a set of training videos that has been well received across the globe, and co-authored the chapter 'Schema therapy' in the *Handbook of Adult Clinical Psychology* (Routledge, 2016). She has a background in the NHS and independent practice in the UK and has also lived in New Zealand, where she worked in a personality disorder team and served on New Zealand's national personality disorders committee. She works with a wide range of psychological difficulties and has a special interest in working with faith in the therapy process.

Joan Farrell, PhD, is an Adjunct Professor of Clinical Psychology at Indiana University-Purdue University Indianapolis and was a Clinical Professor at Indiana University School of Medicine (IUSM), in Psychiatry for 25 years. She is the Research Director of the IUSM/Eskenazi Health Center for Borderline Personality Disorder Treatment & Research. She has co-authored three books on Schema Therapy, which have been translated into multiple languages, as well as book chapters and research articles. Her 40-year career has focused on psychotherapy training and research. She provides Schema Therapy training and supervision internationally. As a contemporary of Jeffrey Young, she worked with Ida Shaw to integrate cognitive and experiential interventions to develop corrective emotional experiences when treating borderline personality disorder (BPD) in groups. This led to the development of Group Schema Therapy in the 1990s. This model was first successfully tested in a trial supported by the National Institute of Mental Health, USA and currently in a five-country trial with 500 patients co-led by Joan and Arnoud Arntz. Joan is an Advanced Level Schema Therapy trainer-supervisor and co-directs the Schema Therapy Institute Midwest, Indianapolis. She was the ISST Coordinator for Training & Certification, 2012–2018 and is now the chair of the ISST Training & Certification Advisory Board.

Cathy Flanagan received her PhD from University College Dublin (UCD), Ireland, and held post-doctoral fellowships with Dr Richard Lazarus at the University of California-Berkeley, and Dr Aaron Beck at the Center for Cognitive Therapy at the University of Pennsylvania. Before relocating to the US, she was Director of Psychological Services, St Patrick's Hospital, Dublin, with teaching positions at UCD and Trinity College Dublin. In her role as Clinical Coordinator and Senior Supervisor at the Schema Therapy Institute of New York with Dr Jeffrey Young, she was involved in the early development of the ST model. As well as providing training and supervision in the US and Ireland, Cathy has published one book, *People and Change*, and written numerous chapters and articles, most recently on psychological needs, coping modes, and internal working models. Cathy is a Member of the Editorial Board, *Journal of Psychotherapy Integration*, and a Founding Fellow, Academy of Cognitive Therapy (ACT). She is on the Schema Therapy Development Programs Committee (STDP) of the International Society for Schema Therapy (ISST), and is Honorary President, Schema Therapy Association of Ireland (STAI). Cathy is currently in private practice in in New York City.

Chris Hayes is a Clinical Psychologist and Advanced Level schema therapist based in Perth, Western Australia. He has had extensive experience in both government and private settings working with clients with complex psychological presentations. Since 2005, he has been practising as an Advanced schema therapist, supervisor and trainer, having completed Certification in Schema Therapy at the Schema Therapy Institute in New York City (USA) with Dr Jeffery Young. He has presented workshops throughout Europe, Asia and Australasia. He is the Director of Schema Therapy Training Australia. In addition to the provision of Schema Therapy training and supervision, he is currently employed with the Health Department of Western Australia as a Senior Clinical Psychologist (within a specialist service working with those who have experienced recent or childhood sexual trauma). He has co-produced two DVD/video releases *Fine Tuning Imagery Rescripting* and *Fine Tuning Chair Work in Schema Therapy*, both of which are highly recommended (and the first of their kind internationally). He has previously served as Secretary of the Board for the International Society of Schema therapy (ISST).

Gillian Heath is a Clinical Psychologist based in London. She was trained by Dr Jeffrey Young at the New York Institute of Schema Therapy and is an Advanced Level schema therapist and trainer-supervisor. She is co-director, with Dr Tara Cutland Green, of Schema Therapy Associates Training, a programme approved by the ISST since 2012. Together, they created the *Schema Therapy Toolkit*, a set of training videos covering core and advanced Schema Therapy methods; and co-authored the chapter 'Schema therapy' in the *Handbook of Adult Clinical Psychology* (Routledge, 2016). She has a background in the NHS and independent practice and has a special interest in working with complex trauma, personality level difficulties and eating disorders, as well as more common mental health problems, such as anxiety and depression.

Chris Irons is a Clinical Psychologist based in London. He has been working alongside Professor Paul Gilbert and other colleagues in the theoretical and clinical developments and adaptations of Compassion Focused Therapy (CFT) (Gilbert, 2009; Gilbert & Irons, 2005, 2014) as a science-based psychotherapeutic approach. In his clinical work, he uses CFT in working with people suffering from a variety of mental health problems, including persistent depression, PTSD, obsessive–compulsive disorder (OCD), bipolar affective disorder, eating disorders and schizophrenia, along with a variety of personality disorders. Chris is a board member of the Compassionate Mind Foundation, a charitable organisation aiming to: 'Promote wellbeing through the scientific understanding and application of compassion'. He regularly presents to academic, professional and lay audiences on CFT and, more broadly, the science of compassion. He is interested in how compassion may improve individual well-being, relationship satisfaction and facilitate positive group and organisational change. Among other things, he is currently researching the role of compassion and rumination in depression; the role of compassion and shame in psychosis; and the role of self and other compassion in relationship quality. He recently published a book on depression, and is currently writing three books on CFT.

Anna Lavender is a Principal Clinical Psychologist at South London and Maudsley NHS Foundation Trust. She has over 20 years' experience in CBT treatment and supervision, and is also a qualified schema therapist and supervisor. She teaches training psychologists on interpersonal processes in therapy, and has worked extensively with individuals with personality disorders. She is joint UK lead on an international trial of the use of Group Schema Therapy with individuals with borderline personality disorder. She is co-author of *The Oxford Guide to Metaphors in CBT* (2010), and is currently co-author, with Dr Stirling Moorey, of *The Therapeutic Relationship in CBT*.

Christopher William Lee works in private practice and has an adjunct appointment at the University of Western Australia. He is a Certified Trainer by both the International Society of Schema Therapy (ISST) and the EMDR International Association. He conducts therapist training workshops on Schema Therapy and trauma treatments throughout Australia and overseas. He has published research on personality disorders, the assessment of schemas, and PTSD. He has received two International Society for Traumatic Stress Studies awards and three International EMDR Association awards for research excellence, the first in 1999 and the most recent in 2019. He was the 2011 recipient of the Australian Psychological Society's Ian Campbell Memorial Award for contributions as a scientist–practitioner to clinical psychology in Australia. He is currently a principal investigator in two international multi-centred randomised controlled trials, one in treating complex PTSD and the other using Schema Therapy for borderline personality disorder. In the past, he served on the ISST Board as the research co-ordinator.

George Lockwood is the Director of the Schema Therapy Institute Midwest, Kalamazoo and is a Founding Fellow of the Academy of Cognitive Therapy. He completed a postdoctoral fellowship in cognitive therapy under the supervision of Aaron T. Beck in 1982, and has training in psychoanalytic psychotherapy and object-relations approaches. He is an Advanced Certified schema therapist trainer-supervisor, was elected to serve on the Executive Board of the International Society of Schema Therapy for eight years, has written a number of articles and chapters on cognitive and Schema Therapy, has played a central role in the development and validation of two new Schema Therapy constructs (Positive Schemas and Core Negative and Positive Parenting Patterns) and three associated inventories. He has trained and worked with Dr Jeffery Young since 1981 (participating in the early development of Schema Therapy), and has maintained a private practice for the past 35 years.

Offer Maurer, PhD, is a Clinical Psychologist, the director of The New Wave in Psychotherapy Program at the Hertzeliya Interdisciplinary Center (IDC) in Israel and the co-founder/co-director of the Israeli Institute for Schema Therapy. He is the former Chairperson of the Israeli Forum for Relational Psychoanalysis and Psychotherapy. Dr Maurer is a guest lecturer at various international programmes on LGBT and sexuality issues, Schema Therapy and psychotherapy integration. He is the founding director of the 'Gay-Friendly Therapists Team' (2001), the first gay-friendly psychotherapy institute in Israel. Based in New York, he offers Schema Therapy informed life coaching for individuals and groups.

Tijana Mirović holds a PhD in Clinical Psychology and is an Advanced Level schema therapist and supervisor with the International Society of Schema Therapy (ISST), systemic family therapist and Rational Emotive Behavioral therapist (Associate Fellow of Albert Ellis Institute). She was an Associate Professor at the university and is now running a counselling centre in Belgrade, Serbia. She did her Master's and PhD theses in Schema Therapy and has published a number of papers on early maladaptive schemas and their relation to societal trauma, family functioning, attachment and various symptoms. Additionally, she has made numerous presentations on Schema Therapy throughout former Yugoslavia and has published the first book on Schema Therapy in the Serbian language. This created an interest in Schema Therapy and led to the opening of the Schema Therapy Centre Belgrade – the first accredited Schema Therapy training centre in the region. Since then, and within this training centre, Dr Mirović has been conducting Schema Therapy training and supervision in Serbia, Croatia, Bosnia & Herzegovina, Montenegro and Slovenia.

Stirling Moorey, is a Consultant Psychiatrist in CBT at South London and Maudsley NHS Trust and Visiting Senior Lecturer at the Institute of Psychiatry, Psychology and Neuroscience, and was formerly SLaM Professional Head of Psychotherapy. He has been clinical lead for psychotherapy departments at Barts and Maudsley Hospitals and has extensive experience of treating complex presentations of depression and anxiety. He is co-founder of the IOPPN Postgraduate Diploma in CBT and has 30 years' experience in training and supervising many professional groups in CBT. He has also trained in Cognitive Analytic Therapy, Schema Therapy and

MBCT. He regularly lectures on alliance ruptures and the supervisory relationship. His research interest is in the field of psycho-oncology and he is co-author of *The Oxford Guide to CBT for People with Cancer* (2012). Other relevant publications include 'Is it them or is it me? Transference and countertransference in CBT', in *How to Become a More Effective CBT Therapist* (2014).

Limor Navot has an MA in Child Clinical and Educational Psychology from the Hebrew University of Jerusalem. She worked for several years as a psychologist in the Israeli Prison Service, with extensive experience in diagnosing and treating prisoners who have committed serious violent offences, as well as treating personality disorders. She is active in the world of Schema Therapy, lecturing and giving workshops at international conferences. She is the head of SafePath Israel, where she gives training and supervision in SafePath, a Schema Therapy based method for working with teams. She has a private practice in Maastricht, the Netherlands.

Anna Oldershaw is a Senior Clinical Psychologist with further training in Emotion Focused Therapy (EFT). She delivers EFT therapy and supervision and is a member of the International Society for Emotion Focused Therapy (isEFT). Alongside Les Greenberg and Robert Elliott, she co-facilitates EFT training at the Emotion Focused Therapy Institute at Salomons Institute for Applied Psychology, in South-East England. Prior to her clinical training, Anna completed a PhD focusing on anorexia nervosa and emotion and has published extensively on the topic. She now works in an NHS Eating Disorder Service. In 2016, Anna received a National Institute of Health Research fellowship to fund the development and testing of an emotion focused therapy for adults with anorexia nervosa (the SPEAKS study), working alongside Dr Helen Startup and Professor Tony Lavender.

Poul Perris, MD, Licensed Psychotherapist and Supervisor, is the Director of the Swedish Institute for CBT & Schema Therapy in Stockholm, Sweden. He was the Founding President of the International Society for Schema Therapy (ISST) from 2008 to 2010, and served as President of the Swedish Association for Cognitive Behavioural Therapies (SABCT) from 2010 to 2016. Poul was originally trained and supervised by Dr Jeffrey Young in Schema Therapy and is a Certified schema therapist, supervisor and trainer for individuals and couples. He specialises in the treatment of personality disorders, and in couples therapy for complex relational problems. Poul has published a handbook on Schema Therapy (in Swedish), and also co-authored several chapters in English textbooks on Schema Therapy. He has been teaching and supervising Cognitive-Behavioural therapists and schema therapists internationally for over a decade.

Eshkol Rafaeli is a Clinical Psychologist (in the US and Israel), a Professor in the psychology department and neuroscience programme at Bar-Ilan

University in Israel, and a research scientist at Columbia University's Barnard College. He is director of the Affect and Relationships lab, which studies close relationship processes, as well as affective and interpersonal processes in psychopathology and psychotherapy. He has been a schema therapist since joining Jeffrey Young's Cognitive Therapy Center of New York in 2002, later becoming a supervisor in the NY programme, and (after his move to Israel in 2009) was one of the founders of the Israeli Institute of Schema Therapy. He has supervised, lectured and written about Schema Therapy extensively. For example, he co-authored (with David Bernstein and Jeffrey Young) *Schema Therapy: Distinctive Features* for Routledge, and more recently contributed chapters to edited volumes on *Working with Emotion in Cognitive Behavioral Therapy* (Guilford Press, 2014) and on *The Self in Understanding and Treating Psychological Disorders* (Oxford University Press, 2016). He has been an editorial board member of several journals, including *Psychotherapy Research*, *Behavior Therapy*, and *Journal of Research in Personality*.

Dan Roberts is a Cognitive Therapist and Advanced Level Certified schema therapist. Dan works with adults at his private practice in North London, where he treats people with developmental and acute trauma, as well as other complex psychological problems. His training encompasses humanistic counselling, integrative psychotherapy, cognitive and Schema Therapy. Dan is also the founder of Schema Therapy Skills, through which he provides training workshops to mental health professionals across the UK. Before retraining as a therapist, Dan was a health journalist for over a decade, writing for many of the UK's major newspapers and magazines. He continues to write articles about psychology and psychotherapy, as well as working to de-stigmatise mental health problems on his website and in the media.

Florian Ruths is a Consultant Psychiatrist at the Maudsley Hospital in London. He is also a trainer and supervisor in CBT. Florian has been co-leading the Maudsley Schema Therapy Service since 2014. He has been Principal Investigator for the International Multicentre Randomised Controlled Trial of Group Schema Therapy for EUPD (Chief Investigator A. Arntz, Amsterdam) for the UK sites. Florian has an interest in investigating the impact of cluster B personality traits on child–parent relationships and has developed a schema-based model of attachment suppression. As lead for the Maudsley Mindfulness Service, Florian has been delivering mindfulness based cognitive therapy groups (MBCT) for patients with chronic depression and anxiety problems for 15 years, with Stirling Moorey. He has also designed a programme based on MBCT to improve well-being and resilience in health professionals. Florian teaches Cognitive-Behavioural Therapy and MBCT on two MSc courses in London and Kent. He has published in the areas of MBCT, anxiety and depression.

Rachel Samson is a Clinical Psychologist, BPsych (Hons) MPsych (Clinical), and co-director of the Centre for Schema Therapy Australia. Rachel has extensive experience working with individuals, couples and families with complex psychological presentations. She is interested in the clinical application of attachment theory across the lifespan. She was trained internationally in the assessment of parent–child attachment and maternal sensitivity in the John Bowlby–Mary Ainsworth tradition. Rachel has Advanced International Certification in Schema Therapy (ISST) and has delivered invited seminars and workshops, published research, and presented at national and international conferences on Schema Therapy, attachment, and high sensitivity. In 2018, Rachel presented an expanded model of Schema Therapy for highly sensitive and emotionally reactive clients with Dr Jeffrey Young and Dr George Lockwood at the ISST International Conference in Amsterdam; the workshop was titled 'Sweeping life transformations: The further reaches of Schema Therapy'.

Ida Shaw is an Advanced Certified schema therapist and trainer-supervisor in individual, group and child–adolescent Schema Therapy (ST) with the International Society of Schema Therapy (ISST). She founded and co-directs the Indianapolis Center of the Schema Therapy Institute Midwest, with ISST Approved Certification Training Programmes in individual, group and child–adolescent Schema Therapy. She provides training and supervision internationally. She has co-authored three books on ST, which have been translated into multiple languages, and numerous book chapters. Ida is Director of Training at the Center for Borderline Personality Disorder Treatment and Research of the Indiana University School of Medicine and Eskenazi Health. She has held the same position for the five-country international trial testing Group Schema Therapy (GST) for borderline personality disorder, and research trials in the Netherlands adapting GST for avoidant personality disorder and social phobia and individual ST for dissociative identity disorder. She chairs the ISST Work Group on Child and Adolescent Schema Therapy that defined certification standards for that area. She has contributed extensively to the experiential interventions of Schema Therapy and, with Joan Farrell, developed and tested a model of Group Schema Therapy which is being used worldwide.

Susan Simpson is a Clinical Psychologist and director of Schema Therapy Scotland. She is an Advanced Schema Therapy trainer-supervisor, providing specialist training on Schema Therapy for personality disorders, eating disorders, and PTSD, both locally in the UK and internationally. Susan is currently secretary of the executive board of the ISST. She has published widely on Schema Therapy for complex eating disorders, and more recently on the role of Early Maladaptive Schemas and modes in burnout among psychotherapists. She recently co-edited *Schema Therapy for Eating Disorders* (2019, Routledge). She currently works part-time within NHS Scotland, and is an adjunct academic at the University of South Australia.

Helen Startup is Consultant Clinical Psychologist and joint Head of Psychology for the Sussex Partnership NHS Eating Disorders Service; she is also a Senior Research Fellow with the Trust and Honorary Senior Lecture with Sussex University. Prior to clinical training, she completed a PhD in Psychological Mechanisms of Anxiety and Worry and publishes widely in academic journals. She has been a co-applicant on four funded multi-site RCTs, testing interventions across various aspects of psychopathology (psychosis, eating disorders, personality disorders). She recently co-authored the *Cognitive Interpersonal Therapy Workbook for Treating Anorexia Nervosa* (Routledge) which is a NICE-adopted psychological intervention. She is an accredited CBT therapist-supervisor and Advanced Level schema therapist. Along with Janis Briedis, she co-directs Schema Therapy School UK Ltd, which offers specialist Schema Therapy workshops and certification training in the UK.

Olivia Thrift is an Advanced Certified schema therapist, trainer and supervisor as well as an experienced CFT practitioner and certified mindfulness and yoga teacher. Originally from the UK, she worked in the NHS and secure forensic settings for over 15 years as a Senior Counselling Psychologist. She specialises in working with people with a diagnosis of personality disorder and complex trauma. Olivia currently lives in Northern California and works with the California Schema Therapy Training Program as a supervisor and instructor. She also works for the San Francisco DBT Center and continues to provide psychological therapy and supervision remotely through The Psychology Company, a UK based therapy practice she founded. She has published research in the area of identity and trauma.

Christina Vallianatou completed her first degree in psychology at the University of Wales, Cardiff and her Doctorate in Counselling Psychology at the University of Surrey. She is an Advanced Level schema therapist, supervisor and trainer and an EMDR therapist. She has worked for the National Health Service (UK) and currently works in private practice in Athens. She has years of teaching experience in different academic settings and has taught Schema Therapy in Serbia and Greece. She has psychotherapeutic experience in complex trauma, dissociation, personality disorders and eating disorders. Her research interests, publications and conference presentations focus on the following topics: Schema Therapy, eating disorders and multicultural issues in psychotherapy.

Remco van der Wijngaart, is a psychotherapist, Accredited schema therapist and clinical supervisor (International Society of Schema Therapy, ISST), and Vice President of the International Society of Schema Therapy, ISST (2016–2018). Remco works as a psychotherapist in a private practice in Maastricht, the Netherlands. Initially trained in Cognitive-Behaviour Therapy, he was trained and supervised in Schema Therapy personally by Dr Jeffrey Young from 1996 until 2000. Remco specialises in borderline patients, patients with cluster C personality disorders as well as anxiety and depressive disorders. Since 2000, he has been frequently giving training courses in Schema Therapy worldwide. He co-produced and directed the audio-visual production *Schema Therapy, Working with Modes*, which is considered to be one of the essential instruments in learning Schema Therapy. In 2016, he published two new productions: *Fine Tuning Imagery Rescripting* and *Schema Therapy for the Avoidant, Dependent and Obsessive–Compulsive Personality Disorder*, and, in 2018, the production *Schema Therapy, Step by Step*.

Michiel van Vreeswijk is a Clinical Psychologist, Certified schema therapist and supervisor-trainer with the International Society of Schema Therapy (ISST); a Certified CBT practitioner and supervisor; and CEO of G-kracht psychomedisch centrum BV (mental health care institute), the Netherlands. He offers regular workshops and supervision in ST in the Netherlands and abroad. Michiel has a special interest in schema group therapy and predictors of treatment effectiveness for group and individual Schema Therapy. He has been the co-developer of several time-limited schema group therapy protocols. Michiel has edited and authored books, chapters and articles on ST, including editing, and writing several chapters in, the *Wiley-Blackwell Handbook of Schema Therapy, Theory, Research, and Practice* (2012). He co-authored *Mindfulness and Schema Therapy: A Practical Guide* (2014).

Tünde Vanko has a PhD in Clinical and Developmental Psychology and is an accredited Cognitive-Behavioural therapist and Advanced Level schema therapist, supervisor and trainer. Tünde completed her CBT training at the University of Pennsylvania, USA, when she was awarded a Fulbright scholarship in 2007. During her Fulbright year, she also started the Schema Therapy training at Dr Jeffrey Young's programme in New York. Tünde is also the co-founder and clinical director of the Hungarian Schema Therapy Association in Budapest, which offered the first Schema Therapy certification programme in Hungary. Tünde worked at the Priory Hospital in London for several years. Currently, she shares her time working in private practice in London and actively managing the Hungarian Schema Therapy Association's training programmes in Budapest.

Jeffrey Young is the Founder of Schema Therapy and the Director of the Schema Therapy and Cognitive Therapy Institutes of New York. He serves on the faculty in the Department of Psychiatry at Columbia University, is a Founding Fellow of the Academy of Cognitive Therapy and is the co-founder of the International Society for Schema Therapy. Dr Young has led workshops for over 20 years throughout the world, including the United States, Canada, the UK, Europe, Australia, China, South Korea, Japan, New Zealand, Singapore and South America. He consistently receives outstanding evaluations internationally for his teaching skills, including the prestigious NEEI Mental Health Educator of the Year award. Dr Young has presented workshops and lectures for thousands of mental health professionals, resulting in strong demand for further in-depth training and supervision in Schema Therapy. Dr Young has co-authored two internationally best-selling books: *Schema Therapy: A Practitioner's Guide* for mental health professionals, and *Reinventing Your Life*, a self-help book for clients and the general public. Both have been translated into many languages.

Acknowledgements

The journey of working on this book together has been a pleasure. We have been inspired and moved by the innovation, skill and clinical compassion inherent in the work of our authors and their patients. We have forged new working connections and friendships along the way and have learnt an enormous amount from experts in our field. Indeed, we have also learnt a huge amount about our own coping strategies and resilience! As co-editors, on this new venture together, our working partnership has been productive and full of good humour, becoming good friends as a result, which is perhaps the most lovely part. We both unite in feeling an enormous sense of awe at the depth of learning and true connection we have gathered from the patients we have worked with over the years. We feel genuinely honoured to do this job and to be in a position to form so many special bonds.

Helen Startup and Gillian Heath

An introduction to Schema Therapy

Origins, overview, research status and future directions

Cathy Flanagan, Travis Atkinson and Jeffrey Young

Schema Therapy (ST) is an integrative therapy that combines 'elements from cognitive-behavioural, attachment, Gestalt, object relations, constructivist, and psychoanalytic schools into a rich, unifying conceptual and treatment model' (Young, Klosko & Weishaar, 2003, p. 1). It belongs in what is called the 'second wave' of cognitive behaviour therapy (CBT) because its primary focus has been the *content,* rather than the context or the process, of mental representations (see Luyten, Blatt & Fonagy, 2013; Roediger, Stevens & Brockman, 2018).

Earlier cognitive-behavioural models were based on a number of key assumptions: that patients could comply with the treatment protocol, gain access to their cognitions and emotions, identify clear therapy goals, change problem cognitions and behaviours through logical discourse, and engage relatively easily in a collaborative relationship with the therapist. Jeffrey Young, who had been trained in the cognitive-behavioural tradition, observed that the existing model was inadequate for patients with characterological disorders. These patients were often stuck in rigidly self-perpetuating and self-defeating cycles and either did not respond to, or relapsed after, existing short-term interventions. So, he set about identifying both the characteristics of these patients and the treatment strategies that might better address their specific needs.

Core concepts

Turning to other therapy models, Young found theoretical inspiration in broader relational perspectives (Ainsworth et al., 1978; Bowlby, 1988) and possibilities for clinical expansion in experiential techniques such as imagery and chair work. In the 1980s, other cognitive therapists were also recognising such problems in treating more complex cases and drawing on interpersonal and relational theories to address them (see Safran, 1984). Of course, generations of clinicians and clinical theorists had faced the same challenge of helping people heal from the long-term effects of adversity in childhood and adolescence (Baer & Martinez, 2006; Bakerman-Kranenburg & van IJzendoorn, 2009; Mikulincer & Shaver, 2012). In other words, the questions Young addressed were not new.

What was truly innovative in Young's thinking, however, was the concept of 'early maladaptive schemas', or EMSs. Postulating five core needs – for secure attachments, autonomy, freedom to express valid needs and emotions, spontaneity and play, and realistic limits and self-control – Young proposed that when these core needs are *chronically* unmet, children will form EMSs, or hypersensitivities, to certain kinds of experiences such as deprivation, abandonment or mistrust (Young et al., 2003; Flanagan, 2010). An EMS was originally defined as a broad pervasive theme or pattern comprising memories, emotions, cognitions and bodily sensations, regarding oneself and one's relationship with others, developed during childhood or adolescence, elaborated throughout one's lifetime and dysfunctional to a significant degree (Young et al., 2003, p. 7). In the intervening years, many contrasting definitions have been offered (Eurelings-Bontekoe et al., 2010; Van Genderen, Rijkeboer & Arntz, 2012; Roediger, 2012).

Every child will try to make sense of, and adapt to, their world even in the face of significant and prolonged adversity. Consequently, in their efforts to understand and process such experiences, a child's view of him or herself and of other people can become systematically biased (Young et al., 2003). It was prescient that Young also emphasised the role of temperament in schema acquisition. Research on what is termed *differential susceptibility* demonstrates that, even in infancy, some children are more impacted by their caregiving experiences than others (Boyce & Ellis, 2005; Belsky et al., 2007) and this can also effect the cargivers' behaviour, thereby generating a self-perpetuating cycle. Thus, temperamentally sensitive children may be more affected by adverse early experiences than their less sensitive peers (see Lockwood & Perris, 2012).

Eighteen core schemas have been identified using the Young Schema Questionnaire and grouped into five broad categories of unmet emotional needs called 'schema domains'. The domains are impaired autonomy and performance, disconnection and rejection, impaired limits, other-directedness, and over-vigilance and inhibition. Finally, EMSs were said to be maintained, or perpetuated, through the *processes* of overcompensation, avoidance, and surrender, which, broadly speaking, correspond to the three basic responses to threat: fight, flight and freeze. In *overcompensation*, people fight the schema by thinking, feeling, behaving and relating as though the opposite of the schema were true. If they felt worthless as children, then as adults they try to be perfect; if they were subjugated as children, as adults they might be defiant or rebel. In schema *avoidance*, the individual tries to arrange their environment so the schema is never activated. They block thoughts or images that are likely to trigger it. They also avoid feeling the schema and may take drugs, drink or eat excessively, or become workaholics, all to escape schema activation. In *surrender*, the individual effectively yields to the schema in order to maintain internal consistency and predictability. They do not try to fight it or avoid it. Instead, they accept the schema as true, feel the pain of it directly and act in ways that perpetuate and confirm it.

The primary goal of therapy was to help patients heal by conquering their EMSs, acquiring new ways of coping and, thereby, getting their needs met in more adaptive ways. The therapy relationship has always been seen as central in providing an environment conducive for the therapist to attune to, and attempt to meet, some of the patient's core needs through a process of limited reparenting (Young et al., 2003). This is discussed further in a later section.

Thus, from the outset, ST operated from a different set of assumptions and expectations than standard CBT. There was a clear focus on the developmental origins of patients' problems, a central emphasis on the patient–therapist relationship and an extensive use of experiential techniques to facilitate corrective emotional experiences. It also contrasted sharply with classical analytic approaches, where the therapist's stance was guided by neutrality and anonymity and also by a minimisation of supportive techniques such as gratifying needs or self-disclosure.

The schema mode model

As ST evolved, it became increasingly clear that for patients with complex presentations, and where there were multiple schemas, a more expedient approach was required. This led Young to create the 'mode' construct, which was initially intended to produce a simplification of the model as well as an elaboration of its treatment options. The idea of modes was first used to conceptualise borderline personality disorder (BPD) and then narcissistic personality disorder (NPD; Young & Flanagan, 1998). Young originally defined modes as: 'those schemas or schema operations—adaptive or maladaptive—that are currently active for an individual' (Young et al., 2003, p. 37) and also as 'a facet of the self, involving specific schemas or schema operations that have not been fully integrated with other facets' (Young et al., 2003, p. 40). As with EMSs, many subsequent definitions have since been offered (Lobbestael, van Vreeswijk & Arntz, 2007; Edwards & Arntz, 2012; Van Genderen et al., 2012; Roediger, 2012).

In the first version of the 'schema mode model', Young et al. (2003) proposed that modes could be grouped into four broad categories: Child modes, Dysfunctional Coping modes, Dysfunctional Parent modes, and the Healthy Adult mode. Child modes are thought to be innate and to encompass universal core needs and emotions. Young suggested four main subtypes: Vulnerable, Angry, Impulsive and Happy Child (Young et al., 2003, p. 273) and, furthermore, that the child's early environment may enhance or suppress their expression.

Dysfunctional Coping modes represent the child's attempts to satisfy unmet core needs in an early environment that was emotionally impoverished, oppressive or destructive, for example. Sadly, even if these modes were adaptive when the patient was a young child, they become both maladaptive and self-defeating in the adult world. The three coping styles are surrender, avoidance and overcompensation. They roughly correspond to the coping *processes* already described. It is plausible that, as with EMSs, a variety of factors influence the development of one style over another, including the specific unmet needs of the individual child, temperament, differential sensitivity to parenting models, and unhealthy reinforcement contingencies within the family system (Cutland Green & Heath, 2016).

Dysfunctional Parent modes can be thought of as internalised representations of the negative elements of parenting experienced by the patient as a child and can take the form of self-critical, menacing and demanding internal 'voices', or self-talk. In other words, the patient temporaraily *becomes* their parent and treats themelves the way their parent treated them when they were children (Young et al., 2003, p. 276).

The Healthy Adult serves an 'executive' function relative to the other modes (Young et al., 2003, p. 277) by moderating and integrating them to meet the patient's core needs. It has parallels with the concept of the Observer Self in Acceptance and Commitment Therapy (Hayes, Strosahl & Wilson, 1999) and the Compassionate Mind in its empathsis on increased awareness and regulation of self-states (Gilbert, 2010). Building and strengthening the patient's Heathy Adult in order to work more effectively with the other modes is the overarching goal of mode work in ST. In so doing, the patient gradually develops an awareness of the feelings and unmet needs they experience in their Child modes, and also the capacity to attune to, validate, and respond in a nurturing and balanced way. Likewise, they learn to recognise, negotiate with, and gradually defuse dysfunctional Parent and Coping modes.

Schema mode conceptualisation

Young adheres to his original conceptualisation of ten modes: Vulnerable, Angry, Impulsive/Undisciplined and Happy Child modes; Compliant Surrenderer, Detached Protector, and Overcompensator Coping modes; and, finally, the Punitive Parent, Demanding Parent and Healthy Adult modes. In the intervening years, however, ongoing research interest in modes has led to a continuously growing register. At present, as many as 22 modes have been proposed (Bernstein, Arntz & de Vos, 2007) and it is thought that 'clinicians and researchers will continue to "invite" more modes because they feel these modes are required to understand specific types of personalities' (Lobbestael, van Vreeswijk & Arntz, 2007, p. 82).

Because modes were developed on the basis of clinical experience, the increase in number was deemed necessary to account for variations in clinical presentations (Young et al., 2007). The Self-Aggrandizer mode was thought to be essential for understanding a feature of the narcissistic personality and, in a similar vein, Lobbestael et al. (2007) mention the addition of the 'Conning and Manipulative', 'Angry Protector', and 'Predator' modes identified from work in forensic settings (Bernstein, Arntz & de Vos, 2007). Likewise, Edwards has suggested 'Surrender to Damaged Child' and 'Spaced Out Protector' modes, and Bamber (2006), viewing managers and supervisors as parent figures, added the 'Nurturing Parent' mode. At a clinical level, the therapist and patient also frequently create idiosyncratic Child and Parent mode labels. These are often variants of the prototypical categories.

Since the endeavour has become increasingly one of identifying which modes appear in the different disorders, however, the challenges of accomplishing such a goal have also become more obvious and questions are now being raised as to the ultimate objective of mode conceptualisation – to continue with these efforts to capture the modes of all the PDs, or to provide a limited set of basic modes to understand PDs in more general terms (Lobbestael et al., 2007; Van Genderen et al., 2012). The latter would seem more in keeping with the original goal of *simplification* (see Flanagan, 2014). In spite of such concerns, since its original application to BPD and NPD, the mode model has been used more widely, and with many different personality disorders, and this has led to a growing body of empirical research (described in a later section).

Not surprisingly, hand in hand with the increased emphasis on identifying modes, there has also been an increasing focus on early attachments and the role of the therapist as a reparenting figure. As a result, ST has consolidated two fundamental and complementary therapeutic stances aimed at facilitating corrective emotional experiences: *limited reparenting* and *empathetic confrontation*. Both of these concepts were adopted from earlier schools of therapy and are now central to the practice of ST (Edwards & Arntz, 2012). In sum, the key orientation for schema therapists has become one of adopting the 'role' of a healthy reparenting figure who is both empathic towards the child's needs and encouraging of his or her healthy expression, while *also* firm without being either punitive or overly indulgent.

As explained, in the evolution of ST, the mode model came later and has been a major focus of expansion in recent years. Depending on the individual patient's needs and schema profile, however, it should be noted that therapists still work with *both* individual EMSs *and* with modes.

We will now provide an overview of the main ST techniques, all of which which will be covered in greater depth in subsequent chapters.

Schema Therapy techniques

In a qualitative study of both patients' and therapists' perspectives on ST, the aspects identified as most helpful were the clarity of the theoretical model, the committed therapeutic relationship and the specific therapy techniques (de Klerk et al., 2016). Since the building blocks of the model have been outlined, we now focus on the nature of the therapist–patient relationship in ST and the creative expansion and application of its therapy tools.

The therapeutic relationship in ST

Much psychotherapy outcome research focuses on comparing the effectiveness of various theoretical and technical approaches while trying to control for the influence of therapist factors. However, because the problems of personality disordered patients are particularly evident in the interpersonal realm, the patient–therapist relationship becomes pivotal to good therapy outcomes. Moreover, evidence now indicates that the therapeutic alliance and specific techniques *can interact with, and influence, one another* and this may serve to facilitate the change processes underlying clinical improvement (see Spinhoven et al., 2007).

Limited reparenting

Limited reparenting stems directly from the basic assumption that schemas and modes arise when core needs are not met. It parallels healthy parenting in that it involves the establishment of an attachment to the therapist who relates as a 'real person' within the bounds of a professional relationship (Arntz & Jacob, 2012). A primary goal of ST is to provide patients with the corrective needs-based experiences they missed as children by meeting any of a range of their needs, such as connection, autonomy, desirability or stability (Flanagan, 2010). Interventions aim to facilitate the experience of authentic warmth, understanding and empathy, safety and protection, validation, freedom of expression and appropriate limits and boundaries.

Irrespective of the specific unmet needs and schemas, the objective is to create a supportive and authentic connection which will allow the therapist to access the Vulnerable Child and also to build a Healthy Adult mode. Effective treatment focuses on *both* connecting with the Vulnerable Child *and* strengthening the Healthy Adult. Patients learn how to face and overcome avoidant and compensatory Coping modes and fight unhealthy Parent modes. As therapy progresses, along with turning to their Healthy Adult to get their needs met, patients also make interpersonal gains by taking calculated risks and reaching out to others (Farrell et al., 2009). The patient–therapist alliance is the binding force without which none of these later changes can unfold (Young et al., 2003; Spinhoven et al., 2007).

As described, and by contrast with other approaches, ST encourages therapists to meet some of their patients' emotional needs directly, believing that as the therapist does so, their care becomes internalised and forms part of the patient's Healthy Adult mode. This secure relationship also sets the stage for patients to risk trusting the therapist as they uncover deeply painful feelings, challenge unhelpful beliefs about their interpersonal style and how it affects their relationships, and eventually experiment with new behaviours. Not surprisingly, schema therapists who provide the patient with care, attention, recognition and praise are more effective (see de Klerk et al., 2016), but equally essential to effective reparenting is empathic confrontation.

Empathic confrontation

Empathic confrontation is a natural extension of limited reparenting and a mode change strategy in its own right. As in normal good parenting, it takes the form of simultaneous tenderness and firmness. Here, empathy is combined with helping the patient tolerate frustration. The pre-established strong alliance allows the therapist to address maladaptive Coping modes with compassion for how they developed, while also confronting them and related unhealthy behaviours. When addressing Coping modes, the therapist explores with the patient how their personal ways of coping evolved, which unmet needs they are trying to satisfy and the perceived benefits and costs of continuing to operate in these ways.

Coping modes such as the Detached Protector or Self-Aggrandiser can present major challenges in treatment, but they also often reflect highly resourceful aspects of the patient's character. Albeit ultimately self-defeating, they represent the person's best efforts to meet their underlying needs. So, an important aspect of empathic confrontation entails the therapist sharing his or her experience of a particular maladaptive mode. It is important that this is done in a skilled way so the patient can trust and tolerate the feedback enough to also step back and gain some objectivity by observing the mode from a distance. In so doing, together the therapist and patient can come to understand the survival role the mode may have played, and start to explore how the patient's needs might be met in more balanced and adaptive ways. During this process, therapists needs to be mindful of their own reactions to their patients' Coping modes so they do not inadvertently reinforce these tendencies to overcompensate or avoid.

In sum, the therapist tries to track and attune to the patient's needs and mode activation and also to adapt in such a way as to actively address them, interrupting when necessary to identify a problem mode, for example, or sharing their experience of the mode's interpersonal impact. While overcompensatory modes may require challenging and limit setting, an enquiring or tentative stance may be more effective with surrender and avoidant modes. For example, the therapist might explore the Detached Protector's efforts to prevent the patient from feeling overwhelmed, or take a graded approach toward change by recognising the benefits of some detachment in certain situations. When working with Punitive or Demanding Parent modes, the therapist empathically confronts the modes using a firm and reassuring stance without being critical or aggressive (Arntz & Jacob, 2012).

There are some pitfalls in limited reparenting and empathic confrontation that can hinder the effectiveness of ST. If a therapist believes that empathy is enough, he or she may avoid setting appropriate limits. Likewise, therapists can be excessively cautious about frustrating or challenging their patients and/ or inadvertently allow dysfunctional coping modes to control the treatment. Therapists who use caring techniques while *also* allowing for frustration achieve better results. In other words, patients need to be encouraged to work with discomfort in order to create change through corrective emotional experiences (de Klerk et al., 2016).

Experiential techniques

Schema therapists trained to focus on practical interventions, rather than on theory, tend to achieve better results, including lower patient dropout rates (Giesen-Bloo et al., 2006; Bamelis et al., 2014). The most prominent experiential tools used in ST are imagery rescripting and transformational chair work. Like limited reparenting and empathic confrontation, these techniques have been adopted from methods used in earlier schools of therapy but they have been expanded within the framework of the schema model and are now central to the practice of ST (see Edwards & Arntz, 2012).

Imagery rescripting

Imagery rescripting uses the powers of visualisation and imagination to identify and change emotionally meaningful experiences in the past and this results in transformation in the present (see Arntz, 2015). Patients can typically 'recall' and retell events when discussing childhood memories but it is important to help them move from 'recollection' to 'experience'. Some patients work with images that are associations rather than memories of specific events. Imagery rescripting involves the therapist activating schemas and modes by intensifying emotions and linking them to biographical memories (Arntz & Jacob, 2012). This process of connecting current triggering events to key childhood images (by creating an 'affect bridge') can elicit powerful feelings, so it is pivotal that therapists understand their patients well enough to tune in to the meaning of their experience. Greater attunement allows for the creation of clearer links to past events (see de Klerk et al., 2016). Not surprisingly, rescripting is the main intervention for traumatic childhood experiences (Arntz & Jacob, 2012).

Although early childhood experiences are usually the focus of imagery rescripting, the therapist may also work on emotionally relevant memories in the patient's adult life. In either case, the details of the memory are not modified but the image is rescripted in such a way that patients can get their needs met. In other words, by confronting schemas and maladaptive modes, the *meaning* of the memory is changed (Arntz & Jacob, 2012; Roediger et al., 2018). Emotions such as anxiety, shame, helplessness and sadness may be experienced in the image. The therapist (and/or the patient's Healthy Adult) tries to attune to these feelings and also to provide an antidote, or alternative, in which the patient's core needs are met. Some imagery work is aimed specifically at developing healthy alternatives such as experiencing a sense of safety, self-confidence, and hopefulness.

Typically, the structure of imagery rescripting may be broken into several parts, either in any individual session or over the course of therapy. First, the therapist invites the patient to create and describe a safe place image. Next, the therapist shifts the patient to an upsetting situation in his or her current life. The therapist *links* the current situation to the earliest memory the patient can access, and asks for a description of the situation, including a focus on the emotions and needs of the Vulnerable Child. The therapist then introduces a Healthy Adult figure, represented by the therapist in the early stage of therapy, and later on by the patient's own Healthy Adult. The Healthy Adult meets the child's needs, starting with physical safety, followed by addressing the child's deeper emotional needs. The therapist may then return the patient to the original upsetting situation and model the same approach of the Healthy Adult by addressing the patient's needs in the here and now (Arntz, 2011).

A primary goal of imagery rescripting is for the therapist and Healthy Adult to empathise with, and validate, the emotions and needs of the Vulnerable Child, so the patient can experience what it is like to have their needs met. Imagery rescripting may also be used to confront Demanding or Punitive Parent modes. Through this repeated process, new meanings can replace, or at least moderate, the negative messages perpetuated by dysfunctional modes (Arntz & Jacob, 2012; Roediger et al., 2018). Evidence suggests that the greater the number of ST sessions that include imagery rescripting, the better the outcome (Morina et al., 2017).

Transformational chair work

Although originally recognised through the work of Perls, the father of Gestalt therapy, chair work is being increasingly incorporated into ST (Kellogg, 2012, 2018). It is based on the belief that there is a healing and transformative power in, first, giving voice to one's inner parts, selves, or modes and, second, in enacting or re-enacting scenes from the past, present or future.

Chair work can provide an additional experiential tool for patients who are unwilling or unable to do mode dialogues, or are resistant to exercises such as imagery rescripting. Because chair work can be used in an exploratory or open-ended way, it can be less threatening than more focused interventions. However, it can also be enlisted to work directly with rigid Coping modes, to address negative Parent modes and to enhance the positive effects of limited reparenting. In other words, chair work can be creatively utilised at different stages of therapy.

There are two main forms of such psychotherapeutic dialogues, or chair work. In the first, the 'empty chair', the patient is invited to sit in one chair and imagine another person with whom he or she has unfinished emotional business in the opposite chair. In the second, 'two chair' form, the patient frequently works with inner conflicts. These forms are now more often referred to as 'external' and 'internal' dialogues. Kellogg (2018) has presented a four-dialogue matrix counterbalancing the polarity of using one or two chairs with the polarity of having an internal or an external dialogue.

Multiple chair work is also used in ST to help patients voice conflicting modes, conceptually similar to different personalities interacting with each other (Roediger et al., 2018). Here, each mode is assigned a chair and the patient rotates between these chairs, placed in a circle. The patient gives a voice to each chair or mode, expressing the view and emotions of each one, thereby making the conflicting perspectives and emotions explicit. The therapist can then work with the patient in their Healthy Adult mode to validate and comfort the Vulnerable Child, invite the Angry Child to express his or her anger and authenticate the experience, or address the Impulsive Child by expressing empathy while also setting limits and boundaries. The Demanding Parent can be counterbalanced by the Healthy Adult both through perspective taking and limit setting, whereas the Punitive Parent is confronted and either completely contained or, at least, pushed back so that the patient's Vulnerable Child feels protected.

With the help of the therapist, the patient can learn to evaluate the disadvantages of their dysfunctional Parent and Coping modes. In multiple chair work, the Healthy Adult can also act as the conductor of an orchestra, emphasising the inherent strengths in the patient's modes (for example, the determination of an Overcontroller or the energy of the Impulsive Child) while simultaneously ensuring that no mode becomes too dominant or blocks the patient from getting their needs met.

It is anticipated that continued clinical research, together with practice-based evidence, will further augment the therapeutic effectiveness of both imagery rescripting and chair work, along with other experiential interventions.

Conclusions and future directions

Edwards and Arntz (2012) define what they see as the three phases of ST. The first was Young's original formulation of the key concepts of ST, as outlined in Young et al. (2003). Second, came the Dutch outcome research and continued efforts to expand the empirical base of the model. Here, the primary breakthrough was in the results of a randomised controlled trial (RCT) which showed ST to be superior to a specialised, highly regarded psychodynamic treatment for BPD (Giesen-Bloo et al., 2006). Many other studies have followed with applications of the mode model to almost all of the PDs, including Cluster C, paranoid, narcissistic, histrionic and antisocial PDs (Bernstein et al., 2007; Bamelis et al., 2011; Arntz & Jacob, 2012; Jacob & Arntz, 2013). Finally, ST has also been effectively applied in group settings. Integrating the principles of group therapy with those of ST added yet another dimension to ST's treatment options. Moreover, the value of this development has been demonstrated in the results of an RCT with BPD patients (Farrell, Shaw & Webber, 2009). Even more recently, Roediger et al. (2018) have advanced what they see as the 'third wave' of ST, *contextual* Schema Therapy. It is likely that, as time goes on, more such expansions of the ST model will appear.

Despite these promising developments, however, we also need to proceed with caution. The results of a recent systematic review of ST across mental health disorders are mixed (Taylor, Bee & Haddock, 2017). The review was limited, among other things, by the small number of studies that met their rigorous exclusion criteria. It also focused specifically on evidence of schema change and symptom change, in that the ST model suggests that change in symptoms should be 'the outworking of change to early maladaptive schemas' (p. 458). They conclude that ST has demonstrated effectiveness in terms of reducing EMSs and improving symptoms in PDs (eg. Nordahl & Nysæter, 2005; Nadort et al., 2009; Renner et al., 2013; Dickhaut & Arntz, 2014; Videler et al., 2014). However, despite increasing interest in the application of ST to the treatment of Axis 1 disorders, such as chronic depression (Malogiannis et al., 2014), eating disorders (Simpson et al., 2010), agoraphobia (Gude & Hoffart, 2008), and post traumatic stress disorder (PTSD) (Cockram et al., 2010), they judge that current evidence of schema change in these disorders is sparse. Predictably, they point to a need for further studies to support schema change as an underlying mechanism of ST. Others are more optimistic in their conclusions. Renner et al. (2016), for example, point to emerging evidence for ST as a promising treatment for chronic depression However, they also emphasise the need to better understand the underlying mechanisms of change in ST.

In other words, ST is an evolving model and will continue to require fine-tuning, both technically and conceptually. Regarding the first of these, Jacob and Arntz (2013) recommend that *direct comparisons* of ST with other well-established treatment approaches such as Dialectical Behaviour Therapy or Mindfulness Based Therapy are needed, along with studies to establish the *comparative efficacy* of group versus individual ST. Furthermore, since a focus on techniques can sometimes come at the expense of exploring the mechanisms of change (Sempertigui et al., 2013; Byrne & Egan, 2018), additional *dismantling studies* are also needed to identify the essential ingredients of ST (see, for example, Nadort et al., 2009). In other words, a better understanding of which techniques are most critical for facilitating change, and in which populations, is essential. Such studies will help tailor interventions to focus on those key elements and, in doing so, increase both the overall efficacy and cost effectiveness of treatment (Jacob & Arntz, 2013; Bamelis et al., 2014, 2015).

As for issues of conceptual integrity, since theoretical unity and the application of coherent principles are essential to any treatment plan (see Chapman, Turner & Dixon-Gordon, 2011; Byrne & Egan, 2018), along with efforts to refine and advance aspects of ST's technical research arm, it is equally important to evaluate the *theoretical* constructs that are central to the model. Here, we are alerted by the conclusions of a review by Sempertigui et al. (2013). They call attention to the fact that, despite supportive evidence for a number of elements of ST, 'the foundation in some cases is not too strong, nor always consistent, and there are also still empirical blanks in the theory' (p. 443). In other words, even though there is evidence in support of the ST model, there are also mixed results which include a lack of specificity of the component parts of the model and significant gaps in the theory.

In this context, it is surprising that, despite the central role of attachment theory in ST, an examination of the relationship between specific EMSs and attachment styles has not been a major focus of research. That said, there are some lines of research which specifically aim to explore such conceptual and theoretical issues. Findings here point to clear but complex interrelationships and also to the observation that ST has focused on the Self and not the Other (Platts, Mason & Tyson, 2005; Bosmans et al., 2010; Simard, Moss & Pascuzzo, 2011). The latter point relates to another apparent lacuna. There is very little reference to the concept of internal working models (IWMs) in schema theory, despite the fact that IWMs of Self and the Other are theorised to be reflected in the different attachment styles. Finally, it is worth noting that all of these recent studies were conducted without reference to the concept of mode. It would seem timely, then, to more purposefully examine all of these interrelated constructs (Flanagan, in preparation). In other words, and in line with the comments of Sempertigui et al. (2013) above, there is a pressing need for ST to refine and expand its conceptual and theoretical base so that the integrity of the model is preserved.

From the outset, ST has been defined as an integrative model borrowing many of its constructs and clinical tools from other schools of therapy, including cognitive-behavioural, Gestalt, object relations and psychoanalytic schools. There are four main models of integration – theoretical, technical eclectic, common factors and assimilative integration. ST belongs in the category of *assimilative integration*, which implies 'remaining anchored in a primary theoretical orientation while thoughtfully integrating techniques and principles from other orientations' (Castonguay et al., 2015, p. 366). The assimilative integration trend has appeal to clinicians and researchers alike. For clinicians, in particular, it allows for an expansion of their clinical repertoire without shaking the foundation of their typical way of practising. For these very reasons, however, it is essential that the *theoretical* underpinnings of the model be further refined in step with empirical research aimed at improving ST's clinical tools and techniques.

In conclusion, as with any developing therapy model, there will inevitably be ongoing technical innovations as well as conceptual advances. The expanding range and effectiveness of ST's techniques are promising and will be elucidated throughout this volume. But we also need to ensure that ST maintains its status as an example of assimilative integration. In other words, as well as conducting comparison and dismantling studies, we will need to be mindful of a simultaneous obligation to consolidate our theoretical base. This will be achieved by tightening the definitions of core terms such as EMSs and modes, keeping abreast of the burgeoning research and developmental literatures on IWMs and attachment styles, and remaining open to ideas and techniques from other schools of therapy – without diluting or distorting the core elements of the ST model in the process (Flanagan, in preparation).

Castonguay et al. (2015, p. 369) recommend that '… one fruitful way to improve the effectiveness of psychotherapy is to build upon our conceptual, empirical, and clinical foundations while opening ourselves to potential contributions of researchers and practitioners working in other communities of knowledge seekers'. Thus, as responsible clinicians, we need to continually update our knowledge about topics relevant to the practice of ST. What techniques should be added to any specific treatment in order to best address the needs of particular patients, and why? How much additional training should therapists receive before attempting to implement interventions foreign to their preferred, or primary, orientation? We also need to ensure that we take the time to check in with ourselves – to compassionately self-reflect – and in so doing, to remain mindful of our own personal vulnerabilities and limitations, 'blind spots' and human foibles. In other words, keeping up to date with evidence-based practice, taking care of ourselves and prioritising the therapeutic relationship in our work will allow us to proceed with a level of healthy optimism and respectful caution appropriate to, and necessary for, handling our precious charges – our patients' lives. It is to these matters we will now turn.

References

Ainsworth, M.D.S., Blehar, M.C., Waters, E., & Wall, S. (1978). *Patterns of attachment: A psychological study of the Strange Situation.* Hillsdale, NJ: Erlbaum.

Arntz, A. (2011). Imagery rescripting for personality disorders. *Cognitive and Behavioral Practice, 18,* 466–481.

Arntz, A. (2015). Imagery rescripting for personality disorders: Healing early maladaptive schemas. In N. Thomas & D. McKay (Eds), *Working with emotion in cognitive-behavioral therapy techniques for clinical practice,* 175–202. New York: Guilford Press.

Arntz, A. & Jacob, G. (2012). *Schema therapy in practice.* Sussex: Wiley.

Baer, J.C. & Martinez, C.D. (2006). Child maltreatment and insecure attachment: A meta-analysis. *Journal of Reproductive and Infant Psychology, 24(3),* 187–197.

Bakerman-Kranenburg, M.J. & van IJzendoorn, M.H. (2009). The first 10,000 Adult Attachment Interviews: Distribution of adult attachment representations in clinical and non-clinical groups. *Attachment and Human Development, 11(3),* 223–263.

Bamber, M.R. (2006). *CBT for occupational stress in health professionals: Introducing a schema-focused approach.* London: Routledge.

Bamelis, I.I.M., Renner, F., Heidkamp, D., & Arntz, A. (2011). Extended schema mode conceptualizations for specific personality disorders: An empirical study. *Journal of Personality Disorders, 25,* 41–58.

Bamelis, L.L.M., Arntz, A., Wetzelaer, P., Verdoorn, R., & Evers, S.M.A.A. (2015). Economic evaluation of schema therapy and clarification-oriented psychotherapy for personality disorders: A multicenter, randomized controlled trial. *Journal of Clinical Psychiatry, 76,* e1432–e1440.

Bamelis, L.L.M., Evers, S.M.A.A., Spinhoven, P., & Arntz, A. (2014). Results of a multicenter randomized controlled trial of the clinical effectiveness of schema therapy for personality disorders. *American Journal of Psychiatry, 171,* 305–322.

Belsky, J., Bakermans-Kranenburg, M.J., & van IJzendoorn, M.H. (2007). For better and for worse. *Differential Susceptibility to Environmental Influences. Current Directions in Psychological Science, 16*(6), 300–304.

Bernstein, D.P., Arntz, A., & de Vos, M. (2007). Schema focused therapy in forensic settings: Theoretical model and recommendations for best clinical practice. *International Journal of Forensic Mental Health, 6*, 169–183.

Bosmans, G., Braet, C., & Leen, V.V. (2010). Attachment and symptoms of psychopathology: Early maladaptive schemas as a cognitive link? *Clinical Psychology and Psychotherapy, 17*(5), 374–385.

Bowlby, J. (1988). *A secure base: Parent–child attachment and healthy human development.* New York: Basic Books.

Boyce, W.T. & Ellis, B.J. (2005). Biological sensitivity to context: An evolutionary-developmental theory of the origins and functions of stress reactivity. *Development and Psychopathology, 17*(2), 271–301.

Byrne, G. & Egan, J. (2018). A review of the effectiveness of mechanisms of change for three psychological interventions for borderline personality disorder, *Clinical Social Work Journal, 46*, 174–186.

Castonguay, L.G., Eubanks, C., Goldfried, M., Muran, C., & Lutz, W. (2015). Research on psychotherapy integration: Building on the past, looking to the future. *Psychotherapy Research, 25*(3), 365–382.

Chapman, A.L., Turner, B.J. & Dixon-Gordon, K.L. (2011). To integrate or not to integrate dialectical behavior therapy with other therapy approaches? *Clinical Social Work Journal, 39*, 170–179.

Cockram, D., Drummond, P., & Lee, C. (2010). Role and treatment of early maladaptive schemas in Vietnam veterans with PTSD. *Clinical Psychology and Psychotherapy, 17*, 165–182.

Cutland Green, T.J. & Heath, G. (2016). Schema therapy. In A. Carr & M. McNulty (Eds), *The handbook of adult clinical psychology*, 1032–1073. London: Routledge, Taylor & Francis Group.

de Klerk, N., Abma, T.A., Bamelis, L.L.M., & Artnz, A. (2016). Schema therapy for personality disorders: A qualitative study of patients' and therapists' perspectives. *Behavioural and Cognitive Psychotherapy, 45*, 31–45.

Dickhaut, V. & Arntz, A. (2014). Combined group and individual schema therapy for borderline personality disorder: A pilot study. *Journal of Behavior Therapy and Experimental Psychiatry, 45*(2), 242–251.

Edwards, D. & Arntz, A. (2012). Schema therapy in historical perspective. In M. van Vreeswijk, J. Broersen, & M. Nadort (Eds), *The Wiley-Blackwell handbook of schema therapy*, 3–26. Chichester: John Wiley & Sons.

Eurelings-Bontekoe, E.H.M., Luyten, P., Ijssennagger, M., van Vreeswijk, M., & Koelen, J. (2010). Relationship between personality organization and Young's cognitive model of personality pathology. *Personality and Individual Differences, 49*, 198–203.

Farrell, J.M., Shaw, I.A., & Webber, M.A. (2009). A schema-focused approach to group psychotherapy for outpatients with borderline personality disorder: A randomized controlled trial. *Journal of Behavior Therapy and Experimental Psychiatry, 40*(2), 317–328.

Flanagan, C.M. (2010). The case for needs in psychotherapy. *Journal of Psychotherapy Integration, 20*, 1–36.

Flanagan, C.M. (2014). Unmet needs and maladaptive modes: A new way to approach longer term problems. *Journal of Psychotherapy Integration, 24*, 208–222.

Flanagan, C.M. (In preparation). Internal working models: Missing link or hidden in plain sight?, pp. 14 and 15.

Giesen-Bloo, J., van Dyck, R., Spinhoven, P., van Tilbureg, W., Dirksen, C., van Asselt, T., & Arntz, A. (2006). Outpatient psychotherapy for borderline personality disorder. Randomized trial of schema-focused therapy versus transference-focused psychotherapy. *Archives of General Psychiatry, 63,* 649–658.

Gilbert, P. (2010). *Compassion focused therapy: Distinctive features.* Chichester: Routledge.

Gude, T., & Hoffart, H. (2008). Change in interpersonal problems after cognitive agoraphobia and schema focused therapy versus psychodynamic treatment as usual of inpatients with agoraphobia and Cluster C personality disorders. *Scandinavian Journal of Psychology, 49,* 195–199.

Hayes, S.C., Strosahl, K.D., & Wilson, K.G. (1999). *Acceptance and commitment therapy: An experiential approach to behaviour change.* New York: Guilford Press.

Jacob, G.A. & Arntz, A. (2013). Schema therapy for personality disorders—A review. *International Journal of Cognitive Therapy, 6*(2), 171–185.

Kellogg, S.H. (2012). On speaking one's mind: Using chairwork dialogues in schema therapy. In M. van Vreeswijk, J. Broersen, & M. Nadort (Eds), *The Wiley-Blackwell handbook of schema therapy,* 197–207. Chichester: John Wiley & Sons.

Kellogg, S.H. (2018). Transformational chairwork: Five ways of using therapeutic dialogues. *NYSPA Notebook, 19,* 8–9.

Lobbestael, J., van Vreeswijk, M., & Arntz, A. (2007). Shedding light on schema modes: A clarification of the mode concept and its current research status. *Netherlands Journal of Psychology, 63,* 76–85.

Lockwood, G. & Perris, P. (2012) A new look at core emotional needs. In M. van Vreeswijk, J. Broersen, & M. Nadort (Eds), *The Wiley-Blackwell handbook of schema therapy,* 41–66. Chichester: John Wiley & Sons.

Luyten, P., Blatt, S.J., & Fonagy, P. (2013). Impairments in self structures in depression and suicide in psychodynamic and cognitive behavioral approaches: Implications for clinical practice and research. *International Journal of Cognitive Therapy, 6*(3), 265–279.

Malogiannis, I.A., Arntz, A., Spyropoulou, A., Tsartsara, E., Aggeli, A., Karveli, S., & Zervas, I. (2014). Schema therapy for patients with chronic depression: A single case series study. *Journal of Behavior Therapy and Experimental Psychiatry, 45,* 319–329.

Mikulincer, M. & Shaver, P.R. (2012). An attachment perspective on psychopathology, *World Psychiatry, 11*(1), 11–15.

Morina, N., Lancee, J. & Arntz, A. (2017). Imagery rescripting as a clinical intervention for aversive memories: A meta-analysis. *Journal of Behavior Therapy and Experimental Psychiatry, 55,* 6–15.

Nadort, M., Arntz, A., Smit, J.A., Giesen-Bloo, J., Eikelenboom, M., Spinover, P., van Asselt, T. et al. (2009). Implementation of outpatient schema therapy for borderline personality disorder with versus without crisis support by the therapist outside office hours: A randomized trial. *Behaviour Research and Therapy, 47,* 961–973.

Nordahl, H.M. & Nysæter, T.E. (2005). Schema therapy for patients with borderline personality disorder: A single case series. *Journal of Behavior Therapy and Experimental Psychiatry, 36,* 254–264.

Platts, H., Mason, O. & Tyson, M. (2005). Early maladaptive schemas and adult attachment in a UK clinical population. *Psychology and Psychotherapy, 78,* 549–564.

Renner, F., Arntz, A., Peeters, F.P., Lobbestael, J. & Hubers, M.J. (2016). Schema therapy for chronic depression: Results of a multiple single case series. *Journal of Behavior Therapy and Experimental Psychiatry, 51*, 66–73.

Renner, F., van Goor, M., Huibers, M., Arntz, A., Butz, B., & Bernstein, D. (2013). Short-term group schema cognitive-behavioral therapy for young adults with personality disorders and personality disorder features: Associations with changes in symptomatic distress, schemas, schema modes and coping styles. *Behaviour Research and Therapy, 51*, 487–492.

Roediger, E. (2012). Why are mindfulness and acceptance central elements for therapeutic change in schema therapy too? In M. van Vreeswijk, J. Broersen, & M. Nadort (Eds), *The Wiley-Blackwell handbook of schema therapy*, 239–247. Chichester: John Wiley & Sons.

Roediger, E., Stevens, B., & Brockman, R. (2018). *Contextual schema therapy*. Oakland, CA: Context Press.

Safran, J.D. (1984). Assessing the cognitive interpersonal cycle. *Cognitive Therapy and Research, 8*, 333–348.

Sempertigui, G.A., Karreman, A., Arntz, A., & Bekker, M.H.J. (2013). Schema therapy for borderline personality disorder: A comprehensive review of its empirical foundations, effectiveness, and implementation possibilities. *Clinical Psychology Review, 33*, 426–444.

Simard, V., Moss, E., & Pascuzzo, K. (2011). Early maladaptive schemas and child and adult attachment: A 15-year longitudinal study. *Psychology and Psychotherapy: Theory, Research and Practice, 84*, 349–366.

Simpson, S., Morrow, E., van Vreeswijk, M., & Reid, C. (2010). Group schema therapy for eating disorders: A pilot study. *Frontiers in Psychology in Clinical Settings, 1*, 182.

Spinhoven, P., Giesen-Bloo, J., van Dyck, R., Kooiman, K., & Arntz, A. (2007). The therapeutic alliance in schema-focused therapy and transference-focused psychotherapy for borderline personality disorder. *Journal of Consulting Clinical Psychology, 75*, 104–115.

Taylor, C.D.J., Bee, P., & Haddock, G. (2017). Does schema therapy change schemas and symptoms? A systematic review across mental health disorders. *Psychology and Psychotherapy: Theory, Research, and Practice, 3*, 456–479.

Van Genderen, H., Rijkeboer, M., & Arntz, A. (2012). Theoretical model: Schemas, coping styles, and modes. In M. van Vreeswijk, J. Broersen, & M. Nadort (Eds), *The Wiley-Blackwell handbook of schema therapy*, 27–40. Chichester: John Wiley & Sons.

Videler, A.C., Rossi, G., Schoevaars, M., Van der Feltz-Cornelis, C. M., & van Alphen, S.P.J. (2014). Effects of schema group therapy in older outpatients: A proof of concept study. *International Psychogeriatrics, 26*, 1709–1717.

Young, J., Arntz, A., Atkinson, T., Lobbestael, J., Weishaar, M.E., & van Vreeswijk, M.F. (2007). *The Schema Mode Inventory (SMI)*. New York: Schema Therapy Institute.

Young, J. & Flanagan, C. (1998). Schema-focused therapy for narcissistic patients. In E. Ronningstam (Ed), *Disorders of narcissism: Diagnostic, clinical, and empirical implications*, 239–268. Washington, DC: American Psychiatric Press.

Young, J., Klosko, J.S., & Weishaar, M.E. (2003). *Schema therapy: A practitioner's guide*. New York: Guilford Press.

Part I

Assessment, formulation and core needs

1 Assessment and formulation in Schema Therapy

Tara Cutland Green and Anna Balfour

Introduction

Skilful assessment and an accurate, collaboratively developed case conceptualisation[1] form the foundation of effective Schema Therapy. This initial phase
involves building a meaningful relationship with your patient,[2] engaging them in
therapy and orientating them to how Schema Therapy brings about change.

Schema Therapy views patients' problems in terms of unmet emotional needs
(past and present),[3] related schemas,[4] coping styles and maladaptive coping modes
(from here on, 'coping modes', 'sides' or 'parts'). You and your patient are
somewhat like detectives, aiming to identify and put together these pieces of the
puzzle to synthesise a picture of their patterns so that you can map a way forward.
This occurs through the curious questioning and exploration that you would use
in a standard psychological assessment, but also by noticing how your patient tells
their story, relates to you and what is evoked between you. Attending to all
aspects of their experience, methods such as imagery and chair work and Schema
Therapy inventories also offer valuable means of gathering further information.

This focused period of exploring early experiences and current life patterns,
and the links between them, can itself provide a meta-awareness that begins to
loosen your patient from unhelpful habits of thought or action. Providing
a framework of understanding in which they can make sense of themselves and
feel accurately and deeply understood can engender hope, confidence in your
ability to help them and motivation to engage in the therapy.

In this chapter, we offer some detailed approaches and creative perspectives
to assessment and case conceptualisation, illustrating them through the case of
Jim and his therapist, Mira.

The role of assessment and formulation

Determining suitability for Schema Therapy

Schema Therapy was originally developed for those whose problems are
long-standing and have their origins in childhood or adolescence (Young
et al., 2003). Aligning with this, the landmark randomised control trials

(RCTs) of Schema Therapy (Giesen-Bloo et al., 2006; Bamelis et al., 2014) have demonstrated good outcomes for Schema Therapy with personality disorders. A number of authors additionally make the case, on theoretical grounds, for the use of Schema Therapy with less complex problems that require shorter term therapy, and provide supporting case studies (e.g., Renner et al., 2013; Reusch, 2015 and contributors to van Vreeswijk et al., 2012). Evidence to support its effectiveness with less complex problems is increasingly emerging (e.g., Carter et al., 2013; Renner et al., 2016; Tapia et al., 2018); however, further studies are much needed.

Thus, while NICE-recommended treatments such as Cognitive-Behaviour Therapy (CBT) might be considered as a first approach for Axis I disorders, Schema Therapy might also be considered for those patients who fail to progress with standard treatments. A recent UK study (Hepgul et al., 2016) reports that around two-thirds of individuals seeking treatment through IAPT – a time-limited, predominantly CBT service for anxiety and depression – have significant personality disorder features, the presence of which will be associated with poorer treatment outcomes (Goddard et al., 2015). Particularly in these more complex cases, Schema Therapy might usefully be considered.

However, Schema Therapy is not suitable for all patients. Original contraindications included active psychosis and chronic or moderate to severe alcohol or drug use (see Young et al., 2003). Nonetheless, clinical reports suggest that formulating psychotic experiences as expressions of toxic parent or dysfunctional coping modes can help point to underlying unmet needs, which can then usefully guide interventions. Additionally, Schema Therapy has been adapted and evaluated for substance-dependent patients, with some initial encouraging outcomes.[5]

Beginning the healing process

The assessment and formulation process allows for a particular expression of limited reparenting. Akin to the healthy parenting of a young child, you show interest in and are attentive to your patient and their activities, validate their unique internal world and offer language and concepts that help them to name and make sense of things. Patients who have lacked such parenting can, as a result, find these initial sessions healing in themselves.

Developing a road map

A full formulation provides an understanding of your patient as a person, not merely their symptoms. It becomes the road map for all that follows, enabling you to be responsive to your patient's needs in any given moment and to draw on a range of change methods within a theoretically consistent framework.

I've always felt, the case conceptualization, if it's off, the treatment won't work, that it's actually central to guiding what you do … if you don't understand what happened in a patient's childhood and adolescence as they're growing up, you can't get them better; you can't do it by just knowing their schemas and their modes, you have to understand how their problems got started.

Jeff Young

Assessment

Case example: Jim

Jim, a 36-year-old construction worker, was referred by his GP for therapy for depression; he also mentioned a recent violent outburst that was concerning Jim.

Jim appeared cold and distant and avoided eye contact as he walked into his first session with his therapist, Mira. She noticed herself feeling a little on edge. When she asked him what had led him to see his GP he looked at the floor and told Mira in an irritated tone that something had happened with his girlfriend, Sarah, and said 'I know she's going to leave me, I just know it. If that happens I may as well end it all.' He said he didn't know why he was there and that 'talking to you isn't going to get Sarah to stay with me.' Mira reflected, 'You're feeling hopeless.' Jim snapped back, 'No, it *is* hopeless.' Mira noticed a slight pang of feeling attacked but girded her empathy, reflecting, 'So what's the point of being here?' Jim responded, 'Yep.'

Mira then enquired, 'What *is* it like for you being here with me in this room?' He said, 'uncomfortable' and started to fidget. 'I've never seen the point of talking about this kind of stuff.' His face flushed, suggesting shame. 'Makes me feel pathetic, weak.' Mira responded, 'Well *I* don't think you're pathetic or weak. It's clearly taken a lot of courage to come here.'

Mira sensed that he might need a bit more help to feel back in control and to regain a sense of self-esteem; it concerned her that his apparent level of discomfort might discourage him from returning for a second session. She commented on how he clearly cared a lot for Sarah and guessed he regretted the argument. He started to open up further, sharing that she was getting fed up of him being miserable – 'and who can blame her' – and thought she was seeing someone else. He said he prided himself on not letting emotions get the better of him but had 'blown it' the other week. On his way home from work he had noticed her car outside a pub; she had said she was going to her mum's that afternoon. When she got home later, he accused her of having an affair, grabbed her phone and smashed it. At this point in the session, he put his head in his hands. Mira said, 'You look pretty upset about that. I'm wondering what you're feeling right now?' He replied, 'That bloody phone cost over £500 to replace!' Mira noticed feeling pushed back by his deflection from her question and his annoyed tone. She paused, reflecting that his anger seemed to be directed at himself, and asked, 'Sounds like you're pretty annoyed at yourself for what you did?' He replied, 'How could I have done something so stupid – what is wrong with me? She was only at the pub to drop off a birthday card to her friend.'

Mira went on to ask more about his relationship with Sarah. Mira heard how she complains that he's emotionally 'cut off' and that while she is lovely, he doesn't put it past her that she will 'screw me over', as previous girlfriends and his ex-wife have done. He also said that it was Sarah who told him he needed to get help after the incident, otherwise she would leave him – but that she hadn't moved out from where they live together and recently had told him she loved him.

Mira asked what he had meant earlier when he'd said he 'may as well end it all' if Sarah left him. He said he just couldn't bear living with another failure, another rejection and being on his own again. He hadn't made specific plans, and wouldn't do it while his mum was still alive but did think about the high bridge nearby that was nicknamed 'Suicide Bridge'.

Before the session ended, Mira shared with Jim, 'I can see that you feel terrible about what you've done and keep having a go at yourself for it as well as being afraid that Sarah will leave you. I know that you're really uncomfortable talking about these things but I'd like to help you feel less rough, help you understand what led to your outburst, get a kinder view of yourself and develop other ways of dealing with moments like those. You clearly care deeply about Sarah but feel insecure about the relationship. I know *you* think differently right now, but it sounds to me like she wants to make it work and I think I can help with that. What do you feel about giving this a try and seeing me again?'

He agreed to 'give it a go'.

In the early sessions there are many layers to your therapeutic work. In the exerpt above, for example, Mira is attempting to create a safe setting for Jim to open up and self-reflect, to engender hope, managing her own feelings and also aiming to formulate the nature of his difficulties at a more cognitive level.

Distinctive features of assessment in Schema Therapy

An assessment interview in Schema Therapy has similarities to a standard clinical interview. A key difference, however, is that whatever you ask, be it about goals for therapy, their history or any previous therapy, you aim to discover their unmet emotional and relational needs and the origins and current expressions of their schemas and modes. You then explore together what is needed to engender desired changes. Identifying unmet needs will also indicate to you the particular qualities of your limited reparenting that will enable healing.

You will more readily help your patient to piece together relevant parts of their 'puzzle' if you have a good understanding of core needs and are familiar with the 18 maladaptive schemas (Young et al., 2003, pp. 14–17) and prototypical schema modes (see Bernstein and colleagues' helpful descriptions (Van den Broek et al., 2011) and *Breaking Negative Thinking Patterns* (Jacob et al., 2015)).

As your patient shares with you, pay particular attention to emotions they mention (for example, fear, loneliness, frustration) or show in their face or body (for example, looking down or bouncing their foot) as these often provide a window to their 'Vulnerable Child' mode. Listen for explicit or implicit negative, self-directed messages, including demands or criticisms, which could express the messages of an inner 'toxic parent' mode. Notice the qualities of their interactions with you and how these have an impact on how you feel, in order to help discern possible 'coping modes', such as self-aggrandisement, excessive compliance or emotional detachment. Finally, attend to signs of your patient's 'Healthy Adult', including strengths[6] – such as creativity or courage – and interests they pursue, which can give rise to meaningful metaphors and playful interaction between you and the patient.

Imagery for assessment is a powerful experiential technique used in Schema Therapy to deepen your and your patient's understanding of the impact of key childhood experiences, the nature of their unmet needs, related schemas and modes and their origins. This method is detailed in Chapter 2, and so will not be described here.

As Mira reflected on Jim's first session, she hypothesised the following schemas and modes and, thus, began formulating even at this early stage.

Jim's averted eye contact, blushing, sense of being weak and his idea that Sarah couldn't be blamed for being fed up with him, all suggested to Mira a Defectiveness/Shame schema. She hypothesised a Punitive Parent mode, knowing that this typically accompanies this schema and delivers shaming messages. This was consistent with Jim's implied self-talk: 'You're pathetic and weak'; 'No wonder Sarah wouldn't want to be with you'; 'What is wrong with you?' She noted that Jim is likely to feel shame in his Little Side, which would, in all likelihood, believe these messages, as a child would believe what they are told by a parent.

Jim's prediction that Sarah would leave him suggested to Mira a possible Abandonment schema. His idea that she was being unfaithful, as previous partners had been, and his general view that others 'screw you over' pointed to a possible Mistrust/Abuse schema. If present, these schemas would give rise to fears and feelings of being abandoned and abused in Little Jim. Mira noted to herself that Jim may be prone to feeling mistrustful towards her and possibly afraid of becoming attached due to fears of feeling abandoned.

Jim's stern demeanour, irritable responses and her sense of being pushed away by him, Mira thought, would be consistent with this, and suggested to her an Angry Protector mode. She reflected that her pang of feeling attacked would make sense, given the passive–aggressive nature of this mode.

Jim's stated view that there was no point in seeing Mira, Sarah's complaints that he was 'cut off' and his pride in not letting emotions 'get the better of him' suggested to Mira possible Emotional Deprivation and Emotional Inhibition schemas and a Detached Protector mode – as did his general avoidance of emotion in the session. If he did typically suppress his feelings and fears this would, she thought, set him up for an emotional outburst.

Mira reflected that Jim's pessimism about his relationship with Sarah and the usefulness of therapy, and his suicidal thoughts, potentially indicated a Pessimism schema and Hopeless Surrenderer-type mode. However, she also held in mind that these could be symptomatic of his depression and current situation, rather than being lifelong characteristics.

Finally, Mira noted that, in spite of this, his Healthy Adult had taken charge and brought him to this initial session, suggesting that a part of him did hold some hope.

In-session emotion

Moments in which your patient displays emotion are particularly important to attend to. This is often their Little Side, or emotional aspects of a coping mode. You may, for example, notice them becoming tearful, their face flushing, a wobble in their tone of voice, subvocal laughs or a sigh and hands going behind their head. Unless you sense that it is too soon – it might feel unsafe or intrusive for some patients until they build trust in you – in these moments, leave the content of the dialogue to one side. Slow down and allow yourself time to attune to their experience in that moment. You might intuit what they are feeling and say, for example, 'That was painful' or 'It sounds like you miss them'. Alternatively, you may share an observation and enquire after what they are feeling: for example, 'I noticed you put your hand on your heart and looked away; how are you feeling?'; or 'I'm wondering what's going on for you right now; you look sad?' Their responses can provide a rich source of understanding and can be explored further.

Consider the following possible responses to the enquiry, 'I'm wondering what you're feeling right now?' and the schemas and modes these might suggest.

1. *I'm not sure – this is what happens: I cry but I don't feel anything.*

Suggests the presence of a Detached Protector mode and an Emotional Deprivation schema, as the patient is not feeling the emotions that are suggested physically through their crying.

2. *Sorry [they take a breath, sit up and smile]. I'm okay.*

Apologising and reassuring the therapist they're all right suggests they may fear their emotions will be too much for the therapist to manage so they change their demeanour. This points to Self-Sacrifice, Emotional Deprivation and/or Subjugation schemas, which tend to fuel this kind of manifestation of a Compliant Surrenderer mode.

3. *[Weeping:] I've never had anyone say that to me, anyone understanding how bad that was for me.*

The Vulnerable Child mode is felt here, expressing invalidation (a form of Emotional Deprivation) as their experienced norm.

The Young Schema Questionnaire

Typically, you would invite your patient to complete a Young Schema Questionnaire (YSQ)[7] at the end of a first session, asking them to return it before the next session to allow you time to score and interpret it.[8] The latest versions of the YSQ are the 90 item YSQ-S3 and the longer 232 item YSQ-L3. Both measure the 18 schemas identified by Young (Young et al., 2003) and tap into primarily cognitive, rather than affective, components. Norms are available for the YSQ-S3 (Calvete et al., 2013) and an interpretation grid accompanies the YSQ-L3, allowing the totals for each schema sub-scale to be identified as low, medium, high or very high scores. Although the YSQ-LS offers more information, the short version is adequate, and a more realistic option for patients.

In addition to using sub-scale totals (or mean averages) to identify the presence and strength of schemas (as advised by Waller et al., 2001), it is important to attend to single items that attract scores of 5 or 6, 6 being the maximum score for each item. Young et al. (2003, p. 75) report: 'We have observed clinically that, if a patient has three or more high scores (rated 5 or 6) on a particular schema, that schema is usually relevant to the patient and worthy of exploration'.

Interpreting and discussing YSQ results

Before discussing your patient's results, ask them how completing the questionnaire was for them, exploring their reactions, as this can provide relevant information. Here are some ways that you might feed back and discuss YSQ results with your patient:

This questionnaire suggests that your strongest schemas are Self-Sacrifice and Unrelent-
ing Standards. I'm interested to know about the ways in which you might resonate
with these themes.

Someone with a Self-Sacrifice schema typically tunes into and complies with others'
feelings and preferences and neglects their own. Does that resonate with you?

This may be to prevent feeling guilty or selfish; or because you have strong empathy
for others' feelings; or you may believe you need to please others in order to be
liked. Do any of these ring true for you – or do you have other ideas about why
you do this?

When we habitually give more than we receive, it's normal to get resentful. Do you
notice that at times?

You also score highly on Unrelenting Standards. This comes in three different forms:

- *Perfectionism*
- *High moral standards that are impossible to meet*
- *A focus on efficiency and accomplishing as much as you can in every*
  moment

Which of these do you relate to?
How do you think that affects your relationships?
I'm wondering what you feel about relaxing or doing something just for fun?

As the above examples highlight, it is important to know the various qualities a schema may have, as this then guides questioning that helps to elicit fine-grained understandings of your patient's schemas and how they manifest. Attending to discrepancies within sub-scales can also be vital to accurate interpretation.

For example, Sophia gave scores of 6 to two Vulnerability to Harm items: 'I feel a disaster (natural, criminal, financial, or medical) could strike at any moment' and 'I worry I'll lose all my money and become destitute and very poor'. She scored other items in this sub-scale '1'. Discussion revealed that her business was struggling and simultaneously her roof required expensive repairs. Further exploration clarified that her high scores did not point to a schema but instead to current, situational anxiety.

Beth gave high scores (5s) only to the Entitlement items: 'I hate to be constrained or kept from doing what I want' and 'I have a lot of trouble accepting "no" for an answer when I want something from other people'. However, rather than pointing to an Entitlement schema, these responses reflected her remembering the times when, as a relief worker in Syria, she had to push through constraints and regulations in order to secure supplies needed by refugees.

Adi, like Beth, gave high scores to Entitlement items relating to a dislike of externally imposed boundaries and low scores to Entitlement items that point to a sense of superiority. Discussion with him revealed that his high scores represented overcompensation for his Subjugation schema rather than an Entitlement schema.

Low YSQ scores

It is important to note that low scores on a YSQ subscale do not necessarily mean the absence of the associated schema. There are a number of possible reasons for this:

- The patient's schema may be out of their view because their current life situation may not contain triggers, perhaps due to avoidant coping.
- They might be pervasively overcompensating for a schema and so not realise that it is driving such behaviour; for example, being dominant in relationships out of fear of subjugation; or frequently having people over for dinner to be at the centre of social gatherings and thus avoiding feeling their Social Exclusion/Isolation schema.
- If their schema attitudes and beliefs are socially undesirable (for example, Self-Aggrandisement, Approval/Recognition-Seeking and Entitlement beliefs) they may deny them when completing the YSQ.
- Their default state may be highly detached and so they be out of touch with a true sense of themselves.
- The schema itself may influence your patient's self-assessment; this is particularly common with Emotional Deprivation. This schema typically originates in contexts in which the patient receives implicit messages that their emotionally depriving experiences are normal and that do not recognise needs, for example, for attunement or praise, as valid. The patient may therefore underestimate the extent to which the needs to which the YSQ's Emotional Deprivation items point, have remained unmet.

When Mira asked Jim how he found filling in the YSQ, he said he had done it quickly and thinking as little as possible – suggesting avoidant coping. He scored very high on Mistrust/Abuse, high on Emotional Inhibition and Pessimism and low on all other schemas. Jim and Mira discussed his strongest themes and Jim felt they resonated with him. Mira continued to hold in mind that Defectiveness, Emotional Deprivation and Abandonment might also be relevant, thinking that Jim's dismissiveness of emotion might explain his low scores on these YSQ items. She invited him to read *Reinventing Your Life* (Young & Klosko, 1994) to see if he might recognise these schemas in himself through reading examples of how they manifest.

Schema Mode Inventory

The Schema Mode Inventory (SMI; Young et al., 2007) may be given to patients at the same time as the YSQ. It has 118 items and taps into 14 schema modes. It can be a useful tool if you are still learning about schema modes, but it should not be relied on to identify all of your patients' modes as it only assesses for a limited number. As mentioned above, we recommend Bernstein and colleagues' list and descriptions (Van den Broek et al., 2011) to orientate you to a broader range of modes. *Breaking Negative Thinking Patterns* (Jacob et al., 2015) describes an even fuller range of mode prototypes and, being written for patients, could be a better way for them to identify and understand their modes than the SMI.

As with other inventories, it is the process of unpacking responses with your patient that is valuable. Ask for specific stories that illustrate their modes in order to understand their particular expressions of them. Wherever fitting, use your patient's language to name their mode: for example, if they have mentioned being 'guarded', you might consider with them, naming their Detached Protector mode 'The Guard'.

Jim's SMI responses gave high scores for Vulnerable Child, Detached Protector and Punishing Parent modes; moderate scores for the Angry Child, Impulsive Child and Healthy Adult modes; and low scores for the other modes, broadly confirming Mira's developing hypotheses.

Family history and upbringing

When asking about your patient's upbringing, including discussions of Young Parenting Inventory (YPI) results (see below), aim to enter into their felt experiences as a child, rather than simply to gather facts. Try to visualise and sense some of what it was like to be them, endeavouring to understand how your patient was uniquely affected by their experiences. You may ask your patient for a picture of them as a child and keep it nearby to help you and them to connect to their Little Side.

Listen for where your patient's childhood needs were and weren't met and why they might have developed coping strategies and modes, considering temperament (see more below) as well as exploring what was modelled or rewarded by parents. For example, they might have been praised for fighting back at school or, alternatively, taught to stay quiet and out of the way.

Asking, 'I wonder what your first memory was?' can be a way to access an early, emotionally relevant memory. Questions of the form 'What it was like to ...'; 'I imagine that was tough – how was it for you, how did that affect you?' can help them to unpack their experiences and give you an opportunity to validate the effects of such. You can also point out positive qualities that their accounts demonstrate, which may help to convey your esteem for them and to counter any internalised critical parental voice by 'jumping on' their strengths rather than any mistakes. Also note whether their answers to your questions focus predominantly on external information: for example, how it was for others at the time, or on their own inner experience. This can point you to how attuned they are to their internal experience or whether this reflects an unmet need, probably in the realm of Emotional Deprivation.

Exploring the origins of a coping mode that is live in-session can provide a way in to exploring formative childhood experiences.

When Jim arrived at his fourth session, Mira commented that he looked particularly down. He snapped back that his week had been 'crap as usual'. Sarah had been out a lot, 'apparently' with her female friends; he thought she was deliberately looking for another man, and that he'd been stupid to start to get his hopes up that she'd stay with him. Mira reflected aloud, 'It seems that you tend to expect the worst, and that when you slip into being a bit more hopeful, your critical side jumps in to have a go at you and pushes you back into expecting the worst, as if this will be less painful somehow.'

Jim nodded and said, 'If you don't get your hopes up you've got nowhere to fall from.' Mira asked 'When did you start thinking that way do you think? How young were you?' Jim paused and said, 'There's one thing that has stuck with me – probably just nothing. It was when I was about seven. I'd made a Lego castle with turrets and a flag and rooms and I was so proud of it. Mum walked by, glanced at it and walked on. I said, "Mum, come and look at my castle!" But she snapped "Stop bugging me!". I went mad – I shouted and smashed up the castle. For a while I gave up making stuff with Lego and I vowed I would never show Mum anything I made ever again.'

Mira said she didn't think this was 'nothing' and that surely every little boy would want their mum to be delighted to see what they'd made, to hear her notice all of the care that had gone into the details, to say how clever he was to have figured out how to do the turrets – perhaps even to have helped him make it in the first place. Jim's eyes teared up, hearing the love and attention he craved expressed and validated by Mira's reparenting stance. 'No wonder, given this level of pain, you gave up playing with Lego for a bit and hoping for your mum's interest – it was a way of protecting yourself from further pain.' They then discussed how giving up and not hoping became a broader strategy to self-protect and named it his 'Give Up' mode.

The Young Parenting Inventory

The questions asked in the 72-item YPI (Young, 1994) are designed to identify parenting received as a child that may have contributed to schema development.[9] Answers are given with reference to each parent separately; if there were other key parenting figures in childhood – say grandparents or a step-parent – a patient can additionally or alternatively answer with reference to them. The YPI would typically be completed following the second session so as not to overwhelm them with too many long questionnaires right at the start of therapy. The inventory was designed as a clinical tool and so subscales should not be summed or average scores calculated. Instead, attend to high-scoring items – 5s or 6s – and ask for examples of these.

As with the YSQ, before asking about the content of the questionnaire, explore how it was for them to complete it. For example, did it evoke pain or anger as bad memories were recalled? Or guilt for portraying parents as imperfect?

This inventory can help prompt your patient to share childhood experiences that they might not otherwise think to mention or shy away from volunteering. Discussions of these can provide an opportunity to explore core needs that may have gone unmet and unnoticed.

Jim's dad left when he was a baby and his mum subsequently had various boyfriends who came and went. Her last boyfriend, Tony, moved in when Jim was six. Therefore, Jim completed the YPI in relation to his mum and Tony. Mira had received general and unclear responses to her questions about Jim's childhood, so enquiring about his YPI responses helped Jim give her a clearer picture.

Jim described his mum as a 'good mum' who took care of his practical needs but gave her scores on the YPI that pointed to Emotional Deprivation. He recalled her as highly stressed and irritable, drunk and loud, or else preoccupied with pleasing the current man in her life. Jim struggled to recall her giving him physical affection or praise, or showing an interest in him. He withdrew, usually playing alone and absorbing himself with Lego, and repeated the story he had told earlier about his mum's disinterest in what he had built. He also remembered crying and feeling sad when he was on his own in his room.

Mira enquiring about Jim's responses to the Mistrust/Abuse questions on the YPI led him to disclose the sexual abuse he suffered from Tony between the ages of seven and 11. He described how, in contrast to when others were around, Tony appeared caring towards him and so Jim didn't think his mum would believe him if he told her.

Introducing Schema Therapy to your patient

As it becomes clear that Schema Therapy might be a good fit for your patient, it can be helpful to outline the model to see how they feel about it. *Reinventing Your Life* (Young & Klosko, 1994), which helps patients deepen and expand their understanding of schemas or 'lifetraps' and coping responses, and *Breaking Negative Thinking Patterns* (Jacob et al., 2015), which uses the schema *mode* framework, can also be recommended to orientate them to the approach.

Mira introduced Schema Therapy to Jim by saying:

'We all have basic needs as children beyond being fed and clothed, including to feel safe, loved and competent. When these aren't met, what we feel and believe about ourselves and others gets distorted – like tinted glasses that colour how we see and react to things. We call these kind of glasses a 'schema'.

'When I think about how Tony treated you, it's clear that your needs to feel safe and valuable weren't met. I guess you learned something like, "others can't be trusted" and "I'm worthless".

'As children, we do the best we know to cope when our needs aren't met. There was no one to help you with your feelings and you even got punished for having them, so one way you learnt to cope was to shut them down.

'We typically carry on coping in life as we did as a child; we don't change just because we are 15, 25, or even 40. But often our coping strategies lose their effectiveness or start to cause more problems than they solve.

'So, for example, by detaching you don't get close to people so they can't hurt you. But then you feel lonely underneath and Sarah complains that you're emotionally "cut off". You don't want to lose her, but it's hard for you to open up because your schemas make it hard to believe she loves and wants to stay with you. It seems that you've been bottling up your fears that she'll cheat and leave, but these feelings don't go away. So when there were just enough signs for you to conclude she was cheating, you exploded. And now you're having a go at yourself for losing control.

'I'd like to help you turn down the volume on the voice that has a go at you, forgive yourself, get better at expressing what you feel and feel more secure with Sarah. Schema Therapy is designed to help weaken your schemas and strengthen your healthy side so that you can feel safe, enjoy fulfilling, loving relationships and feel happier generally.'

Temperament

Temperament is important to consider in understanding your patient, as it influences preferences, values, forms of coping, levels of emotional intensity experienced and so on. You might explore this aspect of your patient by having them ask a trusted family member or family friend how they remembered them being as a child.

Young (Young et al., 2003, p. 86) proposed the following dimensions of temperament as potentially relevant in schema acquisition:

> Labile <> Non reactive
> Dysthymic <> Optimisitic
> Anxious <> Calm
> Obsessive <> Distractible
> Passive <> Aggressive
> Irritable <> Cheerful
> Shy <> Sociable

Research suggests that individuals' sensitivity to the quality of parenting they receive varies (e.g., Belsky & Pluess, 2009). Sensitive individuals thrive more than their less sensitive counterparts when they receive exceptional parenting, and are more adversely impacted by poor parenting. This may explain why some patients with less traumatic histories develop severe schemas (Lockwood & Perris, 2012). Such patients may be more prone to criticise themselves for the intensity of their reactions and severity of their symptoms, especially if, for example, their siblings appear to have been less affected by very similar childhood experiences. For these patients it can be particularly important to explain the effect of temperamental differences and to help them appreciate the strengths and qualities of sensitivity, for example, their vitality or ability to connect with people.

Temperament appears to influence coping style and methods. For example, a child with an optimistic and sociable temperament might seek and elicit need-meeting outside of their nuclear family in a way that a dysthymic and shy child is unlikely to do. A child with a more passive temperament may try to placate an angry parent and develop a Compliant Surrenderer mode, whereas a child with a more aggressive temperament might argue and develop a Bully/Attack mode.

Spirituality, culture and diversity

Faith, class, culture, ethnicity, sexuality and other dimensions of our identity and experience can influence the development and content of schemas and modes. For example, being gay in certain cultures may exacerbate a Social Isolation or Defectivness schema; the Catholic practice of confession may exacerbate cycling between Guilt-inducing Parent and Compulsively Confessional modes; a felt sense of God as a strong, compassionate and wise parent, or meditative practices may enhance a Healthy Adult mode.

Some patients may feel awkward about mentioning an aspect of themselves if it is dismissed or ridiculed in the dominant culture's narrative or if you appear different from them in this respect, perhaps imagining you could not relate to it. It can, therefore, be important for you to enquire proactively: for example, asking if they hold a particular spiritual or cultural worldview. So as not to make faulty assumptions, when working with someone who has a characteristic or is from a culture that is unfamiliar to you, it can be important to take an even more open and curious stance than usual. Additionally, in some instances, it can be helpful to consult others to understand how features of difference or spiritual or cultural expressions, can be upheld in emotionally and relationally healthy ways.

Therapist schemas and the therapy relationship

Tune in to your feelings and internal reactions when you are with your patient. Consider how you feel towards them: connected to them? Irritated by them? Do you feel sad for them or unmoved by their stories of suffering? Does part of their history resonate with you and feel personally painful? What ways of being do they elicit from you – do you have an urge to talk about solutions, to theorise, to flirt, to prove yourself …?

Consider what your responses tell you. For example, being unmoved by accounts of suffering could suggest that your patient has been inhabiting a Complaining Protector mode. Additionally, conceptualising your internal responses in terms of *your* schemas and modes can help you discover what your Little Side needs in order to maintain the presence of your Healthy Adult. It can also help you formulate what your patient may evoke in others when they express themselves from a particular mode, enabling you to hypothesise mode cycles within their relationships. For example a patient in their Complaining Protector mode may cause their partner to switch off (i.e., it may trigger their Detached Protector), leaving the patient feeling invalidated and misunderstood, which then may increase their Complaining Protector's efforts to get some response from their partner.

Supervision and personal therapy are invaluable when our schemas are activated, as this is when our normal level of insight and flexibility plummet. Increasing your awareness of, learning to manage and, ideally, healing, your schemas, will allow you to maintain a healthy reparenting stance and broaden the range of patients to whom you can provide effective therapy. Discussions in supervision or therapy may, alternatively, lead to an equally legitimate outcome of not continuing with a particular patient, if, for example, their coping modes trigger you too intensely at this point in your personal development.

In supervision, Mira explored how her pang of feeling attacked and pushed away by Jim were partly due to her Subjugation and Emotional Deprivation schemas. She reflected that, in each instance, she initially felt a little cowed, then strove to work harder to please and reconnect with Jim as her Compliant Surrenderer coping mode was activated. Mira considered with her supervisor what she might need to stay sturdy and in her Healthy Big Mira mode. They also reflected on what might have been triggered for Jim, given that, in each instance, his irritated tone was preceded by Mira focusing on his feelings. They hypothesised that it was a way of keeping people at arm's length to feel safe because being emotionally vulnerable could trigger his Mistrust/Abuse, Defectiveness or Emotional Deprivation schemas. They agreed that his coping seemed to fit an Angry Protector type of coping mode. Mira then started to imagine that this might be what Sarah experiences and an aspect of her feeling that Jim is 'cut off'. Based on what she had heard about Sarah, Mira hypothesised that her reaction to this may be to criticise. If so, this would trigger Jim's Defectiveness schema, thus reinforcing his felt need to keep others emotionally distant, and so a schema-response cycle would be set in motion.

When Mira next noticed a 'prickly' response from Jim, she asked if they could stop, step back and reflect on what just happened. They unpacked together how he did indeed feel discomfort when she focused on his emotions but hadn't been aware that he responded in a prickly way until now, when she pointed it out. She empathised with why this might be, given his various, understandable fears and also shared that she felt a little 'jabbed' when she was wanting to show care and that it threw her off being fully attuned to him. She emphasised that she knew he wasn't intending to hurt her but simply had developed spikes as a self-defence. To help avert any sense that she was criticising him, she became a little playful and suggested that in these moments he was perhaps 'a bit like a porcupine?' He chuckled. She wondered aloud if Sarah perhaps felt occasionally jabbed by his porcupine spikes and perhaps this was part of her feeling 'cut off' from him.

Formulating

Building a formulation

A formulation is an evolving construct, open to revision throughout therapy as new information emerges. Nonetheless, it is useful to develop an overarching case conceptualisation early in therapy. Formulating essentially involves making links between a patient's early years where schemas were formed due to unmet needs and coping styles were developed, and present day experiences in which schemas are triggered and unhealthy current patterns develop that give rise to dysfunction. The Schema Therapy Case Conceptualization Form (2nd edition, 2018) provides a format that encourages careful and comprehensive thinking about your patients and provides a place to pull together the information you gather throughout your assessment, within a Schema Therapy framework.

Building blocks of Schema Therapy assessment and formulation

In formulating with your patient you are looking to:

- Understand their presenting problems and therapy goals
- Identify schemas, coping responses and modes linked to their presenting problems
- Explore origins of their schemas and modes, including unmet needs in childhood or adolescence, in the context of temperament, social, spiritual, cultural and other perpetuating/protective factors
- Understand mode dynamics in the therapy relationship: what do they pull in you and vice versa
- Identify their needs for limited reparenting, including empathic confrontation
- Identify punitive, demanding, guilt inducing or fear-mongering messages of Dysfunctional Parent Modes and their impact on the patient's Child modes

- Explore active feelings and unmet needs in the patient's Vulnerable and Angry child modes
- Understand the nature, function, benefits and costs of coping modes
- Identify core features and strengths of Healthy Adult
- Develop a treatment plan, based on an understanding of their unmet needs and aspirations for therapy

Schema formulation

For most patients, a mode formulation, which incorporates schemas, is helpful. However, for patients who present with discrete problem patterns, formulating and working at a schema level may suffice.

Consider, for example, Orla, whose single goal for therapy is to reduce procrastination in her work as a teacher. Her most prominent schemas are Insufficient Self-control, Failure and Unrelenting Standards. The latter two appear to stem from underperforming at school, which her high achieving parents viewed back then as a lack of ability, her dyslexia only being diagnosed in adulthood. It may be sufficient to conceptualise her one expression of Insufficient Self-Control that showed as avoidance of lesson preparation – until the last minute – as being a coping response to a fear of failing.

Now when Orla procrastinates, it allows her to attribute any failures to her 'not having done enough work' rather than her feared incompetence. Her fear of failure appears to have arisen from the childhood experiences in which she believed herself to be 'stupid' and is maintained by the unrealistic standards she has of her students – that they all get A grades and behave perfectly in class. The goal of therapy and the focus of change can be formulated sufficiently as meeting the unmet needs signified by her Unrelenting Standards and Failure schemas: realistic goal-setting and the experience of mastery and competence. A range of strategies – for example, childhood imagery rescripting, chair work and reparenting – may be employed to this end.

Table 1.1 summarises Jim's schemas, based on assessment interviews, discussions of YSQ and YPI scores and how he presented and interacted in initial sessions. These have been linked to unmet childhood needs and to particular qualities needed in Mira's limited reparenting.

Formulation integrating schemas and modes

There is not a direct correlation between schemas and modes; they do not neatly correspond. Certain schemas, however, are activated and felt most in

Table 1.1 Summary of schemas, unmet needs and required reparenting

Schema	Unmet childhood needs	Current related unmet needs and most relevant modes	Corrective reparenting needed from Mira
Emotional Deprivation	Mum & Tony: lack of warmth, affection, attention, protection and guidance. Absence of other caring or reliable attachment figures in the family or at school.	Sense of safety, reliable emotional connection, affection, attention, validation, understanding of, and responsiveness to, feelings and needs. *(Little Jim, Porcupine & Wall)*	Sense of safety, reliable nurturing, warmth, empathy, validation of and respsonsiveness to Jim's feelings and needs. Trust-building so as to bypass the Wall and Porcupine and reach Little Jim. Guidance and protection (e.g., in imagery and chair work).
Emotional Inhibition	Mum: unavailable or else annoyed when Jim was upset so he shut down his feelings. Tony: never expressed vulnerable feelings and told Jim he was a 'cry baby' when he showed valid fear.	Open expression of emotions and needs, including safe venting of anger; encouragement to be spontaneous and playful. *(Little Jim, Porcupine & Wall)*	Encouragement to express feelings spontaneously, including his feelings about Mira and the work they are doing together. Modelling of this and also playfulness, by Mira.
Mistrust/ abuse	Tony: sexual abuse, vacillation between being charming/caring and abusive. Sense of betrayal that his mum chose Tony above him.	Experience of trustworthy people who care about him and treat him well. *(Little Jim & Porcupine)*	Genuineness, trustworthiness, honesty, openness.
Defectiveness	Jim took his mum's neglect to mean he was unlovable and her irritability to mean he and his feelings were unacceptable. He took being sexually abused by Tony as a sign of his worthlessness.	Acceptance and love for him by those who know his vulnerabilities as well as his strengths. Compassionate stance towards self. *(Little Jim & Punitive Parent)*	A compassionate stance towards mistakes, praise and compliments. Willingness to show imperfections. Protection of Little Jim from Jim's Punitive Parent.
Abandonment	Jim's dad left when he was a baby, and before Tony came on the scene, Jim's mum was inconsistently available, giving priority to her boyfriends.	Stable, consistently available attachment figure. *(Little Jim, Give Up, Porcupine & The Wall)*	Reliability, regular session times, availability between sessions (within limits), advance notice of, and attention to, reactions to breaks in therapy, e.g., due to vacations.

(Continued)

Table 1.1 (Cont.)

Schema	Unmet childhood needs	Current related unmet needs and most relevant modes	Corrective reparenting needed from Mira
Pessimism	Modelled by mum's bleak attitude that 'things will go wrong, the world is a tough place'. Lack of sustained positive events or experiences at home or at school as a child.	A sense of efficacy, being able to envision a future in which things work out for him. *(Little Jim, Punitive Parent, Give up)*	Modelling of healthy optimism. Having Jim envision and generate more optimistic alternative points of view to his pessimistic stance, including those in which he effects change, rather than provide these herself.

the Vulnerable Child, for example, Abandonment, Emotional Deprivation and Defectiveness. Other schemas show up predominantly in coping modes, for example, Emotional Inhibition (in a Detached mode), Entitlement (in a Self-Aggrandiser mode) and Self-Sacrifice (in a Compliant Surrenderer mode). Other schemas span across modes. For example, the Unrelenting Standards is expressed in the Demanding Parent's 'oughts', 'shoulds', 'musts' and excessive responsibility-giving, felt in the Vulnerable Child as inadequacy, pressure and/or guilt; and acted upon by a Perfectionistic-Overcontroller type of coping mode that strives to meet the parent mode's excessive demands.

The first time you introduce the mode concept to your patient you might begin by using their prototypical names such as those used in the SMI (Young et al., 2007). However, formulating modes involves exploring their idiosyncratic natures, origins, motives and potential downsides; mode names ideally capture these. As previously mentioned, words your patient uses in describing their experience of a mode may help in generating emotionally resonant names. For example a 'Self-Aggrandiser' type of mode may be named 'I'm Amazing!' if this is how your patient describes how it feels to be in it. Similarly, a Compliant Surrenderer side might be named, 'People Pleaser' or 'Keep Others Calm'; a 'Complaining Protector' may be felt as a 'Rescue Me!' mode; an Angry Protector may be called 'Go Away'; a Demanding Parent mode may be named 'The Dictator'.

You might explore modes, or 'ways of being', with your patient that exhibit characteristics of two mode prototypes at once. If so, you can think of this as a 'merged' or 'blended' mode. Examples include:

Workaholic mode = Perfectionist Over-controller + Detached Self-Stimulator
Angry-Superior = Angry Protector + Self-Aggrandiser

Perfect Rescuer = Compliant Surrenderer + Ideal Self form of Self-Aggrandiser

Vengeful Protector = Angry Child + Bully-Attack

When Mira guided Jim through an imagery for assessment exercise (see Chapter 2 for more about this method) Jim struggled to connect to feel he was 'in' the visualisations and kept opening his eyes (displaying emotional detachment). He reported being too conscious of being watched by Mira, suggesting his Defectiveness schema had been triggered. The childhood image that showed up was of being told off harshly by his mum when he was seven years old, after he'd complained and cried angrily that she didn't look properly at the Lego castle he'd built, and smashed it. The current day image to which this childhood image was linked was of him immediately after breaking Sarah's phone, seeing her fear and remembering that she had told him about her friend's birthday. This exercise pointed to the origins of his Emotional Deprivation and Defectivenss schemas and his Angry/ Impulsive Child mode; and unmet needs, including expressing his feelings and needs before they build up and self-compassion.

Formulating self-harm and suicidality

If your patient exhibits risk then it is essential to include this in your formulation. Underlying the risk there will often be a child mode in enormous pain. However, there can be a range of reasons for risky behaviour, and these may sit in different modes, for example:

Vulnerable Child

*   To feel real, if dissociative

Detached Protector/Self-Soother

*   To mask emotional pain with physical pain that feels more bearable
*   For an endorphin release
*   To block out other unwanted feelings/to dissociate
*   To escape from pain permanently via death

Punitive Parent

*   To punish self – an attempt to purge guilt

Angry Child

*   To punish others
*   To communicate anger

Angry Protector

- To keep others away by becoming unattractive

Complaining Protector

- To elicit care from others, indirectly
- To communicate grievance while blocking help due to mistrust

Hopeless Surrender

- To protect from feelings of loss and disappointment

Creative ways to represent formulations

Mapping out your patient's 'big picture' formulation serves a number of functions. It enhances their meta-perspective – that is, their awareness of different sides or parts of themselves. Where some parts are socially undesirable, this overarching view emphasises that less acceptable parts do not reflect *all* of who they are, rather learned ways of being. Finally, it outlines the path towards desired change.

This 'big picture' conceptualisation may develop incrementally, putting together the pieces of the jigsaw one at a time with your patient, or, alternatively, a complete overview may be represented all at once.

Mode map

When using a mode formulation, representing this visually can help your patient hold in mind and recognise modes when they arise. It can also help them to gather a sense of the relationships between their modes. Drawing a 'mode map' (Figure 1.1) is one way to do this and is something they can take with them to refer to between sessions.

When drawing out problem-generating modes, take a compassionate, curious stance. For example, when drawing toxic parent modes with your patient, you might say 'We're designed to learn about the world and ourselves from our parents. It would be odd if you didn't absorb your parent's messages about yourself. The fact you have this Demanding/Punitive Parent side of you shows that you have a brain that learns well. Sadly, it was fed harmful and wrong information and you've been left with this in your head.'

As you draw out coping modes, be careful to acknowledge how they have felt and still feel helpful now, if relevant. Empathise with why they originally

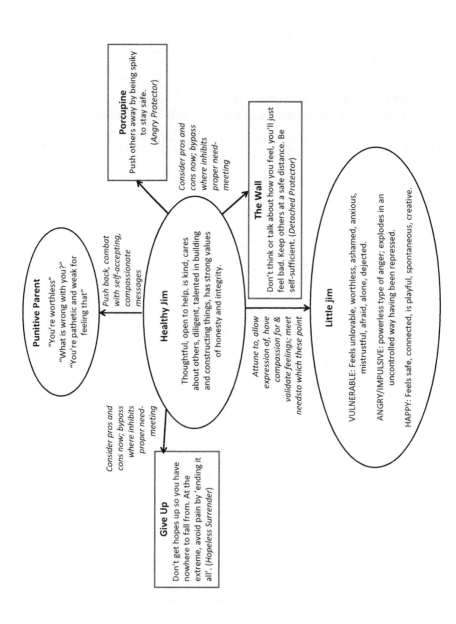

Figure 1.1 Jim's mode map.

developed, considering the context of unmet needs, their temperament, and what was rewarded and modelled to them, maintaining respect for the good intentions of these modes.

In Figure 1.1, the Healthy Adult is placed in the centre, allowing its different roles in relation to other mode types to be shown easily. However, you may prefer to position it elsewhere: for example, at the top of the page, to suggest that it presides over other modes (see, for example, Arntz & Jacob, 2012). Wherever placed visually, it is important to acknowledge your patient's Healthy Side, and to explain that the pathway to their desired changes – to meeting their therapy goals – is to strengthen this, their 'Big Side', in its various roles. You might describe these roles as:

- Being aware of which mode is currently active
- Assessing the usefulness of coping modes and weakening or bypassing them[10] to allow emotional connection with Child modes
- Attending to and meeting the needs expressed by Child modes
- Moderating or combatting toxic parent modes

Chairs

Arranging chairs in the room to symbolise your patient's schemas or modes has the advantages of making them present and immediate and of enabling the relationships between them to be played out.

If used with Jim, he might, for example, be invited to sit in a chair representing his Punitive Parent mode and to deliver its messages, in the tone he hears them in his head, to an empty chair that represents his Little Side. Jim would then be asked to move to the 'Little Jim' chair, to feel what it is like to receive these messages and to take up the posture that shows this. He might, for example, bend over to make himself as small as possible in the chair, his head in his hands. Mira could then intervene in a Healthy Adult role to help Jim experience what the 'Big Jim' side of him could be like. She might protect Little Jim, saying to the empty Punitive Parent chair 'You talk to Jim as if he's worthless – that's not true and I won't let you treat him like this.' She might even take this chair out of the room. She would then turn to 'Little Jim' and give him messages that provide a direct antidote to those of the Punitive Parent. How Little Jim then feels as a result of this intervention would then be explored.

Other modes can be represented in the room in ways and positions that express their characteristics. For example, an Avoidant mode could be positioned facing the door, as if wanting to hide away or escape. Placing a chair symbolising a Detached Protector, such as Jim's 'Wall', between Vulnerable Child and Healthy Adult chairs may powerfully demonstrate how it blocks the Little Side from receiving care. The patient could be encouraged to photograph the chairs' positions so they have a visual reminder to take away with them, to help consolidate this work.

Adaptations with chairs include having different styles or colours of chairs to represent different schemas and modes. For example, both authors use a hard, black upright chair to represent toxic Parent modes, as it instantly evokes a sense of a foreboding presence. Additionally, post-it notes may be stuck to different chairs to label the schema or mode and its messages.

Pictures, symbols and dolls

Some patients like to draw their schema modes, representing them, for example, as stick figures with speech bubbles. Alternatively, they can be symbolised with very basic materials, such as bits of paper of varying size, shape and colour, pipe cleaner figures, or puppets, enabling the playing out of mode interactions. (See Chapter 9 for visual symbols with Dysfunctional Critic Modes and Chapter 11 for more detail on using visual symbols in working with coping modes.)

One of the authors, AB, uses Russian dolls that have five dolls in decreasing sizes encased in the biggest one. If using these, you might suggest that the largest doll represents a Detached or Protector mode, and by placing the smallest doll, the Vulnerable Child, inside the largest one, you can illustrate its loneliness and isolation; it is disconnected from others and unable to get relational needs met. You can then demonstrate how the big Protector needs to be opened up so the Little Side can get their needs met; this can help the patient weaken their attachment to it as a coping strategy. Alternatively, the therapist might place the littlest doll on a chair and ask the patient to sit on a chair facing it. The patient can then be invited to be the voice of, for instance, their Demanding Parent. This visual representation of the vulnerability and powerlessness of their Little Side can help the patient experience how unreasonable this voice is, providing more insight and pointing to what is needed instead.

Bodily representations

Sometimes, a patient's schemas or modes can be represented by the way they express and present themselves non-verbally. Take, for example, a patient with a deferential, quiet tone and a posture in which their shoulders curve inward. As you note this and explore it with your patient, you might identify this as a bodily representation of their 'Suppressor' mode – a form of Compliant Surrenderer that lets others have a voice but pushes down their own desires and needs.

You might notice other schemas and modes aligning with parts of their body or postures. For example, a Self-Aggrandiser mode, expressing an Entitlement schema, may be in evidence when they place their hands on their hips or behind their head, their Healthy Adult may be present when they are sitting upright, and their Abandoned and Abused Child when in a cowering posture. (See Chapter 3 for ways of working with the body to promote therapeutic change.)

As you can see, you and your patient can be creative and also a bit playful together when exploring, expressing and symbolising their inner world

Conclusion

Schema Therapy provides a relational, theoretical framework within which to formulate collaboratively your patient's problematic patterns. Just as the limbs of the body are coordinated via the spinal cord and central nervous system, an accurate formulation guides the timing and choice of therapeutic change methods. In the same way as the sensory nerves in our limbs provide feedback to the central nervous system, a Schema Therapy formulation is developed and revised as new information emerges, and change methods are reflected upon and adapted to best meet the core needs of the patient.

So, while remaining sufficiently adaptable to incorporate new understandings, the formulation provides a 'road map', or 'scaffold', for everything that follows. It can mark the beginning of your patient moving from a place of pain and chaos to feeling contained, understood, no longer alone and having hope for change. It validates their distress and their needs, and points them to adaptive need-meeting and the prospect of greater well-being, strength and flourishing.

Therapist tips

- Become familiar with the 18 schemas and prototypical modes, so you can readily spot signs of their presence.
- Notice what mode your patient is in at any given time and consider this as something to explore.
- Keep to hand a note – or hold in mind – your patient's early life experiences, including names of key figures, that illustrate unmet needs that give rise to schemas and coping modes.
- Inventories can be valuable tools to support your assessment and emerging formulation. However, responses should be understood in the light of discussions of these and what you experience of your patient directly.
- Know your own schemas, modes and vulnerabilities. Personal therapy is critical for thriving as a schema therapist.
- Formulating can be a dynamic and creative process. Use chairs, symbols and playful interaction to bring this process to life.

Further resources

Other inventories you may wish to investigate include:

- Young Parenting Inventory – Revised (YPI-R2; Louis et al., 2018a)
- Positive Parenting Schema Inventory (PPSI; Louis et al., 2018b)

- Young Positive Schema Questionnaire (YPSQ; Louis et al., 2018c)
- Schema Mode Inventory for Eating Disorders (SMI-ED; Simpson et al., 2018)

The Secure Nest is an online tool developed to support patients' work between sessions and to strengthen the patient–therapist relationship. This would ideally be set up at the start of therapy and can be purchased via www.securenest.org.

Picture cards illustrating different modes as cartoon characters are available for purchase online and can be useful if patients find it hard to identify and describe their schemas, unmet needs or modes verbally (see www.etsy.com/uk/listing/665,868,603/core-childhood-needs-educational-mental?ref=shop_home_active_9; https://schematherapysydney.com.au/mode-cards/; and www.i-modes.com/en/shop/imodes-cards-male-or-female-26-cards/).

Schema Therapy Toolkit video 1: Sharing a mode map (Elaine) demonstrates sharing a full formulation and can be purchased at www.schematherapytoolkit.com.

Notes

1 The terms formulation and case conceptualisation will be used interchangeably in this chapter to refer to an understanding of a patient's presentation within a specific theoretical model, in this case ST.
2 The term 'patient' rather than 'client' is used for consistency between chapters and does not imply use of a medical model, which the authors do not endorse.
3 ST postulates five core areas of childhood need for healthy psychological development (Young & Klosko, 2003): secure attachments to others; autonomy, competence, and sense of identity; freedom to express valid needs and emotions; spontaneity and play; and realistic limits and self control.
4 When one or more childhood need goes consistently unmet, in interaction with temperament – and potentially other factors such as culture – the individual may develop early maladaptive schemas (shortened to 'schemas'), defined as 'self-defeating life patterns of perception, emotion, and physical sensation' (Young et al., 2003).
5 Initial small randomised trials showed promising results for this Dual Focus Schema Therapy (Ball, 2007; Ball et al., 2005; Linehan et al., 1999, 2002). However Ball et al.'s (2011) trial suggests that single focus therapy may be more effective, indicating the need for a clear rationale for including a Schema Therapy component in work with substance dependent patients.
6 Referring to the Values in Action character strengths (Peterson & Seligman, 2004) may help you spot, name and affirm positive characterstics in your patient that they overlook or minimise.
7 To order copies of inventories referred to in this chapter, visit: www.schematherapy.org. For a more comprehensive overview of the range of Schema Therapy questionnaires see Sheffield and Waller (2012).
8 If your patient may meet the criteria for borderline personality disorder, it is not advisable to give them a YSQ as they are likely to score highly on most schemas

(Bach et al., 2015), so completing such a questionnaire would be unnecessary and potentially discouraging and distressing.

9 A revised, shorter version, with superior psychometric properties, the Young Parenting Inventory – Revised (YPI-R2; Louis et al., 2018a) is shortly to become available.

10 In some circumstances, a coping mode may concord with a Healthy Adult perspective. For example, in certain contexts, a detached or perfectionistic over-controller mode may temporarily be the best form of coping, for example, when parenting or handling work responsibilities, respectively. The key difference is the flexibility with which these strategies can be applied, as appropriate to different contexts.

References

Arntz, A. & Jacob, G. (2012). *Schema Therapy in Practice: An Introductory Guide to the Schema Mode Approach*. Chichester: Wiley-Blackwell.

Bach, B., Simonsen, E., Christoffersen, P. & Kriston, L. (2015). The Young Schema Questionnaire 3 short form (YSQ-S3), psychometric properties and association with personality disorders in a Danish mixed sample. *European Journal of Psychological Assessment, 33*(2), 134–143.

Ball, S.A. (2007).Comparing individual therapies for personality disordered opioid dependent patients. *Journal of Personality Disorders, 21*(3), 305–321. https://doi.org/10.1521/pedi.2007.21.3.305

Ball, S.A., Cobb-Richardson, P., Connolly, A. J., Bujosa, C.T. & O'Neall, T.W. (2005). Substance abuse and personality disorders in homeless drop-in center clients: Symptom severity and psychotherapy retention in a randomized clinical trial. *Comprehensive Psychiatry, 46*, 371–379. http://dx.doi.org/10.1016/j.comppsych.2004.11.003

Ball, S.A., Maccarelli, L.M., LaPaglia, D.M. & Ostrowski, M.J. (2011). Randomized trial of dual-focused vs. single-focused individual therapy for personality disorders and substance dependence. *Journal of Nervous and Mental Disease, 199*(5), 319–328. https://doi.org/10.1097/NMD.0b013e3182174e6f.

Bamelis, L.L.M., Evers, S.M.A.A., Spinhoven, P. & Arntz, A. (2014). Results of a multicenter randomized controlled trial of the clinical effectiveness of schema therapy for personality disorders. *American Journal of Psychiatry, 171*(3), 305–322.

Belsky, J. & Pluess, M. (2009). Beyond diathesis stress: Differential susceptibility to environmental influences. *Psychological Bulletin, 135*(6), 885–908.

Calvete, E., Orue, I. & González-Diez, Z. (2013). An examination of the structure and stability of early maladaptive schemas by means of the Young Schema Questionnaire-3. *European Journal of Psychological Assessment, 29*(4), 283–290.

Carter, J.D., McIntosh, V.V., Jordan, J., Porter, R.J., Frampton, C.M. & Joyce, P.R. (2013). Psychotherapy for depression: A randomized clinical trial comparing schema therapy and cognitive behavior therapy. *Journal of Affective Disorders, 151*(2), 500–505.

Giesen-Bloo, J., van Dyck, R., Spinhove, P., van Tilburg, W., Dirksen, C., van Asselt, T. & Arntz, A. (2006). Outpatient psychotherapy for borderline personality disorder. *Archives of General Psychiatry, 63*(9), 649–658.

Hepgul, N., King, S., Amarasinghe, M., Breen, G., Grant, N., Grey, N., Hotopf, M., Moran, P., Pariante, C.M., Tylee, A., Wingrove, J., Young, A.H. & Cleare, A.J. (2016). Clinical characteristics of patients assessed within an Improving Access to Psychological Therapies (IAPT) service: Results from a naturalistic cohort study

(Predicting Outcome Following Psychological Therapy; PROMPT). *BMC Psychiatry*, *16*(52). doi: 10.1186/s12888-016-0736-6

ISST. (2018). *The Schema Therapy Case Conceptualization Form* (2nd edition). www.schematherapysociety.org/new-conceptualization-form

Jacob, G., van Genderen, H. & Seebauer, L. (2015). *Breaking Negative Thinking Patterns: A Schema Therapy Self-help and Support Book*. Chichester: Wiley-Blackwell.

Linehan, M.M., Dimeff, L.A., Reynolds, S.K., Comtois, K.A., Welch, S.S., Heagerty, P. & Kivlahan, D.R. (2002). Dialectical behavior therapy versus comprehensive validation therapy plus 12-step for the treatment of opioid dependent women meeting criteria for borderline personality disorder. *Drug and Alcohol Dependence*, *67*(1), 13–26. https://doi.org/10.1016/S0376-8716(02)00011-X

Linehan, M.M., Schmidt, H. III, Dimeff, L.A., Craft, J.C., Kanter, J. & Comtois, K.A. (1999). Dialectical behavior therapy for patients with borderline personality disorder and drug-dependence. *American Journal on Addictions*, *8*(4), 279–292. https://doi.org/10.1080/105504999305686

Lockwood, G. & Perris, P. (2012). A new look at core emotional needs. In: M. van Vreeswijk, J. Broersen & M. Nadort (Eds.), *The Wiley-Blackwell Handbook of Schema Therapy: Theory, Research and Practice*. Oxford: Wiley-Blackwell (pp. 41–66).

Louis, J.P., Wood, A.M. & Lockwood, G. (2018a). Psychometric validation of the Young Parenting Inventory – Revised (YPI-R2): Replication and extension of a commonly used parenting scale in Schema Therapy (ST) research and practice. *PloS One*, *13*(11), e0205605. 10.1371/journal.pone.0205605.

Louis, J.P., Wood, A.M. & Lockwood, G. (2018b) Psychometric validation of the Young Parenting Inventory - revised (YPI-R2): replication and extension of a commonly used parenting scale in Schema Therapy (ST) research and practice. *PLOS One*, *13*(11). https://doi.org/10.1177/1073191118798464 (ISSN 1932-6203).

Louis, J.P., Wood, A.M., Lockwood, G., Ho, M.-H.R. & Ferguson, E. (2018c) Positive clinical psychology and Schema Therapy (ST): The development of the Young Positive Schema Questionnaire (YPSQ) to complement the Young Schema Questionnaire 3 short form (YSQ-S3). *Psychological Assessment*. Advance online publication. 10.1037/pas0000567.

Peterson, C. & Seligman, M.E.P. (2004). *Character Strengths and Virtues: A Handbook and Classification*. New York: Oxford University Press and Washington, DC: American Psychological Association.

Renner, F., Arntz, A., Leeuw, I. & Huibers, M. (2013). Treatment for chronic depression using Schema Therapy. *Clinical Psychology: Science and Practice*, *20*(2), 166–180.

Renner, F., Arntz, A., Peeters, F.P.M.L., Lobbestael, J. & Huibers, M.J.H. (2016). Schema therapy for chronic depression: Results of a multiple single case series. *Journal of Behavior Therapy and Experimental Psychiatry*, *51*(6), 66–73.

Reusch, Y. (2015). The great temptation: Treating impulsivity and binge eating with schema therapy [Die grosse Versuchung – Impulskontrollstörungen und Behandlungsmöglichkeiten aus schematherapeutischer Slcht am Beispiel der Binge-Eating-Störung]. *Verhaltenstherapie und Verhaltensmedizin*, *36*(3), 251–261.

Sheffield, A. & Waller, G. (2012). Clinical use of schema inventories. In: M. van Vreeswijk, J. Broersen & M. Nadort. (Eds.) *The Wiley-Blackwell Handbook of Schema Therapy: Theory, Research and Practice*. Oxford: Wiley-Blackwell (pp. 111–124).

Simpson, S.G., Pietrabissa, G., Rossi, A., Seychell, T., Manzoni, G.M., Munro, C., Nesci, J.B. & Castelnuovo, G. (2018). Factorial structure and preliminary validation of the schema mode inventory for eating disorders (SMI-ED). *Frontiers in Psychology*, *24*(9), 600.

Tapia, G., Perez-Dandieu, B., Lenoir, H., Othily, E., Gray, M. & Delile, J.M. (2018). Treating addiction with schema therapy and EMDR in women with co-occurring SUD and PTSD: A pilot study. *Journal of Substance Use, 23*(2), 199–205.

Van den Broek, E., Keulen-de Vos, M. & Bernstein, D.P. (2011). Arts therapies and schema focused therapy: A pilot study. *The Arts in Psychotherapy, 38*(5), 325–332.

van Vreeswijk, M., Broersen, J. & Nadort, M. (Eds.) (2012). *The Wiley-Blackwell Handbook of Schema Therapy: Theory, Research and Practice*. Oxford: Wiley-Blackwell.

Waller, G., Shah, R., Ohanian, V. & Elliott, P. (2001). Core beliefs in bulimia nervosa and depression: The discriminant validity of Young's schema questionnaire. *Behavior Therapy, 32*(1), 139–153.

Young, J.E. (1994). *Young Parenting Inventory*. New York: Cognitive Therapy Center of New York.

Young, J.E. & Klosko, J.S. (1994). *Reinventing Your Life*. New York: Plume.

Young, J.E., Arntz, A., Atkinson, T., Lobbestael, J., Weishaar, M.E. & van Vreeswijk, M.F. (2007). *The Schema Mode Inventory*. New York: Schema Therapy Institute.

Young, J.E., Klosko, J.S. & Weishaar, M.E. (2003). *Schema Therapy: A Practitioner's Guide*. New York: Guilford Press.

2 Experiential techniques at assessment

Benjamin Boecking and Anna Lavender

Introduction and chapter aims

Comprehensive psychological assessment is key in formulation, treatment planning and the evaluation of therapeutic change. However, patients with personality-level problems often struggle to identify their emotions, cognitions and key problems, thus making accurate assessment via purely discursive means or a questionnaire difficult or incomplete. Moreover, patients' schematic content and maladaptive coping modes can themselves interfere with the collection and valid interpretation of the obtained assessment information.

To help circumnavigate some of these difficulties, Schema Therapy makes use of experiential techniques that therapists apply flexibly in addition to discursive, cognitive and behavioural techniques throughout the course of therapy. In particular, imagery and chair work techniques have special significance during the assessment process. Imagery techniques can help to identify less accessible cognitive and emotional patterns (i.e., schemas) that link triggering situations with distressing childhood memories and associated unmet needs. Chair work techniques aim to assess the origin, impact and function of patients' coping modes. At the assessment stage, Schema Therapy allows for more time than other therapeutic schools. The therapist's guiding principle is to use all information gleaned from any interactions with the patient, including (attempts to conduct) imagery and chair work to aid the formulation.

In this chapter, we describe core imagery and chair work assessment techniques, alongside 'top tips' for commonly encountered difficulties. For ease of reading, we refer to a female therapist and a male patient throughout the chapter.

Core strategies

Imagery for assessment

The use of imagery within the assessment process 'moves the understanding of the schema from the intellectual to the emotional realm' (Young et al.,

2003). Schemas, which can be defined as broad themes formed of memories, cognitions, emotions and physiological responses, may be largely non-verbal, and, thus, difficult to access on a cognitive level. In addition, important experiences that gave rise to schema formation may have occurred at a pre-verbal developmental stage. For these reasons, imagery that triggers schemas at an emotional, physiological and cognitive level can be an invaluable technique for the identification of schematic material.

The therapist begins to use imagery for assessment once a personal history has been taken, and questionnaire measures have been reviewed (see Chapter 1). Imagery work then allows for 'hot' assessment of childhood experiences and 'online' schemas – including the unmet needs that underlie them at their developmental origins. Crucially, it also allows the patient and therapist to link schematic content based on early experiences to the patient's current difficulties.

When first introducing the concept of imagery work, the therapist needs to provide a clinical rationale. For example: 'I'd like suggest we try an imagery exercise. Remember how you described that sometimes you know something in your head, but your feelings say something completely different? Sometimes, this can happen if the meanings of very emotional memories find their way into our current experience without us realising. Imagery exercises can help us understand a bit more about which meaningful memories might be triggered in situations that feel very difficult, and they can allow us to work with these memories and images in ways that can be helpful. They can also help us to connect what's going on in our heads and hearts a bit more. Would you be okay to try this with me?'

When introducing the concept of imagery, a patient may be reluctant and frightened. This in itself can provide useful information about schematic content: does the idea activate a Mistrust/Abuse schema? Does it lead him to feel vulnerable or helpless? What possible coping modes are coming online? Should a patient be reluctant, the therapist can provide reassurance that he will remain in control throughout the exercise and can adapt the set-up so that he feels safe (e.g., by keeping his eyes open). The therapist needs to allocate sufficient time within a session to allow for conducting the exercise, feedback and discussion. This is key in obtaining valid information, containing the patient and strengthening rapport.

The first principle of conducting imagery exercises is to offer as little instruction or direction as possible. This allows the spontaneous emergence of what is most core for the patient. Clients who are more vulnerable may need to choose an image in advance, even in assessment, to feel some control/predictability. It is key to explore the images' *meaning* to the patient – keeping an open mind as to the potential origins of schema formation, and the encrypting of emotional significance, unmet needs, or the possible activation of a coping mode. It is not necessary for a patient to relive core traumatic memories during assessment. For instance, should a patient retrieve an image of an episode of childhood sexual abuse, it is important to pause the image, move to safe place imagery (see below), bring the individual back to the present, and ensure that they feel safe. Therapeutic work on abusive experiences is carried out later in therapy.

A patient might say that no images come to mind and that he 'can't do imagery', which may be a belief he holds, and/or may indicate the activation of a coping mode. In this case, the ice cream exercise (Farrell & Shaw, 2012) can be useful.

The ice cream exercise

Therapist: 'Close your eyes if that's okay for you, or rest your eyes on the floor. Now imagine that the two of us are walking into an ice cream parlour. You are holding a voucher for unlimited ice cream. What does it look like? Is it a modern or more traditional place? What do you see? You are going up to the counter and looking at all the different ice creams. So many colours. So many flavours. Now choose which flavours you'd like, as many as you want. Would you like whipped cream on top? What sprinkles are there? Rainbow ones? Chocolate? Which ones would you like? Can you see the ice cream in your hand? What does it look like? All those different colours and flavours! Can you see the ice creams? Now you can enjoy the ice cream. Imagine that first bite … the cool sensation, the texture on your lips and in your mouth, and the flavours. Can you taste the ice cream? The whipped cream? The sprinkles? Excellent!'

For individuals with eating disorders or weight concerns, the exercise can be adapted to a different, less threatening setting, for example a homeware store, park or other appealing setting to the patient.

When introduced playfully, most patients will engage in this exercise to at least some degree and are often able to report some imagined experiences. The therapist can then build on this experience for future exercises. Occasionally, patients may feel somewhat hoodwinked by the exercise – which again provides useful information about possible schemas or messages of parent modes.

Safe place imagery

Prior to accessing core schema-related memories using imagery, it is useful to introduce *safe place imagery* that centres on constructing an imaginal safe place within the patient's mind (Utay & Miller, 2006). Once developed, the therapist and patient can use the safe place image throughout therapy as an emotional self-regulation tool, and is often used to 'book end' other imagery exercises (see below). At assessment, it is a gentle introduction to the idea of imagery work. Box 2.1 provides an example of safe place imagery dialogue (Vivyan, 2009).

Observations made during preparation and practice of safe place imagery are helpful for collecting information relevant for the formulation. The ease

Box 2.1 Safe place imagery

Start by getting comfortable and take a couple of minutes to focus on your breathing, close your eyes, become aware of any tension in your body, and let that tension go with each out-breath. ... Imagine a place where you can feel calm, peaceful and safe. It may be a place you've been to before, somewhere you've dreamed about going to, somewhere you've seen a picture of, or just a peaceful place you can create in your mind's eye. ... Look around you in that place, notice the colours and shapes. What else do you notice? ... Now notice the sounds that are around you, or perhaps the silence. Sounds far away and those nearer to you. Those that are more noticeable and those that are more subtle. ... Think about any smells you notice there. ... Then focus on any skin sensations in your connection to the earth beneath you or whatever is supporting you in that place, the temperature, any movement of air, anything else you can touch. ... Notice the pleasant physical sensations in your body while you enjoy this safe place. ... Now while you're in your peaceful and safe place, you might choose to give it a name, whether one word or a phrase that you can use to bring that image back, any time you need to. ... You can choose to linger there a while, just enjoying the peacefulness and serenity. You can leave whenever you want to, just by opening your eyes and being aware of where you are now, and bringing yourself back to alertness in the 'here and now'.

or difficulty with which the patient is able to find a safe place helps the therapist to assess the degree of difficulty he has in generating or experiencing an internal sense of safety. Some patients, when guided to 'think of a safe place', will readily say, for example, 'in my grandma's front room', which is a real, experienced memory, suggesting some degree of internal emotion regulation ability. Others may find themselves unable to think of any real place, and can be supported in thinking of an imaginary, made-up place, such as a sunny clearing in a wood. Others may find it nearly impossible to generate a real or imaginary space where they could imagine feeling safe. This would suggest a severe unmet need for safety at a core level. In this case, a safe place may need to be slowly developed as therapy progresses.

Accessing core schema-related memories using imagery: the float back technique

A helpful imagery technique is the *float back* or *bridge* technique. It involves guiding a patient in imagery from the present to the past to access the origins of their core schemas and unmet needs at an emotional level. At assessment, the aims of this strategy are (1) to elicit what core (relational) memories are triggered in presently upsetting situations, (2) to assess what attributes or behaviours caregivers displayed towards the patient and the effect of these on the patient, (3) to assess the reactions of the caregivers, if the patient expresses his thoughts, feelings or needs, and (4) to see how such reactions may have contributed to shaping coping modes.

To collect this information, the exercise below may need to be repeated several times, with the patient directed gently towards each of his primary caregivers and other important people in his past. It is important to keep in mind that accessing core schema-related memories can be quite distressing for patients. Should this be the case, extra care should be provided within and potentially after the session.

Therapist: Okay, so let's start by closing your eyes or resting them at a point on the floor, and trying to bring to mind a time you've felt bad in the last week or so. Maybe a time with another person or people when you felt really upset – sad, bad about yourself, or angry perhaps. Tell me about where you are, and when? Who is there? What can you see and hear? Tell me about what's happening. And how are you feeling? [If the patient is struggling to find words for his emotions, prompt.] Do you feel angry/lonely/rejected/lost/sad? What's going through your mind? What do you feel in your body? Okay, now hold that feeling in your body, enlarge it even, and let the image of the situation fade. Now, just let your mind float back to the past, to an image or memory maybe of a time with your mum or dad that resonates with the emotions you're feeling. The situations don't need to match up, just the feelings. Just let me know when you've landed on a memory.

In conducting the exercise, the therapist is looking for an early memory, ideally during early childhood, when schemas are most likely to have been formed. If the patient describes a memory from adolescence or adulthood, the therapist can choose to stay with this or she can try to float back from this memory to an earlier one, using similar prompts to those described above. If the patient struggles to access any kind of memory, a Detached Protector mode may be at work – attempting to shield the patient's Vulnerable Child from remembering or re-experiencing past distress. It may be useful to try to continue this imagery exercise nonetheless, as it can elicit memories not usually available to patients via their habitual retrieval processes. However, a strong Detached Protector mode may suggest particularly painful memory contents and, thus, the therapist should proceed with sensitivity and ensure time and resources to support her patient in the wake of this.

If the patient does not stay in the present tense, or relates to his experience in the third person, a Detached Protector mode may be trying to protect the patient from the affect associated with the image. The therapist may wish to label the Detached Protector and collaboratively make sense of its activation before trying the exercise again. Sometimes, it may be helpful to practise present-tense descriptions 'offline' beforehand, for example by describing the current situation in the therapy room (What he can see, hear, etc. ...). Once the patient has identified an image or memory:

Therapist: How old are you? Where are you? What can you see and hear? Who's there with you? What's happening? How are you feeling? What's going through your mind?

It might not be immediately obvious why or how the image may be associated with the triggering situation in the present. This can be for various reasons: (1) the patient did not experience 'online' emotion when floating back, (2) an initial image may have been 'blocked' and replaced by a coping mode, or (3) the patient may try to convey a message or impression based on what he believes the therapist wants to hear, or to meet his needs otherwise. Alternatively, the image may code highly relevant information in a subtle or symbolic manner: the therapist needs to finely attune to the patient's experiences in the image and enquire about possible cognitive–emotional omissions that may inform an interpretation of the image. Last, the image may illustrate the patient's unmet needs rather than a source of distress (e.g., the patient reports an image of scoring a goal when playing football with friends – signifying a possible need for acceptance and belonging that is not experienced at home).

Therapist: Okay, now just let that memory begin to fade, and move to your safe place. Just rest there, breathe in the calm, the peace and the safety. Stay there as long as you need, and when you're ready, gently come back towards me in the session.

If the patient is very distressed and cannot experience a sense of safety in the present, it will be important to conceptualise and validate this as the vulnerable child experiencing the pain of the past and to connect this to the emerging formulation. The therapist should use her limited reparenting stance to soothe the patient and to try to meet his need for safety, using grounding techniques as appropriate. If the patient does not feel safe to leave the clinic by the end of the session, the therapist may choose to extend the session, or suggest that he sits in the waiting room until he feels strong enough to leave, and follow this up with a phone call later on.

After the imagery experience, the therapist asks the patient how he experienced the exercise, what the images meant for him, and how the connected memories may link to the originally brought distressing situation by theme or elicited emotion.

One variation on the float back technique involves 'floating forward' or a 'forward bridge' wherein the therapist and patient start with an image – already activated – from childhood and float forward to a current image that resonates emotionally with the childhood experience. This can be useful when a patient attends a session with a particular memory that he feels is important for his emotional state in the here-and-now.

Chair work for assessment

Chair work refers to experiential exercises that involve a rationale-based positioning of chairs and guided dialogues between externalised aspects of the self (e.g., child and coping modes), the self and internalised representations of others (parent modes), or the self and others in the patient's day-to-day life (Kellogg, 2004). Chair work techniques are powerful tools for assessing cognitive–emotional splits in patients' senses of self, that is, modes.

As outlined in a recent narrative review (Pugh, 2017), chair work interventions were initially developed within the school of psychodrama (Gershoni, 2003), further developed in gestalt therapy (Perls et al., 1951), and thoroughly established in Schema Therapy as a core feature of the therapeutic repertoire (Arntz & Jacob, 2017; Kellogg, 2012; Young et al., 2003).

During the assessment stage, chair work techniques aim to identify the 'weaponry' and impact of dysfunctional parent modes on a patient's experience of themselves and others. Moreover, they allow a therapist to use 'interview' techniques to assess the origin, development, function and 'motives' of coping modes with an emphasis on their originally adaptive nature that has since gone awry. For more detailed descriptions of chair work techniques and their current evidence base, see Part III of this text, Pugh (2017), Kellogg (2012, 2014) and Arntz and Jacob (2017).

As with imagery for assessment (and, indeed, all experiential exercises), it is important to

- leave enough time for providing a rationale (e.g., to bring different facets of the patient's self into contact with each other and to explore their origin, functions and needs),
- attune to the patient's emotions on a moment-by-moment basis, and
- leave enough time for debriefing and bridging to potential insights into the patient's life.

During the assessment phase, chair work techniques can be particularly helpful in assessing the experience, expression, function and impact of parent and coping modes.

Chair work to assess the dysfunctional parent–vulnerable child relation

The aims of the exercise are to assess (1) the content of the Punitive Parent's messages (and to form hypotheses about their displaced expression in the here-and-now), (2) the impact of these messages on the patient's Vulnerable Child/emotional experience, (3) coping strategies that the patient might 'flip' into once the Punitive Parent is online, and (4) the Healthy Adult mode's resources to counter the Punitive Parent.

Set-up: Therapist chair, patient chair/Healthy Adult chair, Punitive Parent chair, Vulnerable Child chair.

Therapist: Is there a recent situation that you can think of where you put yourself down or felt a sense of inner pressure or exhaustion, or just felt really bad about yourself? Can you briefly describe the situation? Where were you? What happened?

For some patients, it may have become second nature to criticise themselves, thus making it difficult to identify a particular situation or, indeed, recognise the (omni)presence of a Punitive Parent mode. In this case, the therapist should first label, and then reflect back its presence whenever she notices it has come online.

Therapist: I'd like to find out a bit more about your feelings in this situation. To do this, perhaps we could try a chair work exercise – how does that sound? Over here [points to Punitive Parent chair], I would like to put the Punitive Parent chair; over here [points] the Vulnerable Child chair. Once you sit in the Punitive Parent chair, I would like you to speak to the Vulnerable Child just as your Punitive Parent would. Try to speak directly to the Vulnerable Child and try to use the same kinds of words and emotional tone that the Punitive Parent would.

If the patient struggles to voice the parent mode, the therapist can enquire gently, for example, 'In this situation, what would the Punitive Parent say to you?' While the patient role plays his parent mode, the therapist should closely observe themes of its messages and relate these to the patient's presenting difficulties and coping modes. For example, does the parent mode attack the patient's body image ('You're so ugly'), interpersonal relationships ('Nobody would love you if they really knew you'); sense of identity ('You're a laughable excuse for a man'), ways of thinking ('You're stupid'), emotions ('Only losers feel weak'), or behaviours ('You hide like an animal').

Patients who are very scared of their Punitive Parent mode (for example, some patients with a borderline personality disorder diagnosis) can become overwhelmed by the prospect of sitting in the Punitive Parent chair. In these instances, the therapist can instead allocate an empty chair for this mode, situated well away from the patient, and ask the patient what the punitive part is saying to the Vulnerable Child, thus creating a safe distance from the mode.

If strong Detached or Avoidant Protector modes prevent chair work, through the patient either refusing to engage in the work, or not being able to 'summon' the relevant modes to be worked with, these modes need to be assessed and worked with first. If mode flips occur during chair work (which is common, given that it is a powerful affect-eliciting intervention), express validation and aim to gently re-focus the chair work. During later stages of therapy, add additional chairs and conduct chair dialogues as applicable.

Sometimes, the parent mode's hostility may merge with critical or angry thoughts that the patient wishes to indirectly relay to the therapist ('You can't help anyone'; 'No one will be able to ever understand you'; 'Other people might say you are okay, but they're lying'). If the therapist hypothesises this, it is important to gently enquire after the exercise in a validating manner and to conceptualise any fears that might stop the patient from expressing his concerns more directly.

Therapist [assessing feelings and needs of Vulnerable Child]: Now move to the Vulnerable Child chair and try to connect with your Vulnerable Child [patient changes chairs and sits down]. What's it like for your Vulnerable Child hearing this?

Therapist [assessing difficulties with self-assertion or secondary thoughts about emotions]: When your Vulnerable Child is trying to express his feelings and needs, what does your Punitive Parent say? How does he react? [Patient moves to Punitive Parent chair and continues chair work.]

Therapist [assessing how the Punitive Parent reacts to attempts of self-affirmation by modelling Healthy Adult]: [squatting next to Vulnerable Child chair and addressing Punitive Parent] I've had it with your hatefulness. You say you know everything about me, but you are just being cruel. I'm not listening to you any longer! [addressing Vulnerable Child]: How are you feeling? What does the Punitive Parent say [invites patient to punitive parent chair] ...

The therapist can then conduct a chair dialogue where the patient moves between the Punitive Parent and Vulnerable Child chairs giving support to the Vulnerable Child as needed. Here, the therapist monitors the reactions of the Punitive Parent and the Vulnerable Child, while also assessing how the Punitive Parent reacts to attempts by the Vulnerable Child to express its needs, or speaking up against the parent mode. The therapist may then work with the patient to try jointly to bring insights from the chair dialogue to bear on the presenting problems and maladaptive coping behaviours.

Quite commonly, parent modes can criticise patients for their maladaptive coping modes, thus closing a vicious circle in the formulation ('It's pathetic to use drugs'; 'You're disgusting for binge eating'; 'You're a coward for staying indoors', 'Normal people lead happy and successful lives', etc. ...). In this case, the therapist should validate the coping behaviour and relate it to the parent modes' toxicity ('No you are wrong – it is perfectly understandable why I am afraid to leave the house if you keep intimidating me'). (Disadvantages of the coping modes are addressed below.)

Last, ask the patient to move into their 'original' chair and reflect upon the exercise. The therapist should relate the information to the patient's presenting difficulties. (When does the patient blame himself? How may the parent mode's messages reflect early experiences with caregivers? How does the patient tend to react, once he pressures himself? What makes it difficult to disregard the Punitive Parent? What would have happened in the past, etc.?)

Some patients may refuse to engage in the exercise, as they may feel guilty or scared to 'speak ill' of their caregivers. In this case, the therapist can highlight that the parent modes do not symbolise the parents *per se*, but are internalised personal memories of difficult or hurtful *aspects* of their parents' behaviours. Others may feel ambivalent or confused about the impact of the parent modes (e.g., 'They mean well'; 'They got me to where I am now') – in particular if their caregivers may have mistreated them supposedly 'for their own good'. Such patients may find it difficult to identify any negative impact of the parent modes and the emotions of the Vulnerable Child. Here, the therapist may use the following strategies:

Chair work to assess triggers, origin, function, and downsides of coping modes

This exercise is useful when (1) the therapist wishes to assess the origin and function of a coping mode, (2) observes a coping mode coming online in session, or (3) the patient recounts a situation where a coping mode was present.

Set-up: Therapist chair, patient chair/Healthy Adult chair, coping mode chair.

Sometimes, the very characteristics of a coping mode can influence its assessment. For example, a compliant surrenderer may be seemingly keen to engage in the exercise, only to express what he thinks the therapist might wish to hear. An avoidant mode may refuse to engage for fear of being exposed while a self-aggrandising mode might attempt to criticise or ridicule the nature or set-up of the exercise. The therapist should highlight the voluntary nature of the exercise and gently encourage attempting it while observing the patient's emotional responses throughout (e.g., 'I can see this is uncomfortable and your Superman mode is being critical, perhaps to try to get out of talking about your feeling; but I think another part of you wants to understand what's going on').

Once the therapist (or patient) notices the activation of a coping mode, she invites the patient to move to the coping mode chair.

Therapist: I wonder if a chair work exercise might help us to shed some light on this. I would like to invite you to sit down in this chair and 'become' the coping mode for a while. Try to completely take his perspective, and speak entirely from his point of view. Is that okay? [Therapist begins to interview the coping mode – speaking as if it were a person.] Hello [coping mode]. [Assessing triggers]: When I just spoke to the Vulnerable Child, what brought you up? What happened? How did the Vulnerable Child feel, or what was going through his mind? Are there times where you are very present for him? Are there times where you have to come in as an emergency? [Assessing origin]: When were you first there for him? Can you remember when he used to need you first? What happened at the time? [Assessing function]: Why did you have to be there for him at the time? What would have happened had you not been around? What happened when you did your job well? How did his experience change? How did his relationships change? What do you help him with? What would you need to step back a little?

During the interview situation, it is important to genuinely empathise with the coping mode's motives (e.g., to protect from pain, to motivate care, or to stabilise the patient's sense of self through shielding his Vulnerable Child). Importantly, the therapist should attempt to gain a *nuanced* understanding of its function without jumping to simplified assumptions about its present maladaptiveness. For example, an Angry Protector mode may be adaptive if triggered by genuinely punitive or manipulative others.

To assess the patient's awareness of the coping mode's more maladaptive downsides, the therapist can enquire, for example, 'Does your presence have any downsides for [patient]? When you are around, are there things he struggles with? I understand that you have his best interests at heart and that you genuinely care for him – what if I told you that he feels very lonely when you are around or that it is very difficult for me to relate to him although I genuinely want to?'

Summary and conclusion

Imagery and chair work are key experiential exercises that can be flexibly used to assess the origins of, triggers for, and coping strategies used to contain emotional distress in a multimodal manner. Throughout the assessment phase and, indeed, therapy, these exercises can help bridge the dissociation between 'head' and 'heart' commonly reported by patients struggling with emotion regulation difficulties (Stott, 2007) and access information usually not available through discursive or purely cognitive means. This chapter introduced imagery and chair work techniques for assessment; emphasising several key guidelines such as (1) allowing enough time for the exercises, debriefing, reflection and containment, (2) providing a rationale for each intervention, (3) being attuned to the patient's emotional experience and activation of schemas and modes on a moment-by-moment basis, and (4) not to assume 'prescribed' hypothesised functions of experience, but to curiously allow for contradictions and intricacies characteristic of all of us.

Therapist tips

1. Allow enough time for experiential work – extended sessions may be useful at this phase.
2. Focus on the rapport rather than on the collection of information – a strong rapport will help you to assess your patient's internal world more accurately.
3. Listen out for ambiguities, possible symbols, and personal meaning to identify and map modes as you go along, either internally to yourself, or with your patient.
4. Never oversimplify or assume mode functions – assess idiosyncratically and be prepared to change the formulation when new nuances emerge.
5. Watch out for – and separate – merged modes (e.g., coping mode merging with parent mode) and formulate functions (e.g., self-criticism as an attempt to stabilise the self).

References

Arntz, A. & Jacob, G. (2017). *Schema therapy in practice: An introductory guide to the schema mode approach*. Chichester: John Wiley & Sons.

Farrell, J.M. & Shaw, I.A. (2012). *Group schema therapy for borderline personality disorder: A step-by-step treatment manual with patient workbook*. New York: John Wiley & Sons.

Gershoni, J. (2003). *Psychodrama in the 21st century: Clinical and educational applications*. New York: Springer.

Kellogg, S. (2004). Dialogical encounters: Contemporary perspectives on "chairwork" in psychotherapy. *Psychotherapy: Theory, Research, Practice, Training, 41*(3), 310.

Kellogg, S. (2012). On speaking one's mind: Using chair-work dialogues in schema therapy. In M. van Vreeswijk, J. Broersen & M. Nadort (eds) *The Wiley-Blackwell handbook of schema therapy: theory, research, and practice*. Hoboken, NJ: John Wiley & Sons, pp. 197–207.

Kellogg, S. (2014). *Transformational chairwork: Using psychotherapeutic dialogues in clinical practice*. Lanham, MD: Rowman & Littlefield.

Perls, F., Hefferline, G. & Goodman, P. (1951). *Gestalt therapy*. New York: Julian Press.

Pugh, M. (2017). Chairwork in cognitive behavioural therapy: A narrative review. *Cognitive Therapy and Research, 41*(1), 16–30.

Stott, R. (2007). When head and heart do not agree: A theoretical and clinical analysis of Rational–Emotional Dissociation (RED) in cognitive therapy. *Journal of Cognitive Psychotherapy, 21*(1), 37–50.

Utay, J. & Miller, M. (2006). Guided imagery as an effective therapeutic technique: A brief review of its history and efficacy research. *Journal of Instructional Psychology, 33*(1), 40–44.

Vivyan, C. (2009). Relaxing 'safe place' imagery. Retrieved from www.getselfhelp.co.uk/docs/SafePlace.pdf

Young, J.E., Klosko, J.S. & Weishaar, M.E. (2003). *Schema therapy: A practitioner's guide*. New York: Guilford Press.

3 Somatic perspective in Schema Therapy

The role of the body in the awareness and transformation of modes and schemas

Janis Briedis and Helen Startup

In Schema Therapy we conceptualise schemas as learnt cognitive, affective and behavioural attachment related patterns typically formed over time. Often underestimated is the embodiment of these well-trodden habits, manifesting as idiosyncrasies in posture, gesture and impulse (Ogden et al., 2006). Our proposal is that, at each stage of Schema Therapy, our work can be enhanced by greater attention being given to our patient's somatic world. There are times when our patient's experiences are largely encoded at a somatic level (such as in the case of pre-verbal trauma) necessitating these ways of working. Equally, we also believe that within every psychotherapy session awareness is deepened and clinical change enhanced by greater tracking of, and working at, the level of somatic experience. This chapter outlines core principles and techniques to enable the therapist to work at this level of experience, brought to life by clinical example.[1]

General principles of working with the body

In our experience, the prospect of working with the body can be anxiety provoking for many therapists. For patients, mere mention of the body can trigger reactions of distress and shame. Thus, prioritising safety is of critical importance. The general principles described below should guide the reader towards laying these necessary foundations.

Tracking and contact

The first principle of working with the body involves a shift in stance toward active observation of a patient's somatic ways of being, while gently bringing this to their attention. Kurtz (1990) refers to these stages as 'tracking' followed by 'contact statements'. There is essentially a reorientating of the therapist's attention from engagement with the narrative to close observation of the non-verbal accompaniments to the narrative. These non-verbal cues can be explicit, such as hand gestures, head turning, facial grimace, closing of the eyes, frozen stillness, or more subtle, such as tremors, dilation of the pupils, sweating or changes in skin tone (Rothschild, 2000). The therapist is required to keep attention simultaneously on both the manifest narrative and the implicit narrative told via their body, deepening an awareness of the patient's material. The therapist can then gently name what they have tracked: 'I notice you leaned back when you mentioned your ex-partner's name', or 'it is interesting your feet have been moving ever since we started talking about your work worries'. The ultimate goal of body tracking and contact statements is to deepen the felt sense of the material unfolding and to enhance attunement and a sense of connection between the therapist and the patient.

Focus on core organisers

A fundamental principle of somatically based work is to stretch our awareness of experience to accommodate a greater component of 'felt sense'. Ogden's concept of 'core organisers' (Ogden et al., 2006) provides a useful framework to understand different elements of our experience including: *cognitions, emotions, inner body sensations, movement and the five-sense perception* (sight, sound, smell, taste and touch). Any significant experience can be the focus and the therapist essentially goes on a 'dance with the core organisers' by *tracking* the patient's experience and asking the patient: 'What do you feel in your body when you think of x (where x is the past memory)?' (linking memory with body sensation), or 'What sensations in your body come up when you let yourself feel the sadness?' (linking physical sensation and emotion), or 'If that tremor in your hands could speak, what would it say?' (drawing a connection between sensation and cognition). One of the goals of working with the body is to increase the patient's awareness of their inner processes by exploring their experience through the core organisers. The style of exploring the core organisers is one of genuine open-mindedness, curiosity and mindfulness (see section below), rather than directing them towards any particular appraisal or assumptions about their experience. The therapist adopts a non-directive approach while remaining fully present, attuned and engaged with their patient's phenomenological experience. Hence, the pace is slow and steady.

Working within the Window of Tolerance

Working within a patient's Window of Tolerance (WoT) is core to safe and effective trauma work using a somatic focus (Siegel, 1999). It refers to the patient's capacity to tolerate affect and integrate information adaptively between two limits beyond which the individual is either hyper-aroused (uncontained and feeling overwhelmed by anxiety, panic or terror), or hypo-aroused (uncontained, feeling very low in energy, foggy, depressed, numb and dissociated) (see Figure 3.1).

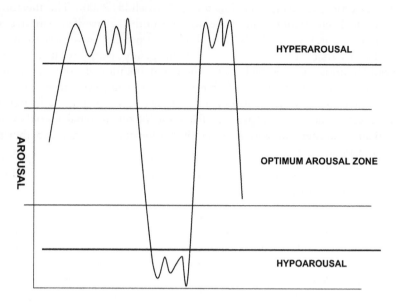

Figure 3.1 Window of Tolerance.

The 'optimum arousal zone' refers to the range between these two extremes where the patient is sufficiently regulated to facilitate the processing of traumatic experiences (Ogden et al., 2006). When the patient is outside their WoT they are considered 'dysregulated' and their integrative capacity and ability to access and process information is significantly compromised. The therapist's task is to *track* the physical and sensorimotor aspects of their patient's experience while monitoring their arousal levels and to help them regulate as necessary using suitable resources. Patients who endured significant childhood trauma are likely to have reduced integrative capacity along with a narrower WoT. Furthermore, focusing on the body directly can become dysregulating, particularly for patients with histories of physical and/or sexual trauma and can bring up overwhelming affect reminiscent of traumatic events from the past accompanied by affective and behavioural avoidance.

In regard to schema mode activity, focusing on the body may trigger the Punitive Critic mode, which may, in turn, trigger a range of 'coping modes'. This creates a difficult dilemma for the patient, who is stuck between a body reliving a past trauma and a self-protective drive to avoid the aversive experience. This can lead to dissociation and other coping responses via the Detached Protector and Detached Self-soother which will hinder the integration necessary for the trauma to be resolved.

The therapist aims to direct just enough attention to the patient's body to facilitate processing, while simultaneously preventing affect dysregulation and the patient breaching their WoT. This work requires close tracking and attunement and a balance between the need for trauma processing and the need for stabilisation. With highly traumatised patients working with multiple core organisers at one time can be overwhelming. It can be helpful to narrow the focus to one or two core organisers at a time (Ogden et al., 2006), more specifically, body sensations and micro-movements, when traumatic aspects of a memory are being processed. So, for example, when the patient is in touch with a very painful, traumatic memory, the therapist might gently notice how they perhaps clench their fists while talking about a particular person, and be curious about other body sensations that may go along with this, yet also guide them to keep in mind that they are no longer in the presence of that person and to connect with their safe place imagery if things feel too much.

A bottom-up vs top-down approach

Sometimes, the safest way into a trauma is via body sensations (*bottom-up approach*) rather than via the associated narrative (*top-down*). Many patients with trauma histories are not helped, and are sometimes harmed, by traditional talking therapies where the traumatic narrative is repeated, leading to a sense of helplessness and a stirring up of distressing affect, without shifting the meaning or emotional intensity of the memory (Van der Kolk, 1994). There are situations when there is simply no amount of talking about the trauma that can undo its effects.

Directed mindfulness

Mindfulness, in this context, describes a non-judgemental observation and awareness of experience as it unfolds, and it encapsulates the style we seek to adopt as therapists when working with somatic material. When in a state of mindfulness, actions are observed, named and normalised, rather than 'thought about' or interpreted, and this is achieved via 'a mindful frame of experience' (Ogden & Fisher, 2015). For instance, the therapist may pause their patient mid-narrative and stretch their awareness by asking: 'What are you feeling right now as you tell me about your experience with X?', creating both contact with, and curiosity about, their experience in that moment.

Experimentation

Similar to cognitive therapy, experiments in body-focused work draw on the principles of collaboration, curiosity and a 'win-win attitude' (Bennett-Levy et al., 2004). An experimental attitude requires spontaneity and openness to study a patient's somatic habits, plus providing an opportunity to disrupt them with a view to gradually generating new, more adaptive patterns. For example, the therapist may suggest to a patient with a slumped posture to straighten their back and to observe the effects of this on their core organisers, or with a patient who feels 'spacey' to press their feet firmly against the ground and to observe the effects of this. Somatic experiments are first conducted together with the therapist and later might be set as homework for patients to integrate into their daily lives. This type of simple regular practice has the potential to eventually disrupt habits that were previously unhelpful and beyond conscious awareness.

Building a somatic resource toolbox

Resources, in this context, refer to strategies that support patients to regulate their arousal levels within their WoT and to gradually expand their WoT over time. There is a distinction drawn between *auto-regulatory* (intrapersonal) and *interactive regulatory* (interpersonal) resources (Schore, 2003) both of which are outlined below.

Identification and development of resources

It is common therapeutic practice to teach patients skills to regulate their emotional state, such as through grounding exercises, distraction, breathing techniques, soothing imagery and the incorporation of transitional objects (see Farrell & Shaw, 2012; Farrell et al., 2014). We find that, with attuned tracking of our patients' experience, we often discover naturally occurring self-soothing strategies that can be fostered. Many of these strategies have a physical component that can be built on, such as closing their eyes when things get 'too much', taking a deep breath, placing their hands on their chest to ground themselves, or rubbing their knees to keep themselves grounded in their bodies. Bringing attention to the already existing resources and linking them to stabilising feeling states can be validating and empowering to patients, helping them tap into the wisdom of their own bodies. It also helps avoid 'reinventing the wheel' where resources are already available which evolved adaptively based on their history and unmet needs. A somatic resource can be brought to attention by simply asking: 'When you do x [e.g., make that movement] does that feel better or worse?'. If it feels even slightly better, it is likely to be a potential positive resource. This resource can then be elaborated by asking the patient to stay with the resource longer, continuing the 'dance with the core organisers' as demonstrated in the example below:

THERAPIST (T):[2] I noticed you put your right hand on your heart as you were talking about that painful loss. What's happening there right now?
PATIENT (P): Yes, I do that sometimes when I feel like I need comfort.
T: Ah, okay. How interesting. What is it like to have your hand there?
P: It feels nice. I can feel the warmth of my own hand on my chest.

T: Lovely. Just let yourself feel that warmth for a moment if you can. What happens when you keep your hand there a bit longer?

P: It feels quite safe actually. Like somebody is there for me and I'm not alone.

T: Lovely. Do you get any images as you tell me this?

P: It reminds me of visiting my gran in the countryside when I was a kid. She lived far away and I remember her hugging me every time we went to visit. It felt so nice and warm.

T: How interesting. What happens in your body as you tell me this?

P: I feel the warmth expanding throughout my whole body.

The pace of the interaction above needs to be slow and deliberate in order to promote a mindful frame of experience, with a view to deepening a 'being/feeling' rather than a 'doing/thinking' state. The attitude is one of playful experimentation and gentle exploration. These strategies are unlikely to be effective unless the therapist and patient take time to 'sink into them together' such that the felt sense is deepened. To reduce the risk of the patient experiencing shame, these practices are carried out together, that is, the therapist mirrors the patient's postures and movements.

The therapist as a resource or as an unintentional trigger for fear

Beyond specific techniques or interventions, the therapist is an important resource for their patient in and of themselves. Many traumatised patients will have a limited range of self-soothing strategies and are unlikely to feel safe around others, including the therapist. Because of their earlier experiences of being emotionally and often physically unsafe, these patients are highly attuned to the movements and mannerisms of their therapist, as a way of monitoring potential threat. With this in mind, the therapist needs to be aware that they may unintentionally communicate signals of danger and activate a patient's sympathetic or dorsal branch of their vagus nerve (Porges, 2011). For instance, for some patients, wide eyes in the therapist's face can imply the activation of the therapist's own defence system and, therefore by proxy, signal danger. For another patient, the therapist slightly turning to one side or breaking eye contact can be interpreted by the patient as rejection or disinterest. Yet, for another patient, a therapist's soothing voice can trigger past memories of being seduced by an abuser. Of course, while it is not humanly possible to avoid all possible threat 'activators', the therapist's awareness of their own body and their openness to explore triggers with their patient can go a long way towards maintaining a sense of safety.

Working with infant modes

Early childhood trauma and associated schemas are likely to be encoded at a pre-verbal level, manifesting as 'infant modes' (Simeone-DiFrancesco et al., 2015). Most commonly, pre-verbal material is encoded physically in the body (Layden et al., 1993). For example, patients may report the activation of an Abandonment schema primarily as a sense of emptiness or hollowness in the solar plexus, or they may report Defectiveness as a tingling all over the body. When working with these infant modes, cognitions are likely to be black and white, emotional reactions are likely to be more extreme and dysregulated and the ability to mentalise will be limited (Simeone-DiFrancesco et al., 2015). An individual in an infant mode is likely to be soothed by the therapist attuning to them using a calm voice, predictable slow movements and soft facial expressions, such as a subtle gentle smile. All of these cues somatically communicate safety and connection, stimulating their social engagement system and fostering a sense of relational cohesion (Porges, 2011). Using touch can be very soothing and the therapist may suggest to the patient to hold one end of a soft scarf or a piece of string while the therapist holds the other, as this can enhance the experience of connection and safety.

There are many ways in which body focused ways of working enhance emotional regulation. Box 3.1 presents a selected list of somatic resources that support both the auto-regulatory and interactive regulatory repertoires.

Box 3.1 A selected list of somatic resources, adapted from (Ogden et al, 2006)

- *Breathing*: using different types of breathing rhythm to activate the parasympathetic (for instance, slower breathing, longer exhalations, resistance breathing, sighing) or sympathetic arousal states (for instance, rapid breathing, sharp in or out breath); using breath to find a common rhythm with the patient ('let's breathe together for a moment').
- *Alignment*: sitting with the back straight; lengthening the spine; rolling shoulders.
- *Centring*: placing one hand on heart and the other on the belly.
- *Grounding*: feeling the feet solid on the ground; standing up and putting weight on different parts of the feet – front, back, sides, alternate feet; sitting or lying on the floor.
- *Movement*: getting up from the seat and walking around the room; stomping feet on the ground; doing yoga-style stretching and holding positions for a period of time; running on the spot; shifting from one foot to the other at varying speed; trying out variable paces and styles of walking; playing games involving activities such as throwing, jumping, running.
- *Orientating*: very slowly turning the head to one side and then to the other while closely observing the environment.
- *Boundary setting*: patient and therapist stand at opposite sides of the room, ask the patient to slowly walk towards you, ask them to 'stop' when it 'feels right', explore how they know where it feels right to draw the boundary, what signals this to them and what it feels like to draw the boundary. Then

> therapist and patient swap roles if appropriate; experiment with saying 'yes'
> and 'no' with various intonations and body postures.
> *   *Relational connection*: therapist reaching out to the patient with one hand, then
>   do this with the other hand or both hands, therapist and patient swap roles
>   and explore what this evokes in them.

Looking at schemas and modes through the prism of core organisers

The 'mindful dance' with the core organisers can be a helpful way of exploring and building an awareness of a particular mode (e.g., helpless Vulnerable Child flipping into Angry Child mode) that repeatedly comes up for the patient:

THERAPIST (T): I can sense a lot of feeling when you talk with me about the argument with your partner. What do you feel now as you describe this to me?

PATIENT (P): I feel really rejected by her. I'm not sure if this relationship will last much longer. We keep going around the same old stuff again and again.

T: I hear the frustration about the same stuff happening again and again. As you describe it, what do you feel in your body?

P: I feel fed up and tired.

T: Where do you feel that tiredness and being fed up in your body?

P: I guess it's in my chest. I feel like I can't do it any more.

T: What exactly do you feel in your chest as you describe this to me now?

P: It's like a feeling of collapse. I can't breathe properly.

T: I notice that your arms and shoulders dropped a little as you describe the collapsed feeling. What's happening in that area of your body right now?

P: I don't know. I didn't notice that before. It's like my body is telling me it can't take it any more.

T: If your shoulders could speak right now what would they say? Are there any words that go with the movement?

P: I guess I'm feeling weak. I know I should leave her but I can't.

T: It sounds really tough. How does it feel when you say these words?

P: Totally helpless.

T: It's interesting you say that because your body is leaning forward. Are there any emotions that go with this leaning forward?

P: I feel so sad and hopeless.

T: Yes. I can sense that too. Are these familiar feelings for you?

P: Oh yes, it's the same stuff going round and round.

T: What mode do you think you may be in now as you say this?

P: I don't know. Maybe the Vulnerable side? I'm so frustrated with myself! Why can't I just pick myself up and do what I need to do?

T: Ah, okay, I can sense some energy there. What mode is this?

P: I feel annoyed and frustrated. The Angry one?

T: That's what I hear too. There is a lot of feeling there. It looks like we have got a clearer picture of what is going on for your Vulnerable and Angry sides when an argument breaks out with your partner.

(*The therapist can then suggest an intervention of working with the Vulnerable Child or Angry Child mode.*)

As demonstrated in this case example, the order in which the core organisers are explored is less important than the steady 'peeling of the layers of the onion' to get closer to the core experiences of the child modes, the core pain and the unmet emotional needs. The exploration can begin with any of the core organisers, usually the one the patient first articulates, then the 'dance with core organisers' continues until there is a sense of deepening into the experience and enough material is gathered to set a session focus and apply one of the standard Schema Therapy techniques. If a coping mode surfaces in the process, it is explored in a similar way with the attitude of curiosity and respect for the underlying unmet needs. Below is an example of exploring a coping mode:

P: [going quiet]

T: What just happened?

P: This is so painful. I don't think I can talk about it any more.

T: That's really fine and I think we need to respect that. How about we take a few deep breaths first? [Pause] I'm so glad that you noticed when it was enough for you and you were able to tell me. What was it that told you you had had enough?

P: I just had the feeling that if I wasn't going to stop now I would explode. Something in me shut down and to be honest I wanted to run, to just get out of here.

T: I'm so glad that you noticed that and also that you stayed in the room. It seems that there is something in you looking out for you that knows when you need to stop.

P: Yes, it's like a voice that tells me to stop talking, or else I will burst.

T: Ah, okay. It's really trying to protect you.

P: Yes. It feels like my whole body shuts down.

T: I see. Are there words that go with that feeling of shutting down?

P: It's something like – Stop! Don't go there!

T: That's very interesting. What exactly does that shutting down feel like in your body?

P: It's like a wave going through my body, almost like mild electric shock, waking me up, telling me that if I don't stop now it will get really bad.

T: Mhm! There is a lot of useful information here. Which mode do you think it is that is trying to shut down and protect you?

P: Well, I'm sure it's the detached wall that we talked about but – honestly – it feels helpful and necessary.

T: I'm sure it is. Would you be willing to explore it further together though?

P: Yes, sure, as long as you're not going to ask me to get rid of it.

T: Of course not. These coping modes are there for a reason and we need to have utmost respect for them because they developed at a time when you absolutely needed them. However, we could explore the effect they are having on your life now. Would that be okay?

In this extract the therapist attaches no particular judgement to any of the modes, and adopts the stance of neutrality, curiosity and gentleness which, in turn, helps create a stronger alliance with the patient, who is more likely to feel understood and validated. In fact, the therapist tries to get *closer* to the coping mode, to get to know it at a deeper 'felt' level, before any focus on change would even be considered. The patient is, therefore, less likely to feel threatened by the process of therapy, via this communication of acceptance and openness to other possibilities.

Enhancing Schema Therapy techniques using a somatic focus

Many Schema Therapy techniques can be enhanced by adding a somatic focus.

Multiple chair work

In chair dialogue exercises, the therapist can ask the patient to explore particular modes through the lens of the core organisers. For instance, the therapist can ask, 'What do you feel (in your body) when you are in this mode/chair?' The therapist may also use their tracking skills and feed back some of their observations about the patient's body posture, or any micro-movements and changes in their voice while sitting in a particular chair representing a mode. For example, the therapist may say, 'Notice how your voice gets quieter and you look at the floor rather than at me when you sit in the "Compliant Surrenderer" chair.' The therapist may further suggest an experiment to disrupt a somatic pattern, for instance by asking a slouching patient to lengthen their spine, look up and make eye contact with the therapist. Their subsequent experience can then be explored through the core organisers to enable the integration of new habits. The somatic disruption of previously learned habitual patterns (unhelpful schemas and modes) therefore leads to the development of new neural pathways and behavioural alternatives ('Healthy Adult' mode) (Ogden et al., 2006; Levine, 2015).

Imagery rescripting

An imagery rescripting exercise can be enriched by asking somatically orientated questions prior to the rescripting phase. By the therapist asking, 'Can you feel Little Luke in your body right now?', and by exploring this experientially through the core organisers, the image can be elaborated and deepened. The 'child mode' can be explored further by asking questions such as: 'What is it like to feel so tense/numb/frozen etc.?', and 'What is that feeling telling you about what you need?', 'Is there an impulse that goes with that feeling?', 'What does your body want to do with that impulse?' Such questions help build connections between past reactions, impulses, the development of coping/critic modes, and current triggers for schemas and modes.

When a satisfactory resolution has been achieved at the end of an imagery rescripting exercise, it can be beneficial to encourage the patient to *stay with* the positive affect to support the integration of new neural pathways. Positive affect can be enhanced with a somatic resource, such as one hand holding the other, stroking the other arm or 'holding' the child in one's arms by giving oneself a 'butterfly hug'. To facilitate affective and somatic integration the patient needs to stay with the new feeling for as long as possible (Dana, 2018). This can be done by exploring the positive affect through the core organisers. Often, patients need active encouragement to stay with these feelings, because, for some patients, positive affect is unfamiliar, anxiety provoking and potentially aversive. Many traumatised patients are scared of positive affect and, therefore, staying with positive emotion may need to be paced and obstacles to it explored. Drawing on the principles of graded exposure in cognitive therapy can be helpful here. The method of titration can support the patient's tolerance for positive affect by gradually increasing the time spent exploring positive transformation at the end of each experiential exercise.

The same process of studying experience through the core organisers can enhance the Healthy Adult mode (may be with eyes closed or open, whichever the patient prefers, as long as the patient is able to stay in a mindful, as opposed to detached or rational, state):

T: How do you feel now at the end of the exercise?
P: I feel good. I really was not expecting that. So much came out. There is a lot to digest.
T: Sure. You did so much work here today. What exactly tells you that you feel good right now?
P: I feel more relaxed. Like I've let something go. And also I feel hope for the future, like there's light at the end of the tunnel.
T: Oh that's so good to hear. Where do you feel that relaxation and hope? Can you locate it anywhere particular in your body?

P: I'm not sure. It's kind of all over my body. It sort of feels like I've let go of a ton of bricks that was lying on my shoulders.

T: Ah, great. And what's that like for you now?

P: I've not felt that for a long time. It's such a relief.

T: Wonderful. Stay with that feeling a bit longer if you can. [Pause] Enjoy it. Absorb it. Make friends with it. Hang out with it as long as you can. [Pause] This is what your Healthy Adult mode feels like, and this is the mode we want to grow and strengthen for you. The more you practise being with these feelings and sensations, the more natural they will feel to you.

P: Ah, okay, that makes a lot of sense. I wish I could feel them more often.

T: If you can feel them now, you can feel them again. It's a matter of practising – gently inviting them, allowing them and staying with them. Sometimes staying with them can feel a little strange because you're not very familiar with them yet, but over time they will become second nature.

Probe experiments

Sensorimotor psychotherapy uses the technique of *probes* (Kurtz, 1990; Ogden et al., 2006), which are similar to the flashcard technique in Schema Therapy but with a greater experiential focus. Flashcards in Schema Therapy are used to enhance the alternative, more adaptive, Healthy Adult perspective, while fighting the unhealthy messages or beliefs from the past (Arntz & Jacob, 2012). Probes can be used to strengthen the Healthy Adult perspective, but also to elicit and study a patient's response to statements that contradict their beliefs. For example, patients who have a strong Unrelenting Standards schema and Perfectionist/Overcontroller and Demanding Critic modes are likely to have beliefs such as 'I always have to work hard', 'relaxation is a waste of time' and 'work must always come first'. To use probes effectively, it is first necessary to identify the beliefs underpinning the schemas and modes that require intervention. Subsequently, the therapist suggests an experiment to study the patient's reaction to statements contradicting their long-held convictions. Often, probe work is spontaneous in that the therapist suggests one or several statements while discouraging the patient from intellectualising or arguing against the probe. The purpose of probe work is to study activation of the sensorimotor and limbic system rather than the cognitive–cortical system. If this turns out to be dysregulating for the patient, probes can be discussed cognitively first and written down in advance of the experiment, or the content of the probes can be adapted to make them less evocative. Probe experiments often form the main focus of the session rather than serving as a cognitive 'add-on' following a piece of experiential work, as is often the case with flashcards. Below is an example of using probes with a patient with a strong Perfectionist/Overcontroller mode:

T: We have talked about your Unrelenting Standards schema and the beliefs that go with this related to the importance of working hard and that relaxation is a waste of your time.

P: Hmm.

T: I wonder if you would be open to doing a little experiment with me today to explore these beliefs further? The experiment will involve me saying a few statements that are different from your beliefs and all I want you to do is to notice what happens in your body when I say them out loud. The purpose of this experiment is not to discuss whether or not you like or agree with these statements, but to study mindfully what happens in your body and to your emotions when you hear these words. Would that be okay?

P: It sounds mysterious but I'm happy to give it a go.

T: Okay, great. So all you need to do is to take plenty of time and tune in to your inner experience. Earlier we talked about mindful awareness, which means stepping out of your intellectual mind and just going with the feelings and with your body. Does that sound okay?

P: Yes, I'll try.

T: Right, the first statement I want to say to you is: [saying slowly and clearly] You don't have to work so hard. [Pause] You don't have to work so hard. [Pause] What do you notice when you hear this?

P: The first thought I get is: it's nonsense!

T: Okay, great that you notice that. Is there an emotion that goes with it?

P: It feels really uncomfortable. It's like you're telling me a lie, like I can't believe a word of it. It goes completely against who I feel I am.

T: Ah, okay. That's really interesting. What exactly tells you that? Where do you feel that discomfort? Is it located anywhere in particular in your body?

P: I notice my body tensing up, especially my arms.

T: Ah yes, interesting! I also noticed your fists clenching slightly and your arms tensing up. If they could talk what would they say?

P: Hmm, I think they might be saying that I always have to fight for what I want.

T: Ah, wonderful! There is a clear message there, isn't there? Does that sound like a familiar theme?

P: Oh yes, that's the story of my life!

T: Sure, it's something you've known for a long, long time. How about I try and say it again and see what happens now?

P: Okay. I'm not sure I like it but let's go for it. At least it's interesting.

T: All right, but do tell me if it gets too much. [*Repeating the same probe again a couple of times, very slowly, with a pause in the middle, giving the patient plenty of space to feel and notice, while the therapist is also closely tracking the patient's body for any changes, e.g., subtle facial expressions, movements, etc.*] What happens now when I say it the second time around?

P: I feel a little less tense. I don't know why. It's strange.

T: Okay, great that you notice that. Stay with it. What tells you that you are less tense this time?

P: I guess my arms are less tense, my breathing has slowed down a bit and I don't feel like I want to fight with you and defend myself so much.

The aim of probe experiments is to explore on a somatic level the impact of a statement that either contradicts an old, unhelpful belief or reinforces a new belief. The aim of probe work is not to coerce the patient into accepting a belief that contradicts their current belief or to change their mind in any way. The work with probes can continue for as long as it is experienced as helpful and productive, that is, when something shifts in the organisation of their experience. Once probe work is under way it can be beneficial to ask the patient to help adjust the wording of the probe, or generate a new probe altogether that would be a better fit, such as what they would like to believe instead of the old belief. Often, patients' initial response to probes is, 'I don't believe it', or 'I intellectually understand it but it does not feel true'. The 'not true' aspect becomes once more a part of the material that is the subject of further curious, mindful, gentle and non-coercive exploration.

The therapist may also suggest that the patient read a list of probes or read the same probe over and over as part of a homework assignment, emphasising to the patient that the primary goal, unlike affirmations used in other forms of therapy, is to gain awareness of their *effect* rather than achieve a particular emotional or behavioural state. Similar to flashcards, probes can be audio recorded and played back on a loop at regular intervals. From our own clinical experience, the typical effect of conducting probe experiments over time is a decrease in the cognitive–affective–somatic split, and a reduction in the intensity of unhelpful beliefs, schemas and modes.

The probe technique can be used with any schemas or modes, and can be especially powerful when working with 'child modes', aiding the process of limited reparenting. Probes such as 'I am here with you', 'You are not alone', 'Your feelings matter', can have a profound effect on the patient who is able to take these in via a state of mindfulness. Patients with strong schemas from the Disconnection/Rejection domain typically report feeling moved by the statements, which strengthens the attachment bond between patient and therapist. Often patients report feeling deeply cared for and 'seen' by the therapist on a relational level. If the patient stays at the level of 'I know it but I don't feel anything', it is likely that a coping mode is active and the patient's capacity to emotionally open up to the experience is still limited. Returning to the mindful study of core organisers can be helpful to further understand what triggered a coping mode or the critic mode, and new probes can be experimented with to 'get to know' and address the relevant mode being triggered.

Conclusion

In this chapter, we describe a number of ways of working with the body to enhance the core techniques of Schema Therapy. These ways of working do not necessarily require a new skill set, but, rather, necessitate a shift in orientation and awareness that brings with it the potential to deepen experiential work, to enhance safety and attunement in the therapeutic relationship and to promote clinical change via a 'somatic route'. For those with histories of trauma, typically encoded in a pre-verbal form, somatic work allows the patient and therapist to more safely make contact with inner experiences that were previously locked tight, too painful to be accessed without overwhelming and dysregulating the patient. The therapist has a range of options via their 'resource toolkit' to explore with curiosity and attunement what is 'happening' for the patient in the moment, using the body and the relationship to help ground this work. In this experiential pause, there is an opportunity for a different level of felt understanding, integration, movement or consolidation. These ways of working provide a safer protected space to 'be with' different elements of the patient's experience with curiosity and acceptance; and only when it feels right might they decide on movement or change. Our hope is that Schema therapists will embrace working with the body with increasing confidence and enthusiasm and will routinely integrate some of these ways of being and relating into their clinical practice.

Therapist tips

- 'The body remembers' – schemas are not only cognitive, affective and behavioural, but also somatic patterns and habits that form over time and stem from early experiences. Learning to read patients' bodies can add much to the therapist's and the patient's own understanding of their internal worlds.
- It is safe to work with the body as long as the patient is supported to modulate their arousal within their 'Window of Tolerance'.
- Deepen your patient's experience via a 'dance with the core organisers' – this is a framework that can enhance all Schema Therapy techniques.
- Dare to play around with somatic experimentation, such as probes, to promote integration of new habits.
- Be mindful, curious and validating of your patient's internal world, and help them to foster this relationship with themselves.
- *Stay with* newly evolving positive affect for as long as possible to enhance the formation of new neural pathways.
- Encourage the patient to trust their body's wisdom and do more of what feels good.

Notes

1 The focus in this chapter will be on somatic techniques that do not necessitate physical contact with the patient.
2 The material presented is written so as to protect patient confidentiality, and session examples are composites of therapeutic dialogues with a number of patients.

References

Arntz, A. & Jacob, G. (2012). *Schema therapy in practice: An introductory guide to the schema mode approach*. Chichester: Wiley-Blackwell.

Bennett-Levy, J., Butler, G., Fennell, M., Hackman, A., Mueller, M. & Westbrook, D. (Eds.) (2004). *Oxford guide to behavioural experiments in cognitive therapy*. Oxford: Oxford University Press.

Dana, D. (2018). *The polyvagal theory in therapy: Engaging the rhythm of regulation*. New York: Norton.

Farrell, J., Reiss, N. & Shaw, I. (2014). *The schema therapy clinician's guide: A complete resource for building and delivering individual, group and integrated schema mode treatment programs*. New York: Wiley.

Farrell, J. & Shaw, I. (2012). *Group schema therapy for borderline personality disorder*. New York: Wiley.

Kurtz, R. (1990). *Body-centered psychotherapy: The Hakomi method*. Mendocino, CA: LifeRhythm.

Layden, M.A., Newman, C.F., Freeman, A. & Byers-Morse, S. (1993). *Cognitive therapy of borderline personality disorder*. Needham Heights, MA: Allyn & Bacon.

Levine, P.A. (2015). *Trauma and memory: Brain and body in a search for the living past*. Berkeley, CA: North Atlantic Books.

Ogden, P. & Fisher, J. (2015). *Sensorimotor psychotherapy: Interventions for trauma and attachment*. New York: Norton.

Ogden, P., Minton, K. & Pain, C. (2006). *Trauma and the body: A sensorimotor approach to psychotherapy*. New York: W. W. Norton.

Porges, S.W. (2011). *The polyvagal theory: Neurophysiological foundations of emotions, attachment, communication, and self-regulation*. New York: W.W. Norton.

Rothschild, B.O. (2000). *The body remembers: The psychobiology of trauma and trauma treatment*. New York: W.W. Norton.

Schore, A. (2003). *Affect regulation and disorders of the self*. New York: Norton.

Siegel, D. (1999). *The developing mind: toward a neurobiology of interpersonal experience*. New York: Guilford Press.

Simeone-DiFrancesco, C., Roediger, E. & Stevens, B.A. (2015). *Schema therapy with couples: A practitioner's guide to healing relationships*. Chichester: Wiley Blackwell.

Van der Kolk, B.A. (1994). *The body keeps score: Memory and the evolving psychobiology of posttraumatic stress*. New York: Penguin.

Young, J.E., Klosko, J.S. & Weishaar, M.E. (2003). *Schema therapy: A practitioner's guide*. New York: Guildford Press.

4 Understanding and meeting core emotional needs

George Lockwood and Rachel Samson

Introduction

The ultimate goal of Schema Therapy (ST) is for our patients to relate to themselves (through mode modification and integration and/or changes in schemas and coping styles) and to others in ways that support their core emotional needs being met. Understanding these needs and the relational process by which they can be met (by the therapist, the patient's Healthy Adult and others) is central to the model and a rich, layered endeavour. Initially, therapist and patient start to link their presenting problems to individual schemas and modes while uncovering possible childhood origins. Part of this process involves the developing awareness of primary parent–child interactions that have shaped the patient's internal world and their ongoing attachment to others. To fully appreciate the nuances of these interactions, the therapist explores their history and attempts to identify the patient's temperament, the characteristics of the parent and the interplay between the two. Close attention is paid to the ways in which the parent–child relationship may have failed to meet certain core emotional needs. Furthermore, in session, the therapist attunes to the patient's unmet needs directly; with a view to adopting a reparenting stance. That is, the therapist aims to provide (within the bounds of a therapeutic relationship) corrective emotional experiences for needs not met in childhood which are perpetuated into adulthood by means of schema maintenance.

It is this process of limited reparenting that we consider to be at the heart of ST; however, relatively little has been articulated about how we might best provide and promote emotionally corrective, schema healing experiences in therapy. This is the focus of this chapter, in which we outline the concept of Positive Parenting Patterns (PPPs) and describe how these can inform our reparenting stance in relation to our patients. We see these as the core positive patterns most central to, and most directly involved with, meeting core emotional needs.

PPPs and core emotional needs

Young, Lockwood and colleagues initially studied possible parental origins associated with Early Maladaptive Schemas (EMS) (Lockwood & Perris,

2012; Young et al., 2003). These were identified via patients' self-report of childhood memories of key negative parenting interactions associated with each of the EMS (Young, 1999). These memories were then used as the basis for developing items to form scales to measure the hypothesised maladaptive patterns. Lockwood and colleagues then conducted factor analytic investigations of the hypothesised structure of these constructs and correlated the resultant factors to those that emerged from the Young Schema Questionnaire (YSQ) (Sheffield et al., 2005). The most recent study with the strongest empirical base identified six maladaptive parenting patterns: Degradation and Rejection, Emotional Inhibition and Deprivation, Punitiveness, Overprotection and Overindulgence, Competitiveness and Status Seeking, and Overcontrol (Louis et al., 2018b).

Having established key problematic parenting patterns, the research group undertook a series of correlational and factor analytic studies (Louis et al., 2018a) to identify the PPPs thought to meet core needs and to be associated with positive mental health outcomes. Seven patterns were found:

1) Emotional Nurturance and Unconditional Love
2) Playfulness and Emotional Openness
3) Autonomy Support: Being believed in and seen as being capable of succeeding at challenging goals.
4) Autonomy Granting: Being given the freedom to be the author of one's own life
5) Dependability: Being reliably present and dependable in providing guidance and support
6) Intrinsic Worth: Providing guidance in the pursuit of intrinsically meaningful life goals while remaining true to oneself and fair and respectful to others
7) Confidence and Competence: Being, and coming across as, confident and competent as a parent

Empirical support for the existence of four broad categories of core emotional needs was recently established and, in a follow-up study, significant positive relationships between these needs and the seven core PPPs were found (Louis et al., n.d.), thus supporting a hypothesis central to both ST and the focus of this chapter.

A PPP is defined as a broad, pervasive theme or pattern comprising behaviours, tone, emotions, attitudes, beliefs and values as recalled by an adult's memories of their interactions with their parent/caregiver that leads to the fulfilment of core emotional needs and the development of a secure attachment, adaptive schemas and adaptive behavioural dispositions.

In this chapter, we focus on how the seven PPPs can inform the dynamic process of limited reparenting in therapy, since these patterns are primarily defined by the positive experiences believed to satisfy our patients' core needs. We see these seven PPPs as adding clarity and definition to the range of corrective emotional experiences that make up the structure of limited reparenting. One possibility is that these seven PPPs are a first step in articulating the optimal conditions for meeting early core needs and, in conjunction with the six maladaptive (negative) parenting patterns, provide valuable guidance with respect to the formation of a patient's early adaptive and maladaptive schemas. Other models of parenting identify, at most, three somewhat more general positive parenting qualities or styles – emotional warmth, being authoritative and being involved (Louis et al., 2018a) – whereas the seven PPPs described here open up a broader, richer and more nuanced understanding of the full range of nutriments parents provide to meet core emotional needs.

The role of temperament

The ST model assumes that temperament plays an important role in the acquisition of maladaptive schemas and modes (Young et al., 2003) and, consistent with this, the recently updated case conceptualisation form (International Society of Schema Therapy, 2018) explicitly invites consideration of temperamental factors in the patient's presentation. However, in general, it has been argued that too little weight is given to temperament in the context of psychotherapy (Aron, 2012) and it is unclear to what degree schema therapists leverage knowledge about a patient's temperament during treatment (beyond conceptualisation). Furthermore, as is discussed further below, ST has not yet addressed the central role temperament is likely to play in the development of adaptive schemas (Louis et al., 2018c). One of the goals of this chapter is to further acknowledge the bright side of this temperament–therapy interaction and how to best leverage it.

The past several decades of research has resulted in a consensus on at least four dimensions of adult temperament: Extraversion–Introversion, Agreeableness–Disagreeableness, Conscientiousness–Spontaneity/Flexibility, and Sensitivity (Neuroticism)–Emotional Stability (Zuckerman, 2012), all of which we believe have an impact on the patient's parenting needs. For example, being lower on trait conscientiousness leads to a greater need for help with impulsivity; being higher on trait sensitivity results in a greater need for attuned emotional support and very stable attachments; being more introverted is associated with a higher need for help in finding and protecting quiet, solitude and a smaller number of deeper relationships. Being high on agreeableness is associated with a greater need for help in advocating for oneself, while being low on agreeableness is associated with a need for help in taking others' needs and feelings into account and establishing reciprocity.

Traits of high sensitivity and high emotional reactivity are also defining features of Borderline Personality Disorder (Trull & Brown, 2013) and, as such, highly relevant to ST. One context within which this high sensitivity and emotional reactivity is brought out clearly is in response to stress.

Underneath the skin, this high stress reactivity is accompanied by a range of more intense physiological responses such as increased heart rate, blood pressure and cortisol. On top of the skin (on a phenotypic level) this is strongly correlated with being very shy (Kagan et al., 1988). Within stressful home or social environments, children and adults with this trait have been found to suffer from a significantly greater amount of behavioural/emotional problems and medical disorders (e.g., infectious disease) and are more likely to be found at the bottom of dominance hierarchies (Boyce, 2019). From this vantage point, this sensitivity and reactivity is clearly a liability and has been viewed exclusively in these terms for decades from the vantage point of what is called the Diathesis/Stress model. Boyce et al. (1995) were the first to discover that these more sensitive children (what he came to call 'orchid' children), when raised in very nurturing and supportive homes, are, in fact, healthier than the less sensitive and more resilient 'dandelion' children (again a term Boyce introduced), having the lowest rates of infectious disease and the lowest rates of emotional/behavioural problems, even lower than dandelion children raised in supportive environments. Orchid children and adults are also more likely to rise to the top of the dominance hierarchies in highly nurturing environments (Suomi, 1997; Boyce, 2019). Thus, rather than sensitivity being a trait involving frailty, it is a trait that is associated with, for better or worse, greater attunement and receptivity. Of particular relevance to limited reparenting, Belsky (1997a, 1997b, 2005), Belsky and Pluess (2009) and Suomi (1997) have studied the impact of highly nurturant parenting in comparison to normal parenting in both primate and human populations. It was found that parents who are exceptionally patient, loving, understanding, warm and responsive in the face of the frequent crises and emotional struggles that are associated with this temperament raise orchid children who develop exceptionally secure attachments and function at a higher level throughout their lifespan than their dandelion counterparts. These orchid children grow up to become highly nurturant parents themselves. The orchid children have a greater capacity to benefit from the more nurturing parenting.

As discussed below, sensitivity is, thus, one of a number of traits that in fact *enable* change and progress when the specific needs associated with the trait are adequately met. For example, for many BPD patients, their sensitivity may contribute to their ability to attach deeply and strongly through the associated greater capacity for vulnerability and receptivity, qualities that enable limited reparenting to have such a strong effect. It could be argued that it is at least partly the dimension of trait sensitivity upon which ST has established its impressive effects with this patient group (Lockwood et al., 2018). Beyond diagnosis, 15–20% of the general population have more sensitive and emotionally reactive temperaments, and these individuals make up the majority of those who seek our help in therapy (Boyce, 2019; Aron, 2013). For this reason, it is one of the groups we focus on in our clinical examples in the discussion that follows.

PPPs: clinical skills and techniques

We provide case examples and discussion for the first four PPPs and, due to space limitations, will briefly highlight some of the central features of the remaining three.

Emotional Nurturance and Unconditional Love

The first PPP, Emotional Nurturance and Unconditional Love, forms the foundation of limited reparenting and is the most multifaceted of the seven. This PPP is made up of three sub-themes that are detailed below: Emotional Nurturance (comprising in turn four discrete elements), Unconditional Love and Strength and Guidance.

1. Emotional Nurturance involves:
    Deep attachment: The experience of feeling deeply understood, feeling free to talk openly and with sufficient emotional space to be oneself, having someone wise and comforting and having sufficient shared time.
    Affection: Receiving physical affection in a well-timed and attuned manner (from parents) from someone who is warm and affectionate. Within a therapeutic relationship, given the complexities of touch, warmth and non-physical affection are the main elements here.
    Day and night availability: Being confident someone is available to meet one's needs and to provide comfort and security during the night, as well as during the day (from parents). Within therapy, this translates to the therapist holding their needs in mind beyond the face-to-face session and being there for them at times of high stress/crisis within appropriate professional limits (e.g., scheduling an additional phone call, organising extra support, providing a transitional object, or providing email reparenting messages).
    Openness: Having someone who is emotionally open, expressive and who uses self-disclosure that helps to foster connection.
2. Unconditional Love: Involves a parent/therapist who is patient and respectful in the face of a child's or patient's mistakes and amid conflict with him/her, who sets appropriate limits in a respectful and caring way when needed and who readily admits her/his own mistakes.
3. Strength and Guidance: Providing help in setting goals and following through on tasks, giving sound advice and direction, and being supportive and encouraging in the face of challenges.

Emotional Nurturance and Unconditional love in a therapeutic sense represents multifaceted, spontaneous and genuine caring, deep appreciation and emotional involvement, but differs from romantic, friendship or familial love in that it occurs within a boundaried therapeutic relationship. As can be seen, nurturance and love are not merely about fostering connection or providing emotional support, but also involve setting limits when needed, as well as supporting the emergence of autonomy. We see optimal integration of these themes as involving an initial attuned response to needs for attachment, affection, availability and openness with a gradual increased focus on autonomy and self-regulation, when the time is right.

Case example: Elijah

The following case example illustrates the four discrete elements of Emotional Nurturance, one of the three sub-themes outlined above, as they are expressed through work with a highly sensitive patient. Elijah, a 20-year-old philosophy student, shifted from extreme emotional isolation to deep connection through the course of treatment. He presented with severe anxiety and depression, emotional dysregulation, alcohol abuse, self-harming requiring medical treatment, was actively suicidal and had the belief he needed to be 'fixed'. Underlying these symptoms was a highly sensitive temperament, profound emotional deprivation and a sense of being fundamentally unacceptable, different and defective.

Elijah had been considered by his parents to be a highly sensitive and 'deep' child. He said, 'No one seemed to be like me, or be able to understand my fears or big existential questions. Mum would often laugh it off, as if it was ridiculous for a child of my age to ask such things ... I internalised all this and believed I was defective. I was too sensitive, too deep. Other people will never understand me. True connection is not possible.'

His father rarely showed any positive emotions and was unresponsive and impatient. He would become blaming and rejecting when Elijah was emotional or depressed and did not understand him or know how to support him without using physical punishment in response to minor misdemeanours. His mother was insensitive and intrusive; she would push for connection but be misattuned. Elijah had no secure attachments and, by mid-adolescence he was depressed, highly suicidal and self-harming.

Being deeply understood, for Elijah, meant first recognising that feeling highly anxious and dissociated was not his fault or something he was doing wrong, but, rather, was due to him having learned, on a neurobiological level through repeated traumatic experiences, that attachment was unsafe and highly threatening.

His therapist understood he would need repeated experiences of sensitivity, attunement and safety, and an understanding that his neurobiological system would set the pace, that there was no way to hurry the process. Following her lead and helping him feel safe being together in verbal and non-verbal ways included periods of silence, non-verbal smiles and eye contact, and him sending emails with songs and images in between sessions. When Elijah 'failed' to put words to his experience in the allotted time, he would become punitive and self-harming, so he was given some extra time. This provided the sense of space needed for a deep attachment. The therapist trusted this process and understood that his silences involved both fear and deep processing on his part. Over time, he began to share what was previously a solitary processing.

Alcohol and self-harm were used to numb unregulated feelings. Reducing these coping mechanisms meant that the therapist needed to be more accessible and available outside the session to help provide regulation and support during this phase. This included her checking in and offering email contact and some phone calls between appointments – a therapeutic parallel to the around-the-clock 'day and night availability' referred to above. As the attachment grew, Elijah began to feel less isolated and to experience the connection as a deeper, more powerful and fulfilling source of regulation. In parallel, his self-harm, alcohol abuse and suicidality reduced dramatically.

A growing trust allowed Elijah's history to be processed within a sense of safety and attunement in the therapy relationship. The depth of understanding grew and his life narrative became more coherent. This led to him feeling more secure: 'I no longer look back at my childhood and feel defective, I now look back and feel grief for not getting what I desperately needed. I also know that there are so many like me (depth-orientated, sensitive) and that I am able to access these connections whenever I need.'

Playfulness and Emotional Openness

We see the PPP discussed above, Emotional Nurturance and Unconditional Love, as primarily involved with the minimisation of negative affect. However, the amplification of positive affect (as involved in the Playfulness and Emotional Openness PPP) is also a key element of secure attachment (Schore, 2001; Schore & Schore, 2007) and of parenting. This PPP involves the parent/therapist being playful, emotionally open and spontaneous. A few of the items defining it were: 'Could act child-like and be silly with me when s/he felt like it', 'Was able to be free and expressive when s/he wanted to be', and 'It was easy for him/her to be playful when s/he wanted to be'.

One of our supervisees discussed imagery work with a female patient imagining herself as a little girl hiding behind the living room couch drawing on a piece of paper and feeling alone and scared. The supervisee's focus in the image was on connecting with her by trying to talk with her about her feelings of fear and sadness. She did not want the therapist near her and did not feel like talking. We suggested taking an interest in what she was drawing and joining her in her imaginative world as a way to connect in a more positive and playful way. Adding this dimension to imagery and, more broadly, in therapy, helped her to open up, connect with her therapist more easily and added an element of fun and enjoyment in their work together. The supervisee became aware that he had, without realising it, been predominately in 'toolbelt mode' in his work with his patients, looking for problems to solve and missing opportunities to more easily and naturally accomplish things such as bypassing the Detached Protector mode through fun and play.

Chapter 10 of this volume (Shaw) and Lockwood and Shaw (2012) also provide an extensive discussion and examples of this theme in action.

Autonomy Support

This PPP involves believing in someone and seeing them as capable of succeeding at challenging, valued goals. It involves looking out for, developing and celebrating strengths and capacities in a positive and respectful way. Part of this means not losing sight of the patient's potential, even during prolonged difficult stretches when things seem to be getting worse. Items defining this PPP include: 'Was proud of me when I succeeded at something important', 'Saw me as strong and resilient', 'Was confident in my ability to solve problems that came up that other children my age could do', and 'Believed in my ability to succeed at challenging goals'.

Autonomy Support is made up of two facets:

1) Looking for and seeing capability (e.g., believing in a person's ability to succeed at challenging goals).
2) Praise and a positive focus (e.g., being proud of someone when they succeed at something important, focusing on what someone did well without needing to point out mistakes or flaws).

Case example: Tamara

Tamara was a 37-year-old single woman with Avoidant Personality Disorder and a highly sensitive temperament. She had had years of previous therapy which had little impact on her social anxiety and dread and avoidance of dating. This treatment included assigned homework that involved putting herself in situations where she might meet someone and to attempt to initiate conversations with men. At these times, she invariably felt intense anxiety and an urge to avoid contact that she was unable to overcome. In the few situations where she went on an actual date, she experienced what she called an 'emotional lockdown', which involved feeling frozen, putting up a wall, and counting the minutes until it was over. Dates rarely progressed past a first meeting, and she rejected the few men that expressed an interest.

She researched different therapeutic approaches and sought out ST in the hope it would help her change on a deeper level. Early on in imagery work, Tamara saw herself, aged six, in a closet doorway curled into a ball and feeling empty, terrified and unwilling to talk. By the time she was an adolescent, she had developed an intense, surly and dismissive Detached Protector mode. The first several months of treatment were focused on developing a warm and secure base (through a primary focus on the

Emotional Nurturance and Unconditional Love PPP discussed above). Through this, Little Tamara, found initially in imagery, began to experience an emerging sense of lovability, confidence, openness, curiosity and even an interest in exploring the world and people around her.

Her Detached Protector mode was still ever-present but not calling all of the shots any more. She found herself responding to a request to take part in a goodbye party for a colleague without dread, and actually found herself spontaneously enjoying some of the interactions. This was a new experience. However, when her thoughts turned to men, she felt the same strong avoidance and overwhelming anxiety. She stated that after 27 years of trying and not having developed any sustained intimate relationships, this showed that she just could not do it. The therapist explained that he understood she was very scared, but that she was also in a different place, on a deeper level. She had previously been dating with a terrified little girl inside, huddled in a ball, but that this little girl now felt better and more open and adventurous. Little Tamara knew her therapist would be there for her, and with the progress she was making, it was a 'whole new ballgame'. She felt buoyed by this perspective and made a plan to put together a profile on a dating website.

At this point, Tamara was reminded of an experience she had with her niece, Paula, who also had a highly sensitive temperament. At four years of age, Paula was partway across a bouncing and swaying rope bridge on a playground with other children crossing back and forth when suddenly she froze, terrified to go further or back up. Tamara, who was standing down below, could see the terror on Paula's face. A couple of parents offered to go up and bring Paula down. Tamara knew this kind of moment well from her own experience, and instinctively knew what Paula needed and said to her, 'It is okay to be scared. You can do it. I am right here. I will be here for you.' Tamara reiterated this a few times and could see the fear lessen. Paula then began to slowly and determinedly walk across the bridge. Tamara met Paula with open arms as she got off the ladder on the other end, and could see the pride on her face as she gave her a big hug.

Her therapist was aware that with Tamara having a newly developed capacity to deal with her fear of dating, and now being in a better position to face and manage it, they were in the same position as Tamera was then with Paula. Her therapist, knowing of this change, had good reason to believe in her, and Tamara began to believe more in herself. This emerging new belief was further fostered by a mode dialogue between Little Tamara, who now felt more lovable, hopeful and open to adventure, and her Detached Protector, as she imagined a first date. It would have been a logical next step to use imagery and mode dialogues to face the process of developing a dating profile. However, in this case, she had a close friend who was ready and eager to help her with this, and it was her clear preference to do this with her (see Autonomy Granting, below). In working with Tamara in this way, her therapist embodied the key principles of Autonomy Support (and, secondarily, Autonomy Granting) in believing in her capability and creating conditions in which she could develop a sense of mastery that included supporting and believing in Little Tamara as she faced a major life challenge.

In the Louis et al. studies (2018a, 2018b) in which the seven PPPs emerged, Autonomy Support was found to have the strongest correlations of all the seven, with dimensions of adaptive functioning as measured by the Ryff Scales of Psychological Well-being (Ryff & Keyes, 1995), which includes measures of six adaptive constructs: Autonomy, Environmental Mastery, Personal Growth, Positive Relations with Others, Purpose in Life, and Self-acceptance.[1]

Autonomy Granting

This involves a respect for an individual making their own choices, their privacy and their ability to navigate and handle their life without frequent monitoring. We see an openness, interest and attunement to a wide range of temperaments, preferences and life choices as a central aspect of this construct. A therapist who is high in this theme will come across to the patient as open, non-judgemental and accepting. This PPP has wide relevance in therapy. We briefly touch on just three examples of Autonomy Granting here.

Example 1: Emotional experience

Robin was a sensitive and expressive patient and said she had always been this way, even as a child. Her father was an emotionally guarded man and highly critical and shaming of how she 'wore her heart on her sleeve' and 'over-reacted to the slightest problem'. She liked her therapist pointing to her father's limitations and the fact he felt she deserved much better. She felt deeply validated and understood, that there was nothing wrong with the intensity of her feelings – this was fundamentally her father's problem. However, Robin did not feel angry with him. Her therapist felt a dilemma at this point, as he wondered if her anger was being suppressed or inhibited. He initially encouraged her to try to connect to any anger in childhood imagery. However, from Robin's reactions, he surmised that her feeling toward her father was *not anger*, despite the fact he found this a little puzzling under the circumstances. He shared his reactions with her with curiosity and acceptance, and Robin said she appreciated him giving her space to feel things out in her own way. The therapist demonstrated the principles of Autonomy Granting in this situation by remaining caring and involved, and through his active curiosity and attunement, while also allowing the patient to determine her own emotional path.

Example 2: Choice of intervention

As schema therapists, we are encouraged to use a range of experiential techniques and other interventions that are understood to facilitate change. For some techniques (such as Imagery Rescripting) there is good empirical evidence for their application, and it is necessary to work with the patient's coping modes to understand a reluctance or refusal to use a technique. Often, therapists are also scared of using the technique and need help in supervision to overcome their fears.

However, we argue that the principles of Autonomy Granting should also be borne in mind when choosing an intervention. For some patients, they make progress in ST without the use of certain techniques, and they may actively and persistently dislike a specific method, rendering it ineffective. There may be a variety of temperamental and personal reasons for this which may not necessarily be "unhealthy," and it is in line with the principles of Autonomy Granting to explore other ways of meeting their needs. For example, Elijah (the patient discussed at the start of the chapter) preferred immediate reparenting experiences with his therapist over imagery, and he found the 'as if' quality of imagery odd and distracting. His therapist was curious as to the potential modes at play (exploring, for example, the Detached Protector's feelings about imagery), but she came to realise that this particular method was not necessary to meet Elijah's needs, and granting him greater autonomy in therapy was more important.

Example 3: Sociability

A subtle lack of Autonomy Granting can also occur in well-intentioned efforts to encourage those with a more introverted temperament to socialise more, develop more friends, or become part of a group in line with the needs of a more extroverted temperament. Without attention to these nuances, our more introverted clients can end up feeling as if their natural and healthy inclinations are a defect.

Dependability

Dependability involves the therapist demonstrating that they can be relied upon to not abandon the patient; stand up for, protect and advocate for her when needed; be steady, consistent and responsible; follow through on promises and tasks (e.g., homework); know when to hold her in mind outside of regular sessions and be available to provide extra support; and be available to guide and support her in developing the discipline and impulse control to pursue central life goals when needed. This also involves developing an overall 'game plan' for the patient, associated with a clear and full case conceptualisation, rather than more of a 'flying by the seat of one's pants' or session-by-session approach. The therapist's traits involve being sufficiently conscientious and committed, and the patient's experience is of being in steady and knowing hands.

Example: Dependable Presence

Chris, a patient with a highly sensitive temperament, was having out-patient exploratory surgery to check for possible cancer. It was likely he would be alone when he heard the result. His therapist agreed to check in by phone soon after Chris spoke with the surgeon, providing support at a critical time. In this instance, the therapist had held Chris in mind and showed he could be depended upon when it mattered most. This was a reparative moment for Chris (who had Mistrust/Abuse schema) and he opened up more fully in subsequent sessions.

Intrinsic Worth

This PPP involves helping a patient learn to prioritise being true to oneself, fair and companionable, on par with, or ahead of, impressing others or winning or acquiring status or money. Central to this is learning to function adaptively within the competence hierarchies the patient finds him or herself in or chooses to take part in, engaging as fully in the pursuit of personal mastery and as competitively with others as one wants, while remaining fair and respectful in regards to pursuing what is personally meaningful.

Confidence and Competence

This PPP was found to be associated with a child experiencing their parent as being emotionally strong, steady and predictable, being effective at getting things done, and having realistic expectations of him or herself. As a therapist, this involves, among other things, coming across as sufficiently secure, confident, flexible, open and assured. Interestingly, this PPP also involves being comfortable with, and open to, tough questions or challenges from our patients and, through this, learning from them in the process of them learning from us.

Summary and conclusions

Central to the process of ST is identifying our patients' unmet emotional needs and, within appropriate boundaries, meeting these needs within the therapeutic relationship through limited reparenting. However, to date, our sense is that limited reparenting has been poorly articulated as a construct, despite being a central and highly nuanced aspect of therapy. We aim to progress things in this domain by proposing that the seven core PPPs provide a potentially useful framework for increasing our awareness, attunement and effectiveness within our limited reparenting role. We provide a description of the relational characteristics that may function as antidotes to some of our patients' core unmet emotional needs. We hope this can help therapists hone their reparenting style as well as provide a useful overview of key relational processes for junior therapists or therapists transitioning from other, less relational, models of working.

Of course, we do not assume that we provide an exhaustive or even comprehensive list of PPPs. Rather, we aim to provide a springboard for the development of a shared language for describing and translating the critical ingredient of limited reparenting within ST. The research described so far would be further enhanced by prospective study designs exploring whether therapist attunement and behaviour in accordance with the proposed PPP predicts better therapeutic outcomes.

Therapist tips

1) It is valuable to hold in mind the seven PPPs as a framework for honing our reparenting skills in a ST context.
2) All seven of these patterns are involved in meeting needs for both connection and autonomy.
3) These seven PPPs help to define the core capacities of the therapist upon which all the technical aspects (e.g., imagery rescripting, chair work, mode dialogues, body work) of ST will ideally be rooted.
4) We believe that a solid grounding in these relational structures of limited reparenting will breathe life into the use of therapeutic tools, lessening the need for a more scripted approach since the techniques flow naturally from the felt and tacit sense of knowing associated with the embodiment of these patterns.

Note

1 While suggestive of parallels with limited reparenting, it is important to keep in mind that these correlations are not based on studies of patients and therapists but of adults' memories of their experiences of being parented as they correlated with measures of adaptive and maladaptive functioning.

References

Aron, E. (2012). Temperament in psychotherapy: Reflections on clinical practice with the trait of sensitivity. In M. Zentner & R. Shiner (Eds.), *Handbook of Temperament* (pp. 645–670). New York: Guilford Press.

Aron, E. (2013). *The Highly Sensitive Person*. New York: Citadel Press.

Belsky, J. (1997a). Variation in susceptibility to rearing influences: An evolutionary argument. *Psychological Inquiry, 8*: 182–186.

Belsky, J. (1997b). Theory testing, effect-size evaluation, and differential susceptibility to rearing influence: The case of mothering and attachment. *Child Development, 68*: 598–600.

Belsky, J. (2005). Differential susceptibility to rearing influences: An evolutionary hypothesis and some evidence. In B. Ellis & D. Bjorklund (Eds.), *Origins of the Social Mind: Evolutionary Psychology and Child Development* (pp. 139–163). New York: Guilford Press.

Belsky, J. & Pluess, M. (2009). Beyond diathesis stress: Differential susceptibility to environmental influences. *Psychological Bulletin, 135*(6): 885–908.

Boyce, W.T. (2019). *The Orchid and the Dandelion: Why Some Children Struggle and How all can Thrive*. New York: Alfred Knopf.

Boyce, W.T., Chesney, M., Alkon, A. et al. (1995). Psychobiologic reactivity to stress and childhood respiratory illnesses: Results of two prospective studies. *Psychosomatic Medicine, 57*(5): 411–422.

International Society of Schema Therapy (2018). Schema therapy case conceptualization form, 2nd edition, Version 2.22, d.edwards@ru.ac.za or office@isstonline.com

Kagan, J., Reznick, J.D. & Snidman, N. (1988). Biological bases of childhood shyness. *Science, 240*(1998): 167–171.

Lockwood, G. & Perris, P. (2012). A new look at core emotional needs. In M. van Vreeswijk, J. Broersen & M. Nadort (Eds.), *The Wiley-Blackwell Handbook of Schema Therapy: Theory, Research and Science* (pp. 41–66). West Sussex, UK: Wiley-Blackwell.

Lockwood, G. & Shaw, I. (2012). Schema therapy and the role of joy and play. In M. van Vreeswijk, J. Broersen & M. Nadort (Eds.), *The Wiley-Blackwell Handbook of Schema Therapy: Theory, Research and Science* (pp. 209–227). West Sussex, UK: Wiley-Blackwell.

Lockwood, G., Samson, R. & Young, J. (2018, May). Sweeping life transformations: The farther reaches of schema therapy. Workshop, International Society of Schema Therapy convention, Amsterdam, Netherlands. www.schematherapysociety.com/Sweeping-Life-Transformations

Louis, J.P., Davidson, A.T., Lockwood, G. & Wood, A.M. (n.d.). Schema Therapy Personality Theory (STPT): Do perceptions of parenting relate to the fulfillment of theorized core emotional needs? Under review.

Louis, J.P., Wood, A. & Lockwood, G. (2018a). Development and validation of the Positive Parenting Schema Inventory (PPSI) to complement the Young Parenting Inventory (YPI) for Schema Therapy (ST) assessment. DOI: 10.1177/1073191118798464

Louis, J.P., Wood, A.M. & Lockwood, G. (2018b). Psychometric validation of the Young Parenting Inventory – Revised (YPI-R2): Replication and extension of a commonly used parenting scale in Schema Therapy (ST) research and practice. *PLoS ONE, 13*(11). DOI: 10.1371/journal.pone.0205605

Louis, J.P., Wood, A.M., Lockwood, G., Ho, M.-H.R. & Ferguson, E. (2018c). Positive clinical psychology and schema therapy (ST): The development of the Young Positive Schema Questionnaire (Ypsq) to complement the Young Schema Questionnaire (Ysq-S3). *Psychological Assessment,30*(9): 1199–1213. DOI: 10.1037/pas0000567

Ryff, C.D. & Keyes, C.L.M. (1995). The structure of psychological well-being revisited. *Journal of Personality and Social Psychology, 69*(4): 719–727.

Schore, A.N. (2001). The Seventh Annual John Bowlby Memorial Lecture, Minds in the Making: Attachment, the self-organizing brain, and developmentally-oriented psychoanalytic psychotherapy. *British Journal of Psychotherapy, 17*: 299–328.

Schore, J.R. & Schore, A.N. (2007). Modern attachment theory: The central role of affect regulation in development and treatment. *Clinical Social Work Journal, 36*(1): 9–20. DOI: 10.1007/s10615-007-0111-7

Sheffield, A., Waller, G., Emanuelli, F., Murray, J. & Meyer, C. (2005). Links between parenting and core beliefs: Preliminary psychometric validation of the young parenting inventory. *Cognitive Therapy and Research, 29*(6): 787–802. DOI: 10.1007/s10608-005-4291-6

Suomi, S. (1997). Early determinants of behaviour: Evidence from primate studies. *British Medical Bulletin, 53*: 170–184.

Trull, T. & Brown, B. (2013). Borderline personality disorder: A five factor-model perspective. In T. Widiger & P. Costa *Personality Disorders and the Five-Factor Model of Personalty* (Third edition, pp. 119–132). Washington, DC: American Psychological Association.

Young, J.E. (1999). Young Parenting Inventory (YPI) (on-line). New York: Cognitive Therapy Centre. www.schematherapy.com

Young, J.E., Klosko, J. & Weishaar, M. (2003). *Schema Therapy: A Practitioner's Guide.* New York: Guilford Press.

Zuckerman, M. (2012). Models of adult temperament. In M. Zentner & R. Shiner, *Handbook of Temperament* (pp. 41–66). New York: Guilford Press.

Part II

Creative methods using imagery

5 Core principles of imagery

Susan Simpson and Arnoud Arntz

Introduction and rationale

A growing body of research indicates that imagery facilitates more direct access to emotions, thereby providing a unique opportunity for change. Indeed, imagery has a greater impact on negative and positive emotions than verbal processing of the same information (Cuthbert et al., 2003; Holmes et al., 2006). In effect, imagery behaves like an 'emotional amplifier' in the presence of both positive and negative affective states (Holmes & Mathews, 2010). In Schema Therapy (ST), imagery plays a key role at every level: assessment, conceptualisation and practice. Imagery rescripting (IR) is a powerful mechanism for facilitating the therapeutic transition from intellectual insight to experiential change through corrective emotional experiences. The power of IR draws on the human capacity to process information more effectively in the presence of affect. Imagery-based work is particularly effective as a mechanism for challenging long-standing and entrenched early maladaptive schemas (EMS) linked to unmet needs and trauma during childhood (Young, Klosko & Weishaar, 2003).

The transdiagnostic nature of images

Since the 1990s, there has been increasing recognition of the link between a range of emotional disorders and both excessive intrusive 'unwanted' mental images and an absence of adaptive imagery. Indeed, negative images play a key role in maintaining psychological distress across a range of presentations (e.g., Harvey, Watkins & Mansell, 2004). Mental images manifest in multifarious ways across diagnostic groups. In post traumatic stress disorder (PTSD), these take the form of recurring nightmares and 'flashback' multi-sensory images associated with past moments of threat or danger. The content of intrusive images reflect variations in perceived threats across disorders, including: embarrassing oneself in public (social phobia); imminent catastrophe associated with loss of control or collapse (panic disorder); being unable to cope with, or escape, imminent disaster such as being trapped, humiliated (agoraphobia); ego-dystonic scenes linked to contamination or feeling responsible for hurting others (obsessive–compulsive disorder (OCD)); negative memories signifying failure, humiliation (depression); distorted body shape linked to negative self-evaluation (eating disorders); being threatened or attacked (psychosis) (e.g., Hackmann, Bennett-Levy & Holmes, 2011; Holmes & Hackmann, 2004). Although intrusive imagery focused on future events are often catastrophic in nature, they can also take the form of 'solutions' that bring short-term relief, such as in the form of visual images of oneself checking in OCD, images of suicide that bring relief from currently unsolvable problems, or visuo-sensory cravings of substances that drive addictions (May et al., 2008).

Working directly with images to alter their affect tone and meaning, IR has increasingly become a central intervention across a wide range of therapeutic models (Arntz, 2012; Holmes & Hackmann, 2004), and has been a core experiential technique utilised in ST since its inception (Young, 1990, 1999). The following section provides an overview of the growth in theory and experimental findings in this developing field, and some of the identified benefits of working with imagery across a range of clinical applications.

Background theory: mechanisms of operation in mental imagery

Mental imagery: theories of operation

Mental images include not only visual aspects, but the whole range of sensory experience, including smell, sound and felt sense (Kosslyn, Ganis & Thompson, 2001), making them seem real, or 'experience near' (Conway, 2001). For example, a mental image of being on a beach might include not only the sight of the blue seas and skies, but also a felt sense of bare feet on the sand, sun on the skin, the scent and taste of salt and sounds of seagulls and the waves.

Imagery has been conceptualised as a 'weak' representation of sensory perception (Pearson et al., 2015). Brain imaging studies indicate that when we close our eyes and picture an event or action, almost the same neural representations are activated as when events or actions are directly perceived in real-time, including at the primary visual cortex (Kosslyn, Ganis & Thompson, 2001; Pearson et al., 2015). This same overlap in neural activity has been found between direct perception and visual imagery (dreams) during sleep (Horikawa et al., 2013). Mental imagery focused on real or imagined unpleasant events consistently activate a higher level of negative affect than verbal or language-based versions of the same material (e.g., Holmes, Arntz & Smucker, 2007; Holmes & Mathews, 2005; Holmes et al., 2006). The theory of 'functional equivalence' proposes that just as direct perception of threat results in activation of bodily responses, such as increased adrenalin and heart rate, mental threat-based images operate through equivalent neural processes and stimulate parallel physiological reactions (Kosslyn, Ganis & Thompson, 2001). Thus, imagery has a direct impact on emotion via the physiological/

bodily aspects of emotional experience. Imagery may provide a route into the sensory–memory components of a deeply embedded EMS (represented by memory images, bodily-felt sense, cognitions and emotions) and, by so doing, provide an opportunity to change the meaning encoded in the early event that contributed to the development of the EMS. For instance, IR may be used to access a mistrust/abuse schema encoded in an early memory of abuse, by accessing the image of a parent's violent behaviour, the sound of their shouting, the smell of alcohol on their breath, and the visceral sense of heart racing and tight chest, along with thoughts of imminent danger. Where the full fear structure is accessed, the possibility of emotional and cognitive change via rescripting is presented.

Storage and recall of visually encoded schemas

Emotional memories, including unprocessed trauma fragments, appear to be laid down and recalled primarily in the form of visuo-sensory images (Arntz, De Groot, and Kindt, 2005; Conway, 2001; Willander, Sikström & Karlsson, 2015). These appear to be more immediately and directly accessible, and more likely to dominate conscious awareness, in comparison with verbal material (Holmes & Mathews, 2005). Further, emotional images appear to be preferentially linked to memories of similar events, which, over time, form specific 'schema memory banks'. An event that triggers a schema in the present (e.g., someone being asked to meet with their manager, thereby triggering a failure schema) is likely to activate the person's memory bank that is composed of prior images that evoked similar emotions (e.g., failing tests at school, disapproving parental facial expressions, being scolded by a teacher, being teased by peers). In IR, it is possible to directly tap into the relevant schema memory bank through the 'affect bridge'. The person is asked to re-imagine a recent experience, then focus on the feelings in their body, and allow their mind to drift back to a childhood memory with similar feelings – thus presenting an opportunity to rescript in order to change schema meaning at a deep felt sense level.

Working with implicational knowledge through images

According to the interacting cognitive subsystems theory (ICS) (Teasdale & Barnard, 1993), implicational knowledge is an integration of images, sensory information, conceptual thought and embodied experience, which operates at a felt sense intuitive level.

In contrast, the verbally based propositional knowledge system is thought to operate primarily at an intellectual level, whereby we may know something to be true factually, but this may not equate to feeling it to be true. In the case of trauma, an event may be stored as implicational knowledge, or situationally accessible memories, whereby the person may have flashback memories of the trauma event, a felt sense of being unsafe, and a bodily felt sense of tension and hypervigilance, with no direct access to their verbally accessible memory system which holds the narrative of the event (Brewin, Dalgleish & Joseph, 1996; Ehlers & Clark, 2000). In the context of therapeutic interventions, direct verbal cognitive challenging may address schemas at an intellectual level, while at an implicational level, they remain intact (e.g., 'I understand that I am not worthless, but it still feels true'). Similarly, a person who has experienced trauma may still feel unsafe at a bodily felt sense level, even though they may understand from a rational perspective that they are no longer in danger.

Early maladaptive schemas (EMS) are experienced largely as 'implicational' knowledge, and perpetuated by self-defeating coping patterns that reinforce this world view. For example, the Social Isolation schema, 'I don't belong, I'm different', may be stored as implicational data (e.g., images of being excluded, a felt sense of being lonely and different to others, thoughts and expectations of being judged by others) and perpetuated by avoidant coping that reduces exposure to novel information that could potentially challenge these assumptions and provide opportunities for change (e.g., Barnard, 2009).

Given the substantive role of flashback images in generating the distress associated with unprocessed trauma experiences, it seems logical that this may be addressed most effectively through working directly with image modification (Holmes, Arntz & Smucker, 2007). Moreover, even when patients don't report flashback images, evidence suggests that imagery-based techniques provide one of the most powerful means of addressing schemas encoded at the implicational level, thereby reducing their dysfunctional effects (Arntz, 2012; Pearson et al., 2015).

Applied imagery techniques in clinical settings

Imagery-based techniques most commonly applied in clinical settings include those based on imaginal exposure (IE) and IR. The majority of research into the therapeutic effects of imagery have focused on reduction of negative images. IE (or evocation) is one of the most established techniques in cognitive-behavioural therapy (CBT) settings, with good evidence for fear-based disorders in terms of stimulating emotional processing and reducing distress (Ehlers & Clark, 2000; Foa & Kozac, 1986). In contrast, IR has been applied in numerous settings as a means of eliciting new meanings associated with images based on memories or imagined events, as well as developing new positive images (Casement & Swanson, 2012; Hunt & Fenton, 2007; Morina, Lancee & Arntz, 2017). Whereas in some cases the IR comprises a complete treatment (e.g., PTSD and nightmares), in other cases (e.g., ST, CBT), IR forms one component of an overarching psychotherapeutic approach.

Preliminary studies suggest that IR may be more effective than IE in targeting images that evoke primary emotions that are not based on fear (e.g., anger, guilt, shame) (Arntz, Tiesema & Kindt, 2007; Grunert et al., 2007), although findings are mixed (Langkaas et al., 2017). In one study where an IE condition was compared with IE plus IR, treatment outcomes on PTSD symptoms were generally equivalent, but in the latter condition the drop-out rate was lower, and there were greater changes in non-fear-based emotions such as anger, guilt and shame. In addition, therapists expressed a preference for IR, alongside reduced feelings of helplessness (Arntz, Tiesema & Kindt, 2007).

Imagery-based therapy techniques: theories of operation

Imagery-based techniques provide a powerful context for cognitive–emotional processing. Several possible theories have been proposed that may explain the mechanisms by which imagery-based processing manifest.

- *Spontaneous change through evocation*: A range of theories propose that spontaneous changes to schema-based meaning and distress may occur simply through exposure to new information. These changes may occur through habituation to feared images, or spontaneous integration of more adaptive images or previously forgotten memories (Hackmann, Bennett-Levy & Holmes, 2011), thereby facilitating the development of a more integrated narrative of trauma memory (Ehlers & Clark, 2000). Further, imagery-based techniques may facilitate integration of the person's worst trauma-based fears with actual eventualities and outcomes (Ehlers & Clark, 2000) as well as providing an opportunity to learn that fears associated with re-experiencing memories (such as loss of control, going 'crazy') are not borne out by reality (Foa & Kozac, 1986; Jaycox & Foa, 1998).
- *Reduction of negative imagery through working memory competition*: Recent research suggests a role for adding visuo-spatial activities to imagery-based processing, which compete for cognitive load on working memory. For example, attentional breathing (Van den Hout et al., 2011), playing computer games (Engelhard et al., 2011), complex spatial tapping (Andrade, Kavanagh & Baddeley, 1997) and eye movements (Gunter & Bodner, 2008) that are executed concurrently with recall of distressing images may reduce the vividness of the distressing image by taxing the visuo-spatial working memory, therein providing potential for a range of therapeutic effects (Lilley et al., 2009). This may also be one mechanism through which Eye Movement Desensitisation Therapy (EMDR) operates in the treatment of trauma images, whereby increased cognitive load on working memory appears to interfere with the encoding of memories, thereby facilitating transmission of information from episodic to semantic/explicit memory systems and integration of new healthy information (Shapiro, 2014). This has implications for the potential role of incorporating visuo-spatial exercises in the context of IR, an area which is at present largely uninvestigated.

- *Actively challenging schematic meaning through IR*: Therapeutic imagery techniques operate through activation of 'hot' images stored in memory, thereby providing an aperture for reflection on what actually happened, and facilitating reprocessing on the basis of new corrective information. In the case of IR, the therapist plays a more active role by intentionally prompting restructuring of meaning. Through activation of emotionally laden images, schematic meanings become more readily accessible and amenable to re-evaluation. IR provides opportunities for the development of powerful new perspectives through creating imaginal alternative realities. Similarly, visualisation of novel positive images 'from scratch' has been utilised in a range of approaches, including ST, as a means of cultivating healthy self-compassion (Lee, 2005; Van der Wijngaart, 2015). Many patients with a history of neglect and/or abuse, report little or no access to self-compassion at the beginning of therapy. In ST, this is partly developed through the internalisation of 're-parenting' images and the felt sense of getting one's needs met (e.g., through attunement, warmth, empathy, closeness) in the context of IR.

Research indicates that mental imagery operates through multifarious mechanisms. Further research is needed to clarify the differential benefits of IR across various clinical populations, particularly in comparison with IE. Nevertheless, preliminary research suggests that IR is a powerful technique for transformation of schematic meaning and reducing emotional distress associated with both intrusive and non-intrusive traumatic memories. IR has been a central tenet of ST from its inception, providing a powerful platform for accessing and challenging the deeply entrenched EMS associated with complex trauma, PDs and other long-standing difficulties. In the next section, we highlight key principles for capitalising on the transformative power of IR.

Applications of IR in therapeutic settings

Target images for rescripting can be accessed either by focusing directly on a known childhood trauma situation, or by starting with a problematic image based on the patient's current life, and then using an 'affect-bridge' to facilitate access to a childhood memory which taps into the same EMS (Figure 5.1). Ensure that there is adequate emotion accessed within the current-life image before utilising an affect bridge to access a childhood image. If a positive image arises, the patient can be guided to find an image that feels 'opposite'. A safe place image can also be used, especially when dealing with severe trauma images, both as a starting point and as an end point after rescripting. The key is to identify early memories connected to patients' core figures from childhood, and elicit emotions linked to their EMS. In addition, patients can be encouraged to keep a record of affect-

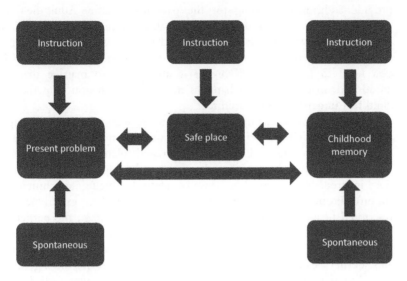

Figure 5.1 Pathways to childhood memories (from Arntz & van Genderen, 2009).

laden dreams and/or nightmares, which are often representative of schemas, and an important target for IR work (Young, Klosko & Weishaar, 2003).

Imagery rescripting of childhood images – three- step protocol

Arntz and Weertman (1999) developed an IR protocol with three main phases.

- (1) *Recall of childhood memory*: The patient recalls a childhood memory linked to their early maladaptive schemas (EMS) and describes this in detail from the child's perspective. The patient is prompted to experience the memory perceptually and emotionally, by describing the situation as the child in the present tense, first person. In the case of severe trauma, this is generally restricted to the time leading up to the abuse/trauma taking place. For example, 'In your mind's eye, see yourself as that little child back in that early situation, and describe what is happening. Now that your uncle is at the top of the stairs, pause the image … what are you feeling? What is happening in your body? What are you thinking? What do you need?'
- (2) *Healthy Adult rescripts*: The patient enters a trauma image as their Healthy Adult self and is instructed to notice the child in the image. They then rescript in order to protect the child from the perpetrator and provide comfort to the child. Alternatively, a significant other (e.g., support person, police, therapist) may initially take on this role or can

provide additional coaching for the patient's Healthy Adult Self. For example: 'Bring your Healthy Adult into the image … what do you see happening? How can you keep the child safe? How do you feel about the child being treated that way? What do you want to do or say? Do you need to make yourself bigger in the image to manage that? Go ahead and do that … what happens next? How can you help the little child feel understood and cared for?'

- (3) *Child re-experiences rescripting:* The patient re-experiences the rescripted image from the child's perspective, noticing how it feels to be protected and cared for by the adult, and is encouraged to imagine any additional changes needed to ensure that the rescripted image meets their needs (i.e., in order to increase their sense of safety, belonging, attachment and so on). From the child perspective, the patient then experiences the rescripted image with additional components added (e.g., the perpetrator is taken away by the police, the child is hugged and reassured).For example: 'Now rewind to when your Healthy Adult entered the image and see her dealing with your uncle … and now see her taking care of you. Listen to her voice and her words. How does that feel? Is there anything else you need? Ask your Healthy Adult for that.'

- *Debrief:* Time should be left at the end of IR sessions for debrief and regulation of the patient's emotions. Sessions are ended with praising the patient for the work and progress they have made and validating their emotional reactions during/following imagery. This protocol has demonstrated effectiveness both in relation to transforming trauma images based in childhood (Weertman & Arntz, 2007), as well as adulthood (Arntz, Tiesema & Kindt, 2007; Arntz, Sofi & van Breukelen, 2013; Raabe et al., 2018). These findings demonstrate the power of IR in reducing traumatisation while changing the meaning encoded in traumatic memories, including self-blame, a sense of being wrong or 'bad', and powerlessness.

Imagery rescripting – key points for implementation

- *Activation of memory 'hotspots':* Allow sufficient time to ensure that the patient is 'in' the image and experiencing it fully by asking them to describe it in detail, in the first person, present tense, noticing perceptual and felt sense aspects of experience. It is essential that mental imagery of the schema-based situation is sufficiently vivid to evoke an emotional response, in order for learning to take place (Lang, 1977). This requires the therapist to find a balance between sufficient activation of affect through exposure to the image, while minimising the risk of re-traumatisation. In the case of severe abuse memories, the memory is paused and rescripting takes place in the moment before the actual abuse takes place. Indeed, the effectiveness of IR depends on sufficient activation of the 'hotspots' of memory. Rescripting of the memory without attendant amplification of affect will be insufficient to bring about schematic change. Moreover, trauma scripts can have several 'hotspots', each of which might need to be addressed (for example, the sexual abuse itself, as well as the rejecting/accusing response of one of the parents later, when the child attempted to approach them for help). Each of these components is likely to hold their own schematic meaning and will need to be acknowledged.

- *Recruit resources to overcome the antagonist:* The therapist (or patient's Healthy Adult) must rescript in such a way that enables them to 'win' the exchange with the antagonist, and can recruit helpers, weapons or defence shields (e.g., a safety bubble) until the child is safe and feels satisfied. The therapist tells the child what they are doing to intervene and instructs the child to notice this.
- *Reparenting through co-regulation:* The therapist (and eventually the patient's own Healthy Adult) is also responsible for soothing the child and provides an antidote to the EMS through correcting misunderstandings whereby the child believes that they are to blame or in some way responsible for the adult. The therapist must draw on their own Healthy Adult self in deciding how to react. It can also be helpful for therapists to close their own eyes and identify their own inclinations that arise while picturing the situation.
- *Transitioning from therapist to patient in Healthy Adult role:* IR can be adapted to match the individual patient's emotional needs and the strength of their Healthy (Compassionate) Adult Self. If the patient's Healthy Adult side is sufficiently well developed, then they are invited to enter the image in order to react to the antagonist and directly address the child's needs. Alternatively, for patients with PDs, who may have a very weakly developed Healthy Adult self, the therapist initially takes the lead and carries out the rescripting while the patient stays within the child's perspective. Through repeated modelling in IR, the patient begins to internalise their own Healthy [Compassionate] Adult self, and is gradually encouraged to take over the role of *internal healthy protector and nurturer* from the therapist. Thereby, they learn to intervene within their own images by stopping, confronting and correcting the antagonist, as well as attuning to their Vulnerable Child self. This transition to the patient developing their own Healthy Adult side is essential for all patients, but may require more prompting and encouragement for those patients with strong Dependence schemas. Over time, these transformed images and schematic meanings become the template for compassionate self-relating in day-to-day life.

Positive imagery: In addition to reducing intrusive negative images, cognitions and affect, imagery has also been shown to function as a powerful mechanism for generating positive schemas and affect more effectively than cognitive processing, providing an important mechanism for promoting healthy emotional maturation. The introduction of compassionate and healing images facilitates healthy emotional development and opportunities for growth, and is potentially an important component of any psychological treatment that aims to cultivate positive change (Gilbert & Irons, 2004; Holmes, Arntz & Smucker, 2007; Lee, 2005). For example, a patient who has developed a Defectiveness schema and thinks of herself as 'bad' as a consequence of childhood abuse, may be guided to use all five senses to develop an image and visceral felt sense of their own inner 'wise being' (Healthy Adult) who is capable of self-nurturance and protection. This image may gradually emerge through internalisation of compassion by the therapist and significant others, or be developed more consciously and systematically. Patients can learn to use an 'anchor' (e.g., hand on their heart) to call on their wise being during times of difficulty, to access self-compassion.

Positive imagery can also be used to develop an image that represents the self as the person wishes to be in the future, as an alternative to the negative self-image, and to strengthen the Healthy Adult mode. The positive image can be symbolic, as long as it facilitates the development of a compassionate internalised self that can meet the patient's emotional needs (e.g., Müller-Engelmann, Hadouch & Steil, 2018). For example, it may take the form of a fantasy figure, ancestor, sacred being (e.g., a guardian angel), or aspect of nature (e.g., a mountain, or tree) (Schwarz et al., 2017).

Imagery rescripting as a highway to behavioural rehearsal and change

Evidence suggests that imagining a future event can increase both how likely we think it is to occur and how likely we are to enact a change in behaviour (Holmes & Mathews, 2010). Adaptive imagery can be used therapeutically to develop healthy coping, while reducing unhelpful patterns of behaviour. Mental rehearsal of tackling a dreaded situation in a calm and composed manner can lead both to a reduction of anxiety and increased self-efficacy (Mathews, 1971; Moran & O'Brien, 2005). In ST, imagery plays an important role in rehearsing behavioural change, as well as identifying 'stuck points' and modes that interfere with healthy change. Mode dialogues can be carried out within IR to facilitate understanding, and to enable patients to move beyond obstacles in order to learn healthy ways of meeting their emotional needs in their day-to-day lives. Therapeutically, flashforward images can be used to reverse behaviours associated with schema perpetuation; for example, a person with a Negativity/Pessimism schema may imagine themselves dancing or telling a joke; a person with an Emotional Inhibition schema may visualise talking about feelings with a trusted other; and someone with a Subjugation schema might be guided to visually rehearse setting limits on a demanding colleague. This may be followed by schema-mode imaginal dialogues when the schema voice (or Inner Critic) blocks the new behaviour (e.g., a conversation where the patient plays the critical voice of the schema ('you don't deserve happiness') and the therapist refutes this from the strong compassionate stance of the healthy voice). Imagery can also be used to dialogue with avoidant coping modes that block experiential therapeutic work, hinder interpersonal connection, or drive dysfunctional coping (e.g., addictions). For example, the patient can be guided to imagine being invited to a social night out with friends, and then to play the part of the avoidant protector mode as a separate 'character' in the image that doesn't believe it's a good idea to give up alcohol misuse, and then respond from the perspective of the Healthy Adult.

Some therapeutic principles for the implementation of IR are described at the end of the chapter.

Conclusions

The abundance of research into the therapeutic effects of imagery in recent years has highlighted the importance of imagery-focused assessment and treatment for psychological disorders with a significant emotional component. The effectiveness of IR takes advantage of the human capacity to process information more effectively in the presence of affect. IR is a powerful mechanism for transforming schematic meaning through corrective emotional experience, facilitating the transition from intellectual insight to experiential change. In ST, IR constitutes a central mechanism facilitating access to deeper level beliefs which are encoded not only in the form of cognitions, but also in memories, affect and somatic experience. The burgeoning research in this field is testament to the growing recognition of the potential of imagery-based techniques for reducing distress and suffering, as well as facilitating the development of positive healthy schemas.

Therapist tips

- *Patient is too detached*: Ensure IR is moving at a reasonable pace in the first person present tense to keep the affect 'hot'. The therapist should frequently check on patient's level of affect and activation of schema modes throughout IR to ensure they are still engaged with full sensory experience of image.
- *Excessive activation leads to dissociation*: Give additional control over the process, and incorporate a signal that indicates a need to return to the safe place. In addition, use a graduated approach, and incorporate methods that facilitate a 'mindful observer' role (e.g., by picturing themselves watching the image in black and white from the back of a cinema). A piece of fleece or other material can also be used, whereby therapist and patient each hold one end of the fleece, and the therapist gently pulls on it whenever the patient starts to emotionally disconnect or dissociate.

- *Patient cannot find a memory*: Slow down the process and explore possible reasons for this. For those with a strong Detached Protector mode, it can help to introduce IR sessions spontaneously, to avoid anticipatory anxiety and avoidance. Patients can be encouraged to gradually build their tolerance for focusing on distressing images through alternating between these and safe place images.
- *Loyalty to the antagonist*: When a patient finds it difficult to accept protection due to excessive loyalty to parents, explain (1) the difference between adaptive and maladaptive loyalty; (2) the survival value of loyalty for children; (3) that IR is directed to parts of the parent's behaviour (rather than their whole self); (4) that IR is directed at the parent as they were in the past (not now); (5) that the patient can choose later how to relate to the parent in person (in their current adult life).
- *Patient is fearful of future consequences*: Ask about potential fears; build in measures to deal with future dangers in the context of IR (e.g., put abuser in gaol; take child to safe place; give child a bleeper to bring the therapist back into the image as required). Following IR with severe trauma/abuse memories, prepare an audio flashcard on the patient's smartphone with the therapist's voice setting limits on Punitive (Inner Critic) mode. Check on the patient by telephone later in the week.
- *Patient fears they will act out of anger*: Reassure that evidence thus far indicates the opposite, that is, IR may be associated with better anger control, even after violent rescripting interventions (Arntz, Tiesema & Kindt, 2007). Intervene in IR as the therapist and model appropriate ways of expressing anger. Recognise and support the child in processing angry feelings in IR and focus equally on any vulnerable feelings underlying anger.

References

Andrade, J., Kavanagh, D. & Baddeley, A. (1997). Eye-movements and visual imagery: a working memory approach to the treatment of post-traumatic stress disorder. *British Journal of Clinical Psychology*, *36*, 209–223. http://dx.doi.org/10.1111/j.2044-8260.1997.tb01408.x

Arntz, A. (2012). Imagery rescripting as a therapeutic technique: Review of clinical trials, basic studies, and research agenda. *Journal of Experimental Psychopathology*, *3*(2), 189–208.

Arntz, A., De Groot, C. & Kindt, M. (2005). Emotional memory is perceptual. *Journal of Behavior Therapy and Experimental Psychiatry*, *36*(1), 19–34. http://dx.doi.org/10.1016/j.jbtep.2004.11.003

Arntz, A. & van Genderen, H. (2009). *Schema therapy for borderline personality disorder*. Chichester: Wiley.

Arntz, A., Sofi, D. & van Breukelen, G. (2013). Imagery rescripting as treatment for complicated PTSD in refugees: A multiple baseline case series study. *Behaviour Research and Therapy*, *51*, 274–283. http://dx.doi.org/10.1016/j.brat.2013.02.009

Arntz, A., Tiesema, M. & Kindt, M. (2007). Treatment of PTSD: A comparison of imaginal exposure with and without imagery rescripting. *Journal Behaviour Therapy Exprimental Psychiatry.*, *38*(4), 345–370.

Arntz, A. & Weertman, A. (1999). Treatment of childhood memories: Theory and practice. *Behaviour Research and Therapy, 37*, 715–740.

Barnard, P. (2009). Depression and attention to two kinds of meaning: A cognitive perspective. *Psychoanalytic Psychotherapy, 23*(3), 248–262.

Brewin, C., Dalgleish, T. & Joseph, S. (1996). A dual representation theory of posttraumatic stress disorder. *Clinical Psychology Review, 103*, 670–686.

Casement, M.D. & Swanson, L.M. (2012). A meta-analysis of imagery rehearsal for post-trauma nightmares: Effects on nightmare frequency, sleep quality, and posttraumatic stress. *Clinical Psychology Review, 32*(6), 566e574.

Conway, M. (2001). Sensory-perceptual episodic memory and its context: Autobiographical memory. *Philosophical Transactions of the Royal Society of London Series B-Biological Sciences, 356*, 1375–1384.

Cuthbert, B., Lang, P., Strauss, C., Drobes, D., Patrick, C. & Bradley, M. (2003). The psychophysiology of anxiety disorder: Fear memory imagery. *Psychophysiology, 40*(3), 407–422.

Ehlers, A. & Clark, D. (2000). A cognitive model of posttraumatic stress disorder, behaviour, research & therapy. *Behaviour, Research & Therapy, 28*, 319–345.

Engelhard, I., Van den Hout, M., Dek, E., Giele, C., Van der Wielen, J., Reijnen, M. & Van Roij, B. (2011). Reducing vividness and emotional intensity of recurrent "flashforwards" by taxing working memory: An analogue study. *Journal of Anxiety Disorders, 25*(4), 599–603.

Foa, E. & Kozac, M. (1986). Emotional processing of fear: Exposure to corrective information. *Psychological Bulletin, 99*, 20–35.

Gilbert, P. & Irons, C. (2004). A pilot exploration of the use of compassionate images in a group of self-critical people. *Memory, 12*, 507–516. https://doi.org/10.1080/09658210444000115

Grunert, B., Weis, J., Smucker, M. & Christianson, H. (2007). Imagery rescripting and reprocessing therapy after failed prolonged exposure for post-traumatic stress disorder following industrial injury. *Journal of Behavior Therapy & Experimental Psychiatry, 38*, 317–328.

Gunter, R. & Bodner, G. (2008). How eye movements affect unpleasant memories: Support for a working-memory account. *Behaviour Research and Therapy, 46*(8), 913–931.

Hackmann, A., Bennett-Levy, J. & Holmes, E.A. (2011). *Oxford guide to imagery in cognitive therapy*. Oxford: Oxford University Press.

Harvey, A.G., Watkins, E. & Mansell, W. (2004). *Cognitive behavioural processes across psychological disorders: A transdiagnostic approach to research and treatment*. New York: Oxford University Press.

Holmes, E., Arntz, A. & Smucker, M. (2007). Imagery rescripting in cognitive behaviour therapy: Images, treatment techniques and outcomes. *Journal of Behavior Therapy & Experimental Psychiatry, 38*, 297–305.

Holmes, E. & Hackmann, A. (2004). A healthy imagination? Editorial for the special issue of memory: Mental imagery and memory in psychopathology. *Memory, 12*(4), 387–388.

Holmes, E., Mathews, A., Dalgleish, T. & Mackintosh, B. (2006). Positive interpretation training: Effects of mental imagery versus verbal training on positive mood. *Behavior Therapy, 37*, 237–247.

Holmes, E.A. & Mathews, A. (2005). Mental imagery and emotion: A special relationship? *Emotion, 5*(4), 489–497.

Holmes, E.A. & Mathews, A. (2010). Mental imagery in emotion and emotional disorders. *Clinical Psychology Review, 30*(3), 349–362.

Horikawa, T., Tamaki, M., Miyawaki, Y. & Kamitani, Y. (2013). Neural decoding of visual imagery during sleep. *Science;, 340*(6132), 639–642. 10.1126/science.1234330

Hunt, M. & Fenton, M. (2007). Imagery rescripting versus in vivo exposure in the treatment of snake fear. *Journal of Behavior Therapy and Experimental Psychiatry, 38*, 329–344.

Jaycox, L. & Foa, E. (1998). Post-traumatic stress disorder. In A.S. Bellack & M. Hersen (Eds.), *Comprehensive clinical psychology* (Vol. 6, pp. 499–517). Amsterdam: Elsevier.

Kosslyn, S.M., Ganis, G. & Thompson, W.L. (2001). Neural foundations of imagery. *Nature Reviews Neuroscience, 2*, 635–642.

Lang, P. (1977). Imagery in therapy: An information processing analysis of fear. *Behavior Therapy, 8*(5), 862–886.

Langkaas, T.F., Hoffart, A., Øktedalen, T., Ulvenes, P.G., Hembree, E. & Smucker, M. (2017). Exposure and non-fear emotions: A randomized controlled study of exposure-based and rescripting-based imagery in PTSD treatment. *Behaviour Research and Therapy, 97*, 33–42.

Lee, D. (2005). The perfect nurturer: A model to develop a compassionate mind within the context of cognitive therapy. In I.P. Gilbert (Ed.), *Compassion: Conceptualisations, research and use in psychotherapy* (pp. 326–351). London: Routledge.

Lilley, S.A., Andrade, J., Turpin, G., Sabin-Farrell, R. & Holmes, E.A. (2009). Visuo-spatial working memory interference with recollections of trauma. *British Journal of Clinical Psychology, 48*(3), 309–321.

Mathews, A. (1971). Psychophysiological approaches to the investigation of desensitisation and related processes. *Psychological Bulletin, 76*, 73–91.

May, J., Andrade, J., Kavanagh, D.J. & Penfound, L. (2008). Imagery and strength of craving for eating, drinking and playing sport. *Cognition and Emotion, 22*, 633–650.

Moran, D.J. & O'Brien, R.M. (2005). Competence imagery: A case study treating emetophobia. *Psychological Reports, 96*, 635–636.

Morina, N., Lancee, J. & Arntz, A. (2017). Imagery rescripting as a clinical intervention for aversive memories: A meta-analysis. *Journal of Behavior Therapy & Experimental Psychiatry, 55*, 6–15.

Müller-Engelmann, M., Hadouch, K. & Steil, R. (2018). Addressing the negative self-concept in posttraumatic stress disorder by a three-session programme of cognitive restructuring and imagery modification (CRIM-PTSD): A case study. *Journal of Behavioral and Brain Science, 8*(05), 319–327.

Pearson, J., Naselaris, T., Holmes, E. & Kosslyn, S. (2015). Mental imagery: Functional mechanisms and clinical applications. *Trends in Cognitive Sciences, 19*(10), 590–602.

Raabe, S., Ehring, T., Marquenie, L., Arntz, A. & Kindt, M. (2018). Imagery rescripting versus STAIR plus imagery rescripting for PTSD related to childhood abuse: A randomized controlled trial. In preparation.

Schwarz, L., Corrigan, F., Hull, A. & Ragu, R. (2017). *Comprehensive resource model: Effective therapeutic techniques for the healing of complex trauma.* New York: Routledge.

Shapiro, F. (2014). The role of eye movement desensitization and reprocessing (EMDR) therapy in medicine: Addressing the psychological and physical symptoms stemming from adverse life experiences. *Perm Journal, 18*(1), 71–77.

Teasdale, J. & Barnard, P. (1993). *Affect, cognition and change: Re-modelling depressive thought.* Hove: Lawrence Erlbaum.

Van den Hout, M.A., Engelhard, I.M., Beetsma, D., Slofstra, C., Hornsveld, H., Houtveen, J. & Leer, A. (2011). EMDR and mindfulness: Eye movements and attentional breathing tax working memory and reduce vividness and emotionality of aversive ideation. *Journal of Behavior Therapy and Experimental Psychiatry, 42*, 423–431. http://dx.doi.org/10.1016/j.jbtep.2011.03.004

Van der Wijngaart, R. (2015). Ways to strengthen the healthy adult. *The Schema Therapy Bulletin, 1*, 7–10.

Weertman, A. & Arntz, A. (2007). Effectiveness of treatment of childhood memories in cognitive therapy for personality disorders: A controlled study contrasting methods focusing on the present and methods of focusing on childhood memories. *Behaviour Research & Therapy, 45*, 2133–2143.

Willander, J., Sikström, S. & Karlsson, K. (2015). Multimodal retrieval of autobiographical memories: Sensory information contributes differently to the recollection of events. *Frontiers in Psychology, 6*(e73378), Article no. 1681.

Young, J., Klosko, J. & Weishaar, M. (2003). *Schema therapy: A practitioner's guide.* New York: Guilford Press.

Young, J.E. (1990, 1999). *Cognitive therapy for personality disorders: A schema-focused approach* (revised edition). Sarasota, FL: Professional Resource Press.

6 Imagery rescripting for childhood memories

Chris Hayes and Remco van der Wijngaart

Adverse childhood experiences, in interaction with a child's temperament and caregiver responses, are thought to form the origins of early maladaptive schemas, modes and coping responses (Arntz & van Genderen, 2011). Imagery rescripting harnesses the emotional power of mental visualisation to assist in changing the meaning and legacy of such negative childhood experiences.

Historically, imagery work in psychotherapy has taken many different forms (Edwards, 2011) and there is growing evidence supporting imagery rescripting as an effective treatment in a range of psychological conditions, including post traumatic stress disorder, social anxiety disorder, obsessive–compulsive disorder and various eating disorders (Morina, Lancee & Arntz, 2017). The intervention within Schema Therapy primarily focuses on changing the meaning of autobiographical memories that may have contributed to the development of schemas and modes. Patients are asked to activate memories and images of childhood events linked to schemas and modes and imagine a more favourable ending that is attuned to the needs of the child (Arntz & Jacob, 2012). Such an approach is in contrast to other imagery-based approaches where the image remains unchanged, such as imaginal exposure (Foa & Rothbaum, 1998), whereby the patient is asked to envisage and 'play through' an emotionally painful experience without changing the outcome. There are various imagery rescripting protocols; however, for the purposes of this chapter, imagery rescripting is defined by protocols outlined by Arntz and Weertman (1999) and Arntz (2014).

Imagery rescripting is a valuable clinical tool for a number of reasons. First, it provides a structure to bypass coping modes which typically block affect, memories and cognitions. This occurs as the process of mental visualisation helps the patient connect more easily with emotionally significant events (Holmes & Mathews, 2010). As a result, core feelings and traumatic material can be directly accessed and worked with. Second, patients are able to make clearer connections with, and have a better understanding of, the origins of early maladaptive schemas, modes and life problems than through discussion alone (Hackmann, Bennett-Levy, & Holmes, 2011). Third, the therapist (and later the patient) is able to provide a corrective emotional experience within imagery rescripting. The process of imagery rescripting is not solely about accessing painful and upsetting childhood memories and images; it is also about changing the image and providing a new outcome and meaning. As a result, patients are able to experience more favourable and restorative emotions that may aid cognitive change (Arntz, 2011; Holmes, Arntz, & Smucker, 2007). In addition, imagery interventions are also thought to help create alternative memories that are more easily accessed by patients (Brewin, 2006; Brewin, Gregory, Lipton & Burgess, 2010).

Core principals of imagery rescripting

Attachment and bonding

Within imagery rescripting, core Schema Therapy tenets of limited reparenting and experiential interventions converge to provide a synergistic effect. Here, the patient can experience the therapist's attunement and ability to meet their needs within the image process, providing a powerful emotionally corrective experience. In contrast to some other imagery rescripting based interventions where the patient is encouraged to change the image on their own (Smucker, Dancu, Foa & Niederee, 1995), imagery rescripting within a Schema Therapy context initially encourages the therapist to rescript the image, enabling the patient to experience some of their emotional needs being met by the therapist. In doing so, the patient experiences a healthy and strong attachment to the therapist. Furthermore, the process models for the patient how to respond to the antagonists and manage emotionally charged childhood situations. In this way, patients often report internalising or drawing on their therapist's stance and capacity. For example, saying that they thought about what the therapist would do or say in a given situation. Moving forward in treatment (akin to a child growing up), the patient is encouraged to take the lead role in rescripting, with the therapist increasingly playing more of a supporting role.

Meeting the needs of the patient

Personality disorders and chronic emotional problems are often associated with neglect, trauma and deprivation of childhood needs (Johnson et al., 1999). In reparenting, the concept of a therapist meeting core emotional needs is a key principal and is seen as an antidote to past deprivation. The meeting of needs in imagery work similarly acts a as guiding principle, leading the therapist's interventions at each stage in the rescripting. In difficult circumstances, where the therapist is unsure of how to proceed, identifying the need for the child in the image is a helpful method to ensure a corrective outcome.

Imagery rescripting process

Selecting meaningful images

At times, it can be challenging to identify potential images to rescript. Some patients report difficulty remembering specific situations from their childhood (sometimes due to schema avoidance or pre-verbal trauma). In contrast, others have limited insight into the emotional impact of their early experiences and do not volunteer specific memories, deeming them irrelevant to their current problems or progress in treatment. There are several ways to identify meaningful childhood images for imagery rescripting.

Information gained from the assessment process and use of inventories, such as the Young Parenting Inventory (YPI; Young, 1996), can provide specific meaningful events and images to rescript. In addition, patients can access images via an affect bridge (or 'float back') from a recent triggering event. Here, the therapist asks the patient to access a recent triggering image, identify feelings and thoughts from this experience, and then links this back to a childhood event with similar sentiments. 'So, that feeling of sadness, like you don't matter, you're overlooked and as if no one is interested? Hold on to that feeling and the sense that you don't matter, and try to get a childhood image where you felt the same way.'

An alternative method to help access meaningful images to rescript is the 'Google Images' or 'Search Engine Technique' (de Jongh, Ten Broeke, & Meijer, 2010), an approach often used in an Eye Movement Desensitisation and Reprocessing (EMDR) context. Here, the therapist suggests to the patient that they are making a 'memory search' into their mental 'search engine' for a particular belief or schema. For example, a patient's 'Google search' for the belief 'I'm worthless, bad' (the cognitive component of a defectiveness schema) might result in a list of related memories that they had previously not connected to this theme. Similar to internet search engines, patients are encouraged to suggest several memories that may be a part of their 'search', with the top 'posting' most linked to the desired search. The therapist may encourage the patient to complete such a task in his or her own time as a homework assignment, and use the exercise to prime the imagery work, or make links throughout the session. Such key memories can then be used for future imagery work.

There are two main stages of imagery rescripting. In Stage 1, the therapist provides the rescript and is the primary agent of change. The therapist acts as an internal model for the patient and aims to provide emotionally corrective experiences by meeting the child's core needs in the image. Stage 2 is when the patient rescripts the image. This typically occurs when the patient's Healthy Adult mode is strong enough to have compassion, insight and some emotional capacity to respond to the needs of the child in the image. Some patients may also choose to imagine significant caring characters in their life entering the image and assisting in the rescripting (for example, a grandparent

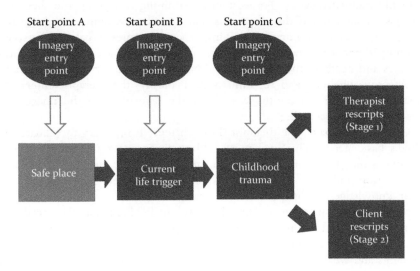

Figure 6.1 Imagery rescripting – process stages 1 and 2

who had a positive impact on the patient). In Stage 2, the patient and therapist may also work together to meet the child's needs in the image.

There are several entry points to imagery rescripting work (Figure 6.1). Patients who are apprehensive about imagery or are more dysregulated may benefit from initially completing imagery to create a 'safe place' (Start point A) *(see Part I, Chapter 2)*. Following this, specific 'Image Targets' for rescripting can be accessed from recent triggering events (or emotional states within the session), such as a recent argument with a partner or feeling tense in session with the therapist (Start point B). Here, the therapist uses an affect bridge to identify earlier childhood touchstone events where the patient experienced similar feelings. Alternatively, the therapist may seek to directly access specifically meaningful images identified in the assessment as pertinent in schema development (Start point C). For example, a patient with a Subjugation schema may identify a memory where they felt intimidated and controlled as a child (with the rescript commencing with this image).

Stage 1: therapist rescripting the historical image

Unlike exposure therapies, imagery rescripting does not require the patient to visualise the most traumatic aspects of the experience. Instead, the therapist aims to rewrite the image at the moment that the child needs the corrective experience to occur. As a result, the therapist seeks to access some of patient's experience in the distressing scene without overwhelming them or moving into reliving a highly traumatic event. To assist in determining this point, the therapists can ask themselves: 'If this were in a real situation involving a child in my care, when would I intervene?' This process requires a balance between coming in too early (and, as a result, having limited access to the child's feelings and needs in the situation) and entering too late, risking the patient feeling overwhelmed and retraumatised. Typically, the therapist enters the image just before the trauma was about the take place in the image and prevents it from occurring.

Once in the image, the therapist does whatever is necessary to validate the child's basic needs. This may mean addressing an antagonist in the image, removing the child from the situation, offering safety, comfort or expressing appreciation and care. The therapist's rescripting can be guided in part by their knowledge of the patient's schemas. For example, if the patient has strong Subjugation schema, the therapist might highlight the need for empowerment and autonomy: 'It's okay to speak your mind, I really want to hear how you're feeling and nothing bad will happen if you express your thoughts and what you need with me.' In contrast, if a Defectiveness schema was dominant, the therapist may highlight the need for acceptance and appreciation: 'I think what you're saying is excellent. There's nothing wrong with you for having these feelings. Anyone in this situation would feel the same. What happened here wasn't your fault.'

The therapist can regularly assess how the patient is feeling in response to their rescripting: 'What is it like having someone there for you?', 'How is it having me speak to mum like this?' Such enquiries offer valuable feedback about how best to meet the child's needs in the image and allow the therapist to adapt their reparenting to make the image feel safer if the patient is distressed or overwhelmed.

After the therapist has met the child's needs in the image, and the patient reports feeling supported and safe, the therapist may ask the child in the image; 'What would you like to do now? What would feel nice for you? We can go out to play, or go for a walk, or just sit together. What would feel right for you?' For example, 'How about we do something less intense, what would you like to do now rather than having to deal with this? Where would you like to go right now? Maybe we could go and play outside?' This conclusion process assists the patient to regulate their emotional state by contrasting intense emotions with enjoyable and relaxed activities. Furthermore, this component of the rescripting process embodies the rescripting principle that the therapist's reparenting (in which the child is safe and cared for) continues beyond the original rescripted scene.

Stage 2: patient rescripts the historical image

Later in treatment, when the patient's Healthy Adult mode is strengthened, the therapist encourages them to take a more active role in rescripting. Here, the therapist invites the patient, as an adult now, to rescript the image and respond to the needs of the child. There are three phases to this stage; (1) the image set-up, (2) The Healthy Adult rescripts, (3) Vulnerable Child experiences the rescript.

Phase 1 – setting up the scene (patient in the image as a child)

THERAPIST: What's happening for Little Peter, how old is he?

PETER: I'm seven, dad has come home and he's angry, He's yelling at mum, asking where I am.

THERAPIST: Where are you?

PETER: I'm in the laundry, scared, waiting for him to find me.

Once the patient has set the scene and their feelings and unmet needs are 'active' in the image, the therapist then moves to Phase 2.

Phase 2 – patient rescripts the image (patient in the image as an adult)

THERAPIST: I want you to pause the image and I want to bring your strong Healthy Adult side, you as an adult, into the image with Little Peter. Be the Healthy Adult now, maybe sit up the way the Healthy Adult does. So now there is Little Peter, you as an adult and your dad. As an adult, how do you feel about what is happening? What do you, as an adult, want to do for Little Peterr?

PETER: I'm sick of this. It's wrong! I feel for that kid, he doesn't deserve this.

THERAPIST: What do you want to do or say?

PETER: I want to protect Little Peter. 'Dad, I won't let you treat Little Peter like that any more, I am not putting up with this. You're dealing with me now!'

THERAPIST: Say that again to him.

PETER: 'You're dealing with me now. What you're doing is wrong and I'm not going to let you give him a hard time any more.'

The patient proceeds with rescripting, responding to the needs of the child and providing safety, care, guidance and support and ultimately prevailing over the exchange.

Phase 3 – child perspective of the rescript (patient in the image as a child)

THERAPIST: I now want you to rewind the tape, to the start of the image when adult Peter arrives, and now be Little Peter – what do you see …

PETER: I'm in the laundry, I'm scared, hiding from dad, then adult me comes in.

THERAPIST: What happens now?

PETER: Adult me is standing over dad saying he's sick of how he treats me, he's saying he's not going to put up with this any more and that he's dealing with him now.

THERAPIST: How does that feel, to hear and see that?

PETER: Awesome, no one speaks to him like that.

The therapist continues to play out the image as before, asking the child what they need. If the child expresses additional needs (such as care, holding, etc.) the therapist encourages them to ask their Healthy Adult to meet their needs.

THERAPIST: What do you need now? [as Little Peter]

PETER: I need a hug.

THERAPIST: Can you tell him that?

PETER: 'Big Peter, can I have a hug?' He's hugging me, saying it's going to be okay. It feels so good.

This type of imagery helps the patient's Vulnerable Child mode to feel able to 'talk' to their Healthy Adult and ask for what they need in current day situations.

Imagery rescripting – types of antagonists

In rescripting, the emotional needs of the child should act as a guiding principle in determining what happens in the image and the therapist and patient's Healthy Adult are free to do whatever is necessary to meet the child's needs. In essence, rescripting offers an opportunity for the child in the image to experience what should have happened but did not happen. Typically, this involves the therapist or the patient's Healthy Adult having a level of strength and influence that is not strictly realistic, in a literal sense, but embodies what the child needed at the time and is, therefore, emotionally credible and usually appreciated by the patient. For example, the therapist or Healthy Adult might put an abusive figure into custody or insist that a neglectful parent listens to how the child feels.

Within the rescripting process, the therapist may encounter an array of different circumstances and 'characters' who are associated with the development of one or more of their schemas.

Punitive antagonists

Punitive antagonists are blaming, abusive and undermining and the therapist needs to take strong and direct action to provide the Vulnerable Child safety and care. When working with such antagonists, the therapist 'pauses' the image, steps between the child and the antagonist and does whatever is necessary to create a feeling of safety, power and generate a sense of reattribution. In order for the rescripting to be credible, the therapist must respond in a determined, confident, firm and uncompromising way that shows they are in charge of what happens, not the antagonist.

Case example

As a child, Sandra was victimised by a violent father who frequently would swear and hit her for mistakes and 'poor behaviour'. During imagery rescripting, Sandra describes the following image:

SANDRA: I'm scared, so scared; he's standing at the door, he's so angry, he's saying I'm a stupid little bitch because I've split some of my drink [patient becoming tearful and upset].

THERAPIST: Sandra ... [Pause] the image, I want you to see me in the image with you, standing between you and dad, can you see me there?

SANDRA: Yeah, I can see you there ... I'm scared, I don't want him [dad] to hurt me.

THERAPIST: What's it like, me being there?

SANDRA: It feels good, a bit safer having you around when dad is like that.

THERAPIST: Do you feel safe with me handling him, or do you think I need to be bigger or need something extra to help?

SANDRA: Yeah, maybe a bit bigger, because he's so angry ...

THERAPIST: Okay, so, I'm bigger, towering over him and I'm speaking to dad now, Little Sandra .... [Tone – strong, determined, uncompromising]. 'Greg [Dad], you can stop right there – You are frightening Sandra, she is a good kid. It's your job to make her feel safe and you're not doing your job, so I'm taking over now to make sure it's safe. I want you to leave right now.' How is he responding?

SANDRA: He's in disbelief that someone is standing up to him.

THERAPIST: [continued strong uncompromising tone] 'You are dealing with me now and I'm not going to let you take your issues out on Sandra any more, you're dancing to our tune now – leave now. (I'm taking your father out of the image.) 'I'm now turning to you, Little Sandra. You don't deserve all this, it's just a can of drink. You're a good kid and he's the one with the issues.' What's it like having someone there for you, to protect you?

SANDRA: No one has ever done that before, it feels good [tearful].

Demanding antagonists

Demanding antagonists apply pressure to perform and achieve beyond what is realistic, balanced or within the patient's resources. There is no time for relaxation, they must work hard at all times and succeed at what they do (e.g., 'I just want you to be the best version of yourself'). Such caregivers want their child to succeed in life and feel that a high level of achievement is a necessary condition for that success. Standing up to these demanding messages requires a different approach compared to combating punitive messages. Here, the therapist takes a more discussion orientated and persuasive approach in which arguments will be put forth as to why relaxation, spontaneity and play are necessary basic needs for children.

Case example

Ben was raised by loving but hard-working parents who never had any time for rest and relaxation. Ben experienced clear pressure to perform. During an imagery rescripting exercise, Ben's father is standing behind Ben, who is 12 years old and who is doing his homework. Ben has been working for an hour and would really like to go and play outside, but his father pushes him to keep working. The therapist addresses the father in the image, recognising his good intentions while making a strong case to allow Ben time to relax and play: 'While I understand that you want what's best for your child, the way you are trying to care for him right now is leaving Ben exhausted. Every battery needs recharging from time to time, to prevent it from running out. I think we both want Ben to be able to look back, years from now, on a balanced, happy life full of experiences of love, connection and fun. I don't want him to look back at a life that was about nothing but deadlines and hard work.'

Guilt-inducing antagonists

Guilt inducing antagonists display disappointment, sadness, withdrawal or other forms of indirect communication. This is often used as a way to discourage self-expression, autonomy, play and spontaneity or as an indirect way to chastise the child. Such messages are often experienced as being punitive ('I'm bad for leaving mum at home sad'), and are often delivered in an indirect, guilt-inducing way. In some cases, where the antagonist has mental health problems or is socially isolated, there may be a desperate but misguided attempt to have the child meet their own emotional needs and remain very close at the expense of the child's need for autonomy.

In their challenge to the parent, the therapist should directly identify the indirect, subtle communication and draw attention to the impact on the child. Next, the unspoken punitive message must be clearly (although less forcefully than with punitive parents) refuted and challenged. The patient can also be provided with psychological education regarding the difference between healthy loyalty and a sense of responsibility. In addition, the therapist may need to provide 'help' and support to the antagonist (for example, the therapist saying they will access support for mentally unwell caregivers).

Case example

Elsa grew up with a depressed and exhausted mother. She presents with chronic low mood and difficulties getting her needs met by others.

ELSA: I'm at home with mum.

THERAPIST: What do you see? How old are you?

ELSA: I'm about eight. I'm in her bedroom. I've come in because I want to go with my friend to the local shop around the corner to buy some snacks – it's the school holidays.

THERAPIST: How is she in the image?

ELSA: She's lying in bed. It's about three in the afternoon. She's speechless, tired looking and she's got sad eyes.

THERAPIST: How are you feeling?

ELSA: I'm sad [becoming tearful], I'm a pain and I shouldn't be bothering her.

THERAPIST: Elsa, I'm going to speak to your mother ... 'I understand that you feel unwell, and I feel for you. However, you are still Elsa's mother, and you are supposed to care for your child – not the other way around. I know you feel unwell and you need help, but it's not right to put it on Elsa. I can arrange for one of my most trusted colleagues to help if you'd like that. But I don't want you burdening Elsa with your pain in this way.' The therapist says to Elsa: 'I want you to look at me right now instead of at your mother, because every time you look at her, you feel responsible and guilty. I'm happy to organise help for her but it's not right for you to have to worry about her. I want you to simply enjoy life and be a child, so you should go buy a treat for yourself right now.'

Neglectful or absent caregivers

Some patients have grown up in an atmosphere of emotional neglect and loneliness where caregivers were physically and/or emotionally absent. While punishing sentiments may be limited, the patient has internalised such depriving experiences with the message 'Your needs don't matter and you are not important or loveable'. In such situations, the therapist may need to focus on the needs of the child with no caregiver present. In these dialogues, the therapist uses limited reparenting to meet the needs of the child and validate their feelings. Often, the therapist's presence, involvement and desire to spend time with the child in the image provides an antidote to their loneliness and the feeling that they don't matter. In situations with physically absent caregivers, the therapist may also need to 'bring in' the offending parent, allowing for an exchange within the imagery. In dialogues with depriving caregivers, the therapist explicitly appreciates the child, highlights their emotional needs and points out the caregiver's responsibilities.

Case example

John describes an image in which he is nine years old and sitting alone in his room. His parents are out; he doesn't know where they are or when they will be home; he's had to make his own way back home from school and let himself in. The therapist steps into the image and comforts the sad and lonely child. He then asks John's mother to join them and stands up for his needs.

THERAPIST: Can you see me there with you and your mum?

JOHN: Yeah, I can see you both there, you're in front of me and mum is to the side.

THERAPIST: I'm turning to your mum. Mary, John is a fantastic child and he needs you, he needs you to notice him, be there for him. He feels like he doesn't matter to you and that's not okay. [Turning to John] How is she responding?

JOHN: She's looking confused, saying she needs to work.

THERAPIST: [to Mary]: I know you need to work, but you need to think about John and let him know that you care about him, that's your job ... [to John] How is she responding?

JOHN: She's saying, '*I need to go to work*', she's almost robot-like.

THERAPIST: [to Mary]: Mary, I know it's hard for you, but ignoring your child like this is damaging him. I'm not going to stand by and do nothing. I'm going to let John know that he matters and that you're lucky to have him. [To John] What's it like me being there, knowing you're not alone?

JOHN: [tearful]: Good ...

THERAPIST: I'm taking mum out of the image now; can you see me there with you? Little John, I care about you, you are very important to me and you matter so much, I'm sorry you're here all alone ... I'm making time for you. What's it like me being there?

JOHN: Really good.

Rescripting stops short of manipulating the antagonist's emotional reactions in any way. In the case above, a neglectful parent is not envisaged as remorseful (unless this is how the patient thinks the parent would react). Rather, the therapist and Healthy Adult do whatever is needed to reparent the child in the image. This is emotionally credible because the patient is aware of the feelings of care and compassion that both they and the therapist have for the child in the image.

Some childhood events may be inevitably associated with huge loss or sadness (for example, in the death of a loved one) and it may not be possible to completely solve the situation for the child. The therapist is able, however, to validate and support the child and provide vital help and a deeply caring presence that was often missing at the time of the event. In this way, the therapist empathises with the unavoidable loss in the situation, without leaving the child alone to cope with their pain.

Emotions in imagery work

Imagery rescripting is designed to access the emotional component of schemas. As a result, the therapist aims to trigger an emotional response in imagery. However, therapists are often concerned about either flooding the patient with excessive affect, or failing to access enough emotion. Here, the Window of Tolerance model (Siegel, 2015) can be a useful framework for the therapist to understand the best level of emotional experience for the client. The Window of Tolerance model describes a zone of optimal emotional arousal for psychotherapeutic work, suggesting that emotional arousal can vary between a state of hyperarousal (excessive or overwhelming emotional experience) and hypoarousal (underactive emotional experience 'numbness'). Between such states, there is a 'window' of emotional experience allowing for effective processing (Ogden, 2009). According to this model, the boundaries of the window are idiosyncratic for each individual, with some patients having a larger capacity and willingness to experience emotion than others. Factors influencing the range of the 'window' can include experience of childhood trauma, temperament, beliefs about emotion and environmental factors.

As a result, the schema therapist should take into account the Window of Tolerance when accessing emotional material. Flooding and overwhelming (and possibly re-traumatising) the patient is not the aim of the intervention. In turn, the therapist also needs to take active steps to access the Vulnerable Child mode when the patient is disconnected from emotional material.

The following strategies can be used to modify the level of emotional intensity in imagery.

Patients recalling and not experiencing

Some patients describe what is happening in the image in a somewhat distant manner, as if they are observing it from afar rather than feeling part of the scene. For example, the patient may be recollecting a childhood event rather than having a visual/perceptual experience ('Dad would come home drunk and yell and scream at me for not doing well at school'). Here, the therapist encourages the patient to be in first person present tense ('I'm coming home from school, I'm a bit late, dad is at the gate drunk, stumbling around yelling at me … saying I'm pathetic'). In addition, the therapist focuses on the experiential (particularly visual) aspects of the experience (Therapist: 'What do you see? What can you hear around you?'). This helps the patient experience their feelings and needs more intensely in the image as they feel they are 'there' and this allows the rescripting to have a more powerful impact.

Therapist uses their influence or fantasy in imagery to manage affect (Window of Tolerance)

Patients often access strong and intense emotions during imagery rescripting and can sometimes feel overwhelmed. In these situations, the therapist can manipulate visual aspects of the scene to help the patient feel safer, more in control and less overwhelmed. For example, the therapist can use a 'remote control' approach to 'fast forward' or 'rewind' particular experiences. In some cases, key antagonists may need to be removed, or safety features such as a glass wall or prison cell used to contain the aversive character. The therapist can also use fantasy to gain a sense of safety and security for the patient in the image. For example, the therapist can increase their size, enter the image with extra assistance (such as the police or child protectors who become imagined adult figures that are safe, strong and protective).

In contrast, specific antagonists may not be in the image and may need to be 'summoned' for effective rescripting. For example, a patient who has an absent parent may not readily have many memories of where the parent was actively interacting with them. In such cases, the therapist may need to bring the antagonist into the scene to allow for a therapist–antagonist interaction. For example, a father who may have abandoned the family might need to be 'brought back' for the therapist to provide a rescript.

Attuning to the patient's experience

The therapist aims to balance attuning to the patient's experience and structuring the process so the child's needs are ultimately met in the image. The therapist aims to 'get' and display to the patient their understanding of the child's needs, rather than merely proceeding with the technical process of rescripting. The therapist aims to attune to emotional material (how are you feeling, as he says that?), related cognitions ('What's going through your mind right now?') and physical sensation ('Where do you notice this in your body?'). In addition, short summaries and clarification in imagery can increase the intensity of the patient's experience ('So, is it kind of like there is nothing you can do right? You're so scared and you have a sense you're just going to get your head bitten off by him, no matter what you do?').

For some patients, imagery rescripting can feel too challenging. For example, a patient may feel overwhelmed, fear being controlled or exposed, or be convinced the technique will not help them. If a patient refuses to complete imagery work, the therapist needs to honour and respect their position. The therapist can ask about their concerns and encourage the patient to give voice to the part of them that is unwilling to do imagery. This allows the patient to weigh up the pros and cons of not engaging with imagery work. Mode dialogues can also be conducted to explore and work through the patient's ambivalence. For example, the therapist might hear from their Vulnerable Child and adapt the imagery to address their fears about being unsafe, or the patient's Healthy Adult might talk back to a Punitive Parent mode about the patient's fear of making of fool of themselves or making mistakes.

Conclusion

Imagery rescripting offers a creative, engaging and flexible way to gain profound insights into the origins of key schemas and modes. It also provides a unique opportunity for the patient to receive corrective emotional experiences that were absent in childhood and pivotal to their growth and well-being. Furthermore, the process provides a forum for the Healthy Adult to strengthen and take a more central role, as they practise meeting the needs of their Vulnerable Child in each rescripting. Such interventions can provide the patient with unique experiences resulting in powerful outcomes.

The process can, however, be limited by the patient's willingness and capacity to experience imagery-based emotional material. Given its emotional intensity, some patients may feel frightened or distrusting of imagery and seek to avoid it. In these cases, therapists should ask about such concerns from the 'part' of them that does not want to do imagery. Often the coping mode's concerns can be understood and accommodated to allow for imagery rescripting, sometimes with creative adaptations to the process.

Imagery rescripting can be challenging. The therapist may not know necessarily what will come up for the patient, or may be unaware of highly distressing childhood experiences that are unexpectedly disclosed. Two guiding principles that can offer the therapist assistance in such challenging circumstances are: 'What would a good caregiver do at this point?' and 'What does the child need and how can I directly meet this need in the image?' In this way, the therapist attunes to the patient's core needs and the patient feels the opportunity to experience something different and more positive for their future self.

Therapist tips

1. *Win the exchange via taking the antagonist out of the image.* Therapists often face hostile or domineering antagonists. The therapist can ultimately 'win the exchange' by removing the antagonist; for example, 'See your father leaving the room now, so it's just you and me. He's not in charge any more.'

2. *Therapist tone.* Change tone and language to be consistent with the character being addressed. For example, when the therapist is addressing the patient as a child, it is helpful for the therapist to use age appropriate language and tone ('Hey Jo, I'm sorry these guys are giving you such a hard time, you can trust me, I'll sort it out'). These changes in tone add a more natural quality to the dialogue and helps the patient feel the therapist's presence and attunement.

3. *Therapist position.* Patients can subconsciously feel that combative exchanges are directed at themselves. In order to manage such issues, it is useful for the therapist to change their body position to face away from

the patient when speaking to the antagonist, turning back at key points to check how the patient is feeling and what they need.

4. *Pace.* The pace is akin to riding a bike: too slow and the bike/process stalls, too fast and the participant is not able to take in the experience. It is important for the speed of the imagery rescripting not to be too slow and protracted, as excessive description has the effect of distracting from emotional material. If the scene plays out too quickly it will not allow the patient to fully experience the image and make contact with their needs and emotions.

5. *Limited instruction.* The therapist should also limit the amount of instruction in imagery, and generally resist directly telling the patient what they are seeing (e.g., 'So, can you see me – I'm coming through the window to help' *vs* 'Bring me into the image, where do you seem me, where am I?' A helpful guideline is that the therapist assists with the creation of an image with the least amount of instruction possible, allowing the patient to lead the process.

6. *Get in and get out of the image.* Prolonging the rescripting for too long may result in the patient re-experiencing other related memories, leaving the therapist with a dilemma as to which scene they should rescript. As a general guideline, once the therapist has met the need, she or he should aim to conclude the imagery process as soon as possible.

7. *'I'm afraid they will hurt me when you leave the image …'* Patients can feel safe with the therapist protecting and advocating for them and then flip to feeling vulnerable and exposed when the imagery comes to an end, fearing the antagonist will return or retaliate. The therapist can use the image of personal alarms or pagers, saying that they will come back and take care of things whenever needed.

References

Arntz, A. (2011). Imagery rescripting for personality disorders. *Cognitive and Behavioral Practice, 18* (4), 466–481.

Arntz, A. (2014). Imagery rescripting for personality disorders: Healing early maladaptive schemas. In Thomas, N. & McKay, D. (Eds). *Working with Emotion in Cognitive-Behavioral Therapy Techniques for Clinical Practice* (pp. 203–2015). New York: Guilford Press.

Arntz, A. & Jacob, G. (2012). *Schema Therapy in Practice: An Introductory Guide to the Schema Mode Approach.* Chichester: Wiley-Blackwell.

Arntz, A. & van Genderen, H. (2011). *Schema Therapy for Borderline Personality Disorder.* New York: John Wiley & Sons.

Arntz, A. & Weertman, A. (1999). Treatment of childhood memories: Theory and practice. *Behaviour Research and Therapy, 37* (8), 715–740.

Brewin, C.R. (2006). Understanding cognitive behaviour therapy: A retrieval competition account. *Behaviour Research and Therapy, 44* (6), 765–784.

Brewin, C.R., Gregory, J.D., Lipton, M. & Burgess, N. (2010). Intrusive images in psychological disorders: characteristics, neural mechanisms, and treatment implications. *Psychological Review, 117* (1), 210.

de Jongh, A., Ten Broeke, E. & Meijer, S. (2010). Two method approach: A case conceptualization model in the context of EMDR. *Journal of EMDR Practice and Research, 4* (1), 12–21.

Edwards, D. (2011). From ancient shamanic healing to 21st century psychotherapy: The central role of imagery methods in effecting psychological change. In Hackmann, A., Bennett-Levy, J. & Holmes, E. A. (Eds). *Oxford Guide to Imagery in Cognitive Therapy* (pp. XXIV–XLII). Oxford: Oxford University Press.

Foa, E.B. & Rothbaum, B.O. (1998). *Treating the Trauma of Rape: Cognitive-Behavior Therapy for PTSD.* New York: Guilford Press.

Hackmann, A., Bennett-Levy, J. & Holmes, E.A. (2011). *Oxford Guide to Imagery in Cognitive Therapy.* Oxford: Oxford University Press.

Holmes, E.A., Arntz, A. & Smucker, M.R. (2007). Imagery rescripting in cognitive behaviour therapy: Images, treatment techniques and outcomes. *Journal of Behavior Therapy and Experimental Psychiatry, 38* (4), 297–305.

Holmes, E.A. & Mathews, A. (2010). Mental imagery in emotion and emotional disorders. *Clinical Psychology Review, 30*(3), 349–362. http://dx.doi.org/10.1016/j.cpr.2010.01.001

Johnson, J.G., Cohen, P., Brown, J., Smailes, E.M. & Bernstein, D.P. (1999). Childhood maltreatment increases risk for personality disorders during early adulthood. *Archives of General Psychiatry, 56* (7), 600–606.

Morina, N., Lancee, J. & Arntz, A. (2017). Imagery rescripting as a clinical intervention for aversive memories: A meta-analysis. *Journal of Behaviour Therapy and Experimental Psychiatry, 55,* 6–15.

Ogden, P. (2009). Modulation, mindfulness, and movement in the treatment of trauma-related depression. In M. Kerman (Ed.). *Clinical Pearls of Wisdom: 21 Therapists Offer Their Key Insights* (pp. 1–13). New York: Norton Professional Books.

Siegel, D.J. (2015). *The Developing Mind: How Relationships and the Brain Interact to Shape Who We Are* (2nd edn). New York: Guilford Press.

Smucker, M.R., Dancu, C., Foa, E.B. & Niederee, J.L. (1995). Imagery rescripting: A new treatment for survivors of childhood sexual abuse suffering from posttraumatic stress. *Journal of Cognitive Psychotherapy, 9,* 3–17.

Young, J.E. (1996). Young Parenting Inventory (YPI). Retrieved from the New York Cognitive Therapy Center: www.schematherapy.com

7 Working with trauma memories and complex post traumatic stress disorder

Christopher William Lee and Katrina Boterhoven de Haan

Introduction

Complex post traumatic stress disorder (PTSD) is understood to be the result of trauma experiences which are often prolonged, repeated and with a childhood onset. It is typically associated with traumas that are interpersonal in nature, such as childhood abuse or torture (Herman, 1992), whereas simple PTSD is associated with single event traumas, such as an industrial accident or one-off physical assault.

While the concept of complex PTSD has attracted much discussion and debate (see Bisson, Roberts, Andrew, Cooper & Lewis, 2013), there remains a lack of consensus in regard to what is considered the 'gold standard' evidence-based psychological treatment. Perhaps unsurprisingly, a recent meta-analysis of psychological interventions for PTSD in those who had endured childhood abuse reported that individual trauma-focused interventions (such as trauma-focused cognitive-behavioural therapy (CBT) and eye movement desensitisation and reprocessing (EMDR)) were more effective than non-trauma-focused approaches (such as CBT adapted treatments that focus on coping, safety and anxiety management) (Ehring et al., 2014). Thus, there is support for interventions that directly address the processing of the trauma.

Key components of trauma processing interventions

There is further debate regarding the necessary components of these trauma-focused approaches. The International Society for Traumatic Stress Studies advocated a phase-based approach to working with complex trauma that identifies the importance of an initial phase of stabilisation to improve patients' distress tolerance, prior to engaging in trauma processing (Cloitre et al., 2012). However, it is unclear whether this phased approach improves outcomes and is a necessary component of trauma-focused therapy (de Jongh et al., 2016).

Imagery rescripting (IR) has been proposed as an effective technique within the treatment of childhood traumas or more complex PTSD presentations. There is growing evidence to support IR as an effective intervention for treating complex PTSD presentations (Morina, Lancee & Arntz, 2017). IR involves rescripting of the patient's aversive experiences in childhood to provide a corrective emotional experience where the patient's needs, as their child self, are met. The key component of IR is not only that it changes the trauma meaning, but also that the experiential nature of the treatment allows patients to truly experience the new meaning as enacted in the rescripting, thus further integrating changes to core beliefs (Arntz & Weertman, 1999).

Models for the treatment of PTSD have long emphasised the importance of addressing cognitive processes during interventions (Brewin & Holmes, 2003) and a range of studies support a possible link between trauma, schema severity and PTSD. Researchers have found that elevated levels of Early Maladaptive Schemas (EMS) are associated with higher PTSD scores for women sexually abused as children (Harding, Burns & Jackson, 2011). Similarly, Ahmadian and colleagues (2015) reported on the difference in schema severity between acute and chronic PTSD patients. In particular, they found an increased impairment in cognitive–emotional processes (schemas) in individuals with chronic PTSD. Schemas have also been found to be more acute in war veterans with PTSD than in those without it (Cockram, Drummond & Lee, 2010). Interestingly, while adverse childhood events have been found in prospective studies to increase the risk of PTSD for soldiers entering war zones (Berntsen et al., 2012), EMS have been found to mediate the relationship between adverse childhood events and whether a war veteran develops PTSD (Cockram, 2009). PTSD treatment programmes that use a schema approach were found, in one study, to lead to more symptom reduction than a traditional CBT approach (Cockram, Drummond & Lee, 2010). Taken together, there are reasons for applying the schema model when working with individuals with complex forms of PTSD.

The IREM trial

In this chapter, we describe the methods used in a recently conducted randomised controlled trial incorporating some novel adaptations to the treatment of complex PTSD (Boterhoven de Haan et al., 2017). The data for the trial is to be published elsewhere and so is not reported within this chapter. However, there are points of clinical learning that were captured from the trial experience that we share here. In the study, we compared two types of trauma-focused therapies, IR and eye movement desensitisation and reprocessing (EMDR), for people with PTSD from childhood trauma experiences. Both treatments were delivered without prior stabilisation. This trial, named IREM, recruited participants via mental health and specialised trauma services across Australia, Germany and the Netherlands who had experienced childhood trauma prior to age 16 years and had a primary diagnosis of PTSD. Participants were randomly allocated to treatment condition where they attended 12 sessions on a twice-weekly basis over a period of between six and eight weeks. The majority of participants had extensive trauma histories with co-morbid diagnoses such as depression and anxiety. Assessment was conducted at several time points from pre-treatment, mid and post treatment, with two follow-up assessments at eight weeks and one year post treatment. The EMDR treatment was based on the protocol developed by Shapiro (2001) and IR was based on the model proposed by Arntz and Weertman (1999). Therapists were assessed on adherence to treatment protocol. Qualitative interviews were conducted with the therapists and participants in the trial to investigate their experience of the trauma-focused treatments (Boterhoven de Haan, 2018). Interviews were conducted at each of the treatment sites and a thematic analysis approach was used to explore the data. This chapter focuses on describing and reviewing some of the key clinical methods and techniques used successfully within this trial to hone trauma reprocessing.

Clinical implications of the IREM trial

We suggest that processing of traumatic experiences for complex PTSD can be improved by sharing a broad schema-based model with the patient. Providing patients with a clear rationale helps to facilitate treatment engagement and willingness to address traumatic material. Research has shown that when patients are given a rationale for how schemas and related coping styles contribute to various symptoms, they are more likely to experience the therapist as attuned to them and to feel understood. Furthermore, they report a greater sense of being able to understand themselves. This greater self-understanding was related to an improved optimism which, in turn, was associated with better treatment outcomes (Hoffart, Versland & Sexton, 2002).

In this chapter, we highlight the use of a trauma map as a form of a case conceptualisation that was developed from information processing models of trauma and informed by schema theory. We describe the IR approach for treating complex PTSD, including how to prepare patients, and strategies for enhancing trauma processing. This approach is illustrated with a case example (Jane) who was treated with IR as part of the IREM study.

Case example

Jane is a 54-year-old bank teller, self-referred for therapy to address her history of childhood abuse. Jane presented with mood swings ranging from low mood to outbursts of 'extreme anger'. She felt distant from others and had difficulty trusting people. In addition, Jane reported hypervigilance to threat and difficulties sleeping. Jane acknowledged that she had endured these symptoms for a long time; however, they had increased 18 months ago when her husband left her after he had an affair. She described strong negative beliefs about herself and the world such as 'I am worthless', 'I am broken' and 'no one can be trusted'.

Jane described a significant trauma history which began when she was put into foster care at age four. Trauma events included physical, sexual and emotional abuse which she suffered almost daily and continued until she ran away at 15 years of age.

Jane and Frank had been married for 36 years and they had one child, Tanner, 34. Jane described Frank as supportive; however, she felt that both Frank and Tanner had 'turned on her' since the separation, in particular, Tanner blaming Jane for Frank having an affair. Jane had recently spoken with Frank about reconciling although she was unsure how she felt about this and whether it was what she wanted.

Jane had a group of friends that she would see socially but she stated that they were not close friends as she did not like talking about herself because it made her feel exposed. Jane said she'd not been in close contact with anyone since her separation as she did not want to bother anyone.

Mapping traumas: implications of information processing models of trauma for schema case conceptualisation

An important part of trauma processing is to share a case conceptualisation with the patient. For this, we suggest the use of a trauma map, which can be used to help identify specific trauma memories. The map can consist of a series of events that resulted in PTSD; and/or emotional experiences that would not, on their own, result in PTSD but their cumulative effect have contributed to EMS development, such as being continually put down by a parent. The mapping process helps to build a shared understanding of how the trauma experiences shaped both the individual's thought processes and behavioural patterns. In drawing the trauma map, the patient typically sits beside the therapist and the diagram is constructed on paper placed on a coffee table. The patient is metaphorically and literally working side by side with the therapist to compile the list of these core experiences. This process is necessarily led by the patient's experience; however, sometimes the therapist is more directive in acknowledging traumas that may have been minimised or dismissed and will add these to the map: for example, sexual abuse or bullying at school. Adding these events to the map needs to be sensitively timed and potentially revisited when the patient has a greater sense of their relevance.

While there are different information processing models of traumas, they also share common features (Schubert & Lee, 2009). A key common feature of various models is that each memory is encoded with three distinct components: information about the stimulus; information about the associated emotional response, which includes affect, physiological sensations and behaviours, and information about its meaning. The meaning component for someone with a complex trauma presentation will mostly be an EMS. It is these three components that need to be assessed for each memory that is the basis of the trauma map.

In the case of Jane, presented above, she described the sexual abuse by her foster father as the most distressing of her trauma experiences. Jane was able to identify a specific memory related to the sexual abuse and the image associated with this was of being in the main bedroom of her foster home. When recalling this memory, Jane was able to describe the sensory aspects, including seeing the light through the crack in the door and hearing footsteps coming up the stairs. In describing this event, she reported feelings of shame and disgust and a tightness in her chest. She added that these feelings of shame also went with the response of wanting to hide. When asked about her thoughts related to this scene and those feelings, she described the sense of worthlessness and being broken, which is indicative of a Defectiveness schema. To help Jane understand her trauma experience, we drew this event and its components as pieces of a pie; the left-hand portion represents the details of the episode, the bottom portion represents the feelings and the responses, and the right-hand portion is the meaning associated with the event (see middle circle of Figure 7.1).

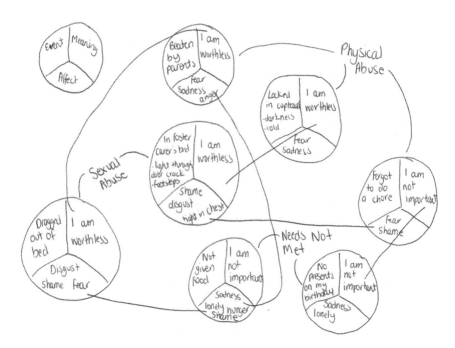

Figure 7.1 An example of trauma mapping with lines indicating similarities in the components of Jane's traumatic experiences.

For complex PTSD presentations, due to the nature and severity of the trauma experiences, we find that some patients have difficulty identifying specific memories due to the similarities across experiences. In these situations, we ask the patient to identify the memories that are the most distressing or the images of their trauma memories that most frequently intrude into their everyday life. As such, it is not necessary for the patient to recall every trauma experience; rather, it is about identifying possible representative targets for processing later in the treatment. In some cases, we find that for patients who have trauma histories but struggle to identify specific memories of major traumas, focusing on memories of other acknowledged schema-related experiences that are less distressing might be better tolerated. When these patients experience a good outcome targeting these lesser traumas, they then may feel ready to progress to targeting the more significant traumas or more distressing events.

The second shared feature of information processing models of trauma is that trauma memories are associative and linked to other experiences in the memory network. During the process of mapping a patient's trauma, we illustrate the links between the person's traumatic experiences, because they either involve similar events, similar feeling states or similar meanings. At this point, the therapist may draw attention to other memories on the map which previously the patient may not have viewed as relevant. In Jane's case, links were made between memories that were similar in nature, such as when she did not have her needs met (i.e., not being given food or presents on her birthday), or because they involved similar schemas such as believing herself defective or worthless. These links can be seen by the connecting lines in Figure 7.1.

After making connections between the content of trauma memories, we then make links between a patient's symptoms and their trauma experiences. The patient's accumulated negative experiences are the etiological foundation of the schema and, in theory, we assume that the person's symptoms result from an interaction between their coping style and their schema (Figure 7.2).

Figure 7.2 A schema informed information processing model of trauma showing how the network of trauma memories give rise to schemas which in turn are maintained by coping styles that combined interfere with healthy adult goals.

Questions that may facilitate this process include: How did your experiences affect the way you thought about yourself (or others, or the world)? Is the way you think now, influenced by what happened to you in the past? How have your experiences shaped the way you live your life now? This type of linking is very similar to the trauma impact statements used in cognitive processing therapy (Resick, Monson & Chard, 2017).

The extent to which the patient responds with the coping styles of surrender, avoidance or over-compensation further entrenches these beliefs through ongoing experiences (Figure 7.2). This, in turn, interferes with the patient reaching appropriate healthy adult goals and gaining a positive sense of self. This includes that they are competent/capable, have a stable sense of connection (loveable/likeable) and a basic sense of safety. So, in Jane's case, she tended to surrender to her Defectiveness schema by allowing her husband and son to verbally abuse and mistreat her, including her son blaming her for his father cheating on her and the marital separation. She also used avoidance strategies which prevented her from receiving incompatible information. For example, when Jane did choose to go out socially, she went out dancing with a group of people where she could easily get away with not talking, therefore not giving her the opportunity to share any personal information and to learn that she was valuable and could be listened to. An example of Jane's over-compensation was her reacting with extreme anger when she felt criticised or rejected.

Subjugation was another schema relevant to Jane. Some of her experiences consistent with this schema included being beaten when she tried to speak up for herself or the other foster children. Through her experiences in her foster home, Jane learnt that if she submitted to her abusers, she could avoid further punishments or beatings. In surrendering to this schema, Jane allowed her husband to make all the decisions in their relationship. In the case of the recent separation, it had been her husband who had cheated on her and his decision to leave, yet he had recently been talking about reconciling. Jane reported worrying that she would not be able to say no to him. Her avoidance of the subjugation schema meant that Jane would not answer phone calls or would hide from people so as to avoid conflict.

The effect of the schema and defensive styles is that they also interfere with gaining a positive sense of self. So, while Jane continues to repeat any one of the above behaviours, her chances of experiencing herself as truly worthwhile are decreased. A further example, in Jane's case, is that she continued to speak with her husband on a regular basis despite having separated eighteen months prior. During these phone calls, he would often criticise her and put her down.

A trauma map is something that we implement in clinical practice outside of IREM. We believe that the drawing of the associated experiences helps prime the individual for schema change. In the first instance, the creation of a trauma map provides visual recognition of a patient's trauma experiences and how these have had an impact on them. In some cases, while it can be challenging for patients, the map also appears to help patients develop a distance from their experiences and, therefore, facilitates understanding of the origins of their schema. Additionally, by making a map that explicitly shows the connections between different events, it incidentally primes the patient for trauma processing, as the information is more readily accessible.

It is often useful to conclude the trauma map session by making links between the individual's past trauma experiences, the process of therapy and their current ways of thinking, feeling and being in the world. In explaining how schemas drive current difficulties and reminding the individual that schemas develop because of events largely in childhood and beyond their control, there is a normalised and non-blaming rationale for their current struggles. Furthermore, hope is instilled that new schemas can bring new ways of thinking, feeling and being in the world. 'Due to these experiences, you started to believe that [*insert schema*] was true. Although you may know that logically this is not true, on an emotional level, it can still feel true. While we cannot change what happened, we can change how these experiences are stored in your mind and how you think about those events. This in turn may help to change how you feel. So, the idea is that [*insert positive belief opposite to schema*] will start to feel more true and therefore it's easier for you to behave in ways that will get your needs met.' (Then give the patient a specific example relevant to their mental health goal.)

Preparation for treatment

In any trauma-focused treatment preparation is important. Our impression is that the process of trauma mapping helps to provide patients with a rationale for treatment through the linking of their past experiences, negative self-beliefs and current behaviours. Thus, even at this early stage of conceptualisation, patients are primed to begin to address their trauma memories. We suggest that the mapping process typically takes one or two sessions, following which the trauma work begins.

Important to preparation is also providing a rationale for the use of IR, such as, this treatment works to help people change the meaning of their childhood trauma experiences by rescripting the event with a different ending so that they learn to feel differently about themselves. In IREM, we used the model proposed by Arntz and Weertman (1999), where the therapist first rescripts and then the patient rescripts. In the first stage of the rescripting, the therapist is able to model a corrective response to the child part of the traumatised patient. Often, patients with childhood trauma experiences or complex PTSD come from backgrounds that are depriving so that they rarely had their needs met, and thus (understandably) don't know how to do this for themselves as adults. The second stage of the rescripting is important for building self-efficacy. The therapist helps direct the patient to enter the image as their adult self and does what is necessary to meet the needs of the child in that memory. This is then followed by the patient going back into the image as their child self, with their adult self by their side responding in ways that meets their needs. This third stage helps integrate corrective information enabling the patient to begin to meet their own needs in the present (Arntz, 2011).

Imagery rescripting: reprocessing trauma memories

In order to build a sense of safety and motivation for the methods, a useful early exercise can be a pilot rescript with a less aversive memory. Where possible, the pilot memory should be unrelated to the main trauma so that there is no risk of activating traumatic material through associated memory networks before the patient feels ready.

After the trauma memories have been mapped and the patient is sufficiently prepared for treatment, a schema formulation can help determine the target memory for processing. A memory that is prototypical of the schema or the most distressing make the best targets. In general, it is also better to choose early memories linked to the schema rather than later experiences where the schema was reinforced. This is sometimes described as choosing the first or worst trauma experience. In the case of Jane, the worst memory she identified was that of sexual abuse depicted by an image of being in her foster parent's bed. The belief she had attached to this memory was worthlessness. Jane was asked to focus on all aspects of the experience in order to activate the trauma memory which was then reprocessed with IR.

A key ingredient of information processing models of trauma intervention is that the individual is connected with information that is incompatible with the trauma meaning (Brewin & Holmes, 2003). In IR, this is done by superimposing the trauma content with a new relational image of their needs being met. These new relational memories are incompatible with the negative messages encoded at the time of the trauma. For example, in working with a patient with a Defectiveness schema, in a scene where the child was punished for having made a mistake, the therapist instead enters the scene and shows compassion for the child and, therefore, facilitates the patient developing more compassion for their Vulnerable Child mode. This work also includes targeting schema related behaviours or coping responses. For example, Jane, during her trauma work, was provided with a corrective emotional experience that reinforced the positive belief that she was worthwhile and important. During Jane's trauma processing, she wanted to run away in the imagery. To address her avoidant behaviour, Jane was encouraged, during the rescripting, to confront the perpetrators and stand up for herself, which was linked back to her treatment goals of wanting to learn to deal with her problems head on and not to run away from difficult situations.

During treatment, the therapist should be mindful that IR can trigger the patient's Punitive Parent mode, where punishing messages internalised from the original abuse or trauma resurface. This mode often relates to schemas such as Defectiveness and Punitiveness where the patient feels they are fundamentally flawed or 'bad' and they deserved what happened in the original trauma memory. The therapist will need to engage with the mode, or a representation of it, to ensure that the patient feels safe and protected and to reattribute any punishing messages to the Punitive Parent mode, rather than being left with these messages as negative 'facts' about their character.

If the patient's sense of their Punitive Parent mode is closely associated with the actual parent or abuser it can be addressed in normal rescripting. In other cases, imagery can be used to manipulate the punitive mode in a manner that reduces its power for the patient. This could be putting a muzzle on a dog or, in Jane's case, shrinking the punitive mode to the size of an ant and blowing it away from her. Depending on the severity of the mode, the therapist may have to guide the patient out of the image and use other techniques, such as chair work, limited reparenting, or psychoeducation as a way of helping the patient become aware of how this punitive mode relates to their ongoing difficulties.

Once a particular memory has been reprocessed, the therapist and the patient review the trauma map and the patient is invited to consider which of the other experiences continue to be associated with distress. This memory then becomes the next target for trauma processing. In the IREM study, we typically process four or five trauma memories in a 12-session programme. It is not often possible to process all of the memories on the map, which is why it is important to target the ones producing the most distress. Also, because of the associated nature of the trauma network, four or five targeted memories seems sufficient for schema change.

Case example: treatment progress and outcome

Jane scored 55 on the Impact of Events Scale–Revised (IES–R; Weiss & Marmar, 1997) prior to beginning therapy. Scores on the IES–R range from 0–88; a score of 55 would be in the severe clinical range for PTSD. She was initially hard to engage in treatment. She reported difficulties in making her scheduled appointments and would often try to avoid engaging in the therapeutic process. Jane's difficulties were explored, and she acknowledged that she was worried that she would get it wrong, 'just like everything else'. Her difficulties were explained in the context of her schema formulation linking them to her problem behaviour and her treatment goals. Jane also struggled to express her feelings and needs in the rescripting: in particular, she struggled to express anger. To help her learn to express herself, Jane was encouraged to think about all the things she would want to include in a statement to explain how her trauma experiences impacted her and her life. It was at this point in her treatment that Jane was given the task to intervene in her own rescripting of the trauma memory. She was encouraged to think about the statement she had written and then to imagine what she would say or do to her foster parents to let them know how much they had hurt her. It was after the sixth session, where Jane allowed herself to express her anger towards her foster parents, that saw her IES–R scores drop to 39, which would indicate that she would be in the moderate range and would still meet criteria for PTSD.

During the course of the treatment, Jane and her husband decided to finalise their separation; however, weeks later she reported that her husband had called and wanted to reconcile. During this conversation Jane reported anger at her husband for 'trying to bully me into changing my mind'. She acknowledged that, in the past, she would have felt pressured and would have eventually complied with her husband's wishes. However, for the first time in a long time, Jane stood up for herself and put her needs first. Experiences like this directly contributed to her evolving sense that she was important and worthwhile. This experience of speaking up for herself was reflected in Jane's IES-R score of 14 at session 10 which would suggest that Jane was in the mild range and no longer met criteria for PTSD. Following this, Jane came to the realisation that she wanted to remain single and was feeling free for the first time in her life. Jane's score at her last session was 5, meaning she was in the subclinical range for PTSD. Although she was scheduled for 12 sessions, Jane felt that after 11 sessions she had adequately addressed her trauma history. The therapist decided that, as part of reparenting her Subjugation schema, it was important to reward her for expressing her needs, so it was agreed that treatment would be terminated at this point.

Summary

Recent studies have demonstrated that it is possible to treat complex PTSD with trauma-focused interventions (Ehring et al., 2014; Van Woudenberg et al., 2018). Simultaneously, there has also been a greater recognition of the importance of treating trauma as a first-line intervention approach. In IREM, we interviewed 16 therapists who participated in the study. One of the emerging themes from the qualitative interviews was that since their involvement in the study, and regardless of what treatment approach, the majority would treat PTSD first and then address other issues as necessary.

A limitation of the generalisability from the study was that all participants had to report PTSD symptoms from childhood, agree to want to try a trauma treatment and be prepared to commit to the 12 sessions. We find, in our clinical practice, that those patients who have trauma history but are vague on whether they experience PTSD symptoms and/or are unwilling to commit to treating their trauma memories do not benefit from a trauma approach initially and need more emphasis on developing the therapeutic relationship and a capacity to tolerate negative emotions.

We have presented a rationale for understanding of the impact of trauma on a patient's schemas using a trauma map and how this can facilitate their engagement in a trauma-focused treatment. This includes drawing links between a patient's various trauma experiences, schemas, current behaviours and coping styles of surrender, avoidance and overcompensation. We then identify positive schemas and relate this to the patient's treatment goals. Once all of this information is collected, the schema formulation is then used to help determine the memory to be targeted for treatment.

Once trauma reprocessing begins, we recommend that the initial memory targeted is either the *first memory* related to the schema (for example, the first time abuse occurred) or the *worst memory* (the memory associated with the highest distress), or the memory that is most *representative of the schema*. The reasons for using these memories is that they are the most critical to the schema network and, therefore, once treated, produce the most emotional change. Furthermore, they also increase the chance that the treatment effects from the initial sessions generalise to other memories related to the schema. Occasionally, the initial memory chosen may not be the first or worst, but one that seems to best encapsulate the schema. After initial processing of a memory, the map is useful in guiding the therapy to the next most relevant trauma memory to be processed. This can enhance the effectiveness of trauma-focused interventions such as EMDR and IR.

In sum, the trauma map operates as a framework for patient and therapist to understand the impact of trauma on many areas of the patient's life and sense of self (their schemas, their coping strategies and their current struggles). The map illustrates why the patient is affected as deeply and pervasively as they are and why their schemas continue to be triggered and perpetuated in their current life. It also makes sense of how imagery re-scripting can help to heal the patient's schemas in a containing and purposeful manner, allowing both patient and therapist to feel more courageous in their endeavours to face, rather than avoid, painful and distressing memories. In imagery rescripting, initially the therapist and later the patient, have the opportunity to give the traumatised child what they needed but never had, and, as such, start a process of much needed schema healing. The map then allows the therapist and patient to regroup after each rescripting and for the patient to integrate emotionally corrective experiences into a broader understanding of themselves and their schemas. Once key developmental experiences have been rescripted, the patient is less likely to be triggered and has a stronger internalised Healthy Adult to meet their needs in everyday life.

Therapist tips

- A schema case conceptualisation provides an important early foundation for preparing patients with complex trauma for intervention work. This shared case conceptualisation identifies trauma memories that are to be targeted and so effectively guides treatment.
- It is recommended that, in general, the first memory, the worst memory or one that is most representative of the schema be used as the target for rescripting.

- However, therapists need to be sensitive to the patient's Window of Tolerance and reluctance to address some memories. Non-core memories are, therefore, occasionally chosen as practice targets, before addressing core trauma memories.
- We encourage a developmental and stepped model for complex patients. The therapist models the appropriate reparenting response for patients before the patient uses their adult self to provide for their needs.
- During processing, therapists should be mindful of the schema that is being targeted and the antidote messages that will be needed to provide schema healing.

References

Ahmadian, A., Mirzaee, J., Omidbeygi, M., Holsboer-Trachsler, E. & Brand, S. (2015). Differences in maladaptive schemas between patients suffering from chronic and acute posttraumatic stress disorder and healthy controls. *Neuropsychiatric Disease and Treatment*, *11*, 1677–1684. doi:10.2147/NDT.S85959

Arntz, A. (2011). Imagery rescripting for personality disorders. *Cognitive and Behavioral Practice*, *18*(4), 466–481. doi:10.1016/j.cbpra.2011.04.006

Arntz, A. & Weertman, A. (1999). Treatment of childhood memories: Theory and practice. *Behaviour Research and Therapy*, *37*(8), 715–740. doi:10.1016/S0005-7967(98)00173-9

Berntsen, D., Johannessen, K.B., Thomsen, Y.D., Bertelsen, M., Hoyle, R.H. & Rubin, D.C. (2012). Peace and war: trajectories of posttraumatic stress disorder symptoms before, during, and after military deployment in Afghanistan. *Psychological Science*, *23*(12), 1557–1565. doi:10.1177/0956797612457389

Bisson, J.I., Roberts, N.P., Andrew, M., Cooper, R. & Lewis, C. (2013). Psychological therapies for chronic post-traumatic stress disorder (PTSD) in adults. *Cochrane Database Systematic Reviews*, *12*, CD003388. doi:10.1002/14651858.CD003388.pub4

Boterhoven de Haan, K.L. (2018). What therapists and adult patients tell us about treating their PTSD from childhood trauma. Presentation to 49th European Association for Behavioural and Cognitive Therapies, Bulgaria.

Boterhoven de Haan, K.L., Lee, C.W., Fassbinder, E., Voncken, M.J., Meewisse, M., Van Es, S.M. … Arntz, A. (2017). Imagery rescripting and eye movement desensitisation and reprocessing for treatment of adults with childhood trauma-related post-traumatic stress disorder: IREM study design. *BMC Psychiatry*, *17*(1), 165.

Brewin, C.R. & Holmes, E.A. (2003). Psychological theories of posttraumatic stress disorder. *Clinical Psychology Review*, *23*(3), 339–376. doi:10.1016/S0272 7358(03) 00033-3

Cloitre, M., Courtois, C., Ford, J., Green, B., Alexander, P., Briere, J. … Spinazzola, J. (2012). *The ISTSS Expert Consensus Treatment Guidelines for Complex PTSD in Adults.* Retrieved from www.istss.org/

Cockram, D. (2009). Role and treatment of early maladaptive schemas in Vietnam Veterans with PTSD. From Murduch University Research Repository http://researchrepository.murdoch.edu.au/id/eprint/1309

Cockram, D.M., Drummond, P.D. & Lee, C.W. (2010). Role and treatment of early maladaptive schemas in Vietnam veterans with PTSD. *Clinical Psychology & Psychotherapy, 17*(3), 165–182.

de Jongh, A., Resick, P.A., Zoellner, L.A., van Minnen, A., Lee, C.W., Monson, C. M. … Bicanic, I.A.E. (2016). Critical analysis of the current treatment guidelines for complex PTSD in adults. *Depression and Anxiety, 00*, 1–11. doi:10.1002/da.22469

Ehring, T., Welboren, R., Morina, N., Wicherts, J.M., Freitag, J. & Emmelkamp, P.M.G. (2014). Meta-analysis of psychological treatments for posttraumatic stress disorder in adult survivors of childhood abuse. *Clinical Psychology Review, 34*(8), 645–657. doi:10.1016/j.cpr.2014.10.004

Harding, H.G., Burns, E.E. & Jackson, J.L. (2011). Identification of child sexual abuse survivor subgroups based on early maladaptive schemas: Implications for understanding differences in posttraumatic stress disorder symptom severity. *Cognitive Therapy and Research, 36*(5), 560–575. doi:10.1007/s10608-011-9385-8

Herman, J.L. (1992). Complex PTSD: A syndrome in survivors of prolonged and repeated trauma. *Journal of Traumatic Stress, 5*(3), 377–391. doi:10.1002/jts.2490050305

Hoffart, A., Versland, S. & Sexton, H. (2002). Self-understanding, empathy, guided discovery, and schema belief in schema-focused cognitive therapy of personality problems: A process–outcome study. *Cognitive Therapy and Research, 26*(2), 199–219. doi:10.1023/a:1014521819858

Morina, N., Lancee, J. & Arntz, A. (2017). Imagery rescripting as a clinical intervention for aversive memories: A meta-analysis. *Journal of Behavior Therapy and Experimental Psychiatry, 55*(Supplement C), 6–15. doi:10.1016/j.jbtep.2016.11.003

Resick, P.A., Monson, C.M. & Chard, K.M. (2017). *Cognitive Processing Therapy for PTSD: A Comprehensive Manual.* New York: Guilford Press.

Schubert, S. & Lee, C.W. (2009). Adult PTSD and its treatment with EMDR: A review of controversies, evidence, and theoretical knowledge. *Journal of EMDR Practice and Research, 3*(3), 117–132.

Shapiro, F. (2001). *Eye Movement Desensitization and Reprocessing: Basic Principles, Protocols, and Procedures* (2nd ed.). New York: Guilford Press.

Van Woudenberg, C., Voorendonk, E.M., Bongaerts, H., Zoet, H.A., Verhagen, M., Lee, C.W. … De Jongh, A. (2018). Effectiveness of an intensive treatment programme combining prolonged exposure and eye movement desensitization and reprocessing for severe post-traumatic stress disorder. *European Journal of Psychotraumatology, 9*(1), 1487225. doi: 10.1080/20008198.2018.1487225

Weiss, D. (1997). The Impact of Event Scale–Revised. In J. Wilson & T. Keane (Eds.), *Assessing Psychological Trauma and PTSD* (168–189). New York: Guilford Press.

8 Current life imagery

Offer Maurer and Eshkol Rafaeli

Introduction

This chapter addresses a variety of imagery techniques focused on recent past, present or future scenes, which can be thought of as adaptations of classic imagery rescripting (ImRs). What is unique about the techniques presented in this chapter is that they direct the patient's (and therapist's) attention to emotionally charged situations in the present day, thus facilitating the understanding, processing, rehearsing and/or rescripting of 'live', sometimes still unfolding, situations.

For most patients, a combination of both childhood and current life imagery over the course of therapy is optimal. Whereas childhood-focused imagery techniques help patients understand the origins of their schemas and unmet needs, the techniques described below afford patients the opportunity of working through their schemas and modes as they operate in their current life.

The immediacy, vividness and relevance of present-day experiences make for a particularly compelling arena in which to work and effect change. In particular, it may lead to one of several benefits, including raising awareness of (and differentiation between) modes, strengthening the patient's Healthy Adult mode (and, particularly, this mode's adaptive capacity to reparent the child modes), and rehearsing behaviour change.

To date, few studies have empirically explored the value of present-day-focused methods. However, a compelling study by Weertman and Arntz (2007) suggested that schema-focused cognitive therapy could progress from a focus on present-day to past-day memories, or vice versa, with equal benefits. Moreover, some present-day imagery methods have been shown to be productive components of evidence-based interventions (including positive imagery techniques: Hackmann, Bennett-Levy & Holmes, 2011; brief anxiety treatment protocols: e.g., Prinz, Bar-Kalifa, Rafaeli, Sened, Lutz, 2019; and mindfulness-based stress reduction: Grossman, Niemann, Schmidt & Walach, 2004).

The chapter is organised around three sections, outlining imagery techniques pertaining to recent past, immediate present, and future scenes. It concludes with some recommendations relevant across all of these techniques.

Imagery rescripting of the recent past

Many therapists familiar with ImRs use present-day experiences as a starting point for accessing much earlier memories. In such instances, the therapist may zoom in on a recent emotionally charged event recounted by the patient (e.g., a conflict with a family member or colleague; the experience of a loss or a rejection, etc.) and invite the patient to close their eyes and bring this scene to mind as vividly as possible. Once the scene is vivid enough, the therapist directs their patient's attention to their emotional experience and bodily-felt sense in this situation, and asks the patient to let the other (more external) aspects of the scene dissipate. Through a focus on their emotions and physical sensations, the patient is asked to traverse an 'affect bridge' (Watkins, 1971) linking this recent event to some earlier event through the shared emotions and sensations. Below is a vignette exemplifying such (classic) ImRs work.

Case example

Adam, a 29-year-old patient came into session feeling defective, ashamed and hopeless, having narrowly missed a car accident due to failing to spot a stop sign. In the current day image, he connected with a sense of despondency about his impaired driving ability and about what this would mean for both his work and his love life. The use of an affect bridge allowed Adam and his therapist to see the emotional similarity between this scene and many earlier instances of humiliation. One salient memory which became the focus of (classic, childhood-focused) ImRs was the repeated experience of being chastised by his father as he was learning to ride a bicycle at age 6–7.

A simple adaptation of ImRs work involves the use of this technique to rescript recent emotionally charged events without pursuing a link to an earlier childhood event. A therapist may choose this strategy for one of several reasons. First, given the reluctance of many patients to engage with historical material, the therapist may opt to pursue recent past focused work in early stages of therapy as a stepping-stone towards more traditional childhood-focused ImRs work later on in therapy, once the patient has seen the utility of experiential/imagery work and the therapy relationship itself feels safer. A present day focus may also be indicated when the recent event is particularly distressing and the therapist determines that emotion down-regulation, rather than the intensification of affect more typical of classic ImRs, is the priority. Finally, a focus on recent past events may be appropriate when these provide a good enough opportunity for strengthening the Healthy Adult, accessing vulnerability, or simply differentiating between multiple modes activated within a scene. Below, we illustrate how Adam and his therapist weave such work into a typical session.

ADAM (A): I've had a really hard week – Tuesday was the worst! When I was at work I was walking out of the elevator and the 'big boss' walked past me, not even acknowledging my existence. Can you believe it? I actually tried to mumble some sort of a greeting, 'good morning' or something … but it was really just a mumble. Her face was totally frozen, almost angry, looking right through me, dead in the eyes.

THERAPIST (T): Wow… What an awful experience. Can you try and tell me – what were you feeling? What was going through your head?

A: For a moment I felt hurt, shocked, enraged. But then I was just flooded with anxiety … I suddenly felt 100% sure that I'm going to get fired! And also, that it's all *my* fault …

T: What a painful situation … such difficult feelings. … And also, I'm thinking … it's so relevant to everything we've been talking about recently, especially the Abandonment schema. Would you be willing to do some imagery work using this scene that you just described? [using the recent experience as a starting point for imagery]

A: Sure. It was so intense … I can still feel this trembling feeling I had as the whole thing played out.

T: I'm sure. It sounds like such an upsetting situation. Would you be willing to close your eyes for a minute and get an image of what you saw right there, outside the elevator? [Adam closes his eyes] Try to get into the situation, and tell me what's happening …

A: I was just getting out of the …

T: Can you try to tell it to me as if it's happening right now … so, 'I'm just getting out of the elevator'?

A: Yeah … Okay. So, I'm walking out of the elevator on my floor, and then around the corner comes the 'big boss' … I'm trying to catch her eye – to speak, to say 'good morning' or something … But as she's moving past me, my words become somewhat slurred or maybe turn into a mumble … and I'm like – this &%$^# is totally ignoring me!

T: I understand … Let's slow down the tempo of this scene. Try to imagine everything in extreme slow motion, maybe starting with the moment you notice her ignoring you … What's going on for you right now? What are you feeling?

A: I'm *so* hurt! And I'm furious! How dare she! What kind of a behaviour is this? What an awful person.

T: You're hurt, you're so angry.

A: Yes … but even more, I'm worried … I'm worried that *she's* angry with *me* … I'm thinking to myself that I must have done something to piss her off and that's why she won't look me in the eye. And then, in a split second, I'm finding myself looking back at all my actions at work and I'm starting to see it all as one big failure … She's going to fire me! She's going to fire me! What will I do? I have bills to pay, I have a mortgage to pay! I have commitments. … What's going to happen next?! I'm all alone. It's like, 'Game Over'.

T: Let's slow things down some more, then. I want to help you find a safe place, somewhere you can be by yourself for a few moments. ... Could you imagine yourself stepping into your office and closing the door behind you? Imagine sitting at your desk? [Trying to down-regulate the patient's emotion, and also enter a space – albeit an imagined one – in which rescripting work can be undertaken.]

A: Yes.

T: Okay ... would it be okay for me to speak with a few of the modes that seem to be coming up right now?

A: Sure, yes.

T: Great. I'd like to start by saying something to the scared part of you, the mode you're so strongly in touch with right now ...

A: Yes?

T: Hey ... I see you, buddy... I can feel how shaken up you are. It was really a pretty nasty situation out there ... Tell me how you are doing now ...

A: I'm just terrified she's going to sack me ... that's it. I can't see beyond this fear right now.

T: I hear you, I really do. Can I bring in another part right now? I'd like to try and get in touch with another part of you ...

A: Yes ... which one?

T: I was thinking of this angry part of you, the part that first got activated when your boss didn't say hi. ... Do I have it right?

A: Yes ... but, ummm ... I'm not so in touch with him right now though ...

T: I know ... but *could* you try and rewind a bit, and go back to those thoughts and feelings you had *right* as you realised she's not making eye contact?

A: Okay, a little bit I think ...

T: Would you speak from this side of you? What do you think? What do you feel?

A: Well, she's an asshole, that's for sure. I mean, I've been working like crazy to get all the stuff ready for the quarter's summary meeting last week. And now she doesn't even *see me*? That's *so not cool*. Not cool.

T: Okay ... good ... I get a feeling you're a bit more into this mode now, right?

A: You bet I am ... Who the hell does she think she is? No, really! I'm asking you!

T: Now let's bring yet another part into the office. ... But wait ... where would you put each of the sides we've talked to so far in the image you have in your mind? Can you look at the scared part and tell me where you see him now? And also, where is the angry part?

A: The scared one is under the desk [*giggling a bit, seems bemused*]. The angry one is standing up near the desk.

T: This is *awesome*. Now please bring in your adult self, the part of you that sees the big picture, too ... where is he going to be?

A: I guess maybe ... I'd be sitting normally at the desk.

T: Great. Could you now *be* this part of you, sitting at the desk, looking at the other two? At the scared part under the desk, and also at the angry one standing near it? [accessing and strengthening the Healthy Adult, helping the patient differentiate between the various modes]

A: Yes ...

T: Try to see if you can say something to each of them. ... Try to reflect on each of their reactions and what they need ... let's take this nice and slow.

As this vignette illustrates, imagery can be adapted to work through recent emotionally charged events without necessarily pursuing a link to earlier childhood events. This image also did not require 'rescripting' in the sense of changing any external events in the scene; instead, it was used to summon the patient's Healthy Adult to help with his schema-driven reactions. A main benefit of such work is that it provides vivid access to the modes activated in recent situations and, thus, enables effective mode work that feels 'live' to the patient, as they are taken back to the full range of emotions, thoughts and feelings evoked therein. Often, this circumvents the patient's more detached or controlled narratives about the situation, which may miss their underlying vulnerability and core needs.

Present-focused imagery techniques

Imagery techniques can also be used to focus on the immediate experience of the patient – that is, on the present moment itself. Such a focus often takes the form of inviting the patient to make contact with a felt sense of their Vulnerable Child mode, to summon an awareness of the qualities and strengths of their Healthy Adult mode and to establish an attuned, nurturing and reparative dialogue between the two.

To connect with the Vulnerable Child through imagery, a therapist may simply invite the patient to close their eyes, and to picture or be their younger side, either in the *first* person (Can you be that younger side of yourself right now?) or in the *third* person (Can you see that younger side of yourself, maybe sitting right next to you?). The therapist may seize on an opportune moment in which sadness, fear, or some other distress is present, and ask the patient whether they would be willing to enter it more deeply. The patient would then verbalize what they (as that younger part) are sensing, feeling and thinking. For example, Adam's therapist may say: 'Adam, can you close your eyes and be, for a moment, the part of you that feels most vulnerable or hurt right now? Be the emotional part of you, the part that's feeling much younger, that isn't necessarily rational, that doesn't try to be in control. How are you feeling right now?'

Alternatively, the therapist may ask the patient to observe or 'see' their Vulnerable Child and to relay back their observations rather than embody that child themselves. This can be helpful when the patient is less adept at expressing vulnerability in a direct way – for example, when the patient is quite new to therapy, does not feel safe enough to cry, or is likely to be overly flooded in this particular instance. 'I can feel your sadness right now ... can you close your eyes and see Little Adam sitting next to you? What does he look like? How do you feel towards him? Can you find out what's going on within him? How's he feeling? Is there anything he wants to tell us? What does he need?'

In either case (i.e., first or third person imagery), the focus is on having the patient – and the therapist – get a clearer and more poignant felt sense of the patient's core pain and of what they need in that moment. This tends to help patients develop compassion for their Vulnerable Child, as they hear its voice in a more raw, uncensored form, quite different from typical internal dialogues in which this voice tends to be masked as the patient flits between different modes. Indeed, patients often express unexpected thoughts and feelings in these moments, ones that may have been dismissed or overwhlemed by other modes. The patient has the chance to unpack feelings, and to learn which one (or ones) ring true at a 'gut' level. This clarity can be a goal in itself; as Greenberg (2015, p. 99) nicely put it, 'we cannot leave a place [or an emotion] until we have arrived there first'; imagery work of this sort helps us do that – that is, fully 'arrive' at that emotional place.

To illustrate this, consider Gabriella, a patient in her early thirties coming into a session saying she feels hopeless and weak. The therapist invites her to focus on this feeling and locate it within her body. Gabriella notes the feeling of being hunched over, just as she remembers herself as a child around the ages of 8–10. She locates the feeling of weakness to her spine – and, specifically, to her sense that she lacks a strong spine of her own and also feels she has no stable 'backing' – no support from family or friends.

Arriving at the deeper emotion and unpacking it can set the stage for reparative work in imagery, in which the therapist offers herself as a reparenting figure or summons Gabriella's own Healthy Adult. The therapist may speak directly to Gabriella's Vulnerable Child, asking her what she most needs and/or suggesting some actions – for example, to imagine that her stronger older self is standing right behind the weaker child, letting her lean back and feel supported. She could ask Gabriella to switch back and forth between the two parts – reporting what she is doing and seeing as the Healthy Adult, and then what she senses and feels as the Vulnerable Child, and so forth.

THERAPIST (T): Do you feel like you could come in and provide that 'back' for your younger self – for little Gabriella? ... Or would it be helpful if I did that too?

GABRIELLA (G): Yes, I think I need you. I can sort of imagine myself standing behind me ... but it would help if you are there too.

T: Of course! I think we can both have Little Gabriella's back. What do you think would help her the most?

G: I dunno. It feels really physical, this thing of being hunched over. Maybe I can put both hands on her back?

T: That sounds perfect. Give it a try ... try to actually see yourself doing that. ... How does it feel?

G: Really good, I feel we're really together, like I'm there for her.

T: And can we ask Little Gabriella what it's like for her?

G: She's liking it, it's comforting for her.

T: Could I hear it straight from her? Can you be Little Gabriella now, telling us what it feels like?

In this situation, the patient's Healthy Adult is active and attuned in meeting the child's needs in the image. In other situations, where the patient feels more unsure or inhibited, the therapist can offer some guidance or coaching to help them ease into their Healthy Adult role in the image. For example, in Gabriella's session described above, if the Healthy Adult proves unable at first to meet Little Gabriella's needs, the therapist might be called in to model a compassionate stance towards the Vulnerable Child as an intermediate step.

G: I dunno. It feels really physical, this thing of being hunched over. But I don't know what to do with it.

T: That's a start ... you're noticing that it's really physical for her. Can we try something? Maybe we can ask Little Gabriella what she needs?

G: Huh?

T: [speaking in a softer voice]: I'm speaking to you now, Little Gabriella; we're here together, your older and wiser self, together with me, and really want to know what can help now.

G: [responding spontaneously as the Vulnerable Child]: I really need a hug, or for you to stand behind me and prop me up ... I feel like a wet noodle.

T: [speaking in a regular voice, aimed at the emerging Healthy Adult]: Okay ... I think she can be our guide here, she's telling us what she most needs. Do you think you could try to do that?

The implementation of present-focused imagery of this sort tends to be relatively brief, and is typically aimed at accessing the Vulnerable Child, recruiting the Healthy Adult, and creating a productive dialogue between the two. However, present-focused imagery can also involve summoning other modes – including the angry or impulsive child, coping modes, or dysfunctional internal critics – as needed. For example, in the above case, Gabriella might be invited to recognise the Surrender Mode she typically slips into when feeling weak. To do so, she would be asked to turn her attention inward, to recognise the feelings and thoughts of this coping mode, to mentally visualise this mode's perspective and to speak from it.

T: I think we're hearing this side we've started to get to know – the Giving Up side, or Hopeless Gabriella. Can I ask you to take a minute and see what this side is feeling … and then speak from this side's perspective?

G: [after a pause]: Yeah …

T: [speaking in a slightly different tone, to mark the change]: So, I'm speaking to you, this Giving Up side, and I want to start by expressing my respect for you, my appreciation for the way you've been there helping and protecting Little Gabriella from what often felt like a much worse fate … from greater hurt or disappointment …

The therapist would then spend some time in imagery getting to know this mode and responding to it empathically, so that it could ultimately be persuaded to permit the patient's Healthy Adult to step in and lead the way towards providing new and different responses to her own Vulnerable Child or to external situations.

More broadly, present-day imagery can be used to help patients deepen their capacity to access and use their Healthy Adult mode. Through the imagery process, patients are offered the chance to 'own' naturally occurring dispositions or inclinations, as well as ones that are introduced or modelled by the therapist. These may take on the form of self-compassion, self-regulation, adaptive interpersonal communication, distress tolerance, and assertive confrontation of external figures or internal voices, to name but few.

Future-focused techniques

Another cluster of ImRs interventions are ones that are focused on future events or scenes. These involve imagery that helps the patient rehearse achieving a desired goal, prepare for a challenging situation (e.g., a date, a job interview, or a necessary confrontation), or develop healthy alternatives to risky or problematic behaviours (e.g., self-harm, suicide attempts, substance abuse, etc.).

At times, future-focused imagery can be used quite simply to allow a patient to train for a particular behaviour or rehearse a particular skill. As Kosslyn et al. (2001) noted, the same neural structures are used when one imagines a skill as when one is actually carrying out that skill. Thus, taking patients through the process of mentally simulating that difficult conversation they've been delaying, the physical activity they've been putting off, or the specific steps that will move them forward toward some important life goal, increases the likelihood that these will actually take place. Like all goal-related activities, such simulation tends to be more effective the more specific, realistic, and concrete the goals/behaviours/skills are. Importantly, as Beck (2011) as well as Hackmann et al. (2011) note, future-focused imagery actually aids in making goals become more specific.

For example, consider Sophie, a 50-year-old woman nearing completion of a course of therapy in which she has been dealing with a lifelong pattern of attempting to exert excessive control in anxiety-provoking situations. For instance, she tended to 'take over' when dining out with friends, dominating the process of ordering food and making others feel intruded upon. Sophie's therapist asked her to imagine an upcoming situation where her whole family would get together at a local restaurant in order to celebrate her husband's birthday. Because she had gained awareness of (and wanted to change) her customary response, the therapist asked her to experience and describe the whole scene in imagery[1] – from greeting her family members in the car park, through the seating and the food order, which is when she usually feels most anxious and tends to exert excessive control. The therapist asked Sophie to imagine herself in these moments, inviting other family members to order whatever items they choose without making any comments about these choices, and without providing directives for sharing the food or for splitting plates with anyone at the table. Instead of acting as she used to, she's invited to simply order her own entrees and continue conversing with the person next to her – or even to imagine herself saying out loud 'I'm not sure what to order; what should I get?' The objective of this exercise was to have Sophie enact the desired behavioural change – first in imagination, and then (as homework) at the actual upcoming family outing.

Some future-focused work (e.g., Sophie's rehearsal of the restaurant scene) is simple to implement and can result in behaviour change without much difficulty. However, many goals prove more difficult to attain and require a more involved approach. Within Young's 'imagery for pattern-breaking' (Young, Klosko & Weishaar, 2003, p. 146) the therapist guides her patient to imagine a desired but hard-to-carry-out behaviour (e.g., going to an office party; initiating a conversation with an attractive stranger). She would then ask the patient to carry out a dialogue between those schemas or modes that block the behaviour (e.g., a failure schema, an avoidant mode, an over-controller) on the one hand, and the patient's Healthy Adult, which encourages him to enter the situation or remain in it, on the other hand. The objective of this work is to help the patient build up the ability to overcome the schema-driven (or mode-driven) avoidance, and engage in the behaviours, even if they prove difficult.

Let us illustrate this idea by returning to Sophie's case. As we noted earlier, Sophie tends to become over-controlling when feeling stressed or anxious in social situations (i.e., when her Vulnerable Child and her Failure and Defectiveness schemas become activated). If this coping response is too strong, she may not be ready at first to embark on the behavioural rehearsal described above. Instead, the session might begin with imagery work aimed at overcoming the disruptive schemas or modes and strengthening the Healthy Adult mode. Following such work, once Sophie and her therapist have determined that the obstacles to more adaptive behaviours have been addressed, the session would ideally progress to the behavioural rehearsal stage.

Both the theory and the practice of pattern-breaking imagery are consistent with social–cognitive research on self-regulation, and with techniques that have been found effective for harder to pursue health-related goals or behaviours. There is strong evidence for the hypothesis that detailed mental simulation (i.e., imagery) of a desired outcome and of the steps involved in reaching the outcome are effective in evoking emotion and desire, motivating action and developing solutions towards multiple goals (for review, see Oettingen & Mayer, 2002; Oettingen & Reininger, 2016; Taylor, Pham, Rivkin & Armor, 1998). Importantly, this research points to a profound difference between simple 'positive fantasies' of desired outcomes, which can backfire, and effective imaginal simulation, which typically leads to more effective outcomes.

The key to effective imaginal simulation seems to be in combining two processes. The first process, referred to as *mental contrasting* (MC; e.g., Oettingen & Reininger, 2016), involves inviting the patient to juxtapose positive fantasies about the future with the possible realistic obstacles to these fantasies' realisation. The second process, referred to as *implementation intention* (II; e.g., Gollwitzer, 1999), involves encouraging the patient to consider specific behavioural steps they would take if they run into the obstacles identified through mental contrasting.

As the following case example illustrates, the processes of MC and II are easy to translate into Schema Therapy terms. David, a depressed and avoidant 35-year-old man, agreed in principle that enrolling in some art classes in a community centre would be in his best interest, but kept putting this off. To help this process along, his therapist (Anna) initiated an imagery exercise which started with vividly imagining the desired outcome (making a new friend or two; having a reason to leave the house on weekends). As David imagined taking part in the art class, Anna enquired whether he felt or noticed anything, and David noted feeling slightly energised by the camaraderie of sitting in front of an easel alongside other painters, and maybe chatting with them a bit. Anna then guided David to imagine performing the specific actions needed to attain this desired end-state (e.g., looking up the community centre's website; calling to enquire about class availability). Invariably, imagining these action steps led David to anticipate various external and internal obstacles. First, he imagined encountering an impatient or discourteous response from the centre's secretary, and felt unprepared to deal with it. Then he noted an emerging feeling of pessimism and deflation about the eventual outcome ('I won't enjoy the art class anyway').

Anna identified this feeling as an expression of David's Hopeless/Avoidant Protector and invited him to assume this coping mode in the image. She invited the Protector to state its concerns and qualms, and to speak about the anticipated obstacles. She responded empathically to these, and then asked the Protector to articulate its goals; as the Protector, David was able to say 'I'm just trying to save him the grief of being disappointed again'. This allowed Anna to continue with an empathic confrontation process, in which she encouraged the Protector to hold on to the emotional goal of protecting David, but to consider the benefits of doing so through other means – like that of permitting David to pursue the desired goal of enrolling in art classes.

Notably, this empathic confrontation can be carried out in one of several ways. If possible, Anna could have asked David's Healthy Adult to speak with the Hopeless Protector, while she listens and gives some pointers. Alternatively, she could have spoken to the Protector herself, modelling this role for the Healthy Adult mode. Finally, if no Healthy Adult mode is accessible at this time, Anna could have asked David for permission to enter the image and carry out the dialogue as a participant within the imagined scene, which would then be located in a particular time and place. Because of David's tenacious avoidance and high level of anxiety in this situation, this was the approach chosen here.

Anna explored with the Hopeless side other ways they, jointly, could protect David, and it agreed to step aside to try these out. Then, Anna again invited David to imagine the behavioural steps involved in making the desired change (i.e., phoning the community centre, having a conversation with the rude secretary, etc.). She also helped him formulate 'if–then' sentences in which he anticipated the re-emergence of obstacles (and, specifically, of the Protector) and came up with specific responses. For example, they collaboratively formed the following sentence, which felt right to David: '*If* I start feeling hopelessness and futility about pursuing art classes, *then I will* pull out my old paint palette and look at it, to remind myself of how much I actually enjoy these art classes'.

Summary, reflection and conclusions

The techniques reviewed in this chapter can be thought of as adaptations of classic past-focused ImRs. Thus, with some exceptions, using them involves adhering to the customary guidelines for imagery work. For example, just as in customary ImRs, safe place imagery may at times be warranted in current day ImRs in order to activate a sense of safety or emotional equanimity before or after the work on the main scene. Additionally, just as in past-focused ImRs, a therapist initiating current day ImRs would invite the patient to imagine the scene as vividly as possible in order to deepen the emotion experienced within it. To do so, the therapist would typically instruct the patient to adopt a first-person, present-tense perspective rather than a more removed outside observer's perspective. Also, as in past-focused ImRs, the therapist would be mindful of the timing and duration of current day experiential work, and allow sufficient time for processing this work both within the same session and in the subsequent one(s).

Beyond these general recommendations, some additional considerations merit special attention when implementing techniques that touch on current life issues. One is the need for special care when working in imagery on scenes that are close to the present, which may very easily (and, sometimes, too easily) translate into real-world action. The freedom afforded by imagery work often allows us (patients and therapists alike) to go quite far in expressing strong emotions and behaviours – even ones containing socially unacceptable reactions such as retaliation or revenge. As a general rule, this is not a cause for concern. Indeed, as Arntz et al. (2007) noted, ImRs has been found to actually *reduce* anger and to increase anger *control* (compared, for example, to simple prolonged exposure in the treatment of PTSD). Nonetheless, the temporal (and often physical) proximity of emotionally significant others – who may be present both in reality and in the imagery of rageful patients – warrants additional care.

For example, when conducting recent past-focused imagery work, a patient might bring up a confrontation with a co-worker or boss. In the course of imagery, the patient may connect with deep and difficult emotions, and may feel as if the best course of (imagined) action is to lash out or strike back at the person who had treated her unjustly. In reality, such behaviour could be ill-advised, unlawful, or even dangerous. This patient's therapist will need to ensure that the patient can distinguish between actions that are best left imagined and ones that are realistically in their best interest. One possible way of doing so would involve repeating the imagery twice: first, with the patient's Angry Child mode lashing out or retaliating, and then, once adequately debriefed, with the Healthy Adult taking over and rehearsing a more moderate response. Still, for patients who struggle with anger and impulsivity, it would be important to use a range of techniques in addition to imagery (e.g., time out, breathing techinques, safe venting, and mode dialogues) to help ensure that they act in their own best interest.

To summarise, the techniques discussed in this chapter enrich the toolbox of schema therapists and have the potential of enhancing mode awareness, facilitating schema healing, and advancing behavioural change. They are aimed at extending (rather than replacing) classic past-focused ImRs techniques, and have the potential to be particularly useful for goal setting, skill development, and problem solving. Additionally, they may serve as an entry point for introducing imagery techniques with some patients, who may at first balk at classic ImRs work with its inherent focus on painful aspects of their past. Finally, this type of imagery allows patients to try out and explore changes that often long eluded them, making their Vulnerable Child heard, their Healthy Adult stronger, and their coping modes understood. Through such work, patients can see and practice new possibilities in their relationships and their lives more generally, creating greater flexibility and opportunity.

Therapist tips

1. Current life imagery can raise awareness of (and differentiation between) modes, strengthen the patient's Healthy Adult mode (and particularly this mode's adaptive capacity to reparent the child modes), and rehearse behaviour change.

2. You might choose to use this approach as a first step in imagery work if your patient is reluctant to engage with historical material, or if the recent event is particularly distressing and requires rescripting.

3. As in other forms of imagery, when patients struggle to express vulnerability, therapists may ask them to observe or 'see' their Vulnerable Child and to relay their observations rather than embody that child themselves. This can give a clearer and more poignant felt sense of the patients' core pain and of what they need in that moment.

4. A major strength of using current- or future-focused imagery work is the ability to harness the power of mode work to affect behavioral change in present life in ways that echo recent recommendations from motivational psychology. In effect, the mode work taking place within imagery follows the logic of mental contrasting.

Note

1   As in other types of imagery, the therapist guides Sophie into the first person field perspective in the present tense: 'I'm going into the restaurant and I can see it's packed, I feel anxious …'

References

Arntz, A., Tiesema, M. & Kindt, M. (2007). Treatment of PTSD: A comparison of imaginal exposure with and without imagery rescripting. *Journal of Behavior Therapy and Experimental Psychiatry*, *38*(4), 345–370.

Beck, J.S. (2011). *Cognitive therapy for challenging problems: What to do when the basics don't work*. New York: Guilford Press.

Gollwitzer, P.M. (1999). Implementation intentions: Strong effects of simple plans. *American Psychologist*, *54*(7), 493–503.

Greenberg, L.S. (2015). *Emotion-focused therapy: Coaching patients to work through their feelings*, 2nd ed. Washington, DC: American Psychological Association.

Grossman, P., Niemann, L., Schmidt, S. & Walach, H. (2004). Mindfulness-based stress reduction and health benefits: A meta-analysis. *Journal of Psychosomatic Research*, *57*(1), 35–43.

Hackmann, A., Bennett-Levy, J. & Holmes, E.A. (2011). *Oxford guide to imagery in cognitive therapy*. Oxford: Oxford University Press.

Kosslyn, S.M., Ganis, G. & Thompson, W.L. (2001). Neural foundations of imagery. *Nature Reviews Neuroscience*, *2*(9), 635–642.

Oettingen, G. & Mayer, D. (2002). The motivating function of thinking about the future: expectations versus fantasies. *Journal of Personality and Social Psychology*, *83*(5), 1198–1212.

Oettingen, G. & Reininger, K.M. (2016). The power of prospection: mental contrasting and behavior change. *Social and Personality Psychology Compass*, *10*(11), 591–604.

Prinz, J.N., Bar-Kalifa, E., Rafaeli, E., Sened, H. & Lutz, W. (2019). Imagery-based treatment for test anxiety: A multiple-baseline open trial. *Journal of Affective Disorders*, *244*, 187–195.

Taylor, S.E., Pham, L.B., Rivkin, I.D. & Armor, D.A. (1998). Harnessing the imagination: Mental simulation, self-regulation, and coping. *American Psychologist, 53*(4), 429–439.

Watkins, J.G. (1971). The affect bridge: A hypnoanalytic technique. *International Journal of Clinical and Experimental Hypnosis, 19,* 21–27.

Weertman, A. & Arntz, A. (2007). Effectiveness of treatment of childhood memories in cognitive therapy for personality disorders: A controlled study contrasting methods focusing on the present and methods focusing on childhood memories. *Behaviour Research and Therapy, 45*(9), 2133–2143.

Young, J.E., Klosko, J.S. & Weishaar, M.E. (2003). *Schema therapy: A practitioner's guide.* New York: Guilford Press.

Part III

Creative methods using chair work, mode dialogues and play

9 Creative use of mode dialogues with the Vulnerable Child and Dysfunctional Critic modes

Joan Farrell and Ida Shaw

Introduction

This chapter describes the use of mode dialogues in Schema Therapy (ST) to provide corrective emotional experiences for the Vulnerable Child mode and to lessen the control of the Dysfunctional Critic modes. In ST, the Vulnerable Child mode is defined as the part of self that feels the pain of unmet core childhood needs (Young et al., 2003). The emotional experience of the Vulnerable Child mode may be primarily sad, fearful or lonely, accompanied by related childhood memories and physical sensations. The Dysfunctional Critic modes (also known as Dysfunctional Parent modes) are defined as the internalisation of negative experiences related to unmet childhood needs, which take the form primarily of negative messages about self or dysfunctional rules about needs and feelings (Young et al., 2003). In this chapter, we focus on two main types: Punitive, focusing on how rules are enforced, and Demanding, focusing on the standards and rules themselves, not their enforcement. The Dysfunctional Critic modes may be Punitive, Demanding, or could combine both elements.

Whether conducted in individual or group ST, creative use of mode dialogues can increase awareness of the effects of the dysfunctional modes on the Vulnerable Child mode and provide significant corrective emotional experiences for patients of any diagnosis. We describe the use of various types of individual and group mode dialogues which target the Vulnerable Child mode and the Dysfunctional Critic modes. Two caveats are necessary for this chapter: (1) ST mode dialogues are not the 'chair work' intervention of Gestalt psychotherapy. We incidentally use chairs as markers for the modes, but could just as easily have patients stand in positions. (2) We have replaced the word 'Parent' with Critic to more accurately describe the internalisation of messages derived from childhood experiences in which core needs were not met with a range of significant figures in addition to parents – for example, coaches, teachers, bullies. This broader label avoids triggering family loyalty responses in our patients that interfere with work to diminish these dysfunctional modes.

Standard mode dialogues

Mode dialogues are conversations between or among the various modes of a person. The standard version of this intervention was developed by Young (Young et al., 2003) for individual ST. In mode dialogues, a patient is asked to move into his or her various modes and to speak from that part. Example: when a patient in a session describes a situation in the present in which modes were triggered, he/she would be asked to connect with, and then verbally express, the Dysfunctional Critic modes related to the situation. He/she would next be asked to move to a second position to connect with the Healthy Adult mode and challenge the accuracy and helpfulness of the Critic mode. The therapist in this exercise might support, encourage, or even speak for the patient's Healthy Adult mode, dependent upon its strength (e.g., 'We don't want to hear any more from you, you are not helpful'). Frequently, a third step is to have the patient connect with the Vulnerable Child mode to express the needs present. The therapist may also speak for the Vulnerable Child mode (e.g., 'I'm scared, I need help'). Finally, the patient would move to the Healthy Adult mode and speak or act to meet the need expressed from the Vulnerable Child mode. The theory is that this exercise facilitates awareness of the maladaptive modes, their dysfunctional messages and interference with the needs of the Vulnerable Child mode being met. Like imagery work, it can provide the patient in the Vulnerable Child mode with a corrective emotional experience of having their need met. This corrective experience allows a new healthy message to be developed: for example, 'My needs are normal and I can meet them'. Preparatory work to use mode dialogues includes understanding of the mode concept, the ability to identify their modes, allow the experience of the mode and be able to express them verbally. Enough safety is needed in the therapy relationship for the patient to access their Vulnerable Child mode and have confidence that the therapist will be able to protect the Vulnerable Child mode from the Dysfunctional Critic modes. Early in the process of using mode dialogues, the patient may want the therapist to sit next to, or even in front of, them when the Dysfunctional critic mode is addressed. A safe place image or safety bubble can be used for additional protection (Farrell and Shaw, 2012).

Creative variants of mode dialogues

Making the modes feel more 'real': effigies to represent the Dysfunctional Critic mode

In response to patients' reports of feeling silly when asked to dialogue with an empty chair or telling us that the experience did not feel real, we created effigies of the modes (Farrell et al., 2014). Using a rectangular piece of muslin or other inexpensive fabric about 4' by 6', we create with the patient (or patients in group ST) a drawing of the Dysfunctional Critic mode with markers. Initial reluctance to participate dissolves when the therapist gets involved in the process. Across cultures, we find that patients do not draw their parents, but, rather, some form of monster or demon. This characterisation is useful as the figure does not look human, underlining the point that these modes are the selective internalisation of only the negative aspects of caregivers, not the whole person. The effigy is used as a canvas for patients to write their Dysfunctional Critic mode messages on. The therapist participates with at least one Dysfunctional Critic mode message. The messages written on the effigy become the script of the Dysfunctional Critic mode in the dialogue. In individual ST mode dialogues, the effigy is draped over a chair to add realism. In group ST, the effigy is is used as a mask for the person playing the Dysfunctional Critic mode in multiple mode dialogues so that the Dysfunctional Critic mode's 'energy' is removed with the mask after the end of the exercise, not left with the patient who played the role.

The Dysfunctional Critic mode effigies evoke a lot of emotion, fear, anger and sadness, which we find intensifies the corrective emotional experience of the mode dialogues. Having this concrete representation of the Dysfunctional Critic modes provides the opportunity to throw these out of the room in experiential work. After the dialogue ends, the effigy can be stamped on, torn apart or locked away in a filing cabinet. We keep it available for additional work, but out of sight. These actions demonstrate and underline the lack of real presence from the Dysfunctional Critic modes today and the role of choice in keeping the their messages alive.

Multiple mode dialogues

In group ST, multiple mode dialogues are a particularly powerful intervention for reducing the intensity or frequency of the Dysfunctional Critic modes. An entire group of healthy adults can be more powerfully challenging to critic modes than a patient who feels like a small child and their therapist. In group ST, there are additional patients to take the roles of the various modes of a single member instead of using empty chairs. Playing out the relationship among modes for an individual allows all group members to feel and see the roles of the various modes in relation to each other. In addition, members are asked to reflect on their experience in the various modes. The tangible experience of the collective strength of the group effectively combating and diminishing the power of the Dysfunctional Critic mode can have powerful effects.

We find that patients are more willing to engage in dialogues with others than with an empty chair and they report that it feels more 'real' to them. We avoid having either therapist play the Punitive Critic mode role and only do so if there is no other option. Because many personality disordered patients are at the concrete operational level of emotional development, they are more able to benefit from experiences that are tangible and concrete, as opposed to more abstract interventions.

The birth of the modes

We developed a multiple mode dialogue called the "birth of the modes" (Farrell et al., 2014), which demonstrates experientially the origin of the maladaptive modes and how they function in the present. Patients and therapists play the roles of modes, thus having both an experience of the mode they play and how it feels to interact with the other modes in a dialogue format. The group or individual patient develops short scripts for each mode. Patients are invited to represent the various mode groups. One group therapist plays the Healthy Adult mode and directs the action to make the point that the Healthy Adult mode is actually in charge of the modes actions. The other therapist plays the Good Parent part of the Healthy Adult mode, who is trying to reach the Vulnerable Child mode to protect, reassure and soothe him/her. Depending upon the size of your group, other patients take the roles of helpers to the therapists or are given specific observer roles. (See Farrell et al., 2014 for therapist scripts, more detailed instructions and diagrams of this exercise.)

We give the Dysfunctional Critic mode actors an effigy to cover themselves with when saying their script so that they are not seen as their role. Patients in the Dysfunctional Critic mode roles do not usually report difficulty playing it as it is familiar to them, but tell us that it can be painful when they see the effect on the Vulnerable Child mode. This experience helps to build compassion for the Vulnerable Child mode. Everyone has a role, even if it is an observational one with a specific task so that they stay connected to the group.

We begin with a demonstration of the steps in which the modes develop:

1. Core childhood needs are not met, early maladaptive schemas form and the Vulnerable Child mode experiences pain, anxiety and suffering. The Vulnerable Child mode says his/her lines about their core needs and feelings – there is no response.
2. The Angry Child mode develops as an innate response to needs going unmet. The Angry Child mode says his/her lines – there is no response
3. The child internalises the negative reaction of significant others to his/her needs, abuse or neglect, negative evaluations and interpretations of the meaning of needs not being met (e.g., 'I am too needy', 'my needs are wrong', 'I don't matter') leading to the development of the Dysfunctional Critic modes. The Vulnerable Child mode, Angry Child mode and Dysfunctional Critic modes all say their lines at once.
4. To survive needs not being met, Maladaptive Coping modes develop. Your group will choose one variant. Now the Maladaptive Coping modess say their lines at the same time as the rest.

After each step in the dialogue, the Vulnerable Child mode is asked whether his/her needs are met. When all of the modes speak at once, no one is heard, and none of the Vulnerable Child mode's needs are met. The Healthy Adult mode and the Good Parent are not heard over the din. Let the ensuing chaos go on for a few minutes then stop the action and discuss what happened. Discussion focuses on the following questions:

1. Was the Vulnerable Child mode's need met?
2. Was the Angry Child mode heard?
3. How did the Maladaptive Coping modes affect the Vulnerable Child mode?
4. Was the Good Parent able to reach the Vulnerable Child mode?

The answer to all of the questions is 'no'. The point is made that this is how the modes came to be and this is how they operate now. The result today is that the Vulnerable Child mode's needs are not met, and the healthy modes cannot reach the Vulnerable Child mode.

The multiple mode dialogue then continues:

5. The Healthy Adult mode takes the effigy from the Dysfunctional Critic modes saying, 'You are not active now – you belong to the past. However, you left these negative messages behind.' [The Dysfunctional Critic modes move out of the scene, and the effigy is left behind on the floor.]
6. The Healthy Adult mode explains to the Maladaptive Coping modes that they did an excellent job of surviving in childhood, but now, with the power of the Dysfunctional Critic modes diminished, they don't have to work so hard and they're now keeping the therapists and safe group members away from helping the Vulnerable Child mode and Angry Child mode. They move off to the side with the understanding that they will be available for emergencies.
7. Now the Vulnerable Child mode, Angry Child mode and Good Parent say their script lines. The Good Parent moves closer and begins a dialogue with the Angry Child mode, listening, validating the anger and encouraging venting.
8. When the Angry Child mode feels heard, the Good Parent moves to the Vulnerable Child mode. The Healthy Adult mode asks all the patients to connect with their Vulnerable Child mode to take in what the Good Parent is going to say. The Good Parent reassures and comforts the Vulnerable Child mode, validates his/her fear and mistrust, identifies needs and meets them in limited reparenting.

Our observation is that the multiple mode dialogue has powerful effects on patients. It allows patients to experience the original role of the various modes, their impact on their present day life and how the maladaptive modes limit their ability to make use of ST. They often remark that now they 'get' some of the modes that they had not understood previously. They experience the input of the Good Parent, providing a corrective emotional experience for their Vulnerable Child mode. This exercise can be adapted to individual work by using voice recordings of the various modes, with the patient playing the Vulnerable Child mode.

Historical multiple mode dialogues

In this type of mode dialogues, the focus begins with a pivotal childhood experience related to a patient's schemas. The event is described, and the modes involved are identified. Other patients are assigned or select the various modes to play, and scripts for them are developed. The protagonist patient plays their Healthy Adult mode with coaching from one of the therapists. The dialogue is played out as it did in the patient's childhood. The pros and cons of the various modes are discussed as they relate to the protagonist's needs being met. The dialogue is played out again, but this time the protagonist, as Healthy Adult mode, interacts with each of the modes to meet the child mode needs, move aside the Maladaptive Coping modes and limit the Dysfunctional Critic modes. The goal of the Healthy Adult mode is to meet the Vulnerable Child mode's needs. This dialogue ends with the protagonist–patient sitting in the centre, and each of the others walks up to him/her, places a hand on his/her shoulder and gives the Vulnerable Child mode a Good Parent message.

A shortened version focuses on a dialogue between a protagonist–patient (Cl.1) in their Healthy Adult mode and their Dysfunctional Critic mode, played by another patient (Cl.2) using the effigy as a mask. This dialogue is carefully arranged so that all patients feel safe. Cl.1 is asked what support they want from the therapist, ranging from the Healthy Adult mode taking that mode role to standing by. Cl.1 is also asked what support they want from other group members. Supported and protagonist Healthy Adult mode are arranged at the distance they want from Cl.2. Cl.2 is also given the support of one or two group members, not for strengthening the Dysfunctional Critic mode, but to support emotionally the Cl.2 as needed. Other group members are assigned roles as observers with specific tasks (e.g., to write down healthy lines from the Healthy Adult mode (Cl.1)).

Example

Karen, in a group session, asked if she could banish her Punitive Critic mode, whom she identified as her mother. With the group's Punitive Critic mode effigy in place, another patient played her Punitive Critic mode with the support of a second group member. We established what support Karen wanted and arranged another patient on each side of her for support and coaching. Karen did a strong job from her Good Parent of telling her Punitive Critic mode (mother) that she was wrong to blame her for the childhood abuse of her step-father, that she should have protected her, that she no longer needed her, etc. At the end of this dialogue, the therapist took the effigy away from the patient playing the Punitive Critic mode and handed it to Karen to do with it as she liked. Karen wadded it up and threw it out of the group room door. She appeared unburdened, and Joan commented on this. Karen said that for the first time she felt free of her 'mean mother'. She also said that for the first time she felt that the sexual abuse she experienced when aged 12 was not her fault.

An after effect of this mode dialogue was that Karen was no longer plagued by the voice she had been hearing that berated and blamed her. She had not previously identified this as her mother's voice, but after the group dialogue she became aware of this and, in a flash of insight, Karen and the group saw that getting rid of the Punitive Critic mode had eliminated that voice. Her 'mean mother' voice had not returned when we last checked nine months later. This example demonstrates the impact on mode change that the experiential work of ST can have.

Multiple mode dialogues in individual ST

A potential limit to the range of mode dialogues to be used in individual ST is our reluctance, as therapists, to ever play a patient's Dysfunctional Critic mode. In limited reparenting, we work to be seen as the Good Parent, so playing the Dysfunctional Critic has the potential to be too confusing for patients when in the child modes. There may be an occasion when we would play the Demanding Critic, but not the Punitive Critic. A way to get around this limitation is to have the patient record their Dysfunctional Critic mode, ideally in video (for example, on their phone) and place it in the position designated for the Dysfunctional Critic and play the recording. The patient can then have the experience of being in the Vulnerable Child mode and hearing their Dysfunctional Critic mode in their voice. This same approach can be extended to allow for the other mode categories to be present via additional recordings of a patient in those modes. It can be particularly useful to record a patient in their Vulnerable Child mode, then play the recording to them when they are in their Dysfunctional Critic mode. Seeing their Vulnerable Child mode in this way can also affect their Healthy Adult mode and encourage their protection and combating the Dysfunctional Critic modes.

Vicarious learning possibilities in multiple mode dialogues

Many patients, in particular those who were abused, are terrified of their Dysfunctional Critic mode, but desperately need to reduce the power of this mode in their adult life. Multiple mode dialogues can set up progressive vicarious learning opportunities to get around what can be paralysing fear. A patient with an underdeveloped Healthy Adult mode too afraid to confront her still powerful internalised Dysfunctional Critic mode even symbolically can start the mode dialogues process by just observing a dialogue like the one described in the example of Karen, above. Depending upon their fear, patients can position themselves behind the therapist for safety, be part of the group supporting the patient in the Healthy Adult mode, or they can stand directly with the patient in the Healthy Adult mode role. While observing, the patient should be in whatever degree of safety she needs – for example, a safety bubble, covered up, holding co-therapist or other member's hand, etc. In a group, the experience of collective strength effectively combating and eventually expelling the Dysfunctional Critic mode has potent effects in diminishing the intensity and power of this mode. We have seen patients begin in fear, take in the group's strength and, in the same session, move to confronting their Dysfunctional Critic mode in a dialogue from their Healthy Adult mode. The same can be true in individual work, as the therapist can join in to support the client and lend strength.

Vicarious learning to increase awareness of the Punitive Critic mode

One of our patients was very resistant to the idea of having a Dysfunctional Critic mode at all, despite horrific abuse by her adoptive parents. Her coping style was to minimise negative childhood experiences, keep others away with an Angry Protector mode and avoid any contact with her Vulnerable Child mode. The group did a mode dialogue in which another patient represented her Punitive Critic mode and Joan played the Good Parent defending the Vulnerable Child mode. After a short, intense interaction, Joan said, 'It is time for you to leave, you old bitch. Get out of here and leave Diana alone!' (this language and approach were appropriate for the patient's experience and the severe abuse from her adoptive mother). The rest of the group applauded, and the patient playing her Punitive Critic mode nodded, smiling. Ida asked her, 'What did you like best of what Joan said in your defence?' Jane, who had been sitting at the edge of her chair while the dialogue was going on, jumped in immediately. 'I loved it when you said, "get out of here you old bitch".' She followed this with talking about how she wished she could do that with her mother but was afraid to. Diana said, 'I can understand that; I was scared at first. I liked everything Joan said to her, and the "old bitch" was the best because that is really what they are. I am sick of living with her in my head; I want her out for good.' As the session continued, Jane shared some more information about her childhood abuse that neither the group nor the therapists had heard before and was able to acknowledge the existence of her Punitive Critic mode.

Vicarious learning 2: a patient observes a historical multiple mode dialogue of her life

Example

Sara, a very avoidant patient with alcohol dependence, volunteered in a discussion of parent messages that she had heard 'you will never be happy'.

She had a childhood of sexual abuse and extreme neglect and, consequently, was not a very happy child. Instead of seeing this as an indication that something was amiss, her mother attributed the unhappiness to her. Sarah was willing to allow other group members and therapists to play her modes in a dialogue between her Punitive Critic mode and the Good Parent of her Healthy Adult mode, but did not feel able to play any of the modes herself. She wanted to sit with a peer on each side of her away from the dialogue during it. The therapist, as Good Parent, said many positive things about Sara and explained to the Punitive Critic mode (her mother was prominent here) that it was a problem if she was not happy now – something was wrong, her needs weren't being met, and she deserved to be happy in the future. She told the Critic that she was doing a terrible job of protecting and nurturing Sara. When the Critic complained about what the Good Parent was saying, the Good Parent made her leave and told her not to send this poison to Sara.

At the end of the dialogue, Sara looked very affected and said, with much emotion, 'I don't know where I would be or how I would feel today if I had heard those Good Parent messages growing up.'

Responses like Sara's suggest the therapeutic effects of even observing mode dialogues.

A next step could be a version of the historical multiple mode dialogues previously described with the adaptation that the event comes from the life of a patient who observes rather than playing the Healthy Adult mode. The observer-patient can take in the effects of the limit setting of his/her peers playing the Healthy Adult mode and their encouragement and comfort for his/her Vulnerable Child mode.

Vicarious learning through mode dialogues in individual ST

Patients with severe personality disorders or complex trauma often have a very fearful Vulnerable Child mode, strong Maladaptive Coping modes and underdeveloped Healthy Adult modes with little accessible Good Parent influence. They have difficulty connecting with their Vulnerable Child mode or Healthy Adult mode using mode dialogues. We have found that opportunities for vicarious learning from the position of an observer can help them to begin this process of mode change work.

Vicarious learning opportunities in individual ST can be constructed by the therapist initially playing the patient's modes. Young (2003) includes this option in standard mode dialogues, and we have expanded upon it. With the abused or fearful Vulnerable Child mode, the therapist may need to provide physical distance and protection from the Dysfunctional Critic modes. When a patient feels they cannot access their Vulnerable Child mode or they reject this part and have no compassion for it, or they are too fearful of their Dysfunctional Critic mode to have a dialogue with it, we set up a dialogue in which the therapist plays the patient's Vulnerable Child mode.

Example of "Tough Susie"

Susie is a patient with borderline personality disorder who has a history of severe abuse, little awareness of her Vulnerable Child mode and robust Angry Protector and Bully Attack Coping modes. She was very adept at playing her Punitive Critic mode and has a weak Healthy Adult mode. I decided to try to reach her Vulnerable Child mode by playing that mode in a dialogue with her speaking from her Punitive Critic mode.

THERAPIST AS VULNERABLE CHILD MODE: I am so scared, you are so mean, and there is no one here to talk to.

SUSIE AS PUNITIVE CRITIC MODE: Stop whining, shut up you little brat.

THERAPIST-VULNERABLE CHILD MODE: [making crying noises and moans]: I'm just a little girl, I didn't do anything wrong, I can't help it that you don't like me.

SUSIE-PUNITIVE CRITIC MODE: I don't feel right saying these things to you. You were probably a good little girl, not like me.

At this point, the therapist stops the action to discuss how Susie was a normal little girl just like the Vulnerable Child mode she was playing, and Susie deserves compassion and support also. She asks Susie to change position to the Good Parent (part of Healthy Adult mode) and talk to the therapist as Vulnerable Child mode.

SUSIE-GOOD PARENT: I don't know what to do with her. She is too sad. I don't like this.

THERAPIST: Let me come and join you from my Good Parent and talk to Little Susie. Susie, you are a lovely little girl, let me rock you and protect you. I will be here for you – you didn't do anything wrong. You are a healthy little girl with regular needs – you are too young to take care of yourself.

SUSIE: I like what you are saying, I never heard anything like that as a kid. Can I take the Vulnerable Child mode chair for a minute – will you say that stuff again to me?

Experiencing the therapist playing Little Susie increased Susie's awareness of and compassion for that part of herself. In essence, she felt compassion for the therapist in the Vulnerable Child mode role and transferred this to her own Vulnerable Child mode. She also began to develop Good Parent skills to care for her Vulnerable Child mode.

Mode dialogue that includes a task

Sometimes, patients have the idea that the Dysfunctional Critic modes and even punishment are necessary or they would not accomplish anything, as this is what they were told growing up. In this case, we need to demonstrate the effects of the Dysfunctional Critic mode in an experiential way through a modified mode dialogue. This is one time when the therapist plays the Dysfunctional Critic mode briefly. This exercise is also used in group ST. We tell the patient that we will alternate playing the Dysfunctional Critic mode and the Good Parent of the Healthy Adult mode just to explore how dialogues with each affect their performance on a simple task. The task is to balance a wooden dowel rod on the palm of one's hand. We use a dowel that is wide enough that the task can be accomplished, but is somewhat difficult. First, we play the Dysfunctional Critic mode and berate the patient and predict that they cannot accomplish the task while they are attempting it. Inevitably, they do not succeed. They report that all they could hear was the Dysfunctional Critic mode and it was too distracting. They also say that they think the task is impossible. Next, we ask them to repeat the task, and we take the role of the Good Parent. We encourage them that they are doing well, say we know they can do it, etc. They often can and, if so, we praise them. If they cannot do it, we give them more tries until they succeed or we tell them how close they were, how we know they just need practice as anyone would, etc. Of course, the Good Parent dialogue feels much better and is more effective in increasing their motivation to keep trying and to succeed. We discuss the application of this experience to their view of the function of the Dysfunctional Critic mode.

Summary

We have adapted the standard format to meet the needs of patients with weak Vulnerable Child or strong Dysfunctional Critic modes, added mode effigies to make the dialogue feel more real and developed multiple mode dialogues for group ST. As with other experiential interventions, it is essential to have the demands and pace match the patient's ability to feel safe and connected to you. Flexibility regarding who plays the mode roles can produce smaller and more manageable steps for the patient to take.

The standard mode dialogue developed by Young can be broadened into multiple mode dialogues for group ST. Multiple mode dialogues allow patients to experience a variety of modes in action and to begin this work by observing others play their modes. This use of vicarious learning can have powerful effects on change in attitude for the Vulnerable Child mode and a different understanding of the drawbacks of the Dysfunctional Critic mode. In individual ST, a form of vicarious learning can be implemented, with the therapist playing different modes of the patient.

Use of an effigy to represent the Dysfunctional Critic mode can make dialogues in individual ST feel more real and believable, and the effigy can act as a mask for the patient playing the Dysfunctional Critic mode in group ST dialogues. The therapist staying attuned to the patient and flexible and creative in implementing mode dialogues lead to furthering the goals of ST to reach and heal the Vulnerable Child mode and to diminish the power of the Dysfunctional Critic mode.

Therapist tips

1. Be sure to check patients' readiness, safety and connection to do Vulnerable Child mode or Dysfunctional Critic mode work and safety before leaving the session. Create contingency safety plans if they have safety concerns. Finish the session with a return to the Safe Place image or Safety Bubble that includes the instruction that the Dysfunctional Critic modes are safely locked away.
2. Allow for steps in confronting the Dysfunctional Critic modes that match the strength of the patient's Healthy Adult mode. Early on, add your Good Parent support to the Healthy Adult mode.
3. Do not play the Punitive Critic mode. You can always use a recording of the patient in that mode. Be flexible with other modes it may be helpful for you to play (e.g., Vulnerable Child mode).
4. Anchor the experiential aspects of the work with some behavioural pattern breaking – for example, flashcard reminder of the experience, Good Parent statements.
5. In the group multiple mode dialogues, give everyone a role. Include in your instructions a reminder for patients to reflect on what they can learn from their experience in another's mode and to take in for their Vulnerable Child mode anything the Good Parent says in the exercise.
6. Allow patients to move out of fear at their own pace by identifying manageable steps for them to take in constructing mode dialogues. Consider the possibility of setting up vicarious learning experiences at the beginning of ST.

References

Farrell, J.M., Reiss, N. and Shaw, I.A. (2014) *The Schema Therapy Clinician's Guide: A Complete Resource for Building and Delivering Individual, Group and Integrated Schema Mode Treatment Programs.* Oxford: Wiley-Blackwell.

Farrell, J.M. and Shaw, I.A. (2012). *Group Schema Therapy for Borderline Personality Disorder: A Step-By-Step Treatment Manual with Patient Workbook.* Oxford: Wiley-Blackwell.

Young, J. E., Klosko, J. S. and Weishaar, M.E. (2003) *Schema Therapy: A Practitioner's Guide.* New York: Guilford Press.

10 Spontaneity and play in Schema Therapy

Ida Shaw

The importance of play

Much has been written about the importance of play in childhood and how it contributes to a child's development. In Schema Therapy, play is a powerful tool and aspect of limited reparenting that helps abused and emotionally deprived patient break through the blocks of mistrust and fear by providing safe experiences where they can feel something other than emotional pain and learn to trust (Lockwood & Shaw, 2012). Many skills are acquired through play, which are vital to one's mental and psychological health. Play is 'work' in the sense of the developmental role it has. It has many important functions: it challenges us to be creative, in it we learn to be spontaneous, it teaches us to problem solve, and we learn in it to communicate wants and needs. These are all important life skills. Wadley (n.d.) summarises it well in the following extract from her poem, 'Just Playing':

> When you ask me what I've done in school today,
> And I say, 'I Just Played.'
> Please don't misunderstand me.
> For, you see, I am learning as I play.
> I'm learning to enjoy and be successful in my work,
> I'm preparing for tomorrow.
> Today, I'm a child and my work is play.

The implications of play deprivation are substantial, because play is essential to the social, emotional, cognitive and physical well-being of children, beginning in early childhood. Even before the United Nations High Commission for Human Rights cited play as a right of every child, philosophers and psychologists, such as Plato, Piaget and Friedrich Froebel, recognised the importance of play in healthy child development (Milteer & Ginsburg, 2012). Typically, our patient have not had a childhood environment that supported them being happy or playful. This may be due to neglect, an impoverished emotional environment, or one in which achievement and work are prioritised and play is identified as frivolous and without purpose. These environments can lead to adults who do not know what they enjoy doing or do not take time for pleasure and may not have developed any hobbies or recreational activities. Play is also an opportunity to develop and explore children's creative side. Play is our earliest experience of connecting, negotiating, meeting, and forming friendships with, others. When play is prohibited, or underdeveloped, people miss out on this foundation developmental experience.

Play and stage of development

Parten was the first to describe the importance of play to the developmental stages of childhood. She states that children's play changes as they develop, going through six distinct stages that generally, but not always, correspond to children's ages. These stages also depend on mood and social setting. They are, in order of development: unoccupied play (0–2 – this is an important setting stage for future play exploration and development); solitary play (2–3 – solitary play is common at a young age because cognitive, physical and social skills have yet to fully develop. This type of play is important because it teaches children how to entertain themselves); onlooker play (common at 2.5–3.5, occurs at any age); parallel play (common at 2.5–3.5 – parallel play is important as a transitory stage for the development of social maturity, which is key to later stages of play); associative play (this type of play typically begins around ages 3 or 4, extending into the pre-school age. This is an important stage of play because it develops necessary skills such as cooperation, problem solving and language development); and cooperative play (late pre-school period, between the ages of four and six, bringing together into action all the skills learned across previous stages, giving the child the necessary skills for social and group interactions). The difficulties our adult patients have with including play in their lives are most likely because of missed or incomplete experiences in these stages of play during childhood, which result in developmental gaps. These cognitive and emotional gaps can be remediated in psychotherapy by introducing the importance of play, and then engaging in play with the therapist in sessions. Adult patients who have little experience with play from childhood have difficulty being playful. Without play, our joy is limited.

Play, by definition, should be fun, but for many adult patients, even the idea of play can be anxiety producing. Early maladaptive schemas (EMSs), core beliefs and coping styles can be triggered when we invite patients to play. For example, we can hear the Punitive Critic mode in patient statements such as: 'This is stupid, it's a waste of time', or 'I don't deserve to have fun and besides play is for babies'. They roll their eyes at others, shake their head with a look of disgust or make disapproving comments such as 'You are acting very immature, if you could see how silly you look you wouldn't be doing that'. Some patients tell us that initially they were afraid of engaging in playful activities because they feared others would see that they didn't know how to play and then they would be judged and feel like a failure, adding to feelings of defectiveness. It is imperative to discuss the importance and value of play with the group, confront and work through the EMSs involved and encourage and celebrate their growth in discovering the joy and benefits of play. For most patients, this conversation diminishes Punitive Critic mode interference, as play also has much intrinsic appeal to all of us. For some, there is not enough freedom from the Dysfunctional Critic modes to allow their participation in play for months. Patience, acceptance of where they are and suggesting that they try to imagine (from their safe place) participating without their Dysfunctional Critic yelling at them.

Accessing the joy of the Happy Child mode can shatter patients' belief that they are 'all bad', the Defectiveness/Shame schema. Play is an enjoyable experience for both the therapist and the patient because it is a safe way to attend to the needs of the Vulnerable Child, the Angry Child and the Happy Child. When we connect to our Happy Child mode, we feel versions of being loved, contented, connected, satisfied, fulfilled, protected, praised, worthwhile, nurtured, guided, understood, validated, self-confident, competent, appropriately autonomous or self-reliant, safe, resilient, strong, in control, adaptable, optimistic and spontaneous. If we are in this mode, our core emotional needs are currently met. Young labeled this mode the Contented Child (Young, Klosko and Weishaar, 2003), but we prefer to focus on the playful and joyous aspects of this mode, so refer to it as Happy Child mode. Learning more about and developing the Happy Child mode will give your Healthy Adult a needed sense of play and fun.

A central aim of play in Schema Therapy is the amplification of positive affect to evoke the Happy Child mode. Play encompasses infinite variability. The form the play takes and its content, rather than being free-form and open-ended, is determined by the patient's needs. Play in a session could end up being free-form and open-ended if the patient's need is for freedom and spontaneity. Alternatively, based on attachment needs, it may be about protection, warmth, love, mutuality and authenticity or about feeling competence (e.g., the example of building a dolls' house). A secondary goal is bypassing maladaptive coping modes (e.g., the Detached Protector mode). Play can often get through the coping modes more quickly than working directly with these modes. However, it will almost always lead to a Maladaptive Coping mode or Maladaptive Critic mode being triggered. Consequently, it is important to watch for this and/or to directly check in on the mode triggered.

Examples of bringing play into the Schema Therapy session

Lego

Playing with Lego in therapy sessions was a breakthrough for my 19-year-old patient with severe depression. I was running late and did not have time to pick up the Lego from the previous session. As soon as Danny came into the room and saw the Lego on the table, his face lit up with excitement, I noticed a positive shift in his energy, his eyes were shining and the beginning of a smile was present. Once he sat down, however, he reverted to his withdrawn, defeated, no eye contact, non-communicative self. I quickly asked if he ever played with Lego before and again his face lit up and the smile returned. He replied that he had. I asked, 'Would you show me what you can make with the Lego?' His smile grew even wider and, without further prompting, he made a remarkable train, caboose and tracks. What was most exciting was that while playing with the Lego, he started talking and sharing things and even made occasional eye contact with me. After my genuine praise of his creation, he sat back and for the rest of the session talked of his love of Lego, the things he could create and how good he felt when he was building them. He spoke of the pain when he was 12 years old, and his mother threw away all his toys, including his Lego, saying he was 'too old for toys'. This session was pivotal in building trust, safety and connection. For the next few months he would begin each session creating something new with the Lego while sharing things about his week. After ten minutes of 'Lego play' he would move into the therapy work relaxed and present. I came to see this as his way to reconnect with me, regulate his initial anxiety and be present. We came to refer to this process as 'landing'. One day he came into the office excited and proud, sharing that he had bought a Lego set. When he said, 'I can now recreate the feelings of happiness that I experience here, at home.' Making room for play in the therapy sessions contributed to the healing of his Vulnerable Child mode, and in the strengthening of his Healthy Adult. At his last session, Danny gave me an amazing cardinal he made from Lego, and said that he was 'now free to soar and enjoy life'.

Finger puppets for all ages

I use finger puppets with children and adolescents to explain the mode model. They have fun picking out puppets that represent their different sides. For example, eight-year-old Billy picked, Sad Billy (Vulnerable Child), or Shut Down Willy (Detached Protector), Wise William (Healthy mode), Punishing Bill (Critic mode) and Happy Billy (Happy Child). Using the puppets with Billy was an effective way to work with his modes to address feeling and needs.

Twelve-year-old Christine was able to quickly pick out her sides/parts. First, she grabbed the queen puppet and said, 'This is my "Diva mode", I walk and talk like a movie star and want lots of compliments' (self-aggrandising Coping mode). Next, she chose the girl pirate puppet, declaring, 'This is my "Mean Mad Missy" part [Angry Child]. I yell and scream because things are not fair, and then my mum yells and says "Go to your room Missy". This is my "Sad and Lonely Christine" [the fluffy baby lion cub puppet]. I feel scared and alone sometimes', (Vulnerable Child mode). She chose the dragon puppet for her Dysfunctional Critic mode, and named it

'Be Better or Else'. For the Happy Child mode she chose the little frog puppet, because it jumps with excitement. And for her Wise Mind Healthy mode, she picked the owl. During one of the family sessions, she showed her parents how using the puppets helped her identify her feelings and needs, and told them about what she still needed help with, especially if she got stuck. After her presentation, her dad picked up three puppets, her girl pirate, a boy pirate and the dad puppet and said, 'When you show me this side of you, I get into my pirate and yell and scream louder but what I really need to do is get into this, the dad puppet, that can help you, not yell at you.' Christine was listening and watching her dad very intently, and when he had finished said, 'Wow! You have parts too. What about you mum, come and show me your sides.' Her mother called me a few nights later to tell me how pleased she was that Christine had a new way to talk to them about her feelings and needs and that she asked for help when she was angry, but, most of all, her mother saw her as being happy again.

Playful regulating imagery: the backpack

Patients often come into the session looking as if they are carrying the world on their shoulders: their concerns, worries, feelings of hopelessness, helplessness and frustration. After the initial greeting, I ask the patient what their favourite colour is. Then I ask them to close their eyes or look down and get an image of just the colour. (For many patients, their favourite colour gives them a sense of safety and peace). Then I say, 'Imagine that I am giving you a brand-new backpack in your favourite colour. Look at all the different sized compartments it has. Now fill it up with all the concerns, worries, feelings and frustrations that you have been carrying around all week. You need a break from all of this. Keep filling the backpack. Feel the weight of your backpack, what a burden it is. Put your filled backpack under your chair and take a deep breath. Feel the release of tension when that load is removed. Now take another deep breath and come back to the room.'

Responses from doing this exercise are frequently, 'I feel lighter, relaxed', 'exhausted, quiet and calm', 'whole, comfortable', 'scared, unsure', 'pain-free, hopeful', etc. The overall goal here is to reinforce the Good Parent message that they do not always have to be working on heavy duty issues, but they need to have activities that will balance their pain. They will need guidance and strategies on slowing down, taking a few breaths, and ways to reconnect to the Healthy Adult mode that will support them in taking a break, even to engage in a playful activity, to re-energise and experience more than pain. Once balance is restored, you can take one thing out of the backpack and explore the feelings and needs connected to the item you selected. With the help from your Healthy Adult mode, you can then focus on techniques or strategies to validate your feelings and healthy ways to get your needs meet.

'Journey Through the Modes Valley' game

Board games, card games, sports, hobbies, travel, reading, puppets, colouring, the list is endless, and all can be used to reach and heal the Vulnerable Child mode and strengthen the Healthy Adult mode A new board game for children by Galimzyanova, Kasyanik and Romanova (2019), 'Journey Through the Modes Valley', brings play into Schema Therapy education. In the game, one may land on the 'Desert of Detachment' or the 'Cave of Self-Criticism', or learn ways to get unstuck in the 'Volcano of Anger'. She has woven the concepts, theory and goals of Schema Therapy in a relatable and effective way in this board game that is fun, but also educates children about feelings, needs, modes, schemas and choices. An adult version of this game is in progress.

Play in supervision: the ugly, scaly, scary, black dragon

When doing supervision on Skype with new supervisees, it is not uncommon to hear their Punitive or Demanding Critic mode when they describe their patient session. 'I should have done this or said something differently. I did it all wrong, I screwed up here, I'm afraid that I cannot do Schema Therapy', etc. I gently point out that their critic is harsh and demanding and getting stuck in this mode can interfere with their connection to the patient and being present. Sometimes words or explanations are not enough to address this stuckness. In these situations, I pull out my large black dragon hand puppet. The dragon has a wing span of three feet, a large mouth with fanged teeth and a protruding, pronged, fiery red tongue, and the entire body is covered in scales that end at its thick pointed tail. When a supervisee flips into their critic mode, I put on the puppet and fill the screen with the black ugly, scaly, scary dragon. This evokes many different reactions from the supervisees: nervous laughter, screams and looks of fear or disgust. Over time they smile at seeing the dragon and make comments such as 'It is so ugly it is cute'. Adding this visual element of play, as well as playful gestures, or light humour, helps them be aware of their Demanding and/or Punitive Critic being triggered and eventually works to lessen it (Farrell & Shaw, 2018).

Examples of play activities for Schema Therapy groups

The face game

Each group member is given a balloon to blow up and soft felt pens. They are instructed to draw a face on the balloon showing how they feel. Before they name how they feel, the other group members try to guess. This is a fun and safe way to begin talking about feelings, why we have them and how we can meet the needs underneath them.

Building a safe house

After a group discussion on ways to take care of the Vulnerable Child mode, one group member told the group that she had an image of a safe house filled with love that she takes her little child to. Several members really liked the idea of a safe house and commented on how nice it would be to have such a place. 'We could all build one in our imagination then share how we decorate it', chimed one. 'Hey, why don't we build a dolls' house together and call it our safe house', said another. This idea turned into the actual building of a dolls' house and was a wonderful learning experience for everyone. The women learned how to work together, use tools, follow a blueprint, dealt with design issues, learned to deal with likes and dislikes, delegated jobs such as sanding and painting and worked out which room they would decorate. They learned how to work within a budget, but, best of all, they shared laughter, joy and a sense of pride and mastery at their contribution to the building of 'the safe house'.

Bringing play into a locked inpatient hospital unit: the Olympics

One evening on the locked inpatient unit where we had a Schema Therapy programme for patients with borderline personality disorder, the patients were complaining about being bored because nothing was on television but the Olympics. I said, 'Let's have our own Olympics.' Soon the excitement spread, ideas were born and plans were made to put on our own games for the viewing audience (the nursing staff). After working together for two evenings constructing banners, flags and costumes, we were ready to start with our opening ceremony. One therapist acted as the master of ceremonies announcing each country (represented by a patient) as they entered the hall. 'Here comes Canada, wearing a beautiful moose hat, waving her maple leaf flag; next is Italy, sporting a lovely jacket in white, orange and green, wait a minute, what is that on her head – yes, it's a plate of spaghetti.' Each country was introduced in this manner and was met with loud applause and cheers. The anthem 'Children of the World' was sung and the games were declared open. The countries competed in downhill skiing, wearing shoe boxes on their feet and carrying an egg on a spoon, the participants had to manoeuvre around various obstacles to the finish line. The same course was used for the luge; lying on the floor on torn cardboard boxes using their hands and feet to propel them was quite the sight to see. Many games were played over the course of the evening and each was met with shared laughter, joy and a sense of belonging. The closing ceremonies ended with hot chocolate and doughnuts. The patients talked about this shared experience many times and always with large grins, smiles and twinkling eyes.

Play activities for the vulnerable child

Keepsakes, memory and connection boxes

We came up with the idea of a making a Vulnerable Child mode box that the patients could use at home, especially during times when the Vulnerable Child mode was triggered. We used shoe boxes and decorated them with colourful and decorative papers. Stickers, cut-outs, buttons, ribbons and various other materials were used as well to adorn these boxes. The patients were encouraged to collect things that would remind them that their Vulnerable Child was safe and cared for and that they mattered. Things like a small smooth stone from the beach, or crayons, bubblegum, pictures, etc. The therapist wrote positive affirmations on cards. Patients made things for each other, such as tapes of relaxing music and bookmarks, all of which worked like transitional objects. Patients reported that they never knew how to comfort their Vulnerable Child before, but now they open their box and read to the child, tell them where the objects came from, read the messages, listen to tapes, blow bubbles, etc. They discovered that by doing these things they were becoming a Healthy Adult taking care of their Vulnerable Child. This activity also targets the emotional deprivation schema.

Dolls

We had a dramatic therapeutic effect with an inpatient patient with dissociative identity disorder. Ann, as one of her young alters, talked about her mother destroying her doll as punishment. I decided to give a baby doll to Ann as a birthday present. She was very touched and valued the doll greatly. We kept it in my office as Ann was afraid that she could not keep her safe on the ward. In therapy sessions, her young alter (who we interpreted as her Vulnerable Child mode) would ask to take the doll out and play with it. My support for her having the doll and playing with it with me was a breakthrough in her allowing her Vulnerable Child mode alter to be in sessions. Trust and safety were increased because I kept the doll safe. Her doll played a major role in some later imagery rescripting, as it came to represent the very young child she felt she had lost because of the sexual abuse she experienced.

Play in imagery

The toy store

We use this imagery primarily in group ST, but it could be adapted to individual work.

'Everyone take a deep breath and listen closely to my story. Allow yourself to become a part of the activity as if you were a child of six years old. Pay close attention to my instructions and your feelings while participating. Begin the exercise: "Oh it is so good to see all of you today. I have a very big surprise for all of you. We are going on an adventure to a huge toy store, the biggest in the world. Wow! I can see how excited this has made you. I am excited too. Once we get to the store you will each have three minutes to pick out two toys that you have always wanted. You do not have to worry about paying for it because I won the lottery and I want to treat all of you. Okay, the time starts now, and the first room we enter is the stuffed animal room. Oh my! Look at the size of that panda bear, it almost looks real! Teddy bears in every size and they feel so soft, giraffes, puppies and kittens, there are so many different kinds and sizes of soft animals here. Only two more minutes left to pick your toys. I see some of you running off to the games room and I can hear lots of laughter and giggles. Oh look! There's a doll room with large and small dolls – Barbies, porcelain dolls in antique costumes, Madame Alexander – some of every type. There is a transformer room, battery operated cars, planes and trucks, science kits, magic tricks and so many books. Someone just dashed off to the Disney room. One minute to go. Hurry, hurry! Wow!! It looks like everyone was successful at selecting two toys. Let's go back to our group room and talk about what you picked and why and what feelings you were aware of. Any mode flips take place?'"

You can add as many fun adventures in imagery as you like following the format above. We include one imagery exercise in each of the Happy Child sessions. We want patients to have positive images to evoke when they need them to balance painful memories. We give them the therapy assignment of practising evoking positive images.

Playing with anger

Anger is very frightening for many patients, particularly those with the mistrust/abuse schema. They associate trauma, abuse, pain and fear at the mere mention of anger. They are often little aware of their Angry Child mode. Asking them to engage in play to deal with anger is met with great hesitancy, fear and scepticism. However, games like tug of war, stamping on and popping balloons are a safe and effective way to release anger. The patients begin to realise that movement and play is a good tool in releasing anger and is much better than shoving it down and numbing out. Making sounds such as who can make the best cow sound or the loudest pig noises is a game that is safe and fun. It can be the beginning step for the patients to claim their voice. Being able to say 'stop' and 'no' when they are feeling anger can be taught through the use of play. The patient also discovers that nothing bad happens when they get angry and that they can control it.

In summary, the use of play to access the Happy Child mode in Schema Therapy has many therapeutic benefits. It can be a safe way to begin to feel, to connect to, one's child modes and to meet the need for spontaneity and play of the Vulnerable or Angry Child mode. Play with the therapist can begin to break through blocks of avoidance, mistrust and fear. It provides experiences in which patients can safely begin to feel and learn to trust. Play is an enjoyable experience for both the therapist and the patient. The shared joy and pleasure of play in the therapy relationship can provide felt evidence against the belief that they are unworthy. It can be an effective way to begin working on banishing the Punitive Critic (the Dragon exercise). Play can become one of the ways the Good Parent part of the Healthy Adult mode meets the Vulnerable Child mode's needs.

Therapists tips

- Engaging the potential benefits of play for the goals of Schema Therapy requires the therapist's ability to be joyful, spontaneous and playful while at the same time keeping track of, and responding to, the schemas activated and modes that are triggered. This requires the therapist's Happy Child mode and Healthy Adult mode to be accessible. Enjoy your own spontaneity and play and share in the benefits from engaging in play.
- When telling a story or playing, the therapist's enthusiasm is important. Patients tend to get caught up in the story despite themselves. The word *enthusiasm* is important to note. As therapists, when we can be open and genuine in sharing our Happy Child mode delight and playfulness in an exercise we lead, it is easier for patients to get caught up in the emotion as well. It is as if we have called their Happy Child part out to play and the 'game' seems like fun.
- Being able and willing to invest our own emotion in our interactions as therapists is crucial for effective play. Just as schema therapists have many differences in personality, temperament and schema profile, there are many different ways to engage with patients. What is critical is that you be genuine and true to yourself. Of course, you must also be aware of times when your schemas and modes are triggered.
- Sometimes a patient says that he/she does not deserve to take part in play. The answer to that is that the therapist thinks so or she would not have invited him/her. The point is that we roll with any negative responses and do not get stuck or try to convince the patient of something that he or she does not feel.
- Patients may have as much difficulty engaging in fun as they do with other experiential exercises. Dysfunctional Critic Modes may be triggered or Maladaptive Coping modes. When this happens, it is important to discuss it and to intervene to banish the Critic from this session or get around the Maladaptive Coping mode. Happy Child work can involve dealing with interfering modes as well as setting up fun.
- Seize opportunities to include play in sessions and to access your and the patient's Happy Child mode.
- Keep some puppets or stuffed animals that can represent modes (e.g., dragons, pirates) and games in your office.

- Be aware of the strength of your Happy Child mode. If it is weak, work on it by seeking out opportunities to play for yourself.
- Patience and acceptance of where a patient's Child modes are developmentally is critical. Play in imagery can act as a first step. They can imagine playing with you in their safe place image and put the Demanding Critic mode out of the image and even send it off in a bubble. Our groups usually made signs for the group room door that announced 'No critics allowed – children at play'.

References

Farrell, J.M. & Shaw, I.A. (2018) *Experiencing Schema Therapy from the Inside-Out: A Self-Practice/Self-Reflection Workbook for Therapists*. New York: Guilford Press.

Galimzyanova, M., Kasyanik, P. & Romanova, P. (2019). *Journey through the modes valley: Schema therapy board game for children and adolescents*. St Petersburg, Russia: Schema Therapy Institute.

Lockwood, G. & Shaw, I.A. (2012). Schema therapy and the role of joy and play. In M. Van Vreeswijk, J. Broersen & M. Nadort (Eds), *The Wiley-Blackwell Handbook of Schema Therapy* (pp. 209–229). Oxford: Wiley-Blackwell.

Milteer, R.M. & Ginsburg, K.R. (2012). The importanvce of play in supporting healthy child development and maintaining strong parent–child bond: Focus on children in poverty. *Pediatrics*, *129*(1), e204–e213. https://doi.org/10.1542/peds.2011-2953

Wadley, A. (n.d.). Just Playing. A poem.

Young, J.E., Klosko, J.S. & Weishaar, M.E. (2003). *Schema Therapy: A Practitioner's Guide*. New York: Guilford Press.

11 Creative methods with coping modes and chair work

Gillian Heath and Helen Startup

Introduction

Chair work is a century-old therapeutic technique originating in the radical ideas of psychoanalyst Moreno (1889–1974), further developed by George Kelly and his Personal Construct Theory and later crafted for adoption into individual Gestalt Therapy by Perls (1969). More recently, through the work of Greenberg, the proposed therapeutic mechanisms of chair work have been operationalised and subjected to empirical scrutiny (Rice & Elliott, 1996, for a review). To date, chair work is a therapeutic tool adopted by most experiential therapies, and it now features as a recent advance in Cognitive Behavioural Therapy (Pugh, 2019). For a succinct, yet informative, overview of the history of chair work, readers are referred to Pugh (2019) or, for a detailed account, to Kellogg (2014). Kellogg has innovated and developed the use of chair work within Schema Therapy (ST), concentrating on both internal and external dialogues (Kellogg, 2014) and his four-dialogue matrix (Kellogg, 2018).

Core principles of working with coping modes

When used in a therapeutic context, chairs are the symbol that objectifies a relationship, be that a relationship between parts of the self (multi-chair technique) or between the self and another (two-chair technique). By objectifying parts of the self, new relational potential emerges. This can come about via the process of 'looking on' at a side of the self in a new way, affording new perspective, or via direct challenge to old self-to-self relationships (such as quietening the Critic to give greater voice to the Little Self). An empty chair can be used to symbolise a person from the past or someone with whom we have 'unfinished business' (see Kellogg, 2014), a technique that is also commonly used in Emotion Focused Therapy (Elliott, Watson, Goldman & Greenberg, 2004). The safety of the symbolic nature of the exercise, alongside the comforting or supportive presence of the therapist, can encourage dialogues between the self and 'other' that may never have been possible before. A goal of chair work in ST is to drive schema and behavioural change, shifting emotional responses between different parts of the self to support our patients to get their needs met in adaptive ways.

Modes, in general, can be defined as the schemas or schema operations (adaptive or maladaptive) that are currently active for the individual (Young, Klosko & Weishaar, 2003). Coping modes, in particular, are thought to develop as a child copes with chronically unmet core needs alongside interactions with their temperament, parental modelling and any reinforcement contingencies at play, including cultural factors. As such, in working with coping modes, we are also interested in the schemas they contain, and the biopsychosocial context in which they evolved.

Using chair work with coping modes

According to the ST model of the self, coping modes aim to protect against various types of threat and also often reflect a person's natural strengths. So, a coping mode may encompass a sensitivity to other people's needs (Compliant Surrenderer), an ability to spot potential threats (Paranoid Overcontroller), the strength to fight (Bully Attack), the capacity to carry on (Detached Protector), to be organised (Perfectionistic Overcontroller), to strive and win (Self-Aggrandiser) or to retreat and regroup (Avoidant Protector). In many ways, coping modes embody a wide range of human capacities that have simply gone too far, taken to the point where our awareness has been lost and we go into autopilot with the coping mode offering a solution that may be a poor fit for the situation.

Coping modes evolve in part from childhood adversity and trauma and, as such, contain a schema bias that typically predicts negative or extreme outcomes (van Genderen, Rijkeboer & Arntz, 2015). As the patient behaves as if the schema is 'right', the pattern becomes entrenched. Coping modes can also hold memories and associations of the patient's core pain and previous traumas. For example, a patient's Wary Mode (a variant of a Paranoid Over-Controller) might be vigilant to being subtly mocked, with a felt sense of years of childhood bullying and social isolation. A Compliant Surrenderer might 'remember' the only way to receive affection was to gauge their parent's mood. Or a Self-Aggrandiser may feel the glow of winning an award at school, while knowing that nothing else would be noticed. These coping mode 'memories' speak to the Vulnerable Child's needs for schema healing, and this is what we can then attune to in our mode dialogues.

In this chapter, we focus on the clinical application of chair work to coping modes within ST. We will describe how chair work, mode dialogues and mode mapping can be used to help patients to overcome the damaging aspects of their coping modes, as well as drawing their attention to the core needs these modes are clumsily trying to fulfil. Methods of working with coping modes are described. These include: awareness raising, interviewing modes for greater understanding, using drawing for mode 'expression', generating agency and motivation, using the therapy relationship for change, empathic confrontation of modes, empowering the Healthy Adult and, finally, using mode dialogues to promote integration of 'all sides'.

The methods described in this chapter can be applied across all three coping styles (avoidance, surrender and overcompensation); however, the therapist may also focus on the more specific core needs embedded in each mode type. Avoidant modes aim to steer clear of schema-driven threats and so there is a focus on facing the patient's underlying fears. Surrendering modes submit to core schemas and there is typically an unmet need for empowerment of some kind. Overcompensatory modes strive for dominance and/or control at the expense of other needs and there is a focus on allowing for, and attending to, the patient's core pain, often previously hidden or denied under these more forceful modes.

Raising awareness of coping modes

An important precursor to chair work is devising a shared mode formulation (see Chapter 1 for further detail of *mode mapping*) in which the patient's mode relationships are drawn out. One way of mapping these relationships is to have the 'Little Self' positioned at the bottom of the diagram, surrounded by the coping modes (Figure 11.1.). The Critic can be positioned somewhere

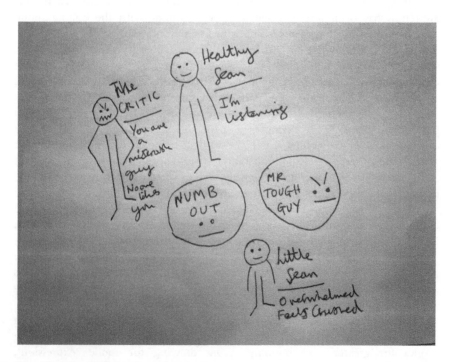

Figure 11.1 An example of a mode map.

above, bearing down on the rest of the self, with the Healthy Adult positioned away from this, grappling for space to grow. By arranging the mode map in this way, it is possible to have a validating discussion about the self-protective developmental function and motives of the coping modes. It is important to stress that we all have coping modes, they are in fact critical to managing in life. However, when the terrain of our earlier lives was such that needs weren't met, our ways of coping had to "wrap" themselves around these failings and "up their game" in order to manage the world back then. Now that the terrain of our life has changed, the challenge is to learn to modify or "turn down" the ease and intensity with which our coping modes come into play.

In order to dynamically bring these ideas to life, it can be invaluable to represent some of these core mode relationships via chairs during the formulation phase. This might involve a couple of chairs, to represent a key mode relationship, but more chairs would be used to help elaborate a patient's sense of their full self.

For example, Sean[1] was only aware of being angry and irritable; he was constantly getting feedback from the world that he was an 'angry person' and needed to 'sort himself out'. As a result, Sean had a limited sense of himself as 'just this miserable angry guy' whom no one liked. Unsurprisingly, he suffered with depression and was socially isolated. However, his therapist was aware that there was much more to Sean. She had heard how, as a child, he had been frequently ridiculed by his father in an unpredictable and aggressive fashion. In order to survive his early home life, Sean described how he learnt to project a 'tough side' to the world that usually manifested as 'attacking others before they attack me' (Bully Attack mode, BA). To get to know this mode, Sean's therapist simply guided him to move chairs each time he flipped into an attacking place. Her aim was to increase his awareness and curiosity toward this side of himself. During later sessions, Sean's therapist guided him to switch chairs as his BA, Little Side and Critic started to speak. When his Little Side started to feel pain and the Bully Attack would kick in, his therapist moved the BA chair so that it was facing slightly towards the door, quietening its influence and creating room for other parts to speak. Sean's Little Side was able to state that he felt overwhelmed and crushed by the presence of the BA. In a later session, his therapist also invited Sean's Healthy Adult to get involved and find his perspective and voice. Sean was also supported to increase awareness and, therefore, reduce the automaticity of the shift into the BA by tracking body signs, such as a dull feeling in the stomach and a clenching of fists,[2] which act as a 'flag' for spotting that the mode has been activated. The aim here is not to challenge the mode directly, but, rather, to increase the patient's awareness of the ways in which different parts of the self are relating to each other, in order to give greater flexibility.

Another valuable use of chairs during formulation is where a patient is seen to rapidly 'mode flip', as can be the case for individuals with borderline personality disorder (Arntz & Van Genderen, 2011). The process of pausing and placing the parts of the self on chairs *slows down* the session and encourages the fostering of meta-awareness and mentalising, processes that are core struggles for this patient group (Bateman & Fonagy, 2004). Again, the goal is not to challenge the modes, rather to slow down the mode flipping, to draw attention to the full self and part self relationships. Keeping a mode diary for homework can further enhance this developing self-awareness.

Working with avoidance

It is only human to avoid pain. Avoidant coping modes aim to protect us by steering clear of strong emotions (Detached Protector), challenging situations (Avoidant Protector) and interpersonal threat (Angry Protector), or by using distraction to soothe or stimulate (Detached Self-Soother or Detached Self-Stimulator). At heart, when we avoid something, we are often frightened of it (or the emotions it may activate) and the methods described here are aimed at helping to face and work with such fears to support our patients to better meet their needs.

Coping modes and the therapy relationship

Rachel enters the clinic room in silence and with almost no expression. She sits down and looks at her therapist with a fixed, slightly unnatural stare and polite half smile. Her therapist feels instantly ashamed, nervous and unsure of herself. She assumes Rachel is probably angry with her because of a letter she'd sent the previous week. In the letter, she had explained to Rachel that it was service policy to discharge a patient if she failed to make contact after a number of missed appointments, and asked her to make contact. The therapist had wrangled with how to phrase the letter and feared it came off as officious. Now Rachel's silent anger confirmed to her that she had in fact made a 'huge mistake' and let her down.

The therapy relationship has the capacity to trigger our own and our patient's schemas from the first encounter onwards. This offers a rich opportunity to understand 'in the moment' mode cycles that often characterise the patient's interpersonal world. This can be emotionally challenging work and the mode concept helps to keep both patient and therapist within their Window of Tolerance (Ogden et al., 2006; Siegel, 1999, 2011), providing containment and distance in working with a part, not all, of the patient or the therapist. This allows both to step back from ruptures (or other important relational moments) and understand together what has happened from a safer distance.

Naming the rupture and relevant modes

The therapist may notice a rupture and pause to share their sense that something has 'happened' in interpersonal terms. There is then often an emotionally charged but profoundly important moment of trying to work out together what is going on. Both patient and therapist maybe intensely triggered in these moments and it often requires a certain kind of therapeutic bravery to talk about, rather than avoid, the rupture. By exploring with our patients how our coping modes might be reacting, we diffuse potential relational toxicity, as there is an implicit assumption that they are, in their own way, trying to help. In the next extract, the therapist (*T*) explores whether Rachel's (*R*) hostile silence might be coming in part from her Wary Protector (a type of Angry Protector mode):

T: Rachel, what's going on? You seem annoyed.

R: No, it's fine. What shall we work on today?

T: Even though you say it's fine, it doesn't feel that way. Has something happened? You seem angry.

R: No, I'm past that. There's no point, I don't want to talk about it.

T: I don't know but I'm wondering if this might be partly about the letter I sent?

R: [Doesn't reply and looks incredulous at what the therapist is saying.]

T: [Gesturing to another part of the room] I wonder if your Wary Protector has come up and doesn't trust me enough to talk?

R: [Nods but remains cross-looking and silent.]

Hearing the coping mode's view of the relational incident

Having created a symbolic space for the most relevant mode, the therapist can ask about this side's thoughts and feelings about the rupture. This technique is especially helpful when the patient is reluctant to own or share their feelings more directly. The therapist concentrates on the present moment and recent/immediate schema triggers to try to understand what has just happened between them:

T: I think there might be good reasons for you to feel angry right now and I want to hear them. [Gesturing again to the same 'Wary Protector' spot.] What is your Wary side saying about talking to me right now?

R: It's saying you don't care, there's no point and it doesn't understand why I came today.

T: [Gesturing again to the same spot.] What did it think when you read the letter I sent?

R: It – and, to be honest, all of me – couldn't believe it. It was so formal. I can't believe you were suggesting we might finish because I've missed a few sessions!

T: What went through your mind about me and about us? What angered you most?

R: I felt you just didn't care – I didn't understand why you would write that.

T: [Again gesturing to the same spot.] And what did that side say about talking to me?

R: That the shutters were down now. That if you were going to criticise me like that for not coming, we're out.

T: Was there anything else that made the Wary side feel I couldn't be trusted?

R: I guess that you didn't talk to me – but I realise I haven't been here. I just felt really lost.

The therapist asks the coping mode questions (What did it say then? How did it feel when …?) to try to understand its concerns about her and their relationship. The patient may have only rarely experienced someone sensitively attending to a rupture in this way. In Rachel's case, the therapist wanting to properly hear from the coping mode allows it to step to one side slightly and for other, more vulnerable, feelings to emerge. Rachel explained that she felt she didn't matter to her therapist and expressed a more desperate feeling about therapy not lasting forever and a lack of readiness to cope on her own. The therapist felt a strong connection to Rachel. She acknowledged she had, in fact, been very worried about losing her trust while writing the letter, and found it difficult to word. She told her that she knew it came off wrong, and that she was sorry it had caused her so much distress.

Bringing ourselves into the mode cycle

At this point, there is an important opportunity for the therapist to bring themselves into the process more fully, speaking to what modes or reactions were pulled in them, and how this might happen with other people in the patient's life, too. The therapist asked if it would be all right to share how she felt at the start of the session, when the Wary Side was strong. Rachel agreed. She said, at that moment, when Rachel wouldn't talk and looked so hostile, she found herself wanting to withdraw – and she wondered if that happened with other people, too? Rachel spoke about how a similar thing had happened with a close friend, who had since broken off contact.

Linking to core needs

Rachel's therapist asked what she might need when she felt let down by her, in situations such as with the letter – was there anything she could say to the Wary Protector? Rachel (looking over at the Wary Protector spot) said that the she could say to it that her therapist had showed she cared many times, and that no matter how bad things looked, she needed to try to talk to her. The therapist said that meant a lot to her, and it would really help her if Rachel could do that or talk to her about her struggles. She, too, would try to be open about her part in things, rather than writing formal letters, so that they could figure out what was going on together.

In this type of mode work, the therapist symbolically separates out the triggered part of the patient and invites them to give it voice, understanding together, at a distance, how it views the relational incident. By locating the mode in a space away from themselves and the patient, the therapist provides some safety and containment to a potentially highly charged situation. The therapist is authentic in sharing their part in the mode cycle, which often has a disarming effect, as the patient feels the therapist's intention to make sense of what just happened between them (not as an observing expert, but as part of the relationship) in the service of remaining connected and making progress.

Separating modes and empathic confrontation

At other times, the therapist may choose empathically to confront a mode more directly, asking permission to '*speak to that side*', again using a gesture to locate the mode away from the patient. The therapist shows empathy for the mode but also clearly and specifically states its impact, in that moment, and asks for the patient's help in doing something different, either for the relationship or to help move things forward in therapy more generally.

T: Asma, you seem shut down and cut off from me right now and I'm wondering if the Protector Side has come up? [Patient has been unresponsive, silent and curled up in her chair for several minutes.]

A: Yes [briefly looking up from the floor at the therapist].

T: Can I talk to that side?

A: Yes.

T: [uses a gesture to locate the mode away from the patient] Protector Side, I'm very glad you've been here for Asma when she needed you most. When things were so bad when she was a child, when it wasn't safe to speak. But right now, I need to hear how Asma's feeling. I know she's had a really tough week but I can't help her if you keep her silent and away from me so completely. I promise we will give you plenty of time to come back, if you need to, before the end of the session. [Looking back at Asma.] Asma, can you try and tell me a little bit about how you're feeling right now? How you're doing?

A: I've had such a bad week. I just can't hack it any more. I feel like I want to throw in the towel, it's too much for me.

Augmenting our understanding of coping modes: the 'interview' technique

As we encounter a dominant pattern of coping, our first task is to explore how and why the patient copes in the way they do. Interviewing modes is a useful approach here, as it allows for a full expression of each side. You can ask about how the mode evolved, its main concerns, how it operates currently and the consequences for the patient. In this technique, the therapist uses a central feature of chair work: for the patient to occupy a side of themselves and learn about it more deeply, without intrusion from other sides or a social pressure to be constructive (Kellogg, 2014). The therapist can ask the patient to sit in a separate chair and 'be the mode', or, if that feels too uncomfortable (for example, if the patient is ambivalent about the mode's presence), the patient can supply words for the coping mode, which is allocated its own empty chair. Thus, the main tasks here are essentially cognitive, and focus on enabling the patient to articulate (1) the origin of the mode (i.e., why and when it developed), (2) the function of the mode (i.e., what does it do for the rest of the self, in what ways is it protective?), (3) the pros and cons of managing in this way in the present day. Undertaking these tasks engenders compassion, as it becomes clear that the coping mode is 'only trying to help'. In addition, a new perspective is afforded in linking the mode's main protective concern to a historical context. Further, by looking at the downsides of maintaining reliance on this mode in the present day, 'wiggle room' is created for new ways of being the world.

Generating agency and motivation: multiple mode dialogues

Coping modes are typically self-perpetuating, as they prevent disconfirmation of a schema bias and reduce the patient's sense of agency and confidence to handle situations differently. In the case of strongly avoidant modes, empathic confrontation alone can backfire, as the patient can feel under pressure from the therapist while feeling unable to face their intense fears. So, a sense of, '*I must but I can't*' can become heightened and an urge increases to then avoid the situation as an exit from the bind.

Formulation is central here, as there is typically more than one mode at play underlying the patient's intense fear. Where avoidance is strong, there is typically a Dysfunctional Critic in the background, undermining the patient's confidence and increasing their sense of inadequacy. The Vulnerable Child is frightened and the Healthy Adult offline with a high sense of threat and low sense of agency. The avoidant mode offers instant relief, as the challenge need not be faced; it can be put off or dismissed as unnecessary.

Naming and locating modes

Multiple mode dialogues can be used to reverse the vicious circle with therapist and patient providing protection from the Critic, connecting with the needs of the Vulnerable Child and moderating the avoidant mode to allow the patient to start to face their fears. The case example below also integrates the use of brief imagery to help the patient 'summon' her

Healthy Adult, raising her awareness of her potential strength in this situation.

Shona expressed her disappointment that, yet again she had failed in her efforts to find some voluntary work. A charity shop had left a voicemail for her a few days ago. Although she knew she should phone back, she was feeling tempted to leave it; perhaps she wasn't ready for this kind of work after all. Her therapist asked what other thoughts went with the feeling of 'not being ready' and Shona said she felt she couldn't handle being around people. Her therapist wondered aloud if the Critic was around; Shona agreed it was.

Locating the Critic by the door (using a hand gesture and looking toward the door), the therapist asked what it was saying about Shona not being able to handle the job. Also looking at the Critic 'spot', Shona relayed back that she would embarrass herself, she would freeze and be unable to talk, everyone would think she was weird, she would humiliate herself. The therapist asked how it felt for Little Shona hearing all of that. Shona said she felt very small. The therapist asked if Shona could feel her Little Self next to her; Shona said she could and that she was very scared.

Gesturing to another part of the room, the therapist asked Shona if she could bring in the Hiding Side (her Avoidant Protector), the part that said perhaps she wasn't ready and maybe she should leave it and not call back. Shona said the Hiding Side thought she was being kind to herself by not calling back, that she didn't really need to and it was best not to force things. Looking back toward Shona, the therapist asked what she thought about the Hiding Side's plan. With a wry smile, Shona said she felt relieved. The therapist, also with a playful tone, agreed it must be a relief, excellent news, she didn't have to do it! Shona then spontaneously said that she didn't feel good about it though, but she also didn't feel ready to call back. The therapist asked how Little Shona was feeling – could they hear from her? By placing Little Shona in a chair she was able to voice that she actually longed for someone to want her enough to give her a chance, yet she was terrified of the rejection and sense of failing that would come from calling up and getting a 'no'. She was able to express some of the pain underneath the coping that so rarely got heard. Her therapist could meet this with compassion and a gentle nudge towards self-belief, instilling in her patient the seeds that she did have the potential to manage this situation and progress towards getting her needs met.

This type of chair work can then be progressed via imagery, for example, to bring in the Healthy Adult, or Shona's 'strong' and 'determined' side to support her to rely less and less on her Avoidant coping mode. Two-chair role play was then used for skills building to support Shona to practise calling the charity shop from the perspective of her Healthy Adult, with the knowledge that her coping modes would be there for her should she need them. Shona's therapist also used role play to prepare Shona for possibly not getting the response she was hoping for, to remain within her Window of Tolerance, and use her Healthy Adult to self-soothe rather than to retreat into a coping mode, or spiral into a self-critical place.

Working with surrender

Surrender is an adaptive strategy in the face of situations that are unavoidable and insurmountable. There are times when most of us, to some degree, accept and give into things we feel we cannot change. The ST literature to date has concentrated on one mode of this type, the Compliant Surrenderer (Van den Broek, Keulen-de Vos & Bernstein, 2011); the patient 'surrenders' by appeasing others and putting their needs or point of view ahead of their own to keep connection or avoid criticism or punishment of some kind. The patient surrenders to schemas such as Emotional Deprivation, Self-Sacrifice and Subjugation, whereby they feel their needs are invisible or unimportant and they have no choice but to put the other person first.

Pessimism and hopelessness (for example, a Pessimistic Predictor or Hopeless Protector type mode) also fall into this coping style, as, by surrendering to the worst-case scenario, the patient feels protected from disappointment and, to some degree, allowed to 'give up' in the face of what feels like inevitable failure. In these modes, the patient surrenders to schemas such as Failure, Defectiveness and Pessimism, often with a sense of making their life more predictable, in that at least they 'know where they stand' and are facing 'how things are' for them.

The Vulnerable Child here may feel like they don't matter, their needs are not important and there are very limited options for them, determined either by others or by their circumstances. Often, there are unmet needs to feel understood, important and empowered: for the patient to be allowed to express themselves, to feel their needs matter and a sense of agency that they can work towards what they want.

Dialogues for empowerment: Vulnerable Child to Healthy Adult

Dialogues between the Vulnerable Child and Healthy Adult can be used to empower the patient, as the patient's feelings and needs are expressed and put centre stage to their Healthy Adult. Having been given an initial opportunity to share their concerns, the coping mode can be asked to observe from the side, providing an opportunity to 'see' the potential for a different way of handling the situation. This can have a surprisingly empowering effect. Surrender is often driven by a sense of an inevitable defeat, whereby other people's needs (in Compliance) or difficult circumstances (in Hopelessness) will preside, no matter what. As the patient turns their attention away from these predictions and toward hearing the feelings and needs of their Vulnerable Child, there is a different dynamic to agency and change, as their

Little Self asks for them to listen, to care and to move things forward in a better direction.

John comes into session looking tense and ashamed. He has agreed to date a friend but feels coerced. His only reason for doing so is because this friend had previously used his connections to help John get a job. The therapist asks him to move chairs and speak from the part of him that feels he must do what the friend wants, his 'Appease to Survive' side (a form of Compliant Surrenderer). This part says he has no choice and he should not have accepted his help in the first place – now he needs just to deal with it – this man could get nasty, it won't kill you, just go along with it. The therapist then asks the patient to move to a chair for Little John, she also puts an empty chair for Healthy John next to her own and moves the compliant chair slightly to one side, so it can observe. She asks John to be his Little Self for a minute and say how he's feeling and what is going on for him. John, as his Little Side, says (more angry than scared) that he hates this man, he doesn't want him anywhere near him, he wants him to go away. The therapist then asks John to move into his Healthy Adult, gesturing to the seat next to her, and to be this strong, caring part of him. She asks how he feels toward his Little Side and John says he's proud of him – proud of the fact he can see this man for what he is. The therapist asks him to say this to Little John, so he can feel it – he does and she adds that she feels bad that he has had to go through this. Now empowered by what his Little Self needs, although still apprehensive about how to deal with the situation, John and his therapist were able to come up with a plan.

Drawing modes for expression and focus

Drawing modes can be illuminating, as the patient often expresses unexpected aspects of themselves that are somewhat beyond language. This process does not require artistic ability; simple representations, such as stick figures and shapes can be remarkably expressive. Patient and therapist have the opportunity to play with different possibilities. Examples include a coping mode taking a well-deserved holiday by the sea, a critic being given its own soundproof lecture theatre, or a Healthy Adult and Vulnerable Child pictured quietly sitting together on a park bench. As with many other mode symbols, drawing allows the patient to change the mode's actions and influence, creating greater flexibility. In drawing, the patient is interacting with the mode rather than being consumed by it.

At other times, particularly in the face of rapid mode shifts, drawing out and writing to each element in a triggering situation can help both therapist and patient to slow down, decentre and land on what the patient needs. Figure 11.2 shows an example of where a patient's defectiveness and shame had been triggered by having a panic attack on the bus. In this situation, the therapist starts by asking what the Critic was saying in the triggering situation (based on his hypothesis that the Critic was driving the mode cycle), then

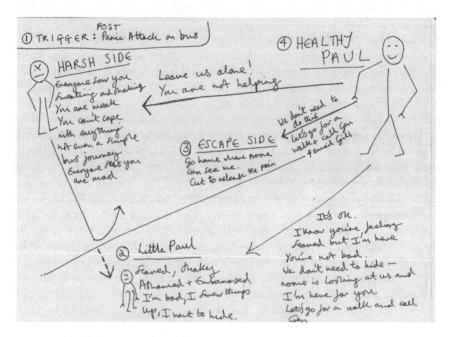

Figure 11.2 Map of Paul's mode activation following a panic attack.

how the Vulnerable Child felt hearing this, and last, how the patient coped. Finally, patient and therapist can work as a team in connecting with the patient's needs and record their plan on the map.

Mode mapping can also be effective in working with dominant and rigid coping modes. These modes can visibly and initially 'have their say' on the map but are then not allowed to squash or take over the process, with the feelings and needs of the Vulnerable Child and Healthy Adult being expressed last, therefore affording proper space for them and, in some sense, the last say (in forming a plan with greater balance).

Working with overcompensation

Overcompensatory modes try to take the opposite stance in relation to the patient's underlying sense of vulnerability to help the patient feel more important (Self-Aggrandiser), powerful (Bully Attack) or in control (Overcontroller). They are active in style and can represent highly valued aspects of a patient's character. As with many coping modes, the therapist encourages a growing sense of mode awareness, moderation and redirection by the Healthy Adult rather than the mode being necessarily rejected outright, as this is often unrealistic and discourages an important channel of communication with the coping mode.

Even with more obviously destructive modes, such as Bully Attack, the coping mode's energy and strength needs to be appreciated and, if possible, harnessed by the Healthy Adult.

Overcompensatory modes typically evolve in situations where the child's vulnerability was unacceptable or unsafe; they learn to rely on active measures (impress, be tough, be in control) to survive emotionally and to steer their own and other's attention away from their core pain underneath. Patients (rightly) sense a high risk of experiencing vulnerability in the therapy relationship and this often activates their overcompensatory modes. A range of reactions can be pulled in the therapist, which can then be explored in the moment, in mode terms.

Dialogues for integration: coping mode to Healthy Adult

This type of mode dialogue can be particularly effective later in therapy to achieve an integration of the coping modes' strengths while developing alternatives where the mode is too dominant, inflexible or overgeneralised. In this particular variant, the therapist (*T*) plays the coping mode and the patient (*P*) the Healthy Adult.

T: Yusef, you seem really aware of the Monitor now but it still seems to take over more than you'd like. Could we try having a dialogue with it, so you can practise having your Healthy Adult respond to it more strongly?

P: Okay, do you mean the chair thing?

T: I was thinking this time I could play the Monitor and you could play your Healthy side and we could have a conversation about our different points of view. How does that sound?

P: Yeah, sounds okay – do you want to start?

T: Sure … So, I'm going to be the Monitor as best I can but correct me if I get anything wrong or it feels off.

P: Sure.

T: [playing his Monitor mode, a form of Paranoid Overcontroller] I don't like the direction we've been heading in therapy. I don't like being stopped from checking my boss's email account. I don't like being asked to desist from writing detailed notes on what she says and does. I don't feel we've got things covered any more. I feel at the end of my tether.

P: Well, I was at the end of my tether. We needed to make a change. Overall, I feel better when we don't check.

T: But what happens if things start to go wrong and I get the sack? I feel you won't even notice it coming at this rate. I'm scared we'll get rejected again.

P: It is scary, you're right. But I think we'll pick up on it if something is going wrong and she should tell me if there's a serious problem.

T: But I don't feel in control.

P: Well, maybe we're not completely – maybe that's not possible.

T: But I don't know if I can cope with that – with not knowing.

P: I don't think we have a choice and we will get in serious trouble if we get caught.

T: But there's no way of her finding out, I've covered my tracks. And what do you expect me to do when I want to check?

P: We don't know that we won't get caught, not for certain. If we got the sack, I know we'd be devastated, it's true, but there's nothing we can do about that right now. I guess we'd figure it out then. If you want to check, you need to pause and go for a walk – we need to ride it out.

The therapist, playing the coping mode, clarifies what the patient is 'up against' between sessions, which can be highly validating. The process also highlights the coping mode's central concern and has the patient answer this (as best they can) from their Healthy Adult. The patient hears the mode in a concentrated form but at a distance, enabling them to form and 'try out' an alternative, more balanced view. The patient typically will rise to the occasion, as they find they don't completely agree with the coping mode after all. At times, of course, the patient may struggle to answer the coping mode – it may feel too convincing or, more often, they may feel they lack a credible alternative. In these cases, the therapist can invite the Vulnerable Child into the dialogue, asking for their view and what they would like to be different. So, for example, in the case above, the patient's Vulnerable Child said they were exhausted and felt frightened by all the checking – that they needed a break. This broke through, and the Healthy Adult promised to give them some respite.

Summary

It is quite rare that patients feel safe enough at the outset of therapy to openly express and turn attention to their core pain. It is usually our patients' coping modes that we first encounter: the sides of the self that function to protect against core pain. An early goal in therapy is, therefore, to support our patients to become consciously aware of these ways of coping and the effects they have on allowing them to get their needs met in the present day. We believe that a powerful and evocative way of introducing this perspective is through the use of chair work. In the early stages, particularly during assessment and formulation, modes are brought to conscious attention as we start to symbolically 'map out' mode relationships using chairs and gently track 'mode flips' as they are experienced in session. For some of our patients (such as those with borderline personality disorder), this simple intervention marks the beginnings of psychological integration. A further function of the chairs is more cognitive in nature and may be about 'getting to know' the coping modes, their function in the past and present, their developmental trajectory and motives. This can produce powerful new perspectives, shifts in schema intensity and sometimes a sense of grief or relief in the awareness that old ways of coping, once relied upon, are now not supportive of well-being.

Chairs can also set the scene for directly challenging the dominance of a coping mode, or for gently encouraging a part of the self, usually crushed (Little Side, for example), to find a position and a voice. It is our experience that chair work is a powerful clinical tool with the potential to foster psychological integration and schema change, as well as deep emotional and relational shifts both within the therapeutic encounter and beyond.

Therapist tips

- Chair work can be a powerful way to delineate and 'map out' mode relationships and bring your formulation to life.
- Where a patient is seen to 'mode flip', use the chairs to *slow* this process down and enhance meta-awareness and the potential for integration.
- Make room for, and get to know, a previously neglected side of the self by *homing in* on a mode via chair work.
- Chair work can support schema change via the technique of 'interviewing' a coping mode, or exploring the pros and cons of its functions, past and present.
- Chair work, at its heart, is about relational and emotional change. Do your best not to take flight into your own coping modes; rather, allow yourself a curious, open and compassionate space for your patient's and your own emotional reactions while working with chairs.
- When you start out, don't take on too many chairs!

Notes

1 The material presented is written so as to protect patient confidentiality, and session examples are composites of therapeutic dialogues with a number of patients.
2 See Part I, Chapter 3 for working with a somatic perspective in Schema Therapy.

References

Arntz, A. & Van Genderen, H. (2011). *Schema therapy for borderline personality disorder.* Chichester: John Wiley & Sons.

Bateman, A.W. & Fonagy, P. (2004). Mentalization-based treatment of BPD. *Journal of Personality Disorders, 18*(1), 36–51.

Elliott, R., Watson, J.C., Goldman, R.N. & Greenberg, L.S. (2004). *Learning emotion-focused therapy: The process-experiential approach to change.* Washington, DC: American Psychological Association.

Kellogg, S. (2014). *Transformational chairwork: Using psychotherapeutic dialogues in clinical practice.* Lanham, MD: Rowman & Littlefield.

Kellogg, S. (2018). Transformational chairwork: Five ways of using therapeutic dialogues. *NYSPA Notebook, 19*, 8–9.

Ogden, P., Minton, K. & Pain, C. (2006). *Trauma and the body: A sensorimotor approach to psychotherapy.* New York: W.W. Norton.

Perls, F.S. (1969). *Gestalt therapy verbatim.* Lafayette, CA: Real People.

Pugh, M. (2019). *Cognitive behavioural chairwork: Distinctive features.* Abingdon: Routledge.

Rice, L.N. & Elliott, R. (1996). *Facilitating emotional change: The moment-by-moment process.* New York: Guilford Press.

Siegel, D. (1999). *The developing mind: toward a neurobiology of interpersonal experience.* New York: Guilford Press.

Siegel, D. (2011). *Mindsight: The new science of personal transformation.* New York: Bantam Books.

Van den Broek, E., Keulen-de Vos, M. & Bernstein, D.P. (2011). Arts therapies and schema focused therapy: A pilot study. *The Arts in Psychotherapy, 38*(5), 325–332.

van Genderen, H. & Rijkeboer, A.A. Theoretical model: schemas, coping styles and modes. In M. Van Vreeswijk, J. Broersen & M.Nadort (2015). *The Wiley-Blackwell handbook of schema therapy: Theory, research, and practice.* Chichester: John Wiley & Sons.

Young, J., Klosko, J.S. & Weishaar, M.E. (2003). *Schema therapy: A practitioner's guide.* New York: Guilford Press.

12 Bridging the gap between forensic and general clinical practice

Working in the 'here and now' with difficult schema modes

David Bernstein and Limor Navot

In his first session of Schema Therapy, the patient refused to make eye contact with his therapist. He answered all questions with one- or two-word responses, leaving his therapist increasingly frustrated, searching for productive topics to discuss. The patient's demeanour was sullen, withdrawn and hostile. Towards the end of the session, the therapist asked, 'What is your goal for this therapy?' The patient replied, 'My goal is that by the end of the therapy, you will know as little about me as you do now!'

Introduction

Many therapists consider forensic and general clinical practice to be two worlds apart. Indeed, in forensic populations, behaviour such as aggression, anger, impulsivity, conning and manipulation are daily occurrences, rather than exceptions. In Schema Therapy, we conceptualise these phenomena in terms of schema modes – emotional states that are active at a given moment, and dominate a person's cognitions, emotions and coping behaviors (Rafaeli, Bernstein & Young, 2011; Young, Klosko & Weishaar, 2003). Research suggests that schema modes could play an important role in understanding criminal and violent behaviour. For example, in a study of hospitalised forensic patients (Keulen-de Vos, Bernstein, Vanstipelen, de Vogel, Lucker et al., 2016), the great majority of violent crimes could be reconstructed in terms of an unfolding sequence of modes. These sequences usually begin with one of the vulnerable child modes (e.g., Abandoned, Abused, or Humiliated Child) and then escalate through modes involving impulsivity (Impulsive Child), anger (Angry Child) and substance abuse (Detached Self-Soother), culminating in reactive or predatory aggression (Bully Attack or Predator mode). In forensic populations, Schema Therapy has been adapted to target these and other 'forensic' modes (Bernstein, Arntz & de Vos, 2007; Keulen-de Vos, Bernstein & Arntz, 2014). In a recently completed randomised clinical trial (Bernstein et al., submitted), Schema Therapy yielded significantly better outcomes than treatment-as-usual in forensic inpatients with personality disorders.

Yet, 'forensic' schema modes also appear in personality disordered patients in non-forensic settings, although in somewhat different or attenuated form. In non-forensic settings, patients usually have relatively greater self-control, less severe attachment problems, less severe personality disorders or traits, and more limited legal involvement (i.e., no offences or less severe offences) than in forensic patients. Nevertheless, they may still exhibit so-called Cluster B personality disorders (e.g., narcissistic, borderline, or antisocial personality disorders), or Cluster B traits that are associated with externalising behaviour problems, such as bullying, harassment or stalking, anger and impulsivity, emotional regulation problems, addictive behaviours, lying and deception. Thus, the phenomena seen in forensic and non-forensic settings form a continuum of severity.

Unfortunately, most therapists in general clinical practice receive little or no training in how to work with the emotional states that are more prevalent and severe in forensic populations. They may not know how to recognise these modes or intervene with them. This can be particularly problematic when it comes to the therapy relationship, when schema modes involve behaviours that cross therapists' boundaries and disrupt the treatment. In forensic settings and in general clinical practice, these schema modes can push therapists out of their comfort zone. For example, patients can put the therapist under pressure through intimidating (Bully and Attack mode), dominating (Self-Aggrandiser mode), or manipulating behaviour (Conning and Manipulative mode). They can keep her at a distance by detaching from emotions (Detached Protector mode) or showing indirect hostility (Angry Protector), or catch her off-guard through sudden displays of anger (Impulsive and Angry Child modes) or reactive aggression (Bully and Attack mode). These modes, occurring in the 'here and now' of the therapy session, often leave therapists feeling helpless and ineffective.

From our experiences with forensic patients, we have developed a systematic framework for working in the 'here and now' with difficult modes, from which therapists in general clinical practice can also benefit. We have written this chapter to bridge the gap between forensic and general clinical practice, providing guidance for therapists in all settings in working with their toughest patients.

We propose that many of the impasses that occur in working with patients with difficult schema modes are attributable to the following three issues:

1. The therapist misrecognises the patient's modes in the 'here and now' of the therapy relationship
2. The therapist chooses the wrong intervention, or doesn't know how to conduct the intervention, and
3. The patient's modes trigger the therapist's modes

We discuss each of these issues, give examples from forensic and non-forensic patients, and provide a systematic approach for how therapists can overcome them.

The therapist's misrecognising the patient's modes in the 'here and now' of the therapy relationship

Schema mode work is based on the assumption that the therapist can recognise the patient's modes that occur in real time and adjust her interventions accordingly. The therapist's goal is to flip or switch patients from maladaptive schema modes into more productive ones, namely, modes involving vulnerable emotions (e.g., Abandoned Child, Lonely Child), or the Healthy Adult mode.

In the Healthy Adult mode, the patient is able to reflect on his emotional state. Rather than enacting his emotional state in behaviour, he is able to take a healthy perspective on it. In the Vulnerable Child modes, the patient directly experiences his painful emotions, related to his unmet emotional needs. When the patient enters a Vulnerable Child mode, the therapist initiates limited reparenting, providing for some of his unmet emotional needs within realistic limits and boundaries.

To carry out schema mode work, the therapist needs to identify the patient's modes in real time and, depending on which is active in the session, chooses a different intervention (see the section headed 'The therapist chooses the wrong intervention, or does not know how to conduct the intervention', below). However, a common problem is when the therapist fails to recognise or misidentifies the modes that occur in the 'here and now' of the therapy session.

Many therapists outside of forensic settings are not familiar with the forensic schema modes, which involve forms of overcompensation: Self-Aggrandiser, Paranoid Overcontroller, Bully and Attack, Conning Manipulator and Predator modes. While these modes are present in non-forensic settings, too, they often manifest in more subtle ways, which can make them harder to identify. In Table 12.1, we present descriptions of how these schema modes often appear when seen in forensic versus non-forensic patients.

In general clinical practice, most patients have relatively stronger Healthy Adult modes than in forensic settings, resulting in less severe forms of the same schema modes. Nevertheless, more subtle manifestations can be harder to identify and distinguish from other coping modes. We give two examples in Box 12.1, along with effective interventions, when the mode is properly specified.

Recognising schema modes is a process of observing both verbal and non-verbal cues, the former involving the content of the patient's speech, and the latter his tone of voice, facial expressions, and body language. The therapist observes the patient's emotions, thoughts, and coping behaviour, and makes inferences about which schema modes might be present. There are several questions that the therapist can ask himself to determine which schema mode is currently active. Naturally, in practice, he will not ask all of these questions each time he sees a schema mode. However, thinking about modes in this

Table 12.1 Common overcompensatory modes as they manifest in forensic versus non-forensic settings

	Forensic	*Non-forensic*
Self-Aggrandiser	Attempts to dominate or control, impose his will on other people. Acts as if he is 'the boss', the alpha male or female who is in charge and in control of everyone and always gets his way.	Acts arrogant or superior, or needs admiration and attention. This mode may also involve dominance in non-forensic settings, but usually to a lesser degree.
Bully and Attack	Threatens and intimidates, makes explicit threats to harm other people, or intimates that he will do so, uses intimidating gestures and body language to get what he wants.	Makes nasty comments, uses put-downs to put other people on the defensive or as payback.
Conning Manipulative	Plays a role to get something he wants indirectly, has a secret agenda or double life, uses charm and manipulation to achieve instrumental ends, lies easily and smoothly, treats the truth as fungible.	Uses flattery, flirtation, 'kisses-up' to people in special positions from whom he wants something (e.g., promotion), plays a role (e.g., the good son or daughter) to gain loyalty or trust, does favours to receive them back. Alliances are made for strategic purposes and are dispensed with when no longer needed.
Paranoid Overcontroller	Always on high alert for harm or threats, sits with his back to the wall to scan the room, scope out trouble, constantly looks for small signs that prove that others are conspiring against him. Bottom line assumption is that no one can be trusted.	Constantly scoping out the competition to see who is trying to gain advantage over him, harm or humiliate him. Not sure whether what other people say can be accepted at face value, or who is a friend and who is a potential enemy or competitor.
Predator	Can injure, kill or destroy to achieve an instrumental end or for revenge. Is indifferent to the harm or suffering that he causes, sees it as 'just business'. Can plan predatory acts for weeks or months in advance, preparing them in secret and carrying them out in a cold, methodical way.	Can deliberately hurt someone whom he perceives has hurt him, ruin someone's career or reputation, smearing someone's name, justifying or rationalising it without genuine appreciation of the hurt he has caused.

way attunes the therapist to the important distinctions between modes, enabling him to rapidly identify them as he gains experience with them.

1. What are you noticing in the 'here and now' with the patient? Is there a mode present that is causing a therapeutic impasse or disruption?
2. What do you observe about the patient's emotional state (e.g., shows no visible emotion, appears tense, angry, sad, or fearful from her facial

Box 12.1 Recognising modes and distinguishing between them

Example 1: In his second session, the patient told his male therapist that he wanted to be transferred to one of his female colleagues at the same institution. He named some of the female therapists who worked at the institute, praising their intelligence, perceptiveness, warmth and empathy. He told his male therapist that it was nothing personal. Female therapists were just better at nurturing than male ones.

Misidentification: The therapist believed that the patient was in a Vulnerable Child mode. He told the patient that he understood his need for warmth and nurturance, and would do his best to provide it, even if he was a male therapist. The therapist attempted to provide limited reparenting, making sure to behave towards the patient in a warm, available and attentive manner. In the next sessions, the patient criticised the therapist's many supposed deficiencies, and continued to request a transfer to a female colleague.

Accurate mode identification: The patient was probably in a Self-Aggrandiser mode. The purpose of the mode was to put himself in the 'one-up' position, and put his therapist in the 'one-down' position.

Effective, mode-matched intervention: The proper intervention with a Self-Aggrandiser mode is usually empathic confrontation. The therapist creates a moment of self-reflection in the patient by bringing his attention to the schema mode that is currently active in the session. The simplest way to accomplish this is to name or describe the mode that the therapist observes, using the language of 'a side of you', or 'a part of you' to refer to the mode.

Therapist: 'John, I know that it is very important to you to have a therapist that nurtures you. I agree that this is very important for you. At the same time, I see a side of you that has a hard time accepting my nurturance. I've been trying to provide what you need, but when I do, this side rejects it, finds a reason to find fault with it. I don't think that you are doing this deliberately. I think that this side protects you. It does it automatically when someone tries to get close to you. I think that it is an old side that you developed to protect you from getting hurt. I also think it would happen with other therapists, even the ones that you see as more nurturing than me. It can take time to trust that someone really cares about you and understands you. I'm willing to take that time with you.'

Example 2: The patient was very angry about her mistreatment by her previous therapist at the same clinic. After she had been transferred to a new therapist, she complained loudly and often about how badly she was being treated. She would yell and curse, raising her voice so loud that some of the therapist's colleagues were alarmed about what was happening in the therapist's office. On one occasion, she took her (empty) plastic coffee mug and threw it against the wall. The patient's angry tirades were so bothersome that the other patients complained about them.

Misidentification: The therapist believed that the patient was in an Angry Child mode. She encouraged the patient to ventilate her emotion and empathised with the patient's feelings of perceived injustice. Rather than getting her emotions out, this intervention appeared to feed the patient's anger, leading to more angry escalations.

Accurate mode identification: The patient was most likey in a Bully and Attack mode. While her outbursts appeared to involve the ventilation of anger, they were so extreme and unceasing that they left everyone at the clinic intimidated, 'walking on egg-shells' every time they saw her.

Effective mode-matched intervention: The most effective intervention with Bully and Attack mode is usually limit setting. The therapist sets limits on the mode that crosses the therapist's boundaries, violating her rights, such as the right to feel safe and be treated respectfully. The therapist's limit setting is firm and consequential, but not punitive. She sets the limits in a personal way, referring to the rights or needs that apply equally to the therapist and the patient and form the basis of the therapy relationship. In the 'stop technique', the therapist first says the word, 'stop', clearly and firmly, often accompanied by a hand gesture (hands raised upwards with palms facing forward) and then carries out the rest of the intervention.

Therapist: Susan, stop! I accept your anger, but shouting and yelling is too much. It's disturbing to me. I need you to express your anger in a way that I can hear it.

Susan: That's your problem if you can't handle it! [continues yelling]

Therapist: Susan, stop! The way that you are expressing your anger is making it impossible for me to work with you right now. You and I both have the right to feel safe here, and to be treated respectfully. I promise you that I will do everything that I can so that you feel safe and respected. But I need the same thing from you.

expression or posture)? What is the mode's primary emotion (e.g., numbness, anger, sadness, fear)?

3. What might have triggered the mode (e.g., the therapist was late starting the session; the therapist questioned the truthfulness of something that the patient told him)?
4. What might the patient be thinking (e.g., 'You betrayed me!', 'I'm the boss here, not you!')?
5. What is the patient's coping style? Does she create distance in the session (i.e., avoidance), put herself above, or try to dominate, the therapist (i.e., overcompensation), or behave in ways that are submissive, dependent, hopeless or helpless (i.e., surrender)?
6. How do you feel when the patient is in this mode (e.g., anxious or inferior, irritated or resentful, detached, needing to give the patient something that she wants)? What mode might you be in, which was triggered by the patient's mode?

We recommend beginning by observing the patient's emotions, because schema modes involve the activation of strong emotional responses. Correctly identifying the patient's emotions rapidly narrows the search for the correct schema mode. For example, if the patient's primary emotion is anger, then the possible schema modes are: (1) Angry Child mode, (2) Angry Protector mode, (3) Bully and Attack mode, and (4) Predator mode. The therapist can then differentiate between these four options by answering the rest of the above questions. If, for example, the patient's anger is open, rather than controlled, the schema mode is likely to be the Angry Child, rather than the Angry Protector. Angry Child mode involves open displays of anger, where the patient ventilates his feelings of unfairness or frustration. Angry Protector mode, on the other hand, involves covert expressions of anger, with hostile non-verbal cues and withdrawn, distancing behaviour. The function or purpose of the Angry Child mode is to 'get the anger out' and protest perceived feelings of unfairness. The function or purpose of the Angry Protector mode is to create a 'wall' of covert hostility, keeping other people, who are perceived as threatening or harmful, at a safe distance.

Differentiating between Angry Child and Bully and Attack modes is largely a matter of whether aggression is absent (Angry Child mode) or present (Bully and Attack mode). The purpose or function of Bully and Attack mode is to threaten or intimidate, while, in Angry Child mode, the purpose is simply to vent anger and signal feelings of unfairness or frustration. Distinguishing between Bully and Attack mode and Predator mode depends on several distinctions. In Bully and Attack mode, the patient's aggression is 'hot' and reactive (i.e., emotionally triggered), while in Predator mode, it is 'cold' and usually instrumental (i.e., with the intention to achieve a certain goal, such as eliminating a threat, obstacle, or rival). In Bully and Attack mode, the patient reacts quickly, moving towards the target of his aggression in a threatening and intimidating manner. In Predator mode, the patient's aggression is contained and in control, and is often premediated. He acts in a 'business-like' or 'robotic' way to carry out his plan, devoid of apparent emotions.

The therapist chooses the wrong intervention, or does not know how to conduct the intervention

To carry out schema mode work in the 'here and now' successfully, the therapist needs to observe the mode that is currently active and choose a 'matching' intervention that takes account of the coping mode's function (e.g., venting anger, in the case of an Angry Child mode) and promotes mode change to better meet the patient's needs. Strategies to achieve this end vary markedly across modes. We show the correspondence between schema modes and effective 'here and now' interventions in Table 12.2.

The maladaptive coping modes – those where the patient makes prominent use of avoidance, surrender, or overcompensation as coping styles – require empathic confrontation or limit setting as interventions (see Table 12.2). Choosing between these two types of interventions is mostly a matter of the severity of the schema mode, and the degree to which it is causing a therapeutic impasse or transgressing the therapist's boundaries. When maladaptive modes violate the therapist's basic rights, such as safety or respectful conduct, the therapist immediately sets limits on the transgressing modes. For example, if the patient behaves in a threatening or intimidating way towards the therapist (e.g., Bully and Attack mode) or demeans the therapist (e.g., Self-Aggrandiser mode), the therapist uses limit setting to 'stop the mode in its tracks'. If, on the other hand, the maladaptive mode is less severe, and does not involve significant violations of the therapist's boundaries, the therapist uses empathic confrontation to create a moment of self-reflection, where the patient comes face to face with his mode and its effect on the therapist. Similarly, when modes cause serious impasses in the therapy that cannot be resolved with other techniques, limit setting is required. Otherwise, empathic confrontation is used. In practice, a combination of limit setting and empathic confrontation is usually required. For example, the therapist might initially set limits on the severe schema modes that are causing impasses or violating boundaries, following by using empathic confrontation to create moments of self-reflection.

The patient's schema modes trigger the therapist's modes: schema mode congruency, complementarity and battles

A third and very common problem occurs when the therapist's own emotional reactions to the patient's schema modes cause him to enter a schema mode himself. When the therapist's schema modes are active, he may lose perspective on the situation. His schema modes, and the early maladaptive schemas underlying them, colour the way he interprets events,

Table 12.2 Correspondence between schema modes and effective interventions in the 'here and now' therapy relationship, with explanations and examples

Schema modes	Interventions
Vulnerable Child (abandoned, abused, humiliated child) or Lonely Child	Limited reparenting: the therapist provides for some of the patient's unmet emotional needs within appropriate limits and boundaries. The therapist adjusts her reparenting depending on the need that is present at a given moment. This is accomplished most directly when the patient is in one of the child modes, where his emotions and needs are most accessible and open to being met directly by the therapist's reparenting. For example, reparenting the Abandoned Child mode involves meeting needs for safety, stability, and connection; the Impulsive Child mode involves the need for limits; and so forth.
Angry Child	Three step process: (1) listen, make room for patient to express her angry emotions; (2) show empathy, acknowledge any realistic aspects of the patient's reactions (showing understanding of the nub of her anger), and validate her emotions; (3) switch the patient to a Healthy Adult or Vulnerable Child mode. In the Healthy Adult mode, the patient can be invited to reflect in a more balanced way on the realistic and distorted or out of proportion aspects of her reactions. In the Vulnerable Child mode, the therapist can provide limited reparenting for the patient's unmet emotional needs (see above).
Impulsive or Undis–ciplined Child modes	Empathic confrontation or limit setting. *Empathic confrontation*: name or describe the mode that you observe. This can be in the form of a statement or a question: 'I see a side of you that … [describe the mode]', or 'Which side of you is it that … [describe the mode]?' You can also name or describe two modes, implying a relationship between them or make the relationship between them explicit. Example of empathic confrontation with an Impulsive Child mode (a single mode): 'Jill, I see a side of you that is really hyped-up right now, that seems to be so fully of energy that you have a hard time sitting still and listening [Impulsive Child mode]. Which side of you is this?' Or with two modes, the Impulsive Child and Healthy Adult modes: 'Jill, I see a side of you that is really hyped-up right now [Impulsive Child mode]. What can we do to help your Healthy Adult side, so that you can settle down and listen?' *Limit setting*: If the mode violates rights or crosses boundaries severely, say the word, 'Stop!', clearly and firmly, then state the rights or needs that make the limit setting necessary. Do the limit setting in a personal way, rather than making reference to formal rules or requirements (e.g., a rule that the patient needs to arrive to the session on time). Example of limit setting without the stop technique with an Undisciplined Child mode: 'John, I know that is hard for you to get out of bed, so you are often late. But this side of you, which just wants to party at night and sleep late in the morning, is getting in the way of therapy. I can't help you if you don't come on time or keep missing sessions. There is no way to do therapy if you aren't here. If it keeps happening, I have no choice but to stop the therapy. We need to find a way to work with the undisciplined side of you, because otherwise, it's too frustrating and difficult for me, and you won't get the help you need.

(Continued)

Table 12.2 (Cont.)

Schema modes	Interventions
	How can we help your Healthy Adult side make sure that you get to therapy on time?'
Internalised Parent modes	Talk back to the modes: the patient and/or therapist talks back to the patient's Demanding Parent or Punitive Parent mode. This is sometimes done in role playing exercises, where the therapist or patient speaks to the patient's Demanding or Punitive Parent mode, which is placed on an empty chair (the empty–chair technique). The patient provides the voice for the mode. Example with the Punitive Parent mode: *Therapist*: What does the punitive side say about John? *Patient*: He says that John is a loser, that he screws up everything that he does. *Therapist*: Punitive side of John, I want to you to stop putting John down. I know John well, and he is a fine person with a lot of good qualities. The way that you put him down is unfair, and it hurts him. You should support him, rather than tearing him down.
Avoidant or surrender coping modes	Empathic confrontation or limit setting Example of empathic confrontation with Detached Protector and Lonely Child modes: 'I see a side of you that keeps you at a safe distance [Detached Protector]. And I get that, but I also feel for the lonely side that needs less distance and more connection [Lonely Child].' Example of empathic confrontation with an Angry Protector mode: 'I see a side of you that is like a porcupine. If I get too close, I'm going to get pricked. Which side of you is this? 'I know that you are not used to expressing your anger. That's okay. But if you are angry with me, or I did something that upset you, then I would like to know it. You deserve that.'
Overcompensating coping modes ('forensic' modes)	Empathic confrontation or limit setting Example of limit setting using the stop technique with a Bully and Attack mode: 'Karen, stop! This side of you that is demanding that I write you a letter for your parole officer is putting me under pressure. I can't help you if I feel like I'm being backed into a corner. You and I both need to feel that the therapy is a place where we feel safe and are treated respectfully. In order to help you, I need to feel that we can have a discussion about whether I should write the letter or not, without your trying to force me to give in to you.' Example of empathic confrontation with a Conning Manipulative mode: 'There is a side of you that sometimes leaves me wondering if you are up to something, if you are being completely truthful with me. I really try to give you the benefit of the doubt, because I think that you deserve my trust. I know that there is a side of you, a healthy side, that is trying do the right thing in the therapy. I also think that there is another side of you that sometimes tries to get what it wants in indirect ways. I want to believe what you tell me, but it is important that I tell you when I am having doubts. If you aren't being completely truthful with me, I assume that there is a reason for it, and I want to know why it's happening.'

producing strong emotional reactions and maladaptive coping responses that interfere with his effective functioning. The therapist's own past, represented by his schema modes, when triggered by the patient's modes, makes it difficult to deal with the 'here and now' therapy relationship.

We have observed three basic patterns of modes triggering modes, which we term 'schema mode congruency', 'schema mode complementarity' and 'schema mode battles' (see Box 12.2 for examples). Understanding how these interactions occur can help therapists recognise the patterns in their own work with patients, beginning the process of gaining healthy perspective on them.

Schema mode congruency. The patient and therapist are both in the same mode, a pattern which, if it lasts for a long time, produces an impasse in the therapy. A very common example is when the patient and therapist are both in a Detached Protector mode. They 'conspire', as it were, to avoiding dealing with emotions or difficult topics, or making genuine contact with each other. Another variation on this pattern occurs when the patient and therapist have an overly intellectual or rational style of relating to one another. They share an intellectualising or rationalising form of Detached Protector mode.

Schema mode complementarity (one-up and one-down). The second pattern is when the patient's and therapist's modes are in a one-up, one-down complementary relationship. Usually, one person is in overcompensatory mode, such as the Self-Aggrandiser or Bully and Attack mode, while the other is in a Vulnerable Child mode (e.g., Humiliated Child mode) or a Compliant Surrender mode.

Schema mode battle. The third situation is a battle of control between two dominant modes, usually overcompensatory modes. For example, when a patient is in a Self-Aggrandiser mode, trying to put the therapist down, and the therapist, as a response, also enters a Self-Aggrandiser mode, trying to bolster his self-image by patronising the patient or putting him in his place.

Box 12.2 Examples of schema mode congruency, complementarity and battle

Congruency: A patient enters a room and begins to talk about his experiences during the week. In a flat or boring tone, he says, 'Everything was okay, nothing special happened. I had a visit. It was nice. I fought a bit with my roommates, but eventually it worked out.' The patient is in a Detached Protector mode, which numbs his feelings and avoids difficult topics or emotional contact with the therapist. As a response, the therapist often enters a Detached Protector mode himself. The therapist becomes bored or fatigued. He may even feel like falling asleep. He may become distracted, thinking about irrelevant things like his vacation plans, or what he needs to pick up at the supermarket after the session.

Complementarity: A patient says, 'I studied psychology once, and, with all due respect, I am older than you, and I have more life experience than you have. So I really don't think that this therapy can go anywhere.' Here the patient is in a Self-Aggrandiser mode, which is motivated by overcompensation for feelings of inferiority. At that moment, the therapist might unconsciously take the position that the patient is steering him into, namely, the one-down position. The therapist might enter a Humiliated Child mode, feeling inferior himself, or enter a Compliant Surrender mode, trying to appease the patient by, for example, expressing a commitment to learn from the patient's greater life experience. The situation can also occur in reverse, when the therapist takes the one-up position, and the patient the one-down position.

Battle: A common example in the forensic context is when the patient is in a Conning Manipulative mode, and the therapist, in response, feels the need to 'unmask' the patient. 'You are not going to make a fool out of me!' says the therapist, implicitly telling the patient, 'I know what you are up to!' Thus, the therapist also enters an overcompensating mode, a Paranoid Overcontroller mode, trying to 'unmask' the patient's Conning Manipulative mode.

Recruiting the therapist's Healthy Adult mode, when the therapist is emotionally triggered

It is inevitable that therapists sometimes become emotionally triggered when they deal with patients with difficult schema modes, which push them out of their comfort zones. However, the therapist's ability to recognise those moments when he enters a schema mode is a function of the Healthy Adult mode. Eventually, that function allows the therapist to accept his own reactions, recover, and move forward with his interventions. To recover in these situations, the therapist needs to recruit his Healthy Adult mode in order to return to a state of psychological equilibrium.

We recommend the following approach, which combines elements of Schema Therapy, Mindfulness, and Self-Compassion, to recruit the therapist's Healthy Adult mode.

1. Notice your reactions to the patient. Accept them. You are allowed to be human.
2. Which side of you (i.e., schema mode) is this? Do you recognise this side from other situations? What triggered this side?

3. What does your Healthy Adult mode have to say to this side?
4. Can you 'park' your schema modes on the side for the moment?
5. Focus on your breathing to ground you in the present moment.
6. Return your attention to the patient.
7. What does your reaction tell you about the patient's schema modes?
8. Choose your intervention with the patient, which matches his schema mode.

Of course, we cannot expect the therapist to carry out all of these steps in the heat of the moment. However, he can learn to slow the process down a bit, giving himself the time to recover his healthy adult functioning. The moment that the therapist notices his own emotions, he begins to return to the Healthy Adult mode. By simply allowing himself to become aware of his experience at that moment – noticing his bodily sensations, feelings, thoughts, and action tendencies (i.e., tendency to fight, freeze, or flee) – the therapist grounds himself in the present moment. Focusing attention on one's breathing can also serve as an anchor, rooting oneself in the awareness of being alive. This attitude of mindful awareness helps the therapist return to his Healthy Adult mode, noticing and accepting his reactions, whatever they may be.

Therapists often experience their reactions during sessions as unwanted and unwelcome. Feeling uncomfortable with the patient can trigger self-punitive thoughts and feelings (Punitive Parent mode) about oneself as a therapist and a person. Therapists often experience painful feelings of inadequacy in such situations, imagining, for example, that one of their colleagues would be able to handle the situation more successfully. Therapists can be very unforgiving of themselves when they fail to live up to their own expectations (Demanding Parent mode). Rather than having a balanced and realistic view of their work, which can be extremely challenging with severe personality disordered patients, they experience setbacks as personal failures. These painful experiences of self-directed criticism only compound their difficulties, making it more difficult to accept their reactions to patients. In fact, therapists have all kinds of reactions to patients: feeling angry, bored, attracted, intimidated, lonely, distracted, and so forth. These kinds of reactions are expectable, when dealing with challenging patients. They simply mean that therapists are human, just like everyone else. The therapist can embrace his own very human reactions, including the self-punitive or demanding sides of himself.

Once the therapist becomes aware of, and embraces, his schema modes, we recommend that he 'parks them on the side'. Thus, the therapist does not reject his modes, but moves them to the periphery of his awareness, leaving his Healthy Adult mode front and centre, so that he can redirect his attention to the patient. The therapist then asks himself, 'Which mode is the patient in right now? What are his emotional needs? Which interventions might I use to switch him into a state of self-reflection (Healthy Adult mode) or emotional vulnerability (Vulnerable Child mode)?'

Summary

In this chapter, we discussed three types of issues that can result in therapeutic impasses in both forensic and general clinical practice: (1) the therapist's misrecognising the patient's modes in the 'here and now' of the therapy relationship; (2) the therapist's choosing the wrong intervention, or not knowing how to conduct the intervention; and (3) the patient's modes triggering the therapist's modes. We reviewed three types of dysfunctional patterns of modes triggering modes which can lead to therapeutic impasses: (1) schema mode congruency, (2) schema mode complementarity, and (3) battle for mode dominance. Finally, we discussed how the therapist can recruit his Healthy Adult mode, accepting his own emotional reactions, 'parking them on the side', and returning his attention to the patient. These concepts and techniques can help therapists overcome obstacles in the 'here and now' therapy relationship, creating emotional space to carry out interventions more effectively in both forensic and non-forensic settings.

Therapist tips

- Hold in mind that phenomena seen in forensic and non-forensic settings form a continuum of severity, with antisocial modes being seen in both populations. In general clinical practice, most patients have relatively stronger Healthy Adult modes than in forensic settings, resulting in less severe forms of the same schema modes.
- In therapy, one of the therapist's goals is to flip patients from maladaptive schema modes into more productive ones, namely, modes involving vulnerable emotions (e.g., Abandoned Child, Lonely Child), or the Healthy Adult mode.
- Consider six factors in identifying an active maladaptive mode: the presence of a therapeutic impasse/rupture, observations of emotional state, potential triggers, cognitions and coping style and your own emotional reaction to the patient.
- To carry out schema mode work in the here and now successfully, the therapist needs to observe the mode that is currently active and choose a 'matching' intervention that takes account of the coping mode's function (e.g., ventilating anger, in the case of an Angry Child mode) and promotes mode change to better meet the patient's needs.
- For overcompensating forensic modes, empathic confrontation and limit setting are usually indicated. Choosing between these two types of interventions is mostly a matter of the severity of the schema mode, and the degree to which it is causing a therapeutic impasse or transgressing the therapist's boundaries.

- There are three basic patterns of modes triggering modes in the therapy relationship: schema mode congruency, schema mode complementarity, and schema mode battles. Understanding how these interactions occur can help therapists recognise the patterns in their own work with patients, beginning the process of gaining a healthy perspective on them and maximising the therapeutic progress.

References

Bernstein, D., Arntz, A. & de Vos, M. (2007). Schema focused therapy in forensic settings: Theoretical model and recommendations for best clinical practice. *International Journal of Forensic Mental Health*, *6*, 169–183.

Bernstein, D.P., Keulen-de Vos, M., Clercx, M., de Vogel, V., Kersten, G., Lancel, M., Jonkers, P., Bogaerts, S., Slaats, M., Broers, N., Deenen, T. & Arntz, A. (submitted). Effectiveness of long-term, inpatient psychotherapy for rehabilitating violent offenders with personality disorders: A randomized clinical trial of schema therapy vs treatment-as-usual.

Keulen-de Vos, M., Bernstein, D. P. & Arntz, A. (2014). Schema Therapy for aggressive offenders with personality disorders. In R. C. Tafrate & D. Mitchell. (Eds.), *Forensic CBT: A Handbook for Clinical Practice*, 66–83. Chichester: Wiley-Blackwell.

Keulen-de Vos, M., Bernstein, D.P., Vanstipelen, S., de Vogel, V., Lucker, T., Slaats, M., Hartkoorn, M. & Arntz, A. (2016). Schema modes in the criminal and violent behavior of forensic cluster B PD patients: A retrospective and prospective study. *Legal and Criminological Psychology*, *21*, 56–76.

Rafaeli, E., Bernstein, D.P. & Young, J. (2011). *Schema Therapy: Distinctive Features*. New York: Routledge.

Young, J.E., Klosko, J. & Weishaar, M. (2003). *Schema Therapy: A Practitioner's Guide*. New York: Guilford Press.

13 Schema Therapy for couples

Interventions to promote secure connections

Travis Atkinson and Poul Perris

Introduction

In distressed love relationships, Schema Therapy (ST) posits that Early Maladaptive Schemas (EMS) prime negative interactions between partners, biasing how each partner experiences the other, creating self-perpetuating cycles of perceived threat or harm. In conjunction with temperament, EMS develop from early life experiences with significant caregivers and can adversely impact current relationships, prompting core relational threats such as being deprived, abandoned, controlled, criticised or abused (Young et al., 2003). States of mind, or modes, evolve from clusters of EMS. They include dysfunctional coping modes, along with child and parent modes. Provoking dysfunctional behaviours between partners, modes stem from schema-driven points of view (Arntz & Jacob, 2013). The bias, dominance and inflexibility of modes block the curiosity, openness and acceptance needed in a healthy love relationship (Siegel, 2012). When a series of coping modes clash repeatedly between partners, a mode cycle emerges as a default pattern of distressful interpersonal relating. This type of mode cycle frustrates each partner's ability to get their core relational needs met (Atkinson, 2012) and, gradually, leads to relationship discord, resulting in poor outcomes for couple satisfaction and longevity (Mikulincer & Shaver, 2016).

The goal of Schema Therapy for Couples (ST-C) is to promote a consistent pattern of secure and stable connection between partners. The therapist orchestrates and supports new experiences within the couple while encoding new meaning to those experiences, debunking each partner's EMS and strengthening their Healthy Adult mode. A central element involves the therapist and couple discovering together how each partner copes when their EMS are triggered in the relationship, discerning how their coping modes attempt to meet their needs in the face of a relational threat through surrendering, avoiding, or overcompensating behaviours. Modes often trigger a partner's schemas, creating distance and tension while reinforcing the core beliefs of the schema at play. Mode cycles usually operate outside of conscious awareness, as partners understand their relational discord through the lens of their own schemas, which can become more entrenched with each cycle.

As a couple becomes aware of, and understands, their mode cycle, they have the opportunity to meet each other's core needs in more emotionally connected, balanced, flexible and adaptive ways. The couple gradually replace dysfunctional coping mode interactions with a positive synergy between the relationship-enhancing Healthy Adult, Vulnerable Child and Happy Child modes: a healthy mode triad. The Healthy Adult identifies and invites the core relationship needs of the Vulnerable Child and Happy Child modes. A new pattern of interaction develops involving reciprocal self-disclosure of vulnerability that invites mutual responsiveness to meet both partners' core needs (Mikulincer & Shaver, 2016). The healthy mode triad honours and differentiates two individual 'me's' within the couple, integrating both partners into one 'we' that defines the whole of the love relationship (Siegel, 2012). Couples are able to effectively repair conflict, heal past injuries and avoid future relationship ruptures (Gottman, 1999).

ST was developed specifically to target entrenched and destructive modes common with patients experiencing traits or meeting the criteria of personality disorders (Young et al., 2003). Empirical support for its use with a range of personality disorders using individual and group modalities (Giesen-Bloo et al., 2006; Farrell et al., 2009; Bamelis et al., 2014) exists. ST-C adapts ST to couples, offering a treatment tailored to more distressed couple interactions. Most existing models of couples therapy do not explicitly address personality disorder traits, possibly contributing to a large subset of couples failing to make significant progress in treatment (Simeone-DiFrancesco et al., 2015). For instance, dissecting the 27–30% of unresponsive couples receiving Emotionally Focused Therapy, the majority suffered multiple injuries from the relationship (Makinen & Johnson, 2006), products of what ST-C would classify as unyielding dysfunctional coping modes.

More severe EMS common in personality disorders are easily activated and discernible in relationships through intense patterns of chaos or rigidity, often expressed through coping modes involving harsh anger or detached numbness that decrease relationship satisfaction and threaten the stability of relationships (Siegel, 2010). This chapter outlines how to work effectively with these mode cycles in ST-C, focusing on six core principles, illustrated by a clinical vignette with a couple:

1. Dual focus: the therapy relationship and tasks/goals
2. Establishing safety: empathic curiosity, validation and protection
3. Conceptualising the mode cycle
4. Strengthening the healthy mode triad
5. Connection dialogues: inviting vulnerability and meeting needs
6. Imagery rescripting for couples: setting the stage and reparenting

The couple in the vignette, Ariana and Hari, have been together for two years. They entered therapy after the overwhelming hurt Ariana experienced when Hari failed to propose to be married while on their latest vacation, dashing her expectations. To illustrate the process in sufficient depth, the vignette focuses more strongly on Ariana. In a full session, the same principles and types of interventions would be used with her partner, Hari, to address his needs. The vignette opens during the couple's tenth session with their schema therapist (*T*), Eva. Both Ariana (*A*) and Hari (*H*) are describing a recent example of their mode cycle.

Dual focus: the therapy relationship and tasks/goals

In ST-C, therapists work toward dual tasks, creating an alliance with both partners using techniques of limited reparenting to help them feel equally understood and cared for, while simultaneously orientating them to address core ST-C tasks and goals, including empathically confronting EMS and dysfunctional mode cycles that can derail progress. Therapists attend to the therapeutic relationship with both partners, while also thoroughly exploring each partner's experiences and modes.

Since one partner is rarely the sole cause of a couple's dysfunction (Gottman, 1999), therapists reinforce the idea that EMS are the source of the mode cycle, which is the culprit of relationship distress. Therapists frame each partner in the relationship as antidotes to the mode cycle, agents of change and healing for EMS. Unlike individual ST, when the therapist is the primary source of reparenting, in ST-C therapists guide each partner to reparent each other. Key interventions in ST-C are choreographed to help each partner fully benefit from the other's corrective influence. Additional resources may be needed, including supplemental individual or group sessions with one or both partners to assist with active reparenting.

In the following segment, the therapist explores Ariana's experience of a prototypical conflict, aiming to assess her part in the mode cycle. However, she is suddenly interrupted by Hari, whose mistrust is triggered by the fact he feels she is misrepresenting the argument. The therapist flexibly shifts from assessing Ariana's modes (a core ST-C task) to using empathic confrontation to acknowledge Hari's emotional reaction (a relational strategy). By validating Hari's emotional reaction, the therapist de-escalates his coping response, allowing her to continue with the task of assessing Ariana's experience and her part in their mode cycle.

T: Ariana, please help me understand what happened when you were driving with Hari?

A: Hari was in the passenger seat, scrolling through his phone, obsessed with it as usual. I was hoping we would get a chance to talk during the drive to make vacation plans.

H: Tell the truth, Ariana. Aren't you leaving out the part about how you started screaming at me!

T: Hold on, Hari [therapist leans in]. Can we let Ariana finish, and then come right back to you?

H: What is the point if she's not telling the truth? What she said isn't what happened. I know where she's going with this.

T: I hear you, Hari. I know it's hard to hear a story you remember very differently. Maybe it's also challenging right now because I'm not stopping Ariana. I'm not here to take sides. I want to understand how both of you remember what happened in the car. I want to find out how your mode cycle played out. Of course, all of us remember things differently. Can you stay with us, Hari, so I can hear the rest of what Ariana remembers? I'll get your side right after that.

Establishing safety: empathic curiosity, validation and protection

Assessing negative patterns of interaction between partners requires a high level of empathic curiosity. Empathy involves identifying with, or imagining, the feelings, thoughts, or attitudes of another person and, for therapists and couples alike, it is one of the most valuable relational tools. Practising empathy can invite the patient's Vulnerable Child to arise, which can, in turn, elicit a complex set of Dysfunctional Parent and coping mode responses. For instance, when therapists bypass a coping mode and connect with the Vulnerable Child, the patient's Critical Parent mode may respond by attacking them for expressing their feelings. This modal reaction is intensified by a fear of how their partner will react to their vulnerability – they may fear their partner will view their vulnerability from a similar stance as their Critical Parent mode – for example, framing them as weak or as a failure. Alternatively, they may anticipate their partner will disappoint them in other ways, such as misunderstanding or invalidating their distress. Finally, they may fear that expressing vulnerability will trigger conflict, anticipating their default mode cycle, making it feel unsafe or futile.

Therapists validate the Vulnerable Child's feelings and protect against the Dysfunctional Parent mode, communicating acceptance and strengthening the therapeutic bond. An open, affirming response to vulnerability by therapists usually elicits empathy and validation from the listening partner. However, if the listening partner shifts into a critical or invalidating mode, therapists are prepared to empathically confront the attack, while remaining focused on caring for the vulnerable partner.

The next step is to help patients soothe and regulate their emotions in the Vulnerable Child mode, a core skill for their Healthy Adult mode when activated in general, and central to remaining emotionally regulated in the session. Core strategies therapists employ to establish safety are illustrated in the following vignette.

A: It is the same old story with him.

T: How so, Ariana? Help me understand.

A: It just seems so pointless.

T: Ariana, can you help me understand what's happening for you right now when you say, 'It seems so pointless?'

A: I really don't know. It's like this void inside of me.

T: Right. Let's look at that void for a moment.

A: Every time I try to say what I think, when I try to share what's important to me, Hari attacks me and shuts me out.

T: Similar to what started a moment ago?

A: Exactly.

T: When Hari jumps in, that is when this void comes up for you?

A: Yes. Maybe there's a part of me that shuts down inside. It's easier to let him have his way. Whenever I fight back, like I did during the drive, Hari gets really angry at me, and it always somehow ends up being my fault. It's a no-win for me because if I say anything, I'm the brat, always asking for too much. Then I start to cry, and really hate myself for saying anything. Why can't I just deal with this on my own, instead of telling him? What is wrong with me?

T: That is a pretty harsh voice attacking you right now, Ariana.

A: Sure, but I have to grow up. Who wants to be with a whiner? How attractive am I if all I do is cry?

T: Look at me, Ariana. [Ariana pauses, then looks up at the therapist.] Great. Take a deep breath with me, and slowly exhale. Excellent. [Therapist pauses, then looks at Hari.] Still with us, Hari?

H: I'm listening.

T: Thanks, Hari, for your patience. I'll come right back to you.

Conceptualising the mode cycle

Effective couple therapy requires therapists and both partners to develop an accurate understanding of the default mode cycle. Therapists identify typical content and triggers that activate EMS with each partner and explore patterns of mode interactions (e.g., attacking or withdrawing behaviours) that define the mode cycle. Mode conceptualisation is informed by the same theoretical principles used during individual ST. However, in couples sessions, therapists are eyewitnesses to rapid and intense interactions that may be hard to fully appreciate from patient's descriptions during individual sessions. Understanding the origins of both partners' schemas also helps the therapist (and the couple) to identify each partner's particular relational sensitivities and prototypical patterns during a mode cycle.

In the next vignette, the therapist assesses the mode cycle of Ariana and Hari that erupts when he interrupts her about what happened in the car. The therapist identifies the presence of Ariana's EMS and modes, beginning with Emotional Deprivation ('I'll never get my needs met') that she coped with by shifting into a Detached Protector mode. Ariana's Defectiveness schema ('I'm flawed for having needs') was reinforced by her Punitive Parent mode.

Finally, her Abandonment schema ('I'll always be alone') appeared as a 'knot' in her stomach, leaving Little Ariana (her Vulnerable Child mode) feeling scared, sad and ashamed.

T: Ariana, a moment ago, you said there's a void inside of you that comes up after Hari jumped in. Can you help me understand what it is like for you to be in that void?

A: What do you mean?

T: Take a moment to put yourself right back in that place, when you were telling me about wanting to talk to Hari about your vacation plans in the car. Hari jumped in, saying you weren't telling the truth. At that moment, you said a void came up inside of you. Can you help me understand what happened for you when you went into that void?

A: There was this incredible pressure in my chest, a tightness, like I was suffocating.

T: Good, Ariana. Imagine yourself in that moment right now. Notice the pressure, the tightness, that part of you that feels like she is suffocating. Where do you feel that in your body right now?

A: Right here [Ariana places her hand on her chest, then moves down toward her stomach].

T: Great, Ariana. What is that sensation in your stomach right now?

A: It's like a knot in the pit of my stomach.

T: Good. Stay in that place, and tune into the knot in your stomach. Can you give a voice to that knot, the sensation that came up after Hari jumped in, when you felt the tightness in your chest, like you were suffocating? What is that knot trying to say?

A: It's that part of me that is terrified. I'm so afraid of being swatted away. It's like I don't exist, I don't matter. What I want, and who I am, doesn't matter.

T: I see. [Therapist monitors Hari, ensuring he is present with Ariana's experience.] It's that part of you that feels like you don't count, and could just be swatted away. Is that right?

A: Yes, I don't matter. I'm alone.

T: Right, Ariana, that knot in your stomach comes up when you feel like you don't matter, and you feel all alone. That is a very scary place to be.

A: Yes, it's all I've known.

T: And then what happens, Ariana, when that part of you feels swatted away, and all alone?

A: I get incredibly sad. That it's all my fault and I'm a brat. That's when I feel the void.

T: And when you feel like you can't take it any more, you pull away, to protect yourself from the pain, and this void appears. Is that right?

A: I have to hide. There's no other way.

T: Can you help me, Ariana, to see if I've got it? When Hari jumps in, you feel this tightness in your chest, a knot in your stomach and you start to feel very sad and alone. Suddenly a blaming voice enters, telling you it's all your fault because you're too much. You feel like pulling back, to protect yourself from feeling more pain and you're left with a deep void inside, an emptiness. Is that right?

A: Yes, that's exactly right. It is empty. I'm alone because I'm not lovable.

Strengthening the healthy mode triad

Breaking a harmful mode cycle requires a couple to develop more flexible patterns of interaction between the healthy mode triad of the Healthy Adult, Vulnerable Child and Happy Child. Prior vignettes illustrate how the therapist guides Ariana to identify her EMS and modes, with a focus on developing awareness and empathy for her Vulnerable Child. Next, the therapist helps Ariana's Healthy Adult to cultivate assertiveness and to express vulnerability, inviting Hari to meet her core unmet needs.

In the next vignette, the therapist helps Ariana build adaptive skills by guiding her to ask for Hari's help to meet her needs rather than making an accusation, replacing 'stop attacking me' with 'help protect me'. The therapist guides Ariana to identify her fears and then invites her to imagine what it would be like if Hari satisfied her needs. Ariana is encouraged to articulate to Hari how he could best respond to her needs. The therapist's validation of Ariana's needs bolsters her Healthy Adult, helping her to advocate for her emotionally deprived Vulnerable Child.

T: Great work, Ariana. If we stay with the knot a bit longer, the part of you scared that she'll be alone and is unlovable, what does that part of you need from Hari? What could Hari do or say that would help loosen the knot?

A: Stop attacking me. Listen to me. Tell me I'm not crazy for just being me.

T: You need Hari to protect you from attacks and to listen to you. You need to know that he accepts and loves you. Is that right?

A: That's right. But I don't think he could ever truly accept me. It feels like I'm destined to be alone.

T: There is that part of you, the knot inside, that fears she'll never be good enough, and will always be alone.

A: It is hard to think it could ever be different.

T: What if we were to imagine how it would be for Hari to listen to you, and to accept you?

A: He would be patient with me. He would stand by my side when I'm scared. He would show me that he cares about me. He would want to know what I think and feel. I struggle to help Hari understand me, and I need his patience to get better at it.

T: Beautifully said, Ariana. One part of you feels like she is tied in a knot, afraid of getting swatted away because there's something wrong with you. This part wants you to pull away to protect yourself. To loosen that knot, you need Hari to patiently listen to you when you're struggling, to unconditionally accept you and to consistently show you that he cares about you. Is that it?

A: Exactly.

Connection dialogues

Part 1: expressing vulnerability and inviting needs

Recent theories of adult attachment suggest that by sharing vulnerability and inviting needs, couples develop a mutual responsiveness to each other that forms a secure, loving bond (Mikulincer & Shaver, 2016). Along similar lines in ST-C, in our experience, couples who regularly engage in connection dialogues are more likely to report relationship satisfaction and longevity. The initial component of the connection dialogues technique incorporates three key elements. First, both partners identify and express vulnerable emotions related to their Vulnerable Child. Therapists work to bypass coping modes in order to access the Vulnerable Child and protect partners against Dysfunctional Parent modes, as needed. Second, both partners identify and share coping mode 'urges' that arise when they experience a relational threat, helping both partners to take responsibility for their coping modes and to make sense of their mode cycle. Third, therapists guide each partner to invite the other to meet their core needs. Therapists work progressively to help partners bypass coping modes, and to become proficient with each element before advancing to the next component.

In the following vignette, the therapist combines all three elements of the first component with Ariana. She invites her to retell the story of the conflict in the car with Hari, interweaving her Healthy Adult and Vulnerable Child modes. Ariana identifies her vulnerable emotions, connects them to her needs and invites Hari to meet her needs. Initially, she struggles with the risk of sharing her vulnerability with Hari and flips into an Avoidant Protector mode. Employing consistent empathic attunement and validation, the therapist guides Ariana to overcome blocks set up by her Avoidant Protector.

The therapist guides Ariana to express her Vulnerable Child's feelings and needs to Hari. She also helps Ariana to identify the meaning of her experience, a crucial aspect of 'name it to tame it' when confronting fearful experiences (Siegel & Bryson, 2011). Expressing her understanding of her struggle strengthens the bond between Ariana's Healthy Adult and Vulnerable Child modes. The therapist emphasises Hari's importance to Arianna as an antidote to Hari's Defectiveness schema, a dominant driver of his part in their mode cycle. Finally, the therapist asks Arianna to rate the level of difficulty of showing her vulnerability to Hari. Although moderately anxiety provoking, she acknowledges it was tolerable for her, increasing the likelihood that she will use connection dialogues outside of the session.

T: Ariana, will you please look at Hari directly, and tell him how scary it is when you feel like you're being swatted away, how this knot comes up inside your stomach, and how you feel like retreating? Can you let him know that what you really need is for him to stay with you, to listen to you, and to understand you?

A: I'll try. [Ariana slowly looks directly at Hari.] When you jumped in, it felt like I was being pushed away, and I got really scared. I thought I was being rejected, so I felt like shutting off, but what I really need is for you to be open, to care about me.

T: Great, Ariana. Now please add the part about what you need from Hari.

A: When I feel pushed away, I get scared, and then I shut down, but what I really need is … [pauses] … this is really hard.

T: I know, and you're almost there. As scary as it is, can you add the part about what you need?

A: I need you to be patient with me. Stay with me and show me that you care about me. Show me that you're interested in what I have to say.

T: Excellent, Ariana. Finally, please share with Hari how much it matters to you for him to be the one to show you that he cares.

A: It would be the best feeling in the world, Hari, to know that you really truly care about me. You matter more than anyone to me.

T: Outstanding work, Ariana. How was that for you to share your fears and how much you need Hari to let you know that he cares about you?

A: Not easy. I felt like I was walking out on a limb.

T: It was very brave of you.

Part 2: responding to the Vulnerable Child

The second component of the connection dialogues intervention involves therapists guiding the listening partner to meet the inviting partner's core needs. This involves three main elements. First, therapists briefly summarise the emotional content shared by the inviting partner who expressed their vulnerability and needs. Second, therapists ask the listening partner questions to help them identify their coping mode in this situation, enabling greater empathy for their own and their partner's Vulnerable Child. Finally, therapists assist the listening partner as they express a response to the inviting partner's needs.

In the following vignette, the therapist explores Hari's initial reaction to Ariana's Vulnerable Child. Accessing his Healthy Adult, Hari uses his knowledge of Ariana's history and relates it to their mode cycle. Ariana's 'knot' reminds him of her fear of her father, enhancing his empathy as he responds to her core need in a genuine and caring way. Since Ariana is not accustomed to Hari's caring response, she is confused. Additionally, her Vulnerable Child is attacked by her Punitive Parent mode for making Hari uncomfortable. The Punitive Parent can shame a Vulnerable Child for causing a caregiver discomfort.

T: Can we check in, Ariana, with Hari now?

A: Yes, please.

T: Hari, how is it for you to hear Ariana share this part of her that feels a knot in her stomach, and is afraid of getting swatted away? You hear Ariana say that she pulls herself away to protect herself. Another part of her knows that you matter to her more than anyone. She needs to know that you care about her, that you want to understand her, and that you accept her. How is that for you to hear, Hari?

H: It's easy to respond to what she's asking for. I feel so much love for Ariana. When you asked her to untangle that knot, I imagined Ariana with her father. He's been such a bully to her. She has struggled with him. I never thought of it like this before, but now I realise that sometimes I probably remind Ariana of how her father makes her feel. I never want to make her feel like that. I want to protect her from him, to help her feel safe so she never feels that knot.

T: It is easy for you to tell Ariana that you love her and want to protect her. I am also curious, Hari, what do you notice right now when you say that sometimes you may remind Ariana of her father?

H: I don't want to be the bad guy like her father, so when I hear Ariana telling a story that makes me look bad, I want to stop her.

T: To cut off your own pain, perhaps the part of you that doesn't always feel so great about himself?

H: Yes, exactly. The last thing I want to do is hurt Ariana, to let her down, so when she starts to go down that road of how disappointed she is with me, I stop her.

T: Right, Hari. I hear you say that you love Ariana and want to understand her pain. When you hear her say that maybe you fell short and could be causing her pain, you try to stop her because it is so upsetting to imagine hurting her.. Am I getting it?

H: Yes, I can't bear to be the cause of her pain.

Having understood the intended function of the partner's coping mode in this situation, the therapist then shifts to help Hari express his underlying core need, in this case for acceptance in the face of making mistakes, an antidote to his Defectiveness schema.

T: That's right. Will you share that with Ariana right now, Hari? Will you look at her directly, and tell her that it is because you love her so much that you never want to disappoint her? Will you share with her that you try to stop her from expressing disappointment toward you because it hurts you so much? Can you ask Ariana to accept you, even when you sometimes let her down? Will you tell her that?

H: Ariana, I know it wasn't easy for you to tell me what you need from me. I see how much it hurts you when I get angry at you and shut you out. I don't want to send you back to that pain you had with your father. I want you to be proud of me, and to know that I want to protect you from that pain.

T: Excellent, Hari. How was it to share with Ariana that you see the impact that you can have on her, and that you truly love her, and want to protect her?

H: It felt great, even though it's hard to admit I sometimes hurt her. I want to untie that knot in her stomach, so she doesn't have to feel scared of me any more.

T: [Looking at Ariana, who begins to cry]. Ariana, I see your tears. How is it for you to hear Hari share his love for you, and to hear that he really wants you to be proud of him?

A: I had no idea that Hari was shutting me out because he cares so much about what I think of him. That feels amazing, but it is hard to believe. There is another side of me that starts to feel badly, like I'm making too big of a deal of this, and should just let him be.

T: It's hard for you, Ariana, to imagine that Hari loves you so much, and doesn't want to let you down? You notice this critical or punitive voice that comes up inside of you that puts you down. Whom does that voice remind you of?

A: It's my father. It is so hard to get him out of my head.

Imagery rescripting for couples

Part 1: setting the stage

Imagery rescripting for couples (IRC) is a core intervention to heal EMS, and is especially helpful when one or both partners have a history of trauma. By undertaking childhood imagery with each partner, it allows the couple to gain a felt sense of unmet childhood needs, both for themselves and their partners. They understand the origins of their EMS, and are able to become a reparenting figure for the other. Therapists conduct imagery in a similar manner as in individual ST, with the significant exception that therapists progressively invite the partner into the reparenting process. The goal is to gradually replace the therapist in the imagery with the partner, as they learn to attune and to meet their partner's needs.

To prepare for IRC, therapists explore details of a partner's childhood when their needs were unmet, similar to the assessment for imagery during individual ST (see Chapter 6 of this volume). Additionally, in ST-C therapists identify any significant past relationship injuries that may reinforce their EMS and current relationship's mode cycle. Therapists invite the listening partner to stay continuously engaged by enquiring about their reactions at key points of the image, enhancing empathy along with an explicit validation of their partner's core pain, when their childhood needs were unmet. This sets the stage for effective reparenting responses by the listening partner.

In the next vignette, the therapist builds on the healing momentum from the connection dialogues intervention by leading an IRC that targets Ariana's Emotional Deprivation schema, the part of her that believes that nobody will ever meet her needs, along with the Punitive Parent mode that tells her she is a 'brat' for being too emotional. The therapist guides Ariana through a toxic memory when she was six years old, involving her father. In the scene, Little Ariana was scared and needed protection and comfort. She relays, and expands on, some of the emotional, sensory and cognitive aspects in her early scene, similar to the process in imagery in individual ST. The therapist then guides her to identify what Little Ariana needed but did not receive, providing the basis for Hari's reparenting responses that are caring antidotes to Ariana's Emotional Deprivation schema. This process also helps Hari's Defectiveness schema, encouraging him to feel important and strong in nurturing Little Ariana.

T: Ariana, I suggest that we focus on the punitive voice of your father. May we do an imagery rescripting exercise together, with Hari's help?

A: Yes.

T: Hari, I'll let you know when to enter the scene, okay?

H: Sure.

T: Ariana, please close your eyes. You said you have this voice that keeps beating up on you, calling you a whiner, and making you feel badly about yourself. See if you can get an image from your childhood, when you're with your father, experiencing the same feelings. Allow the image to emerge, trying not to think too much.

A: I've got one. I'm in our house where I grew up. It's late at night. I don't know why, but I woke up and got really scared. I was alone in my room.

T: How old are you in this scene?

A: Maybe about six years old. I'm wearing my green pyjamas with pink elephants on them that my grandmother gave me when I was six years old.

T: You're in your room and something awakened you. You're feeling scared. What's happening now?

A: I'm lying totally still on my bed, very scared. I hear the TV. My dad usually falls asleep on the sofa with the TV turned on. I wrap myself up in my blanket. I slowly move towards the door, and open it. Sure enough, my dad is on the sofa, but he's not asleep. I'm trying to be really quiet. I decide that I want to lie on the floor and listen to the TV, hoping that my dad won't notice me.

T: And what's happening now?

A: My dad sees me, he's standing up from the couch, he's yelling at me, telling me to go back to bed. He's shouting, 'What the hell is wrong with you!' I'm so scared, I've started to pee. My dad sees the floor getting wet. He's very angry, screaming at me, 'What is fucking wrong with you? What kind of child pees on the floor?' My heart's sinking, and I can't speak. I feel frozen.

T: What a terrifying experience for Little Ariana.

Imagery rescripting for couples part 2: reparenting

As the IRC continues, the therapist shifts to bring Hari into the scene to help reparent Little Ariana. The therapist carefully guides Hari on how to meet the core needs of the six-year-old, terrified by her father. IRC typically elicits a strong reparenting response in partners, as they feel compassion for the child in the image. Therapists can focus on the partner's protective feeling toward the child in the scene, enabling them to express their care and to help their loved one in the image, as needed.

T: Hari, what is your reaction to what is happening with little Ariana and her father?

H: She doesn't deserve to be treated like that. I feel so sad for her, and want to jump in and protect her from him. He's terrifying her.

T: Will you please enter the image as the adult you are now?

H: Definitely!

T: Ariana, does Hari have your permission to enter the scene with little Ariana and your father?

A: Absolutely.

T: Imagine Hari standing next to you in the image, facing your father.

A: It is scary to imagine. My dad can be so mean.

T: I hear you, Ariana. Hari, as you're standing next to little Ariana, how can you protect her from her father?

H: I would tell her father to stop hurting little Ariana, and to see how terrified she is. I would tell him he has to stop treating her like this.

T: Go ahead and confront the father out loud.

H: You have to stop, now! You're terrifying little Ariana. I won't let you continue to scare her like this. She woke up feeling scared and needed comforting. Instead, you screamed at her, terrifying her so much that she panicked and peed in her pyjamas.

T: Yes, Hari, you're on the right track. Now tell Ariana's father how you feel about little Ariana.

H: Ariana is an amazingly wonderful person, and I love her. She deserves your love and protection. Ariana never deserves to be terrified, especially by her father. I won't let you treat her like that again.

T: Exactly. [Turning to Ariana.] What is little Ariana experiencing right now, as she hears Hari standing up to her father to protect her?

A: I'm amazed. My dad looks stunned. Nobody ever confronted him before.

T: What is this like for little Ariana now?

A: I feel relieved. It's strange. It feels great. I was only six years old, and I didn't do anything wrong. It felt so good, Hari, to have you there by my side to protect me.

T: [Turning to Hari.] What was it like for you, Hari, to confront little Ariana's father and to protect her?

H: It was easy. I would never let Ariana be treated like that by anyone. I am always here for you, Ariana, to protect both the little Ariana and the adult Ariana.

Conclusion

EMS are often activated by the people we love most. Understandably, couples can struggle to identify and adequately meet the needs underneath a partner's EMS, falling prey to an interpersonal trap that reinforces core relational pain. Schema Therapy for Couples provides a model to support couples to understand their default mode cycles and their core relational needs. Partners share vulnerabilities, identify core needs, and invite interactions with each other that promote schema healing. Using a range of ST-C strategies, including connection dialogues, IRC, reparenting and empathic confrontation, therapists guide partners to develop a healthy mode triad, consisting of their Healthy Adult inviting their Vulnerable and Happy Child modes to respond in ways that satisfy both partners' relational needs. As a relatively new and innovative approach, we invite further research to demonstrate ST-C's efficacy, especially for highly distressed couples unresponsive to traditional couples treatments.

Therapist tips

1. In distressed love relationships, Schema Therapy posits that Early Maladaptive Schemas prime negative interactions between partners, biasing how each partner experiences the other, creating self-perpetuating cycles of perceived threat or harm.

2. A key element involves the therapist and couple discovering together how each partner copes when their EMS are triggered in the relationship, discerning how their coping modes attempt to meet their needs in the face of a perceived relational threat through surrendering, avoiding, or overcompensating behaviours.

3. One important therapeutic task is to help patients soothe and regulate their emotions in the Vulnerable Child mode, a core skill for their Healthy Adult mode when activated in general, and central to remaining emotionally regulated in the session.

4. Unlike individual Schema Therapy, when the therapist is the primary source of reparenting, in ST-C therapists initially model reparenting to partners, and then guide each partner to reparent each other.
5. Therapeutic interventions help partners develop a sturdy healthy mode triad consisting of the Healthy Adult, Vulnerable Child and Happy Child modes. Partners create enough safety in the relationship to disclose vulnerability and to invite each other to respond in ways that meet their core needs.
6. Therapists can use the full range of ST-C strategies to promote change, including connection dialogues, imagery rescripting for couples, reparenting and empathic confrontation.

References

Arntz, A. & Jacob, G. (2013). *Schema therapy in practice: An introductory guide to the schema mode approach*. Chichester, UK: Wiley-Blackwell.

Atkinson, T. (2012)*Schema therapy for couples: Healing partners in a relationship*. In M. van Vreeswijk, J. Broersen & M. Nadort (Eds.), *The Wiley-Blackwell handbook of schema therapy: Theory, research, and practice* (pp. 323–335). Chichester, UK: Wiley-Blackwell.

Bamelis, L.L.M., Evers, S.M.A.A., Spinhoven, P. & Arntz, A. (2014). Results of a multi-center randomized controlled trial of the clinical effectiveness of schema therapy for personality disorders. *American Journal of Psychiatry, 171*, 305–322.

Farrell, J.M., Shaw, I.A. & Webber, M.A. (2009). A schema-focused approach to group psychotherapy for outpatients with borderline personality disorder: A randomized controlled trial. *Journal of Behavior Therapy and Experimental Psychiatry, 40(2)*, 317–328.

Giesen-Bloo, J., van Dyck, R., Spinhoven, P., van Tilbureg, W., Dirksen, C., van Asselt, T. & Arntz, A. (2006). Outpatient psychotherapy for borderline personality disorder. Randomized trial of schema-focused therapy versus transference-focused psychotherapy. *Archives of General Psychiatry, 63*, 649–658.

Gottman, J.M. (1999). *The marriage clinic*. New York: Norton.

Makinen, J. & Johnson, S. (2006). Resolving attachment injuries in couples using emotionally focused therapy: Steps toward forgiveness and reconciliation. *Journal of Consulting and Clinical Psychology, 74*, 1055–1064.

Mikulincer, M. & Shaver, P.R. (2016). *Attachment in adulthood: Structure, dynamics, and change* (2nd edition). New York: Guilford Press.

Siegel, D.J. (2010). *Mindsight*. New York: Bantam Books.

Siegel, D.J. (2012). *The developing mind* (2nd edition). New York: Guilford Press.

Siegel, D.J. & Bryson, T.P. (2011). *The whole-brain child*. New York: Delacorte Press.

Simeone-DiFrancesco, C., Roediger, E. & Stevens, B.A. (2015). *Schema therapy with couples: A practitioner's guide to healing relationships*. Chichester, UK: Wiley-Blackwell.

Young, J.E., Klosko, J.S. & Weishaar, M.E. (2003). *Schema therapy: A practitioner's guide*. New York: Guilford Press.

Part IV

Empathic confrontation and the therapy relationship

14 The art of empathic confrontation and limit-setting

Wendy Behary

When we engage patients from a sturdy adult posture we become better poised to effectively confront their issues with empathy and care. We may need to challenge their profound avoidance of emotion-focused work, or set limits with a patient who has escalated into a defiant, disrespectful, disparaging, or demanding mode. Some of our anxious/fearful patients will attempt to distract themselves and us from the deeper work of engaging emotions through the use of tangential storytelling, intellectual verbiage and reported amnesia, or simply stating that they are incapable of emotional and sensory awareness. Other patients (especially narcissistic types) may avoid painful emotional material and the risk of exposed vulnerability via (passive–assertive) chronic lateness to sessions or last-minute cancellations, or by (active–assertive) outbursts of anger and criticism when asked to make a commitment to be on time, to respectfully pay for missed time and to comply with the therapy process. All of these coping strategies offer an opportuntiy to dive deeper into their emotional world using our curiosity, empathy, attunement and authenticity. This chapter outlines the meaning of empathy and of being an authentic and sturdy caregiver in ST, as necessary prerequisites to either strategy. I then explore different elements of empathic confrontation including; our empathic lexicon, rising above the incident, making links to the past, implicit assumption, self-disclosure and the empathic preamble.

A sturdy and authentic caregiver

In order to confront and connect with our patients, securing the bond for effective healing and adaptive change, we need to work from a sturdy stance of authenticity and persistent curiosity; making sense of their overly intellectual, submissive, hypervigilant, defensive, angry and, sometimes, intense critical reactions to our efforts to engage with emotion. In other words, we try to step empathically into the patient's skin, to attempt to understand (in a felt way) their emotional reactions and behaviours vis-à-vis the backdrop of their personal narratives. These narratives include their early life experiences, unmet emotional needs, the onset of the activation of early maladaptive schemas (life themes), and the prevailing conditions that continue to trigger their schemas and modes. As postulated by the mirror neuron researcher Marco Iacoboni (2009), 'It seems as if our brain is built for mirroring, and that only through mirroring – through the simulation in our brain of the felt experience of other minds – do we deeply understand what other people are feeling.'

Empathy is not sympathy, nor is it compassion. Empathy is the resonant experience of listening with the intent to try to fully understand how the speaker feels; in addition to understanding his or her ideas, asking yourself the question 'What is it like to be that person sitting across from me?' Showing empathy involves identifying and making sense out of a person's thoughts, behaviours and emotional reactions in a given situation, even if you disagree with them. 'Wonderful things happen when people feel felt, when they sense that their minds are held within another's mind' (Siegel, 2010).

Empathy makes sense

From an empathically attuned posture, we identify patterns such as avoidance or aggression as a schema mode, linking it with a carefully constructed conceptualisation of the patient's makeup, that is, their biopsychosocial preparation for living in the world. We track links to lifelong fears of exposure of shame or inadequacy, fears of being controlled, or fears of being rejected, for example. We feel inevitable compassion for the suffering child in the once-upon-a-time story, one who may have endured confusing messages of manipulation, neglect and conditional acceptance, and we become more mindfully keen in sensing how insecurities of long ago have led to protective masks (for example, detached or overcompensatory attitudes and actions) in the here and now. Making sense out of their blustery, avoidant, charming, arrogant, raging, blaming, self-sabotaging modes also liberates us from the would-be assaults on ourselves from these modes, derived from our own schema activation, those that carry painful messages and labels such as *I am incompetent ... too sensitive ... I am a failure ... I don't try hard enough ... I am not strong enough ... I should be ashamed ... I have no value ...* and more. It is no wonder that studies suggest that 'empathy is a moderately strong predictor of therapy outcome' (Elliott et al., 2011). It is difficult, if not impossible, to be truly present when you are preoccupied with the (naturally reflexive) task of protecting and defending yourself against an angry or critical patient mode. Butressed in a sturdy adult mode we are able to maintain an empathic presence. I will share an example of how to address our own triggers later.

Empathic confrontation

In this stance of collaborative sense-making of the patient's schema driven reactions, and identifying the triggers occurring in the therapy relationship, we ready ourselves to apply empathic confrontation. The use of empathy can foster a connection and sense of shared understanding that draws the patient's attention toward you as opposed to activating their defensive reactions, such as detachment, or aggressive, interruptive counter-attacks. Schema therapists work from a place of 'realness', meaning we come from an authentic sense of self and a desire to be attuned. We respond with empathic statements like: 'Of course you're upset about feeling forced to come to therapy, and blamed for all of the conflict in your relationship; this feels like the story of your life and I can sense the truth in that feeling, but ...' or 'I know how much you value privacy, you were taught to keep family secrets locked away and to always maintain loyalty, but ...' or 'I understand this is a difficult thing to hear, especially given how hard you are trying to prove that you are worthy of trust again, but ...' or 'I fully sense that you didn't mean to be hurtful, but ...'. When we attune in this way, so the patient feels deeply held and understood, we open up a window of opportunity for a real connection. From this place, the patient is more able to 'hear' and tolerate the challenge.

Here is an example of empathic confrontation in the middle of a heated reaction from a narcissistic patient: you are about to confront 'Peter' who has betrayed a partner with acts of infidelity and is (too quickly) growing tired of her mistrust, her upset and what feels like judgements of him, including now his perception of your judgement. He expresses disgust and anger at you (and his partner) for what also feels like 'unfair suspicions' and a 'too tedious and ridiculous process'. He is desperate to be let off the hook of shame, and you know this because you are beginning to understand the boy from the past who could never quite get it right enough for anyone and was made to feel inferior if his performance was anything short of extraordinary.

Lexicon for empathy

Showing your attunement to his vulnerability might start with an empathic linking phrase to the past, for example, 'Must be difficult, Peter, when you feel that familiar spotlight on you as the "failure" or the "bad guy". This has roots in your childhood, yes? You often felt the unfairness of having to measure up to impossible standards and never feeling good enough, even when you met the high bar. You were mostly noticed and admonished for what your dad saw as your weaknesses. And when your partner is angry with you now (because it takes time to restore trust) you feel like you're being made into the bad guy again. ... And you want to cope by asserting that you are entitled to private and pleasurable distractions because you have worked hard, and you are feeling fatigued and under-appreciated. But the problem is that this mode (the part that we sometimes call the "entitled" mode), while helpful when you were young because it allowed you time out from intolerable demands and distress, now only serves to produce (unintentional) pain and heartache for those you love, and leads you right back to the feeling that you have to defend the so-called bad guy. You are hijacked by a deep and familiar pain, Peter, but the wiser part of you knows that healing from a betrayal is not an easy fix and you will need to exercise more tolerance and reassurance in order to repair this relationship. That's hard to do when you are in "combat mode" where you are busy fighting back as if you have to defend the unloveable child.'

This is the schema-perpetuating nature of maladaptive coping modes. Peter avoids his feelings of vulnerability, emptiness and insecurity and opts for a 'pleasurable distraction' – entitled to whatever he wants as a way of feeling special and extraordinary, a means for fighting his Defectiveness and Emotional Deprivation schemas. The problem is that this type of distraction is not spawned by the Healthy Adult mode – one that would thoughtfully guide him to accurately express his upsets to his partner and look for ways to soothe himself without harm to self and others. Instead, it is directed by the long ago constructed Detached Self-Stimulating and overcompensating modes (the Escape Artist, Entitled and Combat modes, as we are calling them) which ultimately serve to promote the feeling of being weak and ashamed (Defectiveness) and disconnected (Emotional Deprivation) from those he hurts with his betrayal and his angry, self-righteous defensiveness.

The therapist shows empathy and understanding for how the patient's current situation (his partner's anger) is triggering a very old theme (of feeling exposed and defective) and how he is drawn to a long established coping mechanism, which is to fiercely defend his schema (from his Combat mode), despite his 'wise side' (or Healthy Adult) knowing better. By sharing her observation of the pattern with empathy, rising above the here and now of the current incident, the therapist simultaneously helps the patient feel deeply understood and gain some distance from his coping modes. She also shares with him how she thinks his coping mode *perpetuates* his core schema and the pain of his Vulnerable Child mode – in this case, how his overcompensatory Combat mode operates on the assumption that he is fundamentally bad and unloveable (linked to his Emotional Deprivation and Defectiveness), both reinforcing his schema and pushing people away.

The message gets lost in the delivery

Another form of empathic confrontation differentiates between intention and impact. We offer the patient the benefit of the doubt in terms of their intentions, while fortifying accountability and setting limits: 'Your input can be such a valuable asset to your team, Dena, but when you take over without discussion or collaboration, your good intentions become overshadowed by that nagging old need to control.'

Notice how the therapist's use of the word 'but' becomes the essence of the confrontation and also predicts the trajectory of self-defeating life themes. The empathic prelude dilutes the impulse to defend or counter-attack when schemas are activated, while the *but* targets the problem and its undesirable effect – the maladaptive reactive modes, that is, the impact of offensive behaviours on others, the obstacles 'we' are facing together in the healing process. So, when Dale is triggered in session, feeling that he is being overlooked (Emotional Deprivation schema), put down (internalised Demanding Critic and Defectiveness schema), not competent enough (Failure schema), or used and controlled (Subjugation, Mistrust and Unrelenting Standards schemas), he easily launches his Bully and Attack mode with a ferocity that can be at worst frightening and at best still profoundly distracting, that is, we momentarily feel the intimidating and insulting wrath that others may experience when Dale is in this mode. In these moments, we are likely to experience the (reasonable) urge to protect ourselves from the onslaught of criticisms, cynical statements, gestures and escalating aggression. For example, this orchestra of schemas and pre-choreographed mode patterns can be easily called to centre stage after a co-worker boldly points out Dale's pattern of avoiding responsibility for any of the conflicts in his life and seems only to blame others for his problems at work (inferring that this is probably the case at home). Dale enters the treatment room fuming with anger expecting you, his therapist, to be in solidarity with an outpouring of insults and castigations against his colleague, starting with 'How dare he ... who does he think he is? ... These morons on my executive team need to get their heads out of their asses!' You attempt to validate the distress underlying the anger without the (requisite) unwavering agreement with the content and, predictably, he turns his attack on you, cynically stating that you are 'no different than the others I have to deal with. ... Maybe you are simply not competent enough to understand my world. ... Therapy is a waste of time and money. ... This is a joke' etc., etc. You feel the ouch, take a deep breath and ask Dale for a moment to figure out what's getting triggered for you in that moment, 'Just give me a moment Dale, this must be something important because even I am feeling triggered, and I am someone who truly knows you' (you close your eyes and raise your hand, indicating a request for his patience and silence for just a moment).

This limit-setting moment is critical for allowing you to restore yourself to your Healthy Adult caregiving mode, and models for Dale how a pause can be an effective strategy for communicating important feelings, as one of his central unmet needs is frustration tolerance when he doesn't get what he wants. With eyes closed, and deep breaths, you quickly conjure up an image of your vulnerable little self and an imaginary safe and calming place, thankful to her (or him) for reminding you of what life in Dale's world might be like, securing your little self in that safe place with the reassurance that you (the Healthy Adult and trained professional) can take care of Dale, your little self does not have to bear this burden and does not have to call upon your coping modes to protect her/him – the ones that might have you avoid Dale's behaviours, surrender to them, or defend yourself against them. You assure your little self with 'I've got this, and it does not have to be perfect, just real'.

With eyes now open, and Dale glaring at you (or staring into the distance), you share the most relevant details of your pause, 'When I feel triggered like that, I run the risk of giving in, giving up, or getting defensive, and none of these reactions would be helpful to you, Dale, despite the fact that it may feel acutely satisfying to the part of you that needs to be right, to assert what feels like the one and only truth without regard for the other person's feelings. This is what others do when faced with your anger or your insults; people who are not trained to understand your make-up and your underlying suffering and are also not responsible to do so. I know it is not your intention to be hurtful [the empathic benefit of the doubt], but [the confrontation] it is off-putting and hurtful and can leave the receiver feeling upset and potentially defensive, or, worse yet, they surrender to your tantrum and then feel resentful towards you. Sad, too, because there was an important [the use of the word "important" brings Dale's attention forward, making clear that what he is failing to express really matters] message you were trying to convey and it got lost in the delivery.' You can then suggest that Dale take another chance to express what he was feeling from his vulnerable side. With some assistance and persistence, he may be able to share that he felt 'very alone ... like there is no one to count on ... no one who understands me ... an old feeling ... not used to not getting the upper hand ... it's hard'. This we can work with, reparent, rescript, and gradually modify behaviours that have been self-defeating for too many years.

Empathic bluntness – setting a limit

Not all of our empathic confrontations have to be chock-full of language, especially when setting a limit where the patient's aggressive words or behaviours cross a line and present a threat. Sometimes, it may be simply put, 'I know you may not intend to be threatening, but right now I'm feeling uncomfortable and this is unacceptable. I have rights and you have rights. And this feels like a violation of my right to feel safe and respected.' The therapist may set a limit by suggesting, 'So, you can take a few minutes to pause and breathe and connect with your vulnerable little Joe, or you can take a walk, take some breaths, a drink of water, and come back so that we can explore what is probably a very important message and meaningful experience you are having underneath all of that distracting anger.'

Some patients will opt for the pause (especially those with abandonment issues) and some will take the walk and almost always return – even if it's just to get the last word in – but the de-escalation allows for better representation of the Vulnerable Child, real feelings behind the anger and criticalness, the 'important' message.

Bypassing detached modes

The use of imagery in Schema Therapy has been shown to be a highly effective strategy for meeting unmet emotional needs and installing adaptive behavioural changes. Another variant of avoidance we often encounter when attempting to use imagery in treatment with challenging patients is the defiantly Detached Protector mode. In this mode, a patient may use forcibly insistent phraseology such as, 'How many times have I told you that I just don't see images. ... I don't remember anything. ... This is silly, the past is done and this is not helping me find a job or save my marriage. ... I've done this before and it doesn't help, in fact it makes me feel worse.'

We know that for patients in this protective mode there is usually a hidden motivation responsible for the defiance, such as (1) fear of being misunderstood, (2) fear of exposing badness or weakness (3) fear of being abandoned, (4) fear of not being able to do the imagery and failing, (5) fear of a loss of control or falling apart and not being able to function, (6) fear of confronting guilt or punishment for revealing secrets/breaking loyalties, (7) fear of being controlled and having to surrender, (8) fear of losing their edge, their specialness, and more.

The more we persist in understanding the Detached mode by asking questions about its role, its origins and its primary function, and by identifying the downside risk of staying in this mode now (albeit helpful in early years as a source of survival for a powerless child), the greater the chance to shore up our appreciation of the hidden driver and begin the process of employing empathic confrontation to weaken and eventually bypass this mode. Using the implicit assumption strategy, a form of empathic confrontation that I developed for treating narcissists but can be expanded to work with many types of difficult patients, assumes there is something implicitly (remembering without realising one is remembering) motivating the drive to detach and disconnect from a painful emotional experience. Making the implicit story an explicit one is a form of sense-making, connecting the dots, a means for allowing us to see a full picture of mode reactions and how these show up under certain conditions that trigger implicitly reminiscent experiences.

Once pulled from the archives and made explicit, we are enabled to execute the reparenting and rescripting work necessary to heal or modify old enduring dysfunctional beliefs and patterns while adopting and fortifying new and sustainable healthy patterns. For example, we might propose something like the following: 'I wonder how scary it must be right now for Little Dena as I look at the "fortress" mode sitting in that chair [this is a collaboratively created label for how it feels when she is in the detached protector mode]? I face the "guard" at the gate [defiant aspect of the mode] who forbids anyone from geting in to see Little Dena and disallows her from coming out and I know it must be very scary because that guard is formidable and angry. And I can understand that, based on what we have figured out together about how exposing the past, the secrets, and allowing yourself to realize that you have rights, feels like a betrayal against your mother, one that will harm you. [Dena nods and drops her head.] And if I could speak with the guard at the gate of this fortress I would like to say thank you for your efforts at protecting Little Dena because, of course, she was helpless once upon a time and had no one to protect her ['of course' is an empathic term indicating a certain knowing, an understanding]. You taught her how to follow rules and how to use her innate sensitivity to be a very good child – even though we know she shouldn't have been expected to be so perfect – and how to keep the peace so she could feel safe. But, she paid a big price by continuing to carry forth into her adult life the idea that she still has no right to assert her ideas, her preferences, her opinions, or to set limits when she is being disregarded or hurt. She has suffered a lot and has paid a big price and now has the chance and the right to be free from this burden. She is no longer helpless, nor is she a performer for her mother to win approval from others. She has me now, and I care very much about her and would like to help her, but I need to be able to access her from within that fortress, because it now only serves to stifle her and make her feel lonely and resentful. She deserves to have a voice and she deserves to know how lovable she is without having to prove anything. And, she has a Healthy Adult in herself and in me who can stand up for her. Perhaps you could step aside for a few minutes so that Healthy Adult Dena and I could connect with Little Dena?'

Negotiating with defiantly Detached Protector modes by using empathic confrontation can be a meaningful step in taking down the walls of the fortress so as to reparent, rescript and unburden Dena from the battle fatigue and loneliness that comes from isolating her realness, giving into (learned) self-imposed demands and expectations of submission, only to become angry and resentful and cutting people out of her life or alienating them with her moody detachment, to reduce and eventually abolish her internalised Demanding Critic, and to fortify her assertiveness and her sense of healthy entitlement and self-worth.

Empathic preamble

This final illustration of empathic confrontation is one I call the pre-emptive measure for empathic confrontation or, simply, the empathic preamble to confrontation. What this means is that you are taking into account what you 'know' (empathy) about the patient's sensitivities to anticipate their probable schema-driven reactions. These sensitivities can be to certain words, gestures and facial expressions that become immediately transcribed by memorised experiences into schema-driven experiences. For example, Joe (who has narcissistic personality disorder) is extremely sensitive to feeling used, inferior and ashamed. He easily shifts into a defensive and critical mode when triggered and threatens to end therapy, followed by a detached distracted mode. So much so that when you attempt to interrupt a tangential flow of approval-seeking storytelling and point out the possibility of his avoidance, and perhaps too much 'proving himself' (as well as reminding him that he doesn't have to do this with you) he harrumphs and shifts into his arrogantly defensive posture, 'Okay, whatever, I was trying to share an important point but I guess it's your show', accusing you of being perhaps too myopic and too controlling, something he also feels towards his partner. One way to prevent this from occurring or to repair it promptly when it does is to use the empathic preamble. It might sound like this, 'Joe, I am sorry to interrupt. I know it makes you feel like I am not interested in what you have to share and that I am just like everyone else you were supposed to trust – that it's my show, my agenda, my expectations of you. Please look at me Joe – it's me, Wendy, the one who cares about you and wants you to have satisfying relationships with others, to let them see you fully from your precious vulnerable side to your bright, talented and witty side, the real you, with nothing to prove. I am not your dad or your competitive older brother … the ones who made you feel used and who sabotaged your efforts, while targeting you for greatness. Look here Joe, it's me. I have no agenda except your happiness and your needs being met so that you can more freely love and be loved, something you didn't have as a child. Now, let's see if we can figure out what activated this shift into your 'entertaining' [approval-seeking] mode and then let's see if we can sidestep it together and take care of Little Joey, you and me as a team.'

Summary

Empathic confrontation promotes a necessary differentiation between past and present experiences, enabling us to connect with the hidden hurts, shame and hopelessness that reside behind strong barricading modes, originally designed as the only source of protection and survival. This strategy also enables us to set healthy limits and ensure adaptive standards for those afflicted with the unmet need for flexibility, frustration tolerance, reciprocity, abiding respect for others, impulse control and the ability to adhere to reasonable rules – all part of a developing child's necessary preparation for living successfully in the interpersonal world of otherness.

Schema Therapy offers a robustly rich and comprehensive conceptualisation, as part of the assessment phase of treatment, one that informs our navigating system in the treatment room, making it possible to confront some of the most immovable impasses in therapy by accurately articulating carefully crafted empathic statements and questions that promote connection to, and healing of, internal suffering. The fundamental role of an effective clinician starts with a sensing, resonating, knowing connection with another and, from this stance, we have the privilege of witnessing the courage of humans as they pursue the most difficult and meaningful emotional transformations.

Therapist tips

1. Use your natural empathy, it is your greatest strength as a schema therapist. Empathy is the resonant experience of listening with the intent to try to fully understand how the speaker feels; in addition to understanding his or her ideas, asking yourself the question 'What is it like to be that person sitting across from me?'

2. Understand your patient's most off-putting moments in terms of their history being played out in the present (an old feeling, an old way of surviving under impossible emotional circumstances) as they desperately try to protect themselves and keep you at arm's length, away from their core vulnerability.
3. Use your rich schema conceptualisation to 'see' and articulate what is happening between you and to navigate the most immovable impasses in therapy.
4. Ground and soothe your own Little Side ('I've got this, and it does not have to be perfect, just real') to enable you to rise above the incident, empathically confront and set limits with your patient.
5. Remember that your patient's Vulnerable Child is there (however hidden and seemingly invisible behind a wall of highly off-putting coping strategies) and your authentic connection, even when challenging, offers the potential for emotional transformation.

References

Elliott, R., Bohart, A.C., Watson, J.C. & Greenberg, L.S. Empathy (2011). *Psychotherapy (Chic)*, *48*(1), 43–49. 10.1037/a0022187

Greenberg, L. *Emotion-focused Therapy: Coaching Clients to Work Through Their Feelings* 2nd edition. Washington, DC: American Psychological Association (APA) (2015).

Iacoboni, M. *Mirroring People: The Science of Empathy and How We Connect with Others*. New York: Picador (2009).

Siegel, D. *Mindsight, The New Science of Personal Transformation*. New York: Bantam Books (2010).

15 Authenticity and personal openness in the therapy relationship

Michiel van Vreeswijk

What do we mean by authenticity in the context of a therapeutic relationship and how important is it to the well-being of our patients? Authenticity can be defined as 'the quality of being real or true' (Cambridge Dictionary, 2017) and concerns relational experiences such as truthfulness, commitment, sincerity, devotion, and positive intention (Wikipedia, 2017). Authenticity shows itself through self-expression, body language and other non-verbal communications and, in the context of therapy, it involves sharing our thoughts, feelings and experiences in the service of our therapy relationship and our patient's goals.

How we orientate ourselves to authenticity depends in part on our therapeutic goals. In offering limited reparenting to the Vulnerable Child, an authentic connection may centre, for example, on the therapist being nurturing, appreciative and encouraging, *deliberately ignoring* off-putting behaviours from a coping mode. As such, an authentic connection here is about seeing past the coping mode to the patient's core feelings and needs underneath. At other times, in reaching out to their to the patient's Healthy Adult, authenticity may involve the therapist sharing their personal reactions to a coping mode or off-putting behaviour much more directly, fulfilling the need to be 'real' and providing a starting point for understanding a mode cycle in the therapy relationship. Further, of course, therapists make mistakes and experience schema-driven reactions to patients that may be sensed by the patient (even if nothing is said), posing another dilemma about how best to name authentically (or not) 'the elephant in the room'.

It could be argued that, in being authentic, the therapist is guided by their patient's overarching need for a level of honesty and openness (for the therapist to be 'real' with them) in the context of thoughtful reflection of their patient's schemas and broader therapeutic needs.

This is challenging work, as we can be 'pulled off' by our own schemas and those of the systems in which we work. There can also be something akin to therapeutic drift, whereby we can be quietly drawn to the path of least emotional resistance with our patients and during supervision – opting for the 'softer' option on the one hand (e.g., being mainly nurturing, understanding and accepting) or technical proficiency on the other (e.g., detailed attention to chair work, imagery, etc.) as ways of avoiding the more challenging task of bringing ourselves more fully into the therapy relationship.

This chapter is aimed at raising awareness of the patterns that may draw us away from being optimally authentic with our patients and to help us step back with curiosity and compassion such that we move towards a renewed commitment to reconnect with our patients.

The patient's experience of authenticity

Have you ever had a patient say to you: 'You're just saying that because you're a therapist, because it's your job.' Or 'This is just one of the techniques you use.'

What the patient may be asking is: 'Are you being authentic with me?' On one level, their question may be driven by their schemas and modes: it might be that their Mistrust/Abuse schema is saying, 'Be careful, this is just a setup to lure you in.' Or their Emotional Deprivation schema might say, 'I cannot believe that this person is genuine and is able to see and connect with how I feel.' Or their Abandonment/Instability schema might say, 'If you start to connect with this therapist, sooner or later he/she will leave and you will be on your own, so is this really worth investing in?'

But what if we set the patient's schemas aside for a moment and ask ourselves: 'Are we being authentic with this patient in this moment?' Probably most of us will say *yes* and either try to prove it or say something along the lines of: 'I wonder what led you to believe that my care for you is just a technique? Is there a schema or a mode activated?' But be honest. Were you really authentic at that particular moment in time? Or were you disconnected, afraid, or even angry with your patient? Perhaps you have unknowingly revealed this non-verbally or verbally, even though you did your best to be present and attuned to their needs. I know I've had many occasions where I was less authentic than I would like to be, often unknowingly and for a range of different reasons. For example, because I was preoccupied by a personal problem, or because I was unsure about where to go next in therapy. Or because I was in doubt about how best to express my thoughts about our relationship. And, yes, there are still moments where I try to persuade myself of my clear and simple intentions (for example, when they say, 'this is just one of the techniques you use') even though something else more complex is going on for me.

Although I would like to say that these moments have become less over time, it is probably more accurate to say that I am more aware of a sense of doubt about my authenticity in that moment. I try to foster this doubt, especially during the moments that are most uncomfortable for me, when part of me would prefer to dismiss them and carry on regardless. This chapter is aimed at helping us face the task of how to be authentic and open in such a way that optimises the therapeutic relationship, to form the foundation for new attachment experiences and limited reparenting.

Exercise 1 How authentic am I?

Do you know where you stand on authenticity? How would your patients answer this question about you, how would they rate your authenticity? What would be the most difficult answer to hear? What would be pleasing to hear?

When am I at my most authentic with my patients? When am I at my least authentic? What stops me from being more authentic? What helps me to be more aware, honest and open, even when my message is sensitive or unwelcome?

Qualities of an authentic therapist

An authentic therapist strives for an honest relationship with his patient at all times, being committed and genuine but not necessarily always sharing everything, especially if it is not in the service of the therapy process. The clinical judgement involved in when and what to share is complex and involves considering both the patient's and the therapist's needs and capacity to handle often emotive interactions, at a particular point in time.

An authentic therapist strives to share both positive and negative reactions to his patient and is open to his patient's reactions to him, even if they are hard to hear or present difficult dilemmas as to the best way forward. Furthermore, I postulate that being authentic as a therapist means that you have to be (a) honest with yourself about your feelings towards the patient and how therapy is progressing, (b) able to question your intrapersonal and interpersonal reactions, (c) be willing and able to share your thinking and some of your experiences with your patient and (d) be willing and able to share your thinking and experiences with your colleagues (e.g., in supervision).

To achieve all of the above you have to have a positive and well-established self-concept; however, as schema therapists, we know this is not a static state as we all have the potential to get pulled off track by our schemas and modes. Supervision and personal therapy have a central role to play in understanding our own reactions, healing our schemas and developing a balanced and positive self-concept.

In my view, authenticity is a necessary ingredient in building a good working alliance in which limited reparenting is possible, ruptures are handled adequately and the chance of drop out is minimised. Continually hiding and masking our feelings from our patients can be both stressful and unnatural. Furthermore, an authentic stance reduces the risk of secondary traumatisation and burnout. This chapter aims to help you to: a) become more attuned to the quality of your own authenticity, b) track how your schemas and modes interact with your authenticity, c) work on harnessing and fostering authenticity, d) use authenticity in case of therapy ruptures and e) become aware of possible pitfalls in being authentic.

Being an authentic therapist and the role of schemas and modes

The case of therapist Quinn: part 1

Quinn is a 58-year-old psychotherapist who has been mainly trained in CBT and EMDR. His father was a sergeant in the military and his mother was a housewife. Quinn's brother is a Member of Parliament and his sister is a Professor of Clinical Psychology. As a child, there were strict rules in his family which everyone followed without question. His father was a dominant, quiet man who showed his anger but did not show any other emotions. His mother was an 'obedient' wife who hid her feelings from her husband and children. Quinn, his brother and sister were educated at international private schools and prestigious universities. Quinn's main schemas are Defectiveness/Shame, Unrelenting Standards and Failure. His most important modes are Detached Protector, Compliant Surrender and Punitive Parent.

The case of the co-therapists couple Yara and Roy: part 1

Yara is a 38-year-old psychotherapist who has been trained in psychoanalysis and mentalisation-based therapy. She has recently undertaken ST training, as she and Roy are soon to work as co-therapists in a randomised controlled trial on group ST. Roy is a 32-year-old clinical psychologist who has been trained in DBT, group therapy and ST. Yara comes from a family in which talking about emotions was not the done thing. Keeping up appearances was more important than sharing your inner thoughts and emotions. Her main schemas are Emotional Inhibition, Unrelenting Standards and Self-Sacrifice and her main modes are Healthy Adult, Happy Child and the Demanding Parent. Roy, on the other hand, comes from a family in which there was never enough sharing of emotions, his mother having borderline personality disorder and his father and sister having attention deficit hyperactivity disorder. Roy's main schemas are Abandonment/Instability, Social Isolation/ Alienation and Failure. His main modes are Demanding Parent, Healthy Adult and Self-Aggrandiser.

In the case of Quinn (Figure 15.1), you can see how several schemas and modes run through the family tree, sometimes skipping one generation, sometimes passed on in the first line. You can also see that the level of authenticity is low in Quinn's family, especially on his father's side. If you were to fill in a genogram for Yara and Roy, using your imagination to fill in the gaps, what would it look like? What would the different members of

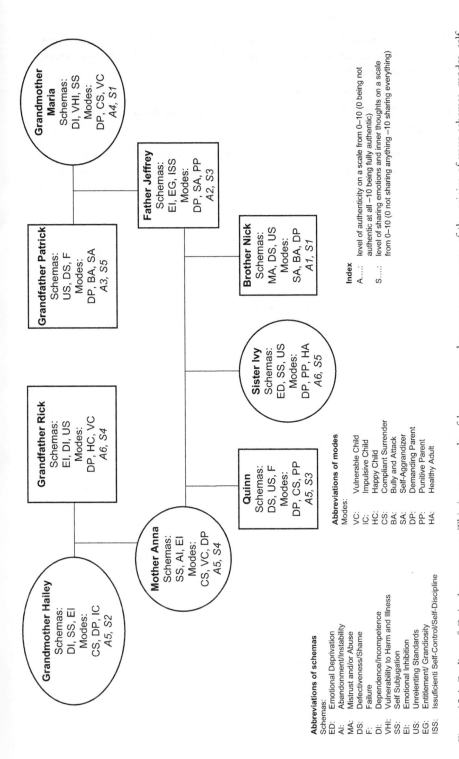

Figure 15.1 Outline of Quinn's genogram. This is an example of how you can become more aware of the origins of your schemas, modes, self-disclosure and authenticity in relationships.

Grandmother Hailey
Schemas:
DI, SS, EI
Modes:
CS, DP, IC
A5, S2

Grandfather Rick
Schemas:
EI, DI, US
Modes:
DP, HC, VC
A6, S4

Grandfather Patrick
Schemas:
US, DS, F
Modes:
DP, BA, SA
A3, S5

Grandmother Maria
Schemas:
DI, VHI, SS
Modes:
DP, CS, VC
A4, S1

Father Jeffrey
Schemas:
EI, EG, ISS
Modes:
DP, SA, PP
A2, S3

Mother Anna
Schemas:
SS, AI, EI
Modes:
CS, VC, DP
A5, S4

Quinn
Schemas:
DS, US, F
Modes:
DP, CS, PP
A5, S3

Sister Ivy
Schemas:
ED, SS, US
Modes:
DP, PP, HA
A6, S5

Brother Nick
Schemas:
MA, DS, US
Modes:
SA, BA, DP
A1, S1

Abbreviations of schemas
Schemas:
ED: Emotional Deprivation
AI: Abandonment/Instability
MA: Mistrust and/or Abuse
DS: Defectiveness/Shame
F: Failure
DI: Dependence/Incompetence
VHI: Vulnerability to Harm and Illness
SS: Self Subjugation
EI: Emotional Inhibition
US: Unrelenting Standards
EG: Entitlement/ Grandiosity
ISS: Issuficienti Self-Control/Self-Discipline

Abbreviations of modes
Modes:
VC: Vulnerable Child
IC: Impulsive Child
HC: Happy Child
CS: Compliant Surrender
BA: Bully and Attack
SA: Self-Aggrandizer
DP: Demanding Parent
PP: Punitive Parent
HA: Healthy Adult

Index
A....: level of authenticity on a scale from 0–10 (0 being not authentic at all –10 being fully authentic)
S....: level of sharing emotions and inner thoughts on a scale from 0–10 (0 not sharing anything –10 sharing everything)

his family say about sharing feelings or being authentic? What ideas might they have about good parenting? What schemas and modes do you think each family member has?

Exercise 2 From present to past, creating your own authenticity genogram

Use the format in Figure 15.1 to map out your own and your family's attitudes and approach to self-disclosure, openness and authenticity. In doing so ask yourself:

1. What schemas and modes do I have? (As a tool, you might fill in the schema and mode questionnaires YSQ and SMI.)
2. Where do I stand on sharing my emotions and inner thoughts?
3. What are my personal values?
4. What are my needs?
5. Where do I stand on being authentic in relationships?
6. Where would I like to be on authenticity in ten years' time?

Now ask these questions also for your siblings, parents and grandparents. Perhaps it's even possible to ask them the questions directly. Do you see any patterns emerging?

Besides becoming aware of your schemas and modes it is also good to realise that schemas are developed (partly) as a result of unmet core needs. Lockwood and Perris (2012) describe per schema the proposed unmet need. From their perspective, Quinn's unmet needs would be unconditional acceptance and love (Defectiveness/Shame), guidance in appropriate standards and ideals (Unrelenting Standards) and support and guidance in developing mastery (Failure). Yara most likely had unmet needs for a stimulating playful and spontaneous environment (Emotional Inhibition), guidance in appropriate standards and ideals (Unrelenting Standards) and balance in the importance of each person's needs (Self-Sacrifice). For Roy, it would be a stable attachment figure (Abandonment/Instability), inclusion and acceptance in a community (Social Isolation) and support and guidance in developing mastery (Failure).

In each case, their unmet needs, schemas and predominant coping styles were highly relevant to their relationship with authenticity in that moment. In the examples above, when their schemas were triggered, the therapists typically tried to hide their feelings or overcompensated, leaving the patient with a sense of something important being missing or unspoken.

Therapist self-awareness gained through life experience, personal therapy and ongoing clinical supervision form the foundations for authentic clinical encounters. For example, if you are aware that you have an Emotional Inhibition schema then it could be important to find family members, friends and colleagues who are more expressive, spontaneous and playful, who inspire you to let your hair down and open up a little. Or, if you have Unrelenting Standards, it is important to find a workplace where standards and ideals are valued alongside having a healthy work life balance. Without this, there is a high risk of burnout for therapists with unrelenting standards (Keading et al., 2017; Simpson et al., 2018) which will be a hindrance to being authentic.

Exercise 3 Imagery to bring you a step closer to your authenticity, needs and personal values

You can either complete this exercise with a colleague/friend or make an audio recording of the instructions on your phone and then play the recording back with your eyes closed.

1. Please close your eyes and let your attention go to your breathing, to that place in your body where you are most aware of your breathing in the here and now without having to change it.
2. Go to that place in your body where you are most aware of your emotions, where you are most aware of your Vulnerable Child. What does that side of you need? Does it need to feel connection and acceptance? Does it need to feel more autonomous, stronger, more confident? Does it need help in finding a balance? Does it need help to find adequate limits?
3. Take your time and listen openly to what your Vulnerable Child is saying to you. When you notice that you are drifting away (perhaps because you anticipate some difficult emotions coming up for you), bring yourself kindly back to your Vulnerable Child. When you notice that you start to judge yourself or this exercise, send this critical and punitive part away as it will not help you to become more aware of what you really need. If you want to, you can always go to your breathing to become more aware of the here and now.
4. Allow yourself to wander off to that place in your body where you are most aware of happiness. Where you feel the energy freely floating. Where you are smiling. Where you are in a playful mood. What is it that your Happy Child is enjoying? What does your

Happy Child like? Is there anything else that makes that part of you feel happy, playful or energetic? Feel free to have it. Enjoy it.

5.   When you are ready, go to that part of your body where you feel able to be accepting, kind and wise. What is this Healthy Adult part of you saying? What do you value? What helps you feel proud of yourself? To feel secure and attached? Are you able to listen to what other people think of your values? Are you open and curious in hearing their views? Let some important other people speak to you. What do they say? How does that feel to you? Please feel free to interact with them in a wise, kind and accepting way. Learn from them what you can and want to learn.

6.   Now go back to your breathing again, to that place in your body where you are most aware of the breathing in the here and now, without having to change it.

7.   Count to three and open your eyes slowly. Take some time to experience what you experience without having to do anything.

It can be helpful to make a drawing of what you have experienced. Share it with somebody you love and trust.

External influences on our authenticity

Schemas and modes are active within and between each subsystem and, equally, have an impact on authenticity. For instance, in group schema therapy there can be a shared schema, mode or coping style which dominates the group dynamic. So, for example, when of the majority of patients in a group have a Social Isolation schema, they are likely to withdraw when they feel threatened, instead of sharing their worries with the group. When the Demanding Parent mode is dominant, the group is likely to focus on solutions and results rather than 'wasting time' expressing and sharing emotions.

In individual therapy, you might try to send the Demanding Parent away, for example, but if the patient goes home to a partner who is demanding, the mode may well get preserved. In a sense, it is needed to help them meet their partner's expectations. Why is this so important in the case of openness and authenticity, you may ask yourself? In a lot of cases, people who have a Demanding Parent struggle with the concept of openness and authenticity as they tend to see this, from the Demanding Parent perspective, as a sign of weakness. In such cases, you are working with their own and, indirectly, their partner's Demanding Parent modes in exploring their options around openness and authenticity.

The case of therapist Quinn: part 2

Quinn hesitantly started to attend ST workshops and supervision three years ago because some younger colleagues in his mental health care institute were trained in ST and were very enthusiastic about it. In their young and energetic way, they described ST as the new 'gold standard' in psychotherapy which could be applied for any presentation. In particular, they liked the focus on the therapeutic relationship and teased Quinn about his 'old-fashioned' view that the therapy relationship was mainly a hindrance and that an emphasis on technique was the way forward. Quinn sought out support for his views from his CBT and EMDR peer supervision groups and from some of his managers, who were originally trained as CBT therapists.

The case of the co-therapists couple Yara and Roy: part 2

Yara is a bit nervous when she realises that she is going to have Schema Therapy supervision together with Roy. She has heard stories about the supervisor, who is apparently very experienced, open and challenging. She has also heard that the supervisor places great emphasis on sharing your own schema and mode triggering in supervision and with patients. She thinks that it will be easy for Roy, as he is always so expressive. At the first supervision session, they are asked to share something about their own schemas and modes and possible pitfalls in their therapeutic relationship. Roy immediately starts to share, in an almost blasé style, about his schemas and modes. The supervisor sees how Yara shuts down and withdraws. The supervisor stops Roy and asks Yara what is going on. Yara manages to say that she is feeling a bit nervous about sharing. That she is not used to doing that. The supervisor asks Roy if he was aware of this and points out to Roy that his blasé style might have triggered Yara. Roy explains he was not aware of that and he thought that he was doing a 'good job' by modelling that he found it easy to talk about his schemas and modes. His Failure schema is then activated and the supervisor reassures him that its normal for co-therapists to trigger each other sometimes and it's good to be able to talk about it. The supervisor underlines the importance of sharing with each other and being there for your co-therapist. The supervisor facilitates a conversation between Yara and Roy about how they might trigger each other and what they need when this happens. Although the conversation was awkward at points, both Yara and Roy seem relieved and closer as a result.

It can happen that we forget to ask our colleagues what we need from them. In some workplaces, it is even taboo and seen as unprofessional. In such working environments, the Unrelenting Standards schema and Demanding Parent mode are likely to be dominant and active much of the time. Having seen many therapists for personal Schema Group Therapy, I have become aware that many of them have learned to cope with emotions in the workplace by pretending that they are in their Healthy Adult or

Happy Child mode while, in fact, they are living with the Demanding Parent (their own and the system's) at their side. Showing vulnerability in these contexts is quite often seen as weakness, so their other reactions and emotions are suppressed.

For some, coming from backgrounds where their parents had a psychiatric illness or if they were bullied or failed at school, they can sometimes experience an added sense of shame about being vulnerable within the workplace. Schemas such as Social Isolation and Defectiveness/Shame are more likely to be activated in workplaces where there is a strong Demanding Parent mode at play, sometimes causing the therapist to withdraw or detach, sometimes to overcompensate, showing only their competent side.

Other workplaces have a culture where the team needs to be like a happy family, in which positive feelings and a certain sort of vulnerability (usually unrelated to the team) is routinely shared and there is a high level of emotional involvement. However, because of the pressure to be a 'happy family', more complex feelings toward each other such as frustration, competition and mistrust are studiously ignored. Obviously, both types of work environments can be toxic and act as a barrier to healthy authenticity among colleagues and between patients and therapists. Finding a healthy balance is a difficult task which sometimes benefits from an external facilitator, but it seems that this is something we rarely do in mental health care.

Exercise 4 Authencity and openess in a wider context

In the case of individual therapy

1. Try asking your patient what other people in their lives would say about an important issue or pattern? What would be their perspective? Invite family members or friends, especially in long-term treatments and/ or cases where there are many interpersonal problems.
2. Use an empty chair to represent the different elements of the outside world. Ask the patient what this empty chair would say when being honest and genuine. Encourage the patient to be authentic in their response. Help the patient by using your own authenticity; for example, by sharing something you have struggled with, something that rumbled your vulnerability.

In the case of group therapy

1. Be aware of dominant schemas, modes and coping styles among the group and how these have an impact on the group's ability to

---

be open and authentic. Encourage the group to discuss their collective schemas and group coping styles. Helpful questions can be: If the group were a person, what would be their most dominant schema or mode? What's the dominant coping style of this group?

2. Do (historical) roleplays, involving group members playing an important person in the life of a particular group member, to figure out what messages have been transmitted about being vulnerable and the capacity to be open about feelings.

In the case of your working environment

1. Start gently testing out with colleagues whether there is capacity to share in open and genuine ways.
2. Try to involve an external facilitator to support your team's relational development.

Working on your authenticity

Having read so far, what is your perspective on your authenticity? Is there anything you want to change? What would it look like if you made some adjustments to your level of openness? How might it change your relationships with your patients, colleagues, or in your private life?

The case of therapist Quinn: part 3a

Quinn was invited by his younger colleagues to participate in a Schema Therapy peer supervision group. As part of supervision, the group practised expressing some of their needs to each other. This contrasted strongly with the more technical approach Quinn was used to; however, in this context, he discovered that it felt okay to share and to show something of his vulnerable side, that it was actually more comforting and helpful in some situations when he received emotional support instead of technical tips. It enabled him to open up more at work with colleagues and patients and in his private life.

The case of therapist Quinn: part 3b

Quinn meets a new client, Roger, who is 23 years old. Roger smells of sweat when he enters the room and his hand feels sticky as they shake hands. Quinn feels queasy because of the smell but tries not to show it to Roger. Roger looks at him tentatively and says, 'Do you have kids, 'cause you look like an old unmarried guy to me? I ask because I'm wondering if you know anything about how it is to be young these days and I'm definitely not looking for an old therapist who is going to give me advice from the 1960s and 1970s.'

Quinn's automatic urge is to distance himself and to think of a technique he can use to help 'the boy' understand that this kind of narcissism will not help him in life. Feeling this urge, he remembers something from his last Schema Therapy peer supervision: the importance of sharing. Quinn takes a moment to become aware of what he is feeling, the schemas and modes enlivened in him. He then says to Roger, 'Roger, I notice that I feel offended and I'm just working out why. I think it's because it felt as if you were devaluing me by saying the things you have just said. I would like us to get to know each other better instead of being judgemental. I do not like to start this way. Can we please have a new start?'

Roger is taken aback. He is not used to people being this open and direct and he can see that Quinn is sincere in what he is saying.

The case of the co-therapists couple Yara and Roy: part 3

In supervision Yara practised being more open and showing different sides of herself. She learned to talk to the Vulnerable Child in Roy and reveal something of her Vulnerable Child to him. Roy learned to listen more deeply to Yara's experience and no longer hid behind his Self-Aggrandiser. They discovered how it was helpful to share with each other what they needed and how, as 'parents', they formed a healthy couple for group members. By being all right in sharing some vulnerabilities and differences of opinion as a 'couple' in the group, Yara and Roy made it feel easier and safer for group members to be more authentic, even around sensitive topics that had been previously avoided.

Reading these cases, what would you need from a colleague to help face and work with your emotional reactions with these patients?

Exercise 5 A future, more authentic you

1. Ask patients, colleagues, friends for feedback on your authenticity and see what you think of it. Is there anything you want to change?
2. If you want to make a change, make a plan with goals. What would you notice if you changed in this way? Decide how and when you would evaluate the changes. Be as specific as possible. Share your plan with somebody who is close to you.
3. Make a drawing of your future authentic self or do an imagery exercise in which you make contact with your future authentic self, envisage what this side looks and feels like.

4. Place a large mirror on a chair and position it so it's facing you. Imagine you are facing and talking with a future, more authentic you about your hopes and fears. What do you need from this side of yourself to begin the change process?

The limits of disclosure and authenticity

A common mistake can be in the timing with which we share our thoughts and feelings with our patients. Sometimes, our Demanding Parent pushes us to act hastily, demanding solutions or wanting to be the 'good therapist' who can reparent by sharing personal material. Or, in our Detached Protector mode, we miss vital cues about our patient's needs in that moment. It is always good to check in with ourselves about what are we sharing, why, and how we plan to deliver the message. Are our own needs (for example, our need for an emotional connection with the patient) and schemas being activated? If so, then we should pause and perhaps address this need in ourselves before considering sharing, which is another form of being genuine.

We also need to understand that making mistakes is all right as long as we are prepared to acknowledge this to our patient in a suitable manner. Saying nothing when a rupture or strong feeling is present in your relationship is often the worse thing to do, as the patient is left feeling that something is profoundly unreal or absent in your therapeutic connection. An example from my own work: a patient sends me a long and personal e-mail about some things she dared not to say in the session because she felt too ashamed. It was at the end of my working day and I responded briefly, asking her some questions, but not mentioning why I was responding briefly or, more importantly, explicitly acknowledging the depth of her emotions. Essentially, there was a critical absence from me while my patient was in distress. The patient e-mailed me back, furious, saying that if I did not have the time or was too tired to answer properly I should not have bothered to e-mail at all. While her response was partly schema driven, she was also accurate in the part I played in her distress. When I acknowledged my role in her distress, she softened and we had a beautiful conversation about taking care of our Vulnerable Child sides. It deepened our therapeutic relationship.

Sharing our feelings can certainly shake things up and is very likely to trigger schemas; however, it usually allows for something that the patient may rarely have experienced before: an honest, open, sharing of feelings, completely in the service of your relationship and an authentic connection, because they matter to you. Unsurprisingly, this often unlocks stuck patterns in other relationships, too, as they grow in their capacity to absorb feedback, without unravelling or losing themselves. In this process, often the therapist grows and learns just as much from their patient as the other way round.

The case of therapist Quinn: part 4

Quinn's patient Sara tells him that she is missing her father, who died four years ago. Quinn feels for her and shares a little bit about the loss of his own mother, who died last year, mentioning that he knows how painful this can be. When he does, he sees Sara looks uneasy and realises that perhaps this is not what she was looking for. He expresses his thoughts out loud and Sara, feeling a bit ashamed, admits that she just needed him to listen and be there for her.

The case of the co-therapists couple Yara and Roy: part 4

At the end of a Schema Therapy group session, Yara and Roy mention to the group that they did not find the group 'active' today and they felt that the group was avoiding addressing various irritations with each other. One group member lashes out at them, saying that she doesn't understand why they are saying this now, right at the end of the session. She feels that the therapists are dropping a bomb on the group and then walking away. Although Yara and Roy have a general tendency to overcompensate, on this occasion they acknowledge the poor timing of their reflections, but do not overrun, finishing the group on time. They say sorry to the group with real feeling and vow to return to their mistake and what happened next time. They acknowledge that it's hard to leave it there, but also that it's important to stick to a time boundary.

What has Quinn done right? What have Yara and Roy done right? What do you learn from this?

In the case of Quinn, Sara might respond by not opening up to Quinn any more in order to protect him, as he has lost a parent as well (triggering her Self-Sacrifice schema). Or she could get angry with him for not being emotionally attuned enough to her needs (triggering of Emotional Deprivation and/or Unrelenting Standards). If Quinn did not address this as he did, a rupture was likely. Now he has a chance to explore with his patient what she needs and feels in relationship to him (for example, the need of a father figure).

Yara and Roy did well not to overcompensate by prolonging the group session time, and, by so doing, adhering to a key group therapy rule which creates structure, predictability and, hence, safety. Furthermore, by acknowledging their mistake and making the commitment to return to the issues at the next session they role modelled that mistakes are manageable (as long as you take responsibility for them) and also that the group is strong enough for repair to occur gradually, rather than needing an immediate fix. It is a challenge for most therapists and patients not to try to solve this kind of conflict immediately. In the short term, it feels so much easier and safer to lengthen a therapy session or offer an extra individual session with the group member who lashed out, but this risks giving a message that conflict needs to be resolved immediately in order to survive. In the long term you can provide a good role model when you do not give in to your avoidant or overcompensating coping styles.

Questions to ask yourself if you're avoiding being authentic with a patient:
What am I afraid of? What is the cost of staying quiet? What do I need to be more authentic?

Questions to ask yourself in your efforts to be more authentic with your patients:
Why am I thinking of sharing my thoughts, feelings or experience? How might this oppeness serve my patient and our relationship? Are my needs, schemas and modes involved? Is there a balance between my Healthy Adult, Vulnerable Child and any other modes in the intervention I am going to make?

Reflections

Being authentic with our patients and our colleagues is not always the easiest route. However, when well considered and well timed, I believe authentic responding can provide a pathway to a new and genuine depth of connection with the people we care about. Authenticity is rarely something we explicitly learn about in our core training. Programmes tend, instead, to concentrate on patient pathology and technique at the expense of relational processes, as if authenticity is a natural and relatively easy encounter once you understand your patient and have the right 'toolkit' to treat them. And yet, when therapy is not going so well or there is something your patient needs but can't voice, all too often therapists call upon their 'tool kit' rather than what already sits between them and their patient, that little voice that can offer something real and genuine. It is hoped that this chapter has stimulated you to reflect *and* to act upon the concept of yourself as an authentic therapist.

Therapist tips

1. Invest time in becoming aware of your own schemas, modes, needs and personal values. Who do you want to be in your relationship with your patients, colleagues and family and friends?
2. Ask for feedback on authenticity from your patients, colleagues, family and friends.

3. Make use of supervision or personal therapy to work on your own authenticity.

References

Cambridge Dictionary. (2017). https://dictionary.cambridge.org/dictionary/english/ authenticity

Keading, A., Sougleris, C., van Vreeswijk, M.F., Hayes, C., Dorrian, J. & Simpson, S. (2017). Professional burnout, early maladaptive schemas and physical health in clinical and counselling psychology trainees. *Journal of Clinical Psychology,* 73 (12), 1782–1796.

Lockwood, G. & Perris, P. A new look at core emotional needs. In M.F. van Vreeswijk, J. Broersen & M. Nadort (2012). *The Wiley-Blackwell Handbook of Schema Therapy. Theory, Research and Practice.* Oxford: Wiley-Blackwell, pp. 42–66.

Simpson, S., Simionato, G., Smout, M., van Vreeswijk, M.F., Hayes, C. & Reid, C. (2018). Burnout amongst clinical and counselling psychologists: The role of early maladaptive schemas and coping modes as vulnerability factors. *Clinical Psychology and Psychotherapy.* doi:10.1002/cpp.2328

Wikipedia (2017). https://en.wikipedia.org/wiki/Authenticity

16 Therapist schema activation and self-care

Christina Vallianatou and Tijana Mirović

As therapists, we aim to care for others. At our best we are empathic and skilled in ways that help our patients process difficult, sometimes traumatic, life experiences. We aim to attune to their unmet needs and to offer a reparenting stance. We may feel guilty when we give 'too little' and exhausted when we give 'too much'. Many of us have a sensitive temperament, a personal history of caring for others, grew up as 'parentified' children or in a family that did not prioritise our needs. Some of us may have been emotionally deprived or traumatised, carrying our own pain inside. As adults, we struggle at times to meet our own needs while being emotionally attuned to the needs of others. In the therapy relationship, our schemas may be triggered by our patient's and the ensuing 'schema chemistry' can aggravate dysfunctional patterns for both. This situation can also contribute to therapist burnout, as the therapist faces the combined stress of schema perpetuation and potentially failing to help their patient.

Studies show that burnout among psychotherapists is high and has different contributors, such as work overload, lack of control, insufficient reward and problems in the organisational environment (Skovholt & Trotter-Mathison, 2016). Fewer studies have explored the role of personal factors (such as schemas) in levels of stress and burnout. It makes sense that not caring adequately for ourselves, our unmet needs, or past traumas could add to our levels of emotional exhaustion and potentially trigger unhelpful coping modes. In these situations, it is likely that our schemas are intensified and our wounded little self doesn't have the chance to heal. It becomes clear that balancing other-care and self-care is highly important.

When our life circumstances are complicated, our capacity for self-care and schema healing is often compromised. As schema therapists, we are not separate from the wider social environment and the socio-political forces that act within it. In fact, we are typically exposed to similar or the same sociocultural circumstances and national events as our patients, which we may unknowingly bring into the therapy relationship. The way in which cultural, historical or political factors may contribute to the development of our schemas, our ability to meet core emotional needs and our self-care, is not adequately understood and often given only token consideration.

This chapter explores the role of our schemas in the therapy relationship and how they impact on our self-care. We will also delve into some culture-specific schema patterns and how these may play out in the therapy process. Drawing mostly on our experiences as trainers and supervisors, we offer specific recommendations that promote creative, compassionate self-care. Our interest in this topic emerged from living and working in countries that have been through serious economic problems, massive political changes and societal trauma.

Therapist schema and mode activation

Research findings indicate that a significant proportion of mental health professionals report adverse childhood circumstances (e.g., Simpson et al., 2018). Professionals who have experienced trauma or neglect growing up may have increased capacity for empathy, but may also be more at risk of developing maladaptive beliefs, coping mechanisms and associated psychological distress (Simpson et al., 2018). Studies indicate that three of the most common schemas among mental health professionals are Self-Sacrifice (SS), Emotional Deprivation (ED) and Unrelenting Standards (US) (e.g., Haarhoff, 2006; Saddichha, Kumar & Pradhan, 2012). Recognising and addressing these and other maladaptive schemas is essential, since they may bias clinical reasoning and negatively affect the therapeutic relationship (Saddichha, Kumar & Pradhan, 2012).

Self-Sacrifice and Emotional Deprivation

Self-Sacrifice schema is one of the most common schemas among therapists (Haarhoff, 2006; Saddichha, Kumar & Pradhan, 2012). Therapists with this schema are acutely sensitive to their patients' reactions to them and may fear abandonment or experience guilt that they have not done enough to help. If a therapist surrenders to an SS schema s/he can engage in a number of self-defeating behaviours, going 'overboard' to meet the patients' needs while ignoring signs of fatigue and exhaustion. Our SS schema may especially be triggered in the face of demanding patients (such as those with borderline personality disorder (BPD) or narcissistic personality disorder (NPD)) who push for more time or more engagement. At the same time, a therapist with an SS schema may struggle to act assertively and set appropriate boundaries resulting in overextending the therapy hour, reducing fees, tolerating missed appointments, etc. (Haarhoff, 2006). Also, when SS is present, the therapist may feel a pull to avoid techniques (such as imagery, empathic confrontation or limit setting) that they anticipate might upset the patient or cause conflict. One of our trainees put it like this:

I have a hard time practising these new schema techniques on patients. I feel as if I am using them for my own training and for my own good. As if I push them to feel pain just so that I could practise.

Self-Sacrifice is often linked with ED, as the therapist may have learnt to meet others' needs in order to maintain an emotional connection. These schemas (especially if combined) push therapists to give too much, while neglecting their own needs. This might go as far as forgetting, or not having time to, properly eat and sleep, or overworking with no time for socialising or fun. Being 'accustomed' to ED, therapists are often unaware that their needs aren't being met or experience a tremendous amount of guilt if they are. Although, at a rational level, most trainees acknowledge the importance of self-care, they may be thinking: 'I will rest/eat/socialise as soon as I finish with my patients/projects, etc.'. However, as soon as that is done, they take on new patients and new projects. This excessive level of sacrifice in the context of feeling pressure to achieve and succeed increases therapists' vulnerability to burnout (Simpson et al., 2018).

Coping with SS and ED schemas requires attention to our little self. Our healthy mode keeps in mind our tendency to self-sacrifice or emotionally deprive ourselves and gradually learns to prioritise our wishes and to take care of our unmet need for connection. It is essential to remember that our little person is important and to be proactive about self-caring time. We can brainstorm helpful ways to calm our little self, such as creating a self-care playlist or keeping an image of our safe place handy. We can regularly practise a soothing imagery exercise in which we offer our little person connection, our compassionate healthy self-listening and attuning to their needs and feelings. In other self-care imagery exercises, our little self might feel soothed in a scene with animals or safe people. We can talk to our little self, ask him/her what s/he needs and make this a priority. It is also important that we actively adapt our personal lives so that meaningful relationships and personal experiences enhance positive feelings and provide schema healing. In our supervision groups, we actively explore ways to take care of our little self. We also encourage our trainees to think about their needs and communicate them in the group. With the group's help, many trainees with SS and ED are able to experience a deep sense of relief and a lifting of shame in expressing and prioritising their needs, providing a direct antidote to past schema messages.

Unrelenting Standards

Unrelenting Standards is another very common schema in therapists and has also been linked to burnout (Simpson et al., 2018). Therapists' US are often triggered when their patients fail to progress 'fast enough' or if the patient is critical of their approach. In supervision, a therapist with US may feel reluctant to try out new things, provide taped sessions, use experiential techniques or engage in role plays, fearing that the supervisor would think less of him/her, if their failure to meet a high standard was exposed.

As with SS, when we surrender to US schema we may push ourselves too hard, seriously neglecting our needs for rest, spontaneity and play. Here, however, there is a drive for perfection or an unrealistically high standard, rather than necessarily being excessively sensitive to the patient's feelings. We might work long hours, see too many patients or fail to take breaks. Additionally, we might use weekends to go to additional trainings or study because 'we don't know enough and there is so much more to learn'. Surrendering to US schema is like surrendering to the demanding/inner critic mode. This mode can rob the therapist of job satisfaction, lead to unnecessary frustration with the progress or duration of therapy and undermine therapist confidence (Perris, Fretwell & Shaw, 2012). One of our trainees explained it like this:

> I often have a large number of patients during the day ... I work without a break and without any options to relax. I know that my body and my mind suffer but I still do it. I brought this on myself because I don't reduce the number of hours I work, plus I don't turn down new patients. If I did, I would feel guilty ... then I feel guilty for not being able to give my patients my maximum ... for not being able to better prepare for the sessions.

We need both our compassionate healthy mode and our happy child to balance and counteract our US, which is often heard as a form of a demanding critic mode. In this situation, we need to be able to accept mistakes and setbacks, practise self-compassion and incorporate more balance and fun activities in our lives. Although it may not be easy to escape in the moment from our demanding/critical mode, in order to concentrate on our unmet needs, the broader desires of our little self and our life goals can keep us on track with a nourishing self-care plan. Fighting our US and inner critic is not easy and we might have a hard time doing this alone. Therefore, it might be necessary to address this through peer-sharing, supervision or personal therapy. It is especially powerful when a supervisor shares the mistakes and misjudgements that s/he made. This normalises mistakes, encourages suitable clinical reflection, as well as fostering acceptance and a healthy, self-compassionate model of self-care.

Therapist–patient schema chemistry

Therapists' and patients' schemas work in interaction, in a self-perpetuating loop (Young, Klosko & Weishaar, 2003). A common example is when a therapist's SS schema comes into contact with a patient's Entitlement or Dependence schema. Here, the patient may expect more, alongside a therapist who feels compelled to accommodate this, even if it comes at huge personal cost. The therapist neglects his/her own needs, is unable to set limits (or push for independence) and, consequently, fails to reparent the patient's core unmet needs. Another common example is when a detached/ avoidant patient triggers our US schema. The patient may not be showing the desired progress and so the therapist starts to feel that s/he is underachieving and wasting the patient's time and money. To cope, the therapist may refer the patient on, potentially triggering the patient's Defectiveness, Emotional Deprivation, or Abandonment schemas by fostering the pre-existing idea that they are a 'difficult' person that no one (not even a therapist) can accept and care for. In situations like this, supervision can facilitate a better understanding of the schema chemistry and provide a healing space. In our supervision groups, we use experiential exercises, such as imagery rescripting, chair work and mode dialogues, that focus on the inner critic. As such, the group provide a reparative antidote to the Critic and the therapist is encouraged to practise using their compassionate healthy mode in the face of prototypical triggers.

Additional problems occur when therapists flip into one of their coping modes, such as the Detached Protector, when their patient is overwhelmed or when their own Vulnerable Child is triggered. Typical examples of therapists' detachment include intellectualising and minimising, overuse of cognitive techniques, failure to provide comfort and reparenting, referring patients to another therapist, avoidance of new/experiential/confrontational techniques, etc. Avoidance in the therapist may trigger the patient to sense a lack of attunement or emotional connection, such that their schemas 'take this personally'. For example, a patient with a Defectiveness schema may interpret their therapist's detachment as the result of them not being 'a good patient, interesting or lovable enough', etc. Depending on his/her coping style in this situation, the patient might then back off, become angry or try to please the therapist to regain the connection.

Sometimes, a therapist overcompensates for his/her Defectiveness or Failure schemas when the patient is not progressing by reacting with anger and impatience (pushing patients toward change prematurely), becoming too confrontational, or blaming the patient ('You don't want to get better'). This, too, can retraumatise a patient, undermining his/her faith in therapy and himself/herself. Research (Haarhoff, 2006) suggests that around three quarters of therapists had what they termed a 'special superior person' schema to some degree. When this schema is activated, the therapy situation becomes an opportunity to achieve excellence and the therapist may have grandiose expectations for their own performance. If therapy is going well, there may be a tendency to idealise the patient, or, conversely, the therapist may devalue or distance themselves from a patient who does not improve or comply with treatment (Haarhoff, 2006).

As therapists, we need to explore in supervision when and why we flip into detachment or overcompensation. Discussing our 'special therapist' moments may feel awkward but we can gently remind ourselves that this kind of overcompensation is not uncommon and is understandable in the context of the high levels of uncertainty and responsibility entailed in our role. Furthermore, we may have come from families where achieving highly or being the best was very important. At times, we may be blind to our overcompensation and need our supervisor's support to unpick this. Many therapists with strong overcompensation may feel under pressure and lonely, without necessarily knowing why, and good supervision (and personal therapy) can provide an opportunity to connect with being 'good enough' (without necessarily being exceptional), to admit mistakes and to accept help. It can be helpful to work through the self-reflection workbook for schema therapists (Farrell & Shaw, 2018) or to write your own case conceptualisation. This helps us better understand ourselves as therapists, the origins of our modes and the needs of our little self.

Schema Therapy potentially entails a greater risk of burnout due to the level of empathy required and the high prevalence of trauma in our patients (Perris, Fretwell & Shaw, 2012). In addition to this, some schema therapists work in societies where there is high incidence of trauma in the general population through war, poverty and other adverse events. Therefore, we need to be mindful of cultural and societal stressors and their impact on therapists and their patients. We will address these issues next.

Therapist's schemas, culture and society

One of the most obvious ways society impacts all of us is through the value system and norms that are passed down through our upbringing. Society, in its various guises, passes on a whole raft of cultural norms to our caregivers and teachers, who subsequently pass them on to us and we continue to pass them on to our children. Although many of us strive to be aware of, resist and even rebel against, certain cultural norms, they have an often unconscious impact on our schemas and coping responses. So, for example, Western women often strongly challenge media pressure to be classically beautiful, while at the same time, in private, investing huge time and energy trying to meet this cultural norm. Some schemas (e.g., Enmeshment, Emotional Inhibition, Unrelenting Standards) appear not only to 'run in families' but tend to be more predominant in certain societies (Young, Klosko & Weishaar, 2003).

The relationship between sociocultural or political factors, personal strains, reparenting and self-care is often complicated. Take the example of a therapist and patient who both have an Enmeshment schema and have been brought up in a culture that encourages enmeshment and discourages autonomy among family members. Through supervision, the therapist realises s/he holds deep-rooted beliefs about the role of the family that are very common in his/her and the patient's cultural background. This affects his/her ability to meet his/her own need for autonomy and reparent his/her patient's emotional need. Working in collectivistic societies such as Greece and Serbia, we often see how enmeshment stops grown-up children from differentiating and separating from their parents. Guilt about putting some distance between adult children and their (guilt inducing) parents remains one of the prevalent topics in our work.

It becomes even more complicated when a patient wants to distance themselves or cut off from an abusive family. The whole society sends the message that it is wrong because 'no one loves you more or wants better things for you than your family'. Having been raised with these messages as well, therapists often find themselves stuck between the need to support their patient's autonomy and a kind of societal guilt about the patient cutting off from their family. Often, therapists struggle with guilt or ambivalence while confronting the parental figure in experiential exercises, or they rush to diminish the anger patients express toward their parents. Many of our trainees brought these issues to supervision, expressing how burdened, confused and stressed this made them feel. Supervisors who come from different (less traditional and more individualistic) backgrounds sometimes struggle to understand and validate the level of tension and difficulty posed by these issues.

Culturally induced guilt can also discourage therapists from engaging in self-care. In a supervision group based in a society that places high value on collective rather than individual needs, over half the group expressed guilt about self-care. They told us: 'I feel guilty when I do something for myself because we were all taught to think it is selfish and wrong. ... Even when you say no, you are considered selfish and rude'; 'If you take care of yourself, if you put yourself first, you are weak, narcissistic and should be ashamed of yourself ... this is the message we got.'

Our supervisees from other (Western) cultures talked about feeling pressured by a different kind of value system, with a greater emphasis on achievement, appearance and status. Here is a typical comment: 'I feel huge pressure to be successful at what I do ... our whole country is competitive and in an "it is never good enough mode".' In other instances, the problem might be that the dominant culture over-values emotional inhibition/control, detachment and intellectualisation at the expense of emotional connection and support, making it harder for schema therapists to be more open and spontaneous in their work.

Schemas and modes develop not only through the transfer of values but also through shared experiences and shared trauma within a particular region. Within the context of therapy, shared trauma is defined as the affective, behavioural, cognitive, spiritual and multimodal responses that clinicians experience as a result of dual exposure to the same collective trauma as their patients (Tosone, Nuttman-Shwartz & Stephens, 2012). Research conducted in former Yugoslavia (Hadžić & Mirović, 2016), suggests that schemas can also develop as a result of adverse social conditions and societal trauma such as poverty, exile, war, exposure to violence and corruption. These types of adverse experiences seem to cultivate and strengthen Vulnerability to Harm and Mistrust/Abuse schemas (ibid.).

Mistrust/Abuse schema (MA) originates from experiences of abuse or mistreatment and entails the expectation that others will deliberately hurt or betray us in some way. Vulnerability to Harm entails an exaggerated fear that a catastrophe will strike at any time and that no one will be able to prevent it. This schema typically originates in childhood environments that are experienced as physically, emotionally or financially unsafe (Young, Klosko & Weishaar, 2003). These two schemas can also develop in later life if we live in a chronically unsafe or unstable environment: for example, in countries experiencing severe financial crises or war. We have noted in our supervisees (and in ourselves), even with a high level of awareness and self-care, it is very difficult not to be anxious in situations that seem to be going from bad to worse. We, as therapists feel vulnerable, too, and yet we put that to one side and help patients who share the same experiences, the same uncertainties and the same collective traumas. Recent research also suggests that psychologists with MA schema may be most at risk of experiencing strong sympathetic–empathic responses to distressing patient presentations, due to activation of, or over-identification with, their own traumatic experiences (Simpson et al., 2018). Thereby, within environments that strengthen and perpetuate MA schemas, there is a particular risk of therapists with this schema struggling to meet their own emotional needs. Two case examples follow that demonstrate the difficulties and challenges that working with shared societal trauma entails.

Therapist schemas and economic crisis: case example 1

In Greece, research suggests that the economic crisis of 2008 has had severe consequences on the population's mental and general health, with a significant increase in suicide rates (Simou & Koutsogeorgou, 2014). Furthermore, there has been marked escalation in feelings of uncertainty and hopelessness for large segments of the population (ibid.). Unemployment, austerity cuts, increases in crime, and the social and political upheaval that emerged often affect both the therapist's and the patient's life. The situation influences the therapist and the therapy relationship in different ways (Vallianatou & Koliri, 2013). Patients talk openly about the consequences of the economic crisis in their lives and therapists are often living through very similar experiences. One supervisee spoke to the group about how unsafe and anxious she felt, how the crisis was reinforcing her Vulnerability to Harm schema ('the economy will collapse completely and we will lose everything') and how she found herself flipping into detachment and working on autopilot. Other supervisees agreed. A group experiential exercise revealed some of the childhood origins of her Vulnerability to Harm: her mother was often catastrophising and her father was not in a position to give her reassurance or make her feel safe. Patients talking about the economic crisis often triggered her vulnerable little self in the sessions and her autopilot felt like the only way to cope. Her Self-Sacrifice schema was also triggered when complex or poor patients needed more treatment and she knew they wouldn't get the help they required due to austerity cuts in health care. During this time, our supervision focused on identifying ways of taking care of her little self. Although initially the idea of self-care was difficult for her to accept (her Self-Sacrifice schema saying that others were much worse off), the therapist gradually learnt to support her little self without needing to detach and her Healthy Adult became stronger. In our experience, when a country goes through a collective crisis or trauma, it is very important that the supervisor initiates discussions around the effect of the crisis or the trauma on the therapist and the therapy relationship. We have observed that talking to other colleagues with similar experiences had a reassuring effect, enabled a deeper understanding and a sense of mutual support and belonging.

Therapist schemas, war and displacement: case example 2

In the period of 1991 to 1999, Serbia was engaged in four armed conflicts and exposed to NATO bombing. The country suffered extreme economic hardship (exacerbated by international sanctions and the worst ever recorded hyperinflation) combined with a huge influx of refugees and internally displaced people (Mirović, 2014). Most of our therapists and trainees grew up in this context and, since the economic and social hardships have only increased, most therapists had little time to 'breathe' or process the events occurring around them. Working as therapists in Serbia, we daily encounter patients who share the same traumatic experiences.

For many of us, having learnt that we should be the 'strong ones' and that the patient's needs come first, there is an inevitable pull to detach and look away from our own traumatised little child. This was even more heightened with a cultural imperative that runs strong in Serbia along the lines of: 'You have to be tough and leave it all behind without looking back. Anything else is weakness!' So, many therapists detached, pretending that it never happened. When we raised this issue in one of our group supervisions, a trainee said, 'In [all the] years of my training and my personal therapy, I talked about everything, except the fact that I was a refugee … not a lot of people even know this about me.' A colleague added, 'It is the same with me, I was drafted and spent months on the frontline … never talked about it.' I (TM) only recently opened up about flashbacks and traumatic memories related to bombing. Needless to say, we all see patients that talk about these experiences on a daily basis.

This tendency to push ourselves to act 'tougher' than we are has been documented in psychotherapists from other cultures as well. Mental health workers have a propensity to minimise their own vulnerability while continuing to expose themselves to excessive work pressures (Simpson et al., 2018). This vulnerability is, among other things, characterised by self-blame for showing signs of stress or vulnerability, striving to reach higher standards while denying personal needs and emotions, and a reluctance to set boundaries and ask for support due to fears of letting others down (ibid.). Clearly, this is not the best way to self-care, especially since there is a high risk for vicarious traumatisation among those who are highly empathic and have personal histories of trauma (Perris, Fretwell & Shaw, 2012). So, what is the best way to prevent this and self-care? We address this issue next.

Therapist self-care

Several studies indicate that not taking adequate care of ourselves, combined with unhelpful coping patterns, intensifies the possibility that we will experience burnout, compassion fatigue, or vicarious trauma (e.g., Thomas & Morris, 2017; Simpson et al., 2018). It seems that many of us do not automatically practise self-care when we become psychotherapists. Instead, this may be something we have to learn and actively continue to implement throughout our working lives. Below, we offer specific recommendations regarding schema and mode activation and self-care.

Schema awareness

First and foremost, it is necessary to develop awareness of our own schemas, modes and maladaptive patterns. This could usefully take place during psychotherapy or psychology training as well as during personal therapy. In our clinical setting, we begin by building our own case conceptualisations. Using this as a guide, we teach our healthy adult to observe when our schemas and modes are triggered, especially during sessions with patients. With the help of our trainers or supervisors, we outline strategies for anticipating and addressing schema chemistry in the therapy relationship. We may use imagery to establish a deeper understanding of our patterns. As we do with our patients, we can focus on a feeling that is triggered in a particular session and potentially 'float back' to an image earlier in our lives to enable connection with the schema of origin and unmet need.

Creating a self-care programme

Awareness alone does not translate into a self-care plan. It is important that we step back and take time to create a self-care programme that is suitably personalised to focus on our unmet needs, that is nurturing and energising and isn't experienced as another task on our to-do list. While doing this, we need to be mindful of our US and inner critic and engage in mode dialogue if necessary. As described above, we need to learn to accept mistakes and setbacks, practise self-compassion and incorporate more fun activities in our lives. We need to concentrate on our unmet needs and to keep on track with our self-care plan.

Culturally shared schemas

Culturally defined schemas can be more difficult to identify, as they are more likely to be widely shared by the society of origin and, therefore, normalised. Our healthy self can take a step back and engage in conversations around the particular characteristics of our culture and history. This will deepen our understanding of our shared experience and will enable us to name our culture-related schemas. It is also recommended that training programmes and supervision initiate and facilitate discussions about this topic. On a personal level, exploring our unmet needs and values means that our compassionate healthy self can make conscious decisions about the extent to which we conform with culturally defined norms. If, for example, Enmeshment is one of our culture-specific schemas, it may be important for us to decide how closely tied we want to be with our immediate family, extended family and other people in our community group. If our country has gone through a lot of unrest and, therefore, Mistrust/Abuse is one of our culture-specific schemas, we may need to learn who we can trust when circumstances are difficult. If our country has been through wars, financial problems, or other serious transitions and we have developed a Vulnerability to Harm schema, directing our attention to being reliably present and soothing to our little self (no matter what is happening externally) can be healing.

Shared trauma and shared healing

Self-care when shared trauma occurs can be challenging for us. We suggest that shared trauma may be dealt with by shared healing. Peer supervision groups that are safely managed seem to offer an excellent opportunity for dealing with shared trauma (Tosone, Nuttman-Shwartz & Stephens, 2012). In these groups, we can explore ways to manage personal stress, our emotional reactions during sessions, grey areas of professional practice and to problem solve where necessary. Our little and adult selves will probably feel safer and less lonely. The group can also organise soothing activities that promote wellness, such as mindfulness practice, going for walks and other nurturing activities. Usual self-care recommendations, such as exercise, hobbies, personal therapy and further training, may not always be possible due to financial limitations (or other problems) and the group may need to work together to develop creative adaptations.

The literature on self-care in psychotherapy emphasises the importance of work–life balance (Simpson et al., 2018). We propose that our self-care plan is guided by a compassionate Healthy Adult stance. A compassionate Healthy Adult, first, seeks to find balance between his/her personal and professional lives. Regarding professional life, attending supervision, seeking further training and support groups may provide an adequate foundation. In our personal life, seeking life satisfaction, connectedness and finding healthy ways to manage stress and anxiety is important. Finally, a compassionate individual recognises his/her own suffering and commits to prioritising well-being for him- or herself.

Summary

As therapists, we try to understand and help our patients. This is often a highly complex and challenging process and there can be a natural tendency to focus outwards on the patient, steering away from our own emotions, needs and schemas. Cultural factors pull on our reactions, too, sometimes unknowingly creating a tension between societal norms and the individual's needs. Often, we enter a mode cycle with our patients where their coping modes activate our schemas and there is the risk of schema perpetuation for both patient and therapist. Another layer is added when therapists are working with shared societal or national traumas, such as armed conflict and/or economic crisis. Here, the therapist may struggle to find the space and resources to care for their own traumatised little self. In general, as a group, therapists are prone to underestimate their own vulnerability and need for self-care (Simpson et al., 2018). We argue that it is a central professional task to explore how our schemas are activated with our patients, how we are affected by cultural norms and by traumas that we may have in common with our patients. As part and parcel of this process, there is a need to connect with our little-selves and create ways of caring for ourselves that allow us, as well as our patients, to heal and thrive as best we can.

Therapist tips

1. Be mindful, curious and compassionate with your schemas and modes.
2. Self-Sacrifice, Emotional Deprivation and Unrelenting Standards are particularly common in therapists. If you have one of these schemas, it is very important to take care of your needs for connection, self-kindness and realistic limits.
3. Develop your reflective practice. Explore your cultural values/beliefs and the role they may play in your schemas and modes and in your work.
4. Formulate a self-care plan that fits with your needs and life circumstances.
5. Look for opportunities for shared schema healing: find colleagues or groups to talk about your shared experiences/shared trauma. Other schema therapists may benefit from your openness and wisdom.
6. Look after your little self! Remember to engage in Happy Child activities to help you relax, laugh and feel good.

References

Farrell, J.M. & Shaw, I.A. (2018). *Experiencing Schema Therapy from the Inside Out: A Self-Practice/Self-Reflection Workbook for Therapists*. New York: Guilford Press.

Haarhoff, B.A. (2006). The importance of identifying and understanding therapist schema in cognitive therapy training and supervision. *New Zealand Journal of Psychology*, 35(3), 126–131.

Hadžić, A. & Mirović, T. (2016). *Afektivna vezanost, Rane maladaptivne sheme i stresna iskustva*. Banja Luka: Filozofski fakultet.

Mirović, T. (2014). Growing up in political and economic turmoil: The effects in adulthood. In M.T. Garrett (Ed.) *Youth and Adversity – Psychology and Influences of Child and Adolescent Resilience and Coping* (pp. 117–132). New York: Nova Biomedical, Nova Science.

Perris, P., Fretwell, H. & Shaw, I. (2012). Therapist self-care in the context of limited reparenting. In M. van Vreeswijk, J. Broersen & M. Nadort (Eds.) *The Wiley Blackwell Handbook of Schema Therapy* (pp. 473–492). Chichester: John Wiley & Sons.

Saddichha, S., Kumar, A. & Pradhan, N. (2012). Cognitive schemas among mental health professionals: Adaptive or maladaptive? *Journal of Research in Medical Sciences*, 17(6), 523–526.

Simou, E. & Koutsogeorgou, E. (2014). Effects of the economic crisis on health and healthcare in Greece in the literature from 2009 to 2013: A systematic review. *Health Policy*. http://dx.doi.org/10.1016/j.healthpol.2014.02.002

Simpson, S., Simionato, G., Smout, M., van Vreeswijk, M., Hayes, C., Sougleris, C. & Reid, C. (2018). Burnout amongst clinical and counselling psychologists: The role of early maladaptive schemas and coping modes as vulnerability factors. *Clinical Psychology and Psychotherapy*. 10.1002/cpp.2328

Skovholt, T.M. & Trotter-Mathison, M. (2016). *The Resilient Practitioner. Burnout and Compassion Fatigue Prevention and Self-Care Strategies for the Helping Professions*. London: Routledge.

Thomas, D.A. & Morris, M.H. (2017). Creative counsellor self-care. *Ideas and Research You Can Use: VISTAS Online*. https://pdfs.semanticscholar.org/ca07/bc9628a8d1f26cb5 fe02f6934c0bcf8b1608.pdf

Tosone, C., Nuttman-Shwartz, O. & Stephens, T. (2012). Shared trauma: When the professional is personal. *Clinical Social Work Journal*, 40, 231–239.

Vallianatou, C. & Koliri, M.E. (2013). The economic crisis and its implications on same-culture identities and the therapeutic relationship. *European Journal of Psychotherapy and Counselling*, 15(4), 346–360. http://dx.doi.org/10.1080/13642537.2013.85524

Young, J.E., Klosko, J.S. & Weishaar, M.E. (2003). *Schema Therapy: A Practitioner's Guide*. New York: Guilford Press.

Part V

Developing the Healthy Adult and endings in Schema Therapy

17 Developing a compassionate mind to strengthen the Healthy Adult

Olivia Thrift and Chris Irons

Introduction

One of the principle theoretical underpinnings of both Schema Therapy (ST) and Compassion Focused Therapy (CFT) is that the self is made up of multiple parts. In ST, the multiple parts are organised around child, parent and coping modes (Arntz and Jacob, 2013). In CFT, these multiples, among others, are organised around different emotions (e.g., anger, sadness) and motives (e.g., compassionate, competitive) (Gilbert, 2010). A central tenet in both approaches is to develop a resilient and robust part of the self, a part that has strong meta-awareness and, thus, acts as an observer to all other parts of the self. This is a part that is akin to the captain of the ship, steady at the helm, holding course even in the roughest of seas and a part that can engage with all other parts of the self with empathy, understanding and wisdom. In ST, this part is known as the Healthy Adult mode, and in CFT it is referred to as the Compassionate Self. This is not to suggest that the two concepts are the same; however, we believe there is much overlap. For example, both the Healthy Adult and Compassionate Self observe, respond and steady the other parts of the self, helping patients stay within their window of tolerance and move towards integration of the self, leading to greater potential for health and growth.

There has been discussion within ST about the potential benefits of integrating ideas from other therapeutic approaches (e.g., Acceptance and Commitment Therapy (ACT)). In this chapter, we explore how ST – and, in particular, the Healthy Adult mode – might benefit from integrating ideas from CFT (Gilbert & Irons, 2005; Gilbert, 2009). CFT was proposed for use as a multimodal therapy rather than belonging to a single 'school of therapy' and was founded by Paul Gilbert (Gilbert & Irons, 2005). It was initially developed in response to the needs of patients with high shame and self-criticism. Gilbert found that many of his patients engaged in therapy interventions (such as thought challenging) with angry, hostile or shame-based inner voice tones. When trying to help patients to create warmer, more caring and supportive tones, many struggled to do this and, in fact, could find this aversive. Gilbert realised that to help patients overcome their difficulties they needed to develop a different way of relating to themselves, which led to the development of CFT. Although in its infancy, CFT has an emerging evidence base demonstrating its utility in working with a variety of mental health problems, including depression, eating disorders, personality disorder and psychosis (Gale et al., 2012; Gilbert & Procter, 2006; Laithwaite et al., 2009; Lucre & Corten, 2012). It is beyond the scope of this chapter to fully review the theoretical underpinnings and evidence base for CFT; readers who are interested are directed to the following summary (e.g., Gilbert, 2010, 2014). CFT draws from evolutionary psychology, attachment theory, developmental and social psychology, neuroscience and physiological research, as well as ideas and interventions from other psychotherapeutic approaches (e.g., Cognitive-behavioural Therapy (CBT)). It is also influenced by ideas and practices from Buddhism.

In this chapter, we focus on four key CFT skills that we believe can enhance Healthy Adult work in ST: mindfulness, stabilising physiology, imagery, and cultivating a compassionate self-identity. We believe integrating these CFT skills will help a patient's Healthy Adult mode have a stronger, wiser counter-dialogue to their punitive and demanding parent modes, will better equip the Healthy Adult mode in emotionally regulating and tolerating the distress of the Vulnerable and Angry Child modes and, finally, will support the Protector modes and soften their self-protective function.

Core concepts of CFT

CFT is rooted in a number of key 'reality checks' about how and why we suffer (see Gilbert, 2009, 2010, for more detail). For example, we have a set of genes that we did not choose, a body and brain that is ageing, decaying and prone to illness and, ultimately, death; we have been bestowed with a variety of emotions that, while crucial for our survival, can be very painful and lead to much suffering in our life; we are shaped by social circumstances, many of which (e.g., bullying, abuse) we have little control over. Through cultivating the skills of a compassionate mind, we develop the wisdom to understand this, to de-centre from the challenges (i.e., that this is 'not our fault') and, crucially, learn to take *responsibility* for bringing change. The core concepts of the CFT model are listed below.

1.   *We have tricky brains*

Over the past million years or so, our ancestors evolved along a line that led to rapid expansion of cognitive competencies. This 'new brain' led to our capacity for imagination, planning, rumination and self-reflection/monitoring and provided evolutionary advantages for our survival and thriving. However, beneficial evolutionary changes commonly bring disadvantages, and our minds frequently operate on non-rational heuristics (Gilbert, 1998). So, our new brain abilities can stimulate ancient (old brain) motives (e.g., to seek safety and avoid danger, to compete), emotions (e.g., anger, anxiety and disgust) and behaviours (e.g., fight, flight, freeze and submission). These, in turn, influence the focus, content and process of our new brain abilities and create the conditions for 'loops in the mind' to form, which can drive much distress.

A common example we use to elaborate this point is to imagine that if a grazing zebra is chased by a lion and then escapes, relatively soon after this it will begin to calm down and return to eating again. However, if we are in a café eating lunch, and manage to run away when we see a lion running towards us, it is unlikely we would calm down quickly. Instead, under the effect of powerful old brain emotions (e.g., anxiety) and motives (e.g., harm avoidance), our new brains are guided to focus on the threat; we are likely to worry about what could have happened if the lion had caught us, or become concerned that they might show up again tomorrow. We may even start to imagine what the impact of our death would have been for other people in our life. These new brain patterns of thinking and imagining send signals back to our old brain, and can keep emotions stimulated, even though the threat (the lion) is no longer present. While this is not our fault, it's important to help people learn how to notice and work with these loops in a wise and helpful way. We shall return to this below.

Based on a variety of scientific theories (Depue & Morrone-Strupinsky, 2005; LeDoux, 1998; Panksepp, 1998), CFT suggests we have three major emotion regulation systems, referred to as threat, drive and soothing, each of which organise our mind and body in particular ways (Figure 17.1).

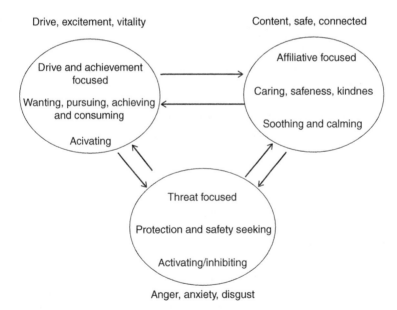

Figure 17.1 The three system model.

The threat system and its emotions of anger, anxiety and disgust evolved to make us pay attention and respond to threats. Upon recognising a threat, a variety of physiological changes in the brain and body will occur, often linked to the sympathetic nervous system and the hypothalamic–pituitary–adrenal (HPA) axis. These physiological systems prime us to respond to threats in particular ways (e.g., fight, flight, shut down and so forth), guide attention (e.g., narrow and focus on the threat) and thinking (e.g., better safe than sorry). Although biologically rooted, this system is shaped by conditioning processes (e.g., operant and classical), as well as social–relational experiences.

The drive system is linked to emotions of excitement, joy and anticipation and evolved to make us pay attention to, and pursue, resources (e.g., food, status and sexual opportunities) that are beneficial for us. When successful in these pursuits, we may feel the activation of positive emotions (associated with the sympathetic nervous system and neurotransmitters such as dopamine) that are pleasurable and reinforcing.

The *soothing affiliative system* is not just the absence of threat or drive, but is linked to brain and bodily changes linked to the parasympathetic nervous system and the release of neurotransmitters, such as endorphins, that give rise to feelings of contentment, calmness and peacefulness. This process is sometimes referred to as 'rest and digest', and, given its physiology, this system helps to balance those of the other two systems.

Evolution – particularly with the emergence of mammals, attachment and extended caring – shaped the soothing system to be highly sensitive to signals of care, affection and kindness from others. So, this system can also be activated when other people (or internally through self-talk and imagery) are caring, kind and reassuring to us. Given that many of our patients have had attachment and relational experiences that have not included regular, consistent or appropriate care and affection, part of CFT involves helping patients strengthen their soothing and affiliative system. This is achieved by creating the brain and body (physiological) states that have evolved to play a powerful role in regulating threat states (e.g., physiology, emotions and so forth). We will explore this in the section below.

1.   *The nature of compassion*

CFT uses a definition of compassion rooted in motivation and intention, regarding it as a sensitivity to suffering in one's self and in others with a firm intention to alleviate and, if possible, prevent it (Gilbert, 2014).

This definition holds two psychologies:

i.   The ability to pay attention to, turn towards and engage with, distress (a type of engagement psychology). This involves six key competencies which can be directed to oneself or others: care for well-being, sensitivity to distress, sympathy, distress tolerance, empathy and non-judgement

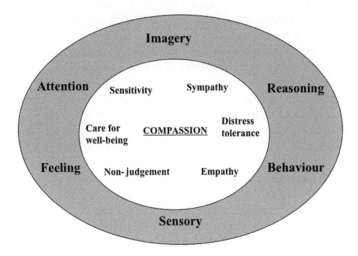

Figure 17.2 From Gilbert, *The Compassionate Mind* (2009), reprinted with permission from Constable & Robinson Ltd.

(inner circle of Figure 17.2, see Gilbert, 2009, 2010 for how these are developed).

ii. A type of action psychology, linked to motivation and wisdom to know how to alleviate distress (an action psychology). This can involve helping patients to develop multimodal skills (see outer ring of Figure 17.2) that, once practised and developed, can help to alleviate their own and others' distress. These include developing compassionate attention, imagery, reasoning, behaviour, sensory focus and feelings. We shall return to some of these below.

Therapeutic techniques to develop a compassionate mind

Alongside helping patients develop a de-shaming sense of their difficulties with an appreciation that 'this is not my fault', it's also important to develop their capacity to become aware of, and regulate, unhelpful threat and drive system processes. We will illustrate four CFT strategies[1] to achieve this (mindfulness, stabilising physiology, imagery, and cultivating a compassionate self-identity) using the case example of Leon, a patient experiencing anxiety and depression. We have used ST language with CFT terms in parenthesis.

Leon was in his late 30s and he came to therapy as he felt unable to move on from Donna, who abruptly ended their relationship three months before they were due to get married. This was two years before he sought therapy, but over this period he had been gradually feeling increasingly anxious and depressed (overactive threat system and blocked drive system).

Leon's therapist helped him make sense of his anxiety and depression by developing a schema formulation, including a mode map which is represented in Figure 17.3.

Leon's anxiety and depression were partly perpetuated by a vicious critical mode, which he named 'The Despiser'. The Despiser held him entirely responsible for the relationship breakup, told him on a daily basis how pathetic he was for feeling so upset and was full of contempt for his being single as he approached his 40s. This part of him (which frequently triggered his threat system) had been internalised from his emotionally invalidating parents (who had not met his core needs for love and support) and had ridiculed any sort of emotional expression or struggle.

Leon's demanding parent mode, which he named The Perfecting Pressuriser, fuelled The Despiser by constantly reminding him that he should be buying a house, getting married and starting a family (Leon would often get stuck in an overactive drive system). He felt unrelenting pressure to show himself and the world that as well as achieving success in his professional life, he was also 'successful' in his personal life. Leon's Perfecting Pressuriser mode had internalised many of the values and messages of his parents, who were not able to meet his needs for realistic expectations and unconditional acceptance. When he didn't live up to his parents' ideals, they would become very critical, in much the same way that when Leon now doesn't live up to the unrelenting standards of the Perfecting Pressurizer mode, The Despiser

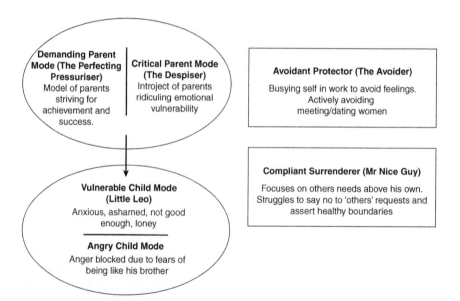

Figure 17.3 Leon's mode map.

mode is quick on the scene. His Perfecting Pressurizer mode is constantly trying to prove to others and himself that he is not useless and worthless (a key fear for Leon) with the unintended consequence that he feels under constant pressure to prove himself.

The shame of 'not achieving' in his personal life was overwhelming and weighed so heavily on Leon (Leon referred to his Vulnerable Child mode as Little Leon) that he was barely leaving the house other than to go to work. His threat system was ramping up and before starting therapy he was not aware of needing to engage in his soothing affiliative system (and certainly did not know how to engage this system, due to emotional deprivation as a child) to better support himself. The breakup had triggered schemas (or 'key threats/fears in CFT) in the rejection/disconnection domain including Abandonment, Emotional Deprivation and Defectiveness/Shame and Little Leon was feeling overwhelmed with loneliness and shame. At the beginning of therapy, anger was not within Leon's emotional repertoire, as his angry child mode was blocked, which made sense given that his older brother was extremely emotionally volatile and aggressive. Leon had learnt it was not safe to connect with anger (one of his key fears was becoming like his brother, 'losing control' and hurting others and had coped with this fear by blocking his anger, which led to the negative unintended consequence of not being fully emotionally connected with himself or able to assert appropriate boundaries when needed). The angry child mode was still drawn on his mode map as his blocked anger was going to be important to work on in therapy and was something he would need his Healthy Adult (Compassionate Self) to help him with.

Leon coped with his feelings largely through his Avoidant Protector (he called this The Avoider) coping mode, which typically manifested as suppressing his feelings through overworking but also showed up in his avoidance of getting back on the dating scene (both of these avoidant type behaviours would be seen as coping strategies in CFT in response to key fears of being emotionally overwhelmed and rejected). He also had a strong Compliant Surrender mode (named Mr Nice Guy); being extremely sensitive to interpersonal conflict, Leon felt safer suppressing his needs than risking tension in his relationships (in CFT, this would be seen as drawing upon submissive behaviour as an evolved coping strategy to manage conflict, with the unintended consequence of leaving him subjugated and unable to form healthy reciprocal relationships). Mr Nice Guy mode also led him to overwork, as he had great difficulty setting boundaries around others' requests of him (a coping strategy in response to fears of rejection with the negative unintended consequence of the risk of burnout). Other people assumed Leon was confident and relaxed, given he had a good job and superficially socialised with colleagues; however, this was largely an apparent competence that masked how hard he was actually finding it to function and feel any sense of enjoyment in his life.

Mindfulness

Leon was introduced to mindfulness in order to cultivate greater awareness of his mind, and, in particular, the types of 'loops in the mind' he regularly got caught up with, and how to ground himself in the 'here-and-now'. Over time and with practice, Leon became more aware of how much his thoughts were driven by The Despiser (threat system thinking) and came to see how this threat-based thinking triggered his old brain emotions of shame and anxiety (threat-based emotions) which flipped him into the mode of Little Leon.

Leon and his therapist explored the links between his Despiser mode and his threat system and Leon came to recognise how his self-criticism activated his threat system, flooding him with stress hormones, leaving Little Leon feeling ashamed and anxious, fuelling further self-criticism. He also realised how the reverse could happen, that when Little Leon was feeling very low or anxious (old brain threat system activation) his Despiser mode would more easily take over his thinking (new brain), perpetuating his distress. Through psychoeducation, Leon came to understand that the reason it was so hard for him to have any balanced thinking when he was in Little Leon mode was because the threat system influences and biases new brain competencies such as mentalising, empathy and self-reflection and that under these conditions, attention acts as a spotlight, 'lighting up' everything that confirms his modes and schemas.

Leon's therapist introduced him to various 'focused attention' mindfulness practices (e.g., sounds, body scan and breathing) to illustrate how attention can be consciously directed. He was also encouraged to develop a regular formal mindfulness practice at home so he could practise sustaining attention at a single point of focus (e.g., the breath), shift attention of his own accord (e.g., moving between points of focus) and let go of judgement (for example, when his mind started wandering). After several months of engaging in a formal mindfulness practice, Leon began to notice when he was getting caught up in the storyline of his thoughts and redirect his attention. The main aim was for Leon's Healthy Adult (Compassionate Self) to have a meta awareness of his threat system and to notice and step out of the loops in his brain and bring awareness back to the 'here-and-now'.

Stabilising physiology

There is increasing evidence that a range of body-based practices, such as controlled breathing and yoga, can enable the frontal cortex to act as a regulator to the amygdala and HPA axis system, which is central to the development of the compassionate mind and Healthy Adult functioning (Schmalzl et al., 2015)

Posture helps 'the body support the mind' and can build capacity for tolerating distress. In the initial stages of therapy, Leon's therapist modelled to Leon's Healthy Adult (Compassionate Self) how to support Little Leon using bottom-up techniques such as embodying a posture reflective of strength, roundedness and confidence. She would instruct him first to anchor his feet on the floor, lift and lengthen his spine, relax his shoulders and hold his body in a way that reflects confidence, stability and openness. She then encouraged him to imagine he was looking at someone he deeply cared about and hold this facial expression (see Irons & Beaumont, 2017, for further elaboration). Once Leon had embodied a dignified and alert posture, his therapist enhanced his physiological coherence by guiding him into a soothing rhythm breathing. Over time, Leon's Healthy Adult (Compassionate Self) felt confident in knowing what he needed to do to help stabilise his physiology and no longer needed his therapist's guidance. His sense of agency helped reduce his fears about becoming emotionally overwhelmed and have faith in himself that he had the wisdom and skills to step in and help regulate his emotional arousal when needed.

Before any practical skills were introduced, Leon's therapist had explained the science behind breathing, including the impact breathing has on the autonomic nervous system, vagus nerve and heart rate variability. Understanding the science of breathing increased Leon's motivation to engage in regular breathing practices between sessions. He focused on rhythm and smoothness when he was practising breathing, and, over time, reduced his breathing rate to between five and six breaths a minute (see Lin et al., 2014).

Smell, sound and touch can also be used to stabilise physiology and support the capacity for compassion. Certain sounds and smells can stimulate our threat system (e.g., police siren, smell of burning) and other sounds/smells can stimulate our soothing system. Leon and his therapist spent time exploring what sounds and smells enhanced his sense of grounding and could thus support Little Leon and they would bring these into the therapy room: for example, burning neroli in an oil diffuser and playing the sound of a crackling fire when engaging in a breathing practice. Outside of sessions, Leon explored how touching different textures could aid the stimulation of his soothing system, which would bring comfort to Little Leon in times of distress, and he began to stroke his dog to the rhythm of his breathing, which had the added benefit of enhancing his sense of affiliation and connection.

Developing a kitbag, for example, with flashcards of breathing instructions, objects to touch, sounds to listen to and smells to inhale, can help patients access their soothing system. When the patient's threat based system is activated (and cognitive flexibility temporarily narrows) they can be encouraged to use these resources, which can increase capacity for Healthy Adult functioning.

Compassion-based imagery

Both ST and CFT use imagery as a therapeutic intervention. One main function in CMT is to stimulate the soothing affiliative system (e.g., parasympathetic, vagus system), regulate threat physiology, and to help patients to access qualities of compassion (e.g., empathy, distress tolerance). In ST, we would want the Healthy Adult mode to understand these purposes so it can better support the vulnerable child and, therefore, we encourage therapists to explain this to their patients in a very direct way.

There are various imagery exercises we can use to activate the soothing affiliative system and build compassion. Schema therapists will be familiar with safe place imagery; however, a helpful addition to the regular instructions is to ask patients to imagine that their safe place has a caring, appreciative and friendly awareness of them – that the 'place' welcomes them and wants them to be there so it can support and comfort them. In this aspect, safe place imagery in CFT aims to stimulate the physiological and emotional aspects of the soothing system, while also developing the affiliative, caring and relational (attachment system) aspects that this system is also associated with.

To help Leon connect to the feeling of being cared for and supported (and to bring his soothing affiliative system online, which may have an additional benefit of countering his emotional deprivation schema), his therapist introduced him to 'ideal compassionate other' practice, helping him to develop an image of a person (or being) that has certain key aspects of compassion (those linked to Figure 17.3 earlier in the chapter) but also, more broadly, wisdom, strength and commitment (see Gilbert, 2009). To help Leon develop his ideal compassionate other, he was asked to recall someone who had been compassionate towards him in the past and to think about their qualities. Although this was a struggle, he did remember a teacher from Year Nine who had been patient and kind when, due to dyslexia, he struggled in his English class. Alongside these qualities, Leon was encouraged to imagine his ideal compassionate other as having great wisdom. He understood all Leon had been through, what it means to be human and how his difficulties were not his fault. Furthermore, this ideal compassionate other had an aura of strength and authority with a confidence in his ability to help even when Leon was struggling the most. Finally, he had a deep motivation to care for and support Leon no matter which mode he was in.

The ideal compassionate other has many of the same qualities of the good parent provided in limited reparenting. This imagery technique might be an additional way of helping patients experience their attachment needs being met and of feeling safe in times of distress, thus down-regulating their threat system. Once the therapist has guided a patient in developing and accessing their compassionate other, then it is important that they help the patient do this for themselves to ensure they are continually expanding the repertoire of emotional regulation and distress tolerance skills the patient's Healthy Adult can draw upon. For example, the Healthy Adult might see the loneliness of their Vulnerable Child and bring to mind their compassionate other in order to give the child some extra support over and above talking warmly and kindly to the child mode.

Developing a compassionate self identity

Compassionate self-identity is rooted in a compassionate mind, and is linked to developing a 'part' of oneself that is *wise, strong and committed* (Gilbert, 2009, 2014). It has overlaps with the Buddhist concept of Boddhicita and Boddhisatva, and is rooted in the motivation to develop skills that can facilitate the two psychologies of compassion – engagement with, and skilful alleviation of, distress. Given this, it is likely to support the development of the Healthy Adult mode, and enable the Healthy Adult to meet and reduce the distress of the Vulnerable Child, and empathetically yet assertively engage with parent modes. This can be done in many ways, one of which is through utilising skills and techniques commonly used by actors – for example, using memory, empathy, imagination, observation and embodiment to step inside the mind and body of a part of them (or character) who has wisdom, strength and caring commitment.

The first dimension of the compassionate self is *wisdom*. Here, wisdom is to understand the causes of suffering and to know how to alleviate and prevent it (linked to the two psychologies of compassion). Leon's Compassionate Self learnt to recognise that he (like everybody) finds himself here with a tricky brain, designed for us, not by us, that he (like everybody) can so easily get caught in loops in the brain and that he (like everybody) has had experiences that have shaped him: for example, frustration of core needs that led to the development of his schemas and modes (or, using CFT language, Leon recognised he had experiences that he did not choose that shaped his threat system and led to key internal and external fears which he coped with by developing protective strategies that led to unintended consequences, none of which was his fault). Furthermore, wisdom enabled Leon's Compassionate Self to appreciate that suffering is part of life, and he is part of the whole human race that suffers through things like illness, grief, rejection, disappointments and death (sometimes referred to as 'the reality check'; see Gilbert, 2009). These kernels of wisdom helped to deepen Leon's Healthy Adult appreciation that suffering is not his fault. When the Healthy Adult can hold this wisdom in mind it is a very powerful response to the judgement of the punitive critical mode and can lessen the shame of the Vulnerable Child. Furthermore, when clients feel less ashamed, they can often move more easily into taking responsibility for the difficulties experienced in life. For example, because Leon felt less ashamed by his emotions, he was more open to accepting them and engaging in helpful emotion regulation strategies.

The second quality of a compassionate identity is *strength*. If Leon's Healthy Adult was going to face the suffering of Little Leon, then qualities such as groundedness, stability, determination, resilience, assertiveness and confidence were essential to staying anchored. Strength can be embodied, so Leon was encouraged to pay attention to his posture and breathing rhythm. His therapist also provided examples (e.g., the high diver or gymnast, who moves into action from a position of stability and roundedness), and images that represent grounding or strength (e.g., a tree with deep roots, or a mountain). It is essential that a patient's Healthy Adult mode (Compassionate Self) embodies strength in order to fight the parent modes and gain the confidence of the child and protector coping modes.

Wisdom and strength, however, need to be integrated with *commitment* – to be caring, to be helpful, to be supportive. The Compassionate Self wants to alleviate distress and foster well-being and flourishing – both in others and oneself. These same motivations should sit at the core of the Healthy Adult. Leon struggled with bringing this commitment to himself. This is common in CFT, and forms an important aspect of the therapeutic work, which is identifying and working with fears, blocks and resistances to compassion (see Gilbert, 2010; Irons & Beaumont, 2017 for further discussion). Leon's therapist helped him to get into contact with the feeling of caring–commitment by engaging a 'flow' of compassion (CFT suggests there are three flows of compassion: to others, from others and to self) that Leon was more familiar and comfortable with – to others. With guidance, Leon explored how the qualities of the Compassionate Self may relate to someone else who was struggling, and through this began to turn them towards himself.

Although explaining the three qualities of the compassionate self is important, therapists should help patients connect to their compassionate self through guided imagery in order to ensure this is an experiential, not cognitive, intervention and to enable their Healthy Adult to get a felt sense of these qualities. Just as you have to get wet if you're going to learn to swim, the qualities of the Compassionate Self need to be experienced and developed in creative ways and through different methods and practices (see Irons & Beaumont, 2017).

Bringing the compassionate self into core strategies for change

Once schema therapists have introduced CMT to their patients the next stage is to help patients connect to their compassionate self to strengthen their Healthy Adult mode (Compassionate Self) and to support them in the therapeutic work, including experiential, cognitive and behavioural interventions.

Chair work

Chair work lends itself nicely to integrating multiple self work from CFT, as both ST and CFT seek to explore how different parts of a patient think and feel about a situation and what each part needs and wants to do. As explained at the beginning of the chapter, in CFT multiple self work can take on many forms, including focusing these on different emotional parts of the self (e.g., anxious, angry, sad, shamed) and/or motives (e.g., competitive, caring). In this sense, CFT uses this exercise to fully explore both the Vulnerable and Angry Child modes and schema therapists might benefit at times from separating out the Vulnerable Child mode into chairs representing the different emotions that sit within this mode. This enables both the therapist and client to notice if there are overly dominant or non-explored emotional experiences (see Irons & Beaumont, 2017). This was very helpful for Leon, whose anxious and shamed self tended to dominate when speaking from the chair of Little Leon (especially when exploring his feelings about the breakup of his relationship) and his sad self was pushed to one side and his angry child (referred to as Angry Self in CFT) denied.

Chair work was a common feature of the work Leon and his therapist engaged in, and was used many times to explore his feelings about Donna leaving him. Little Leon was often full of anxiety (this is referred to as Anxious Self in CFT), and was fearful of never meeting anyone else. His Despiser mode made him believe he was to blame for Donna leaving and his Perfecting Pressuriser was constantly reminding him of what his life should look like (e.g., how he should be in a relationship), which triggered a lot of shame (referred to as Shamed Self in CFT). Leon found it far harder to move into his sad and angry self and had to practise embodying and connecting with these over time.

Through Socratic questions and the help of his Compassionate Self, Leon was able to engage with his Healthy Adult mode and use this to come to appreciate his struggles with his emotional parts, especially in the light of his early experiences. For example, he recognised that sadness was a difficult emotion, as his father had often told him 'big boys don't cry' and that to him, sadness left him feeling vulnerable and exposed. In terms of anger, Leon recognised that he saw anger as very dangerous and destructive, and had memories linked to his brother being verbally and, at times, physically violent. During the course of therapy, Leon came to realise that internalising rather than externalising anger was a lifelong pattern for him as his angry self often triggered Little Leon (and, more specifically, his Anxious Self), which then flipped him into Mr Nice Guy mode (protective strategy of appeasing others to avoid fear of connecting to, and expressing, anger and losing control).

During chair work, Leon used his Healthy Adult (Compassionate Self) to support the different emotional parts of Little Leon, including parts that were both under- and overregulated. Furthermore, his Healthy Adult (Compassionate Self) helped him accept all parts of himself, including facilitating his Anxious Self to accept his Angry Self. With the

Compassionate Self (acting like a safe haven/secure base) supporting him to explore all his emotions related to the breakup, Leon began to recognise that he had become stuck with the ending of his relationship partly because his sadness and anger had been blocked. With the growing capacity to now explore the whole range of human emotions through his Healthy Adult (Compassionate Self), Leon was better able to experience, process and express his emotions in ways that were valuable in guiding him through life difficulties.

With the help of his therapist, Leon learnt to embody his compassionate self; he would pause, engage in his soothing breathing and spend a few moments imagining and embodying the qualities of his compassionate self (wisdom, strength and commitment). He connected with his wisdom by reminding himself that all humans struggle and that the difficulties he was having in life were not his fault. He then embodied strength by engaging his soothing rhythm breathing, grounding his feet on the floor, lifting his spine and adopting a facial expression of calm and confidence. Finally, he looked at the chairs representing the different emotional parts of his child modes (Anxious Self, Sad Self, Shamed Self and Angry Self) and connected to a caring–commitment state (helped by bringing his attention to his heart and gut, which were the areas in his body where he felt a sense of caring commitment most strongly) to be supportive to all parts of himself. This helped him regulate the physiology of his threat system and engage self-empathy. This enabled him to respond skilfully to the different emotional parts of him and view the problems he was facing from a more balanced perspective.

Leon found that when he engaged in his Compassionate Self and turned towards the relationship breakup, he was quite shocked at what emerged. His Healthy Adult (Compassionate Self) could see that while Donna had treated him very poorly in the way that she had ended the relationship, he had also been unhappy during their time together. However, he hadn't been able to express this to Donna due to his Nice Guy mode (or protective strategy of suppressing anger/dissatisfaction) and he couldn't even acknowledge it to himself as Little Leon (and specifically Anxious and Lonely Self) because he was so scared about being on his own (key fear of abandonment). His Healthy Adult (Compassionate Self) was able to recognise that Donna had her own difficulties in life, and struggled to share her feelings, even with her family and friends. In that sense, he could see that there were understandable reasons why she had ended things in the way she did. Alongside this, Leon's Healthy Adult (Compassionate Self) felt motivated (partly because it had spent some time exploring what his Angry Self thought and felt) to contact Donna and to assertively communicate that the way she had ended things had been unhelpful for him.

Imagery rescripting

Leon also felt better placed to support Little Leon during imagery rescripting. The work he had done around commitment to his well-being – and, in particular, wisdom – enabled him to be more open and sensitive to Little Leon's suffering. Furthermore, he could now embody the wise and strong father figure Little Leon never experienced and he began to rely less on his therapist to reparent little Leon. Leon's Healthy Adult – linked directly to his compassionate self – also had more confidence in how to help Little Leon in times of overwhelming distress and would often coach Little Leon to steady his breath and would breathe with him with words of kindness and support. He was able to tell Little Leon that his struggles were not his fault.

Cognitive work

When Leon first started therapy, he over-identified with his thoughts. However, during CMT his Healthy Adult (Compassionate Self) came to understand that evolution has set us all up to have thoughts biased towards threat-based focusing to ensure survival. Developing wisdom in understanding the evolved nature of thinking was the first step Leon needed to cultivate compassionate and balanced thinking.

Through the course of ST, Leon also realised that The Despiser mode thrived off threat-based focusing, which was also perpetuated by being unable to satisfy the unrelenting demands of his Perfecting Pressurizer mode. Furthermore, many of his schemas (key 'internal' fears in CFT language), such as defectiveness/shame and negativity and pessimism, also perpetuated this type of threat-based attention. The capacity for balanced thinking was increased when Leon was able to connect with his compassionate self to help him regulate his physiology with his soothing breathing rhythm, thus bringing his prefrontal cortex online. This enabled the focus of his thinking to be open and broad, as well as less repetitive and ruminative. As he connected to his Compassionate Self, the content of his thoughts also began to change from threat-based negative thoughts to thoughts underpinned by care, warmth and compassion. Finally, his intention changed from punishment (The Despiser mode) to support (Healthy Adult mode).

Leon would frequently get pulled back into unhelpful threat-based thinking but, by using his mindfulness skills, physiological regulation and Compassionate Self, he now had a way of moving out of this. Over time, he started to notice that he was ruminating less and spending less time in his Avoider mode. He reflected he was better able to tolerate being still and attributed this to becoming less fearful and, thus, less avoidant of his own mind.

The Compassionate Self and behavioural work

Strengthening the Healthy Adult mode by establishing behaviours that enable patients to get their needs met is already an important element of ST, especially in the later phase of the work.

Compassionate behaviour has many faces, but one that is often overlooked is the courage to face something difficult. Leon's therapist emphasised the importance of courage by reflecting that a good parent supports their child to brave the world even when it can feel frightening to do so, and a strong compassionate identity works in much the same way. Leon used his compassionate self to engage in graded exposure to situations he found anxiety provoking, such as asserting himself in interpersonal situations (thus lessening the strength of both The Avoider and Mr Nice Guy) and to stay mindful of his desire for relationships and connection (the needs of Little Leon and his Healthy Adult).

Perhaps the most significant step for Leon was asking Lucy, a woman he had become friends with through his book club, out for a date. The multiple self work Leon had done around his breakup with Donna had helped him grieve that relationship and enabled him to open up to the possibility of dating again. Still, asking Lucy on a date required Leon to draw upon the courage and strength (qualities of compassion he was integrating into his Healthy Adult mode) to be vulnerable and risk rejection, as, while this scared him, he recognised that fear was a core part of being human, rather than being something shameful or weak about him. Furthermore, his Healthy Adult (Compassionate Self) was able to regulate his threat-based emotions (through mindfulness, soothing breathing rhythm and imagery) so he didn't become paralysed by anxiety and/or flip into The Avoider mode (protective strategy of distancing himself from his feelings). He recognised that, as Little Leon felt less destabilised by intense emotions, he felt safer within his own body and mind and this gave him the foundation he needed to be courageous. The relationship with Lucy didn't work out but, at the point therapy ended, Leon had been on two other dates and he was feeling much more hopeful that his future self would find love again.

Summary

Strengthening the Healthy Adult mode is one of the most important objectives of ST. Helping patients develop a compassionate mind can be seen as one (of many) potential ways of doing this. ST is an integrative approach and, as ST and CFT/CMT continue to evolve, schema therapists have a rich and exciting opportunity to explore how CMT might enhance their work, especially in fostering a strong, resilient and compassionate Healthy Adult mode.

Therapist tips

1. Introduce psychoeducation early on, especially reality checks around how and why we suffer to strengthen wisdom.
2. Introduce physiological regulation during the early stages of therapy to help build the capacity for Healthy Adult functioning.
3. Have fun creating a soothing system kitbag.
4. It doesn't matter if patients do not think they possess compassionate qualities, focus instead on encouraging them to imagine what it would be like if they did have them.

5. Give just as much weight to courage and strength as to kindness and warmth when discussing compassion.
6. During multiple self exercises, take time to explore each emotion within the Vulnerable Child mode, even if one or more emotions aren't immediately obvious. Also, explore the relationship each emotion has with others.
7. During chair work, encourage the patient to take a few minutes to practise their soothing breathing rhythm and connect to the wisdom, strength and commitment of their compassionate self when they first move into the Healthy Adult chair.

Note

1 For a comprehensive description of Compassion Mind Training skills, see Gilbert (2009); Irons and Beaumont (2017).

References

Arntz, A. & Jacob, G. (2013). *Schema Therapy in Practice: An Introductory Guide to the Schema Mode Approach.* Chichester: Wiley-Blackwell.

Depue, R.A. & Morrone-Strupinsky, J.V. (2005). A neurobehavioural model of affiliative bonding. *Behavioural and Brain Sciences, 28,* 313–395.

Gale, C., Gilbert, P., Read, N. & Goss, K. (2012). An evaluation of the impact of introducing compassion focused therapy to a standard treatment programme for people with eating disorders. *Clinical Psychology and Psychotherapy* advance online publication DOI: 10.1002/cpp.1806.

Gilbert, P. (1998). The evolved basis and adaptive functions of cognitive distortions. *British Journal of Medical Psychology, 71,* 447–463.

Gilbert, P. (2009). *The Compassionate Mind.* London: Constable & Robinson.

Gilbert, P. (2010). *Compassion Focused Therapy: Distinctive Features.* London: Routledge.

Gilbert, P. (2014). The origins and nature of compassion focused therapy. *British Journal of Clinical Psychology, 53*(1), 6–41.

Gilbert, P. & Irons, C. (2005). Focused therapies and compassionate mind training for shame and self-attacking. In: P. Gilbert (Eds), *Compassion: Conceptualisations, Research and Use in Psychotherapy* (pp. 263–325). Hove: Routledge.

Gilbert, P. & Procter, S. (2006). Compassionate mind training for people with high shame and self-criticism: A pilot study of a group therapy approach. *Clinical Psychology and Psychotherapy, 13,* 353–379.

Irons, C. & Beaumont, E. (2017). *The Compassionate Mind Workbook. A Step-by-step Guide to Developing Your Compassionate Self.* London: Robinson.

Laithwaite, H., Gumley, A., O'Hanlon, M., Collins, P., Doyle, P., Abraham, L. & Porter, S. (2009). Recovery after psychosis (RAP): A compassion focused programme for individuals residing in high-security settings. *Behavioural and Cognitive Psychotherapy, 37,* 511–526.

LeDoux, J. (1998). *The Emotional Brain: The Mysterious Underpinnings of Emotional Life.* New York: Simon and Schuster.

Lin, I.M., Tai, L.Y. & Fan, S.Y. (2014). Breathing at a rate of 5.5 breaths per minute with equal inhalation-to-exhalation ratio increases heart rate variability. *International Journal of Psychophysiology*, *91*(3), 206–211.

Lucre, K. & Corten, N. (2012). An exploration of group compassion-focused therapy for personality disorder. *Psychology and Psychotherapy: Theory, Research and Practice*, *86*(4), 387–400.

Panksepp, J. (1998). *Affective Neuroscience*. New York: Oxford University Press.

Schmalzl, L., Powers, C. & Blom, E.H. (2015). Neurophysiological and neurocognitive mechanisms underlying the effects of yoga-based practices: toward a comprehensive theoretical framework. *Frontiers in Human Neuroscience*, *9*, 1–19.

18 Building the Healthy Adult in eating disorders

A schema mode and Emotion–Focused Therapy approach for anorexia nervosa

Anna Oldershaw and Helen Startup

Background to anorexia nervosa

Anorexia nervosa (AN) is an eating disorder (ED) characterised by self-starvation driven by weight, shape and eating concerns and extreme dread of food, eating and normal body weight (American Psychological Association (APA), 2013). Low weight is achieved through the adoption of abnormal eating habits to severely restrict food intake, usually including restriction of both the amounts and types of food consumed. This can occur alongside excessive and extreme exercise or purging behaviours (e.g., vomiting or taking laxatives).

The annual UK incidence of AN is approximately 14 cases per 100,000 for females (Micali et al., 2013). In their lifetime, as many as 4% of women and 0.24% of men are affected by broadly defined AN (Smink et al.,2013). For girls, the peak age of onset is 15–25 years; for boys it is 10–14 years (Micali et al., 2013). AN is reported to have the highest mortality rates of all psychiatric disorders (Smink et al., 2013) and is associated with significant comorbidities. Approximately three-quarters of adults with AN have comorbid Axis I disorders (Herzog et al., 1992), and around a third experience comorbid personality disorders, associated with poorer treatment outcomes (Link et al., 2017). ED symptoms particularly relate to personality disorder symptoms, including unstable relationships, affective instability, emptiness, identity disturbance, inappropriate anger, dissociation/paranoia and suicidal behaviour (Miller et al., 2019).

Treatment of AN

In the UK, the National Institute for Health and Care Excellence (NICE, 2017) suggest that the treatment of choice for adults with AN is talking therapy. AN is notoriously considered 'difficult to treat', however, and randomised controlled trials indicate that speciality adult out-patient treatments do not out-perform each other or control comparisons post-therapy or at follow-up, with only small, non-significant effect sizes of change (Watson & Bulik, 2013). Emerging evidence suggests that early intervention improves outcomes (McClelland et al. 2018); however, this may have limited application for those with significant comorbidity or longer illness duration. Thus, interventions facilitating greater change are crucial (Bulik, 2014; Startup et al., 2015).

Refocusing the clinical spotlight: emotional difficulties and schema for people with AN

Among the complexity and physical risk inherent in working with someone with AN, it can be difficult to maintain a focused psychological intervention, resulting in lengthy therapeutic encounters with shifting foci. Improved psychological interventions for other complex presentations are thought to be achieved by focusing on a core, clearly defined model with one key putative maintaining process, hypothesised, therefore, to have a subsequent broader impact on primary symptomatology within a reasonable time frame (cf. targeting worry, sleep, self-esteem to effect change across psychosis symptoms; Freeman et al., 2015). We propose a similar refocusing of attention when working with AN, specifically towards an 'emotional self' as outlined below in our SPEAKS conceptualisation (Specialist Psychotherapy with Emotion for Anorexia in Kent and Sussex). In this chapter, we describe the SPEAKS theoretical model and outline proposed clinical change processes, describing the primary influences from Emotion Focused Therapy (EFT) and Schema Therapy (ST) in facilitating this change.

A core psychological mechanism in AN

Emotional difficulties

An important and promising development to ED models is the inclusion of difficulties with emotions (Sala et al., 2016). Indeed, emotional avoidance and submissive behaviours are promising predictors of post-treatment clinical outcomes (Oldershaw et al., 2018). In SPEAKS, we understand emotions as learnt or instinctive responses to our external or internal stimuli, informing about our immediate environments, our relationships and our needs. Emotions have been described as the conductor of an internal orchestra of the self, directing cognitive, behavioural, physiological and social functions (Oldershaw et al., 2015). Difficulties in processing and regulating emotion are of relevance to many psychological disorders, including EDs (Aldao et al., 2010) and are significant in the development and maintenance of AN (Treasure & Schmidt, 2013). Systematic reviews indicate that people with AN experience difficulties in emotional awareness, including alexithymia and poor emotional clarity (Oldershaw et al., 2015). There exists a pattern of over-regulation of emotion, relying predominantly upon unhelpful strategies (Oldershaw et al., 2015), including extreme avoidance of emotion triggers and suppression of emotion, particularly to avoid interpersonal conflict.

Emotion and schemas in AN

In AN, we suggest that early life experiences shape the development of schemas that leave the patient vulnerable to experiencing emotion as overwhelming and confusing. In ST terms, maladaptive schemas develop when basic needs go chronically unmet. People with AN rate themselves significantly higher than controls on all schema subscales, with largest differences for Defectiveness, Social Isolation, Subjugation, Dependence/Incompetence and Emotional Inhibition. Schemas affect adult relationships in that they are the 'lenses' through which one makes sense of the motivations and intentions of others, organising subsequent behaviour (Lavender & Startup, 2018). If early life experiences included being emotionally overwhelmed and burdened by the needs of a parent, for example, then it will be almost impossible to attune to, and express freely, one's own emotions and internal experiences. It might have been adaptive to attune to the emotional fluctuations of the parent to 'stay safe' or 'be accepted', with the resultant requirement to cope with one's own overwhelming emotion by 'numbing' emotional experience, surrendering to the belief that emotions aren't 'necessary' or 'of value' (possibly via a flight into an 'intellectual' side of the self), or squashing emotion through overcompensatory coping styles such as perfectionism, worry and procrastination (Startup et al., 2013). Such coping strategies move one further away from a clear sense of the 'emotional self', favouring the view of others, and schemas such as Defectiveness, Subjugation, Social Isolation, Dependence/Incompetence are perpetuated.

The SPEAKS theoretical model of AN

SPEAKS argues that the emotional avoidance cycle and its impact upon the development and awareness of a core 'emotional self' are both crucial for treatment. If we cannot access our bottom-up emotional experiences because we seek to avoid emotional experience or fundamentally rely on, or privilege, the experience of others, we struggle to navigate the world, ourselves and relationships. We cannot connect with important emotional information and needs. In short, we are without an internal emotional conductor to guide us (our emotional sense of self (Oldershaw et al., 2019)).

The SPEAKS integrative model of change

The SPEAKS conceptualisation of change draws on therapeutic theory and practice from ST alongside EFT. EFT is based on the premise that emotion is fundamental to self-construction and must be articulated in narratives with our 'parts of self' to promote change (Angus & Greenberg, 2011). Similarly, ST rests on the principle of self-multiplicity, with the self being composed of a number of interacting 'parts' (Pugh, 2020). At the heart of the self in ST terms is core vulnerability (the Vulnerable Child (VC)) and associated maladaptive schemas and unmet need, with other parts of the self largely attempting to express distress (such as the angry child) or manage this pain (such as via coping modes). It is clear from the outset, therefore, that EFT and ST draw parallels in terms of their approach to therapy as one that considers the whole person and values an understanding of how the self is constructed, including how parts of the self (or modes) might interact.

Emotions across both EFT and ST are understood to be significant in informing an individual of an important need, value, or goal that may be advanced or harmed in a situation. Therefore, their relevance to the SPEAKS conceptualisation of AN is clear. ST adopts a limited reparenting relational stance to support this, which is quite simply the involvement of the therapeutic relationship as an active vehicle for change by going some way (hence the 'limited') to meeting the unmet needs of the patient in the present moment. EFT utilises the therapeutic relationship to facilitate key principles of emotion change (awareness, expression regulation, reflection, transformation and corrective emotional experience), understanding that 'the only way out is through' (Pascual-Leone & Greenberg, 2007). EFT understands emotions as representing different 'levels' of experience. People often present to therapy with 'secondary emotions', diffuse, vague or secondary to the core issues; they are not directly linked to a core unmet need. The secondary emotion is important in that it represents the patient's current emotional state and requires attunement and validation, but connecting with this emotion is seen as a means to move beyond it. Primary emotions are more central to therapeutic change and represent an opportunity to connect with unmet needs, usually with developmental origins. They take one of two forms: representing stuck emotional patterns (perhaps helpful in the past, but now disruptive) relating to coping modes interfering with relationships and life goals, or they can provide important information giving access to core needs and appropriate behavioural responses (Elliott et al., 2004).

Both approaches seek to understand how an individual learnt to cope with their 'core pain' and the costs of this way of coping. In ST, this can be through surrendering, avoiding or overcompensating in relation to core maladaptive schemas. In EFT, this is conceptualised as 'blocks' to core emotional experience and needs by the parts of the self acting as coaches, critics or guards.

A SPEAKS mode map conceptualisation

The SPEAKS treatment model captures the core principle of self-multiplicity via an idiosyncratic AN mode map (Talbot et al., 2015). Typical AN modes include: The *emotional self* or VC, which, in AN, is often partially dissociated and sometimes non-verbal. This is typically silenced or condemned by a Critic mode (often with characteristics of being both demanding and critical), or 'managed' via some of the core ED schema coping modes, such as an 'Over-Controller' keeping rigid control behaviourally (such as via perfectionism) or cognitively (such as via worry, rumination, obsessionality), a 'Detached Protector' that numbs or squashes emotion at a superficial level, or a 'Detached Self-Soother' that transforms manifest emotion into something different (such as via bingeing and vomiting, using drugs, alcohol or other perseverative activities). The heterogeneity of AN is such that there may be diverse schema modes of relevance, which would be named and integrated into the conceptualisation. Indeed, in EFT, the parts of self are considered to emerge through the guiding and following of the patient in their emotional processes and are idiosyncratic to the individual. In the SPEAKS model, we recognise that there are common 'parts' or modes that will emerge.

The Healthy Adult (HA), however under-developed and unintegrated, is considered absolutely key to the SPEAKS model of change and is named and worked with from the outset. A core premise of this way of working is that accessing core pain through the process of removing blocks to emotion and making contact with emotional experience leads to a subsequent self-reorganisation of the individual; there is an emergent sense of self that gradually learns to 'take in' and be guided by this new emotional material with self-agency – the conductor of the orchestra (HA).

People with AN are often thought to have trouble expressing themselves or lacking in imaginal understanding. Therefore, SPEAKS seeks to actively bring a patient's attention and understanding of these parts within the mode map. Also, SPEAKS seek to encourage the patient's own 'bottom-up' exploration and conceptualisation of self. For this reason, toys are used to enable the patient to 'construct' their map. The toys are chosen by the patient, and the choices explored with the therapist. Therapists question and comment on the nature of the toys and their qualities to deepen the patient's understanding of the attributes associated with their parts and invite them to construct them together in the manner of their choosing. Figure 18.1 is an example of a patient-constructed mode map using toys. The experiencing self/VC is a small rubber toy that is malleable and cannot sit or stand. The critical self is a dragon and has been placed by the patient to stand over the VC, with its mouth fixed open, perpetually critical. There is a 'Compliant Surrenderer' coping mode in the form of a doe-eyed dog, submissive to needs of others, and a 'Detached Protector' ape that can squash down emotion with its clenched fist. The Detached Self-Soother looks playful, and is, therefore, seductive, but facilitates unhelpful behavioural ways of distracting from and blocking emotion. Finally, the figure chosen for the HA represents strength, agency and assertive anger, but was placed as far away as possible because she feels distant and out of reach, currently unavailable to the patient.

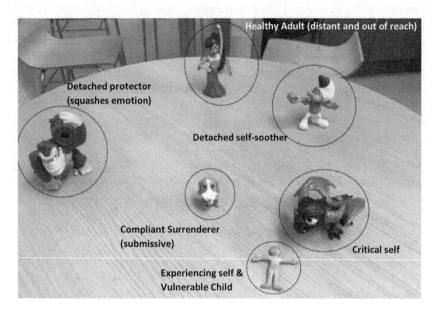

Figure 18.1 Mode map represented using toys selected by the patient to illustrate modes

Mechanisms of change in building the healthy adult

The SPEAKS treatment approach is a process-based model, divided into five phases laid out in a 'guidebook' for therapists. Each phase is described in terms of its treatment stage goals and the hypothesised mechanism of change (i.e., the change processes by which that goal might be achieved). There are therapeutic 'tasks' designed to facilitate the mechanisms of change, each with associated in-session 'markers' to highlight their relevance. Clinical indicators outline for therapists whether a phase has been fully worked through, but recognises that patients may move forwards and backwards through phases. The guidebook approach was taken to respect the clinical skill and experiences brought by therapists and offer them flexibility in the way they approach the material with each individual patient, while also providing a clear central framework in terms of a formulation and coherent process of change to work within.

At the heart of the approach is accessing and activating emotion within a secure, validating therapeutic relationship and, ultimately, transforming it through a connection with adaptive emotion and needs to build and strengthen the HA. In brief, this is achieved by working with: (1) blocks to core vulnerability/emotion to facilitate the expression and processing of these, and (2) the integration of this emotional material into an emergent self-reorganisation to generate a core sense of self – the Healthy Adult. Figure 18.2 illustrates the SPEAKS hypothesised process of change.

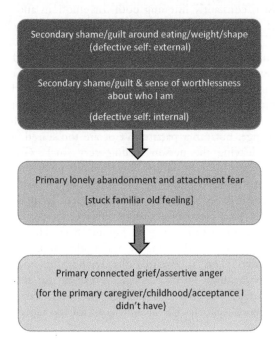

Figure 18.2 The SPEAKS hypothesised process of emotional change

Below, we describe a full course of SPEAKS for a patient called Jemma.[1] Only one or two pertinent tasks are described in each phase, but the overall intervention would involve several tasks to target one mechanism of change and/or the repetition of the same task with deepening of the emotional experience and connection to needs. The SPEAKS theoretical model is evidenced based (Oldershaw et al., 2019), and the preliminary clinical translation described is under empirical investigation via a feasibility trial.

Phase 1

The initial phase of SPEAKS focuses on building the therapeutic relationship in which feared emotions can safely emerge. It seeks tentatively to help the person build a narrative away from eating, weight and shape as the core issues and consider broader contexts and associated emotions. The therapist demonstrates from the outset the practice of 'following' (following the pain to uncover the patient's emotional process) and 'guiding' (deepening emotional contact by guiding towards unsaid emotions 'pointed at' by the patient). As described, a core goal of SPEAKS is to 'follow the pain' to build connection with an emotional world and deepen this understanding (Pos & Greenberg, 2007).

The therapist is constantly listening both for emotions and parts of the self as they emerge. Forms of the critical voice emerge early, such as the eating disorder voice provoking guilt and shame around body image and food. Other parts might include coping modes: a Detached Protector or a Compliant mode blocking access to core vulnerable emotion. These can be named and conceptualised. Anxiety splits are common, by which anxiety (as a secondary emotion process) is blocking other forms of emotional processes. For those with AN, we often see a motivational split, in which part of the self wants to change, but other parts don't or are too scared, and these cancel each other out, leaving the person feeling very stuck. Gradually, through exploration and empathic responding, the therapist helps the patient to map out these parts of the self by drawing the patient's attention to them as they emerge. This can then be 'illustrated' for the patient using a mode map and chairs to represent these parts/modes or by inviting the patient to choose and arrange toys (see Jemma's mode map in Figure 18.1). The therapist responds to the patient's emotions with empathy and understanding, linking back to their new narrative. This is essential for relationship and trust building, particularly given the high levels of shame prevalent for this patient group. A validating, strongly empathic relationship offers the start of a 'corrective emotional experience' that lays the groundwork for the remainder of therapy

Phase 2

Jemma was anxious as therapy started and consumed by guilt over the amount of food she was eating. Her ED critic told her that she was fat, lazy and didn't deserve to eat or to get well. She spoke about having to put the needs of others (her mum and sister) first (Compliant Surrenderer) and that there was no space for her (or her feelings). In one session, Jemma described what happened when she had tried to follow her new eating plan, and the ED part became very active and vivid. The therapist first used chairs to slow things down and increase her meta-awareness of the relationship between these parts of the self. She invited Jemma to use the chair to differentiate this ED part of the self, and initiate a dialogue, thereby allowing exploration of the emotional impact of this. When Jemma switched back into the 'experiencing' chair (the part of her that is on the receiving end of these emotions, collaboratively called 'Little Self'), she initially agreed with the eating disorder voice and the critical things it told her. By drawing her attention instead to the emotional impact of hearing these critical statements, Jemma was able to begin describe more fully the guilt and shame she experienced and how this kept her from making changes.

Connection with these initial emotions was not an easy or brief task. As described above, this patient group find it particularly difficult, overwhelming and threatening to connect to emotional experience and are, therefore, 'over-regulated' in their emotional experience. It is crucial that the therapist supports the patient's connection with emotional experience and avoids them experiencing a 'cognitive', or head-only, level of experience (indicating a flip into a coping mode) which can cause the task to stall. In this instance, the therapist offered empathic validation and gently helped Jemma to explore the bodily felt experience of shame and guilt deepening her emotional experience (see Part I, Chapter 3). The therapist understood this guilt and shame about food, eating and her weight as very real for Jemma and in need of validation, but secondary to the deeper core pain that she believed Jemma was protecting herself from via the use of her ED and other coping modes.

Phase 3

Phase 3 is entered when the patient begins to move beyond secondary emotions, and ED focus, to differentiate into deeper primary emotions. At first, these emotions usually reflect stuck old feelings linked to core schema and relational patterns (e.g., shame, guilt and worthlessness of self, and lonely abandonment; see Figure 18.2). As described, in SPEAKS terms, it is through connection with these primary emotional experiences, and associated needs, that the HA can emerge, facilitating a change in behavioural and relational experiences.

Gradually, through working with the ED part of self, Jemma had begun to reveal a broader Critic, one who told her she was never good enough for others, would always let others down and never achieve anything. The therapist saw this as a sign that the emotional experience of her Little Self had deepened and the patient was beginning to access more primary emotional experiences reflecting core schema. In this case, that meant emotions that related to a sense of worthlessness, feeling not valued or accepted within the family. This was quite subtle for Jemma and equated to a sense of feeling different from mum and her sister, but desperate to be truly accepted by them. Again, the therapist used two-chair work to explore the emotional experience provoked by this criticising part. When Jemma switched into the experiencing chair, the Little Self began to vocalise a sense of lonely abandonment and fears that she might be rejected by others. At this stage, another side emerged, the Compliant Surrenderer, who put the needs of others first and suppressed her own emotions for fear of losing other people. This was understood as a block to allowing and deepening emotions and in accessing 'healthy' emotion processes, which could help to transform these old stuck emotional and interpersonal patterns. The therapist again used chairs, this time with the Compliant Surrenderer blocking her emotional needs as it told Jemma, 'You must always do as others want, otherwise they won't love you'. Gradually, they began to understand the experiencing part of self (Little Self) as a Vulnerable Child, which had little voice and a poorly developed emotional world. The therapist responded in a reparenting, empathic, soothing tone, in keeping with the young developmental age of the vulnerable self at this point. The therapist showed commitment to connecting with this side of the self in a sensitive and non-intrusive manner, enabling the abandonment and attachment fears to be deeply felt and expressed.

To further deepen the feelings of lonely abandonment, while Jemma sat in her Vulnerable Child chair, she was gently guided to close her eyes and elaborate the experience of these emotions via her body with gentle probes such as: 'Where do you feel that loneliness in your body?', 'What does it look like?' and then 'Can you make the feelings large ... I know it's tough ... but can you stay with and have the feelings of loneliness and sadness fill your body.' The 'float back' technique (see Part I, Chapter 2) was used to support Jemma to 'let go' of any current thoughts and to let her mind wander until she fell upon a memory earlier in her life with a similar emotional 'flavour'. Jemma described vividly and with powerful emotion a memory of being left by the side of the road watching on as her parents rowed aggressively in the town centre. Previously, she had only expressed shame about this event, but now feelings of abandonment and despair emerged, associated with having to soothe and comfort her own mother following the row. Jemma described a deep despair and loss, that no one was there for her, that no one could see her needs. The therapist gently asked permission to 'enter' the image (a way of working common to their sessions which Jemma was comfortable with), and Jemma asked her to stand in the image between her and her mother. As can be the case with this type of relational trauma, it can be too much to ask the child in the image what they needed in the moment; it can feel too challenging to the parent–child relationship that, of course, was relied upon at the time. Rather, the key is to have the patient's needs met in imagery. In this case, with Jemma's guidance and the therapist's suggestions, Jemma was taken out of the situation by the therapist and to her aunt's house, a place where she often felt listened to, safe and cared for.

In a later debrief session, Jemma identified this work as being pivotal in getting her in touch with the emotion/pain (desolation, despair, abandonment, sadness) underneath the shame, to link this to unmet need (to be parented and all this involves, rather than parenting) and to learn that this core pain could be responded to with validation, kindness and soothing. It was clear, therefore, from the float back that the lonely abandonment Vulnerable Child was most strongly felt in relation to mum and her unmet needs for individuation, emotional validation and care. The therapist sought to help Jemma understand these links and then gently suggested using empty-chair work to further connect with, and transform, this core pain. Through the experience of imagining mum in the chair in front of her and describing the lack of connection and acceptance she felt, Jemma was able to experience her shame and abandonment in the context of the maternal relationship, where it originated. Once emotions were activated, the therapist encouraged Jemma to tell her mum what she had needed. The expression of needs of acceptance, protection and unconditional love to the introjected mother imagined on the empty chair immediately triggered a sense of grief; a deep sense of loss for the childhood and mothering that she longed for but never had. She began to recognise and process her deep longing for this relationship. By then enacting her mother, Jemma explored her response of surprise and also her indignation, her retort that she had tried her best. Jemma was able to further respond to her mother with a sense of assertive anger that she had been the child and she had deserved more, thus representing the beginning of the HA in the context of this key developmental relationship.

Phase 4

In Phase 4, the patient has arrived at, and worked to transform, their core pain. They are now beginning to connect their transformed emotional experiencing to alternative intra- and interpersonal ways of responding that reflect a more resilient and integrated sense of self (Pos & Greenberg, 2007), that is, directed by the HA. This may involve relationship boundary setting, such as the expression or healthy assertion of their own needs. The intrapersonal experience of self-compassion often emerges here. Previously, Jemma had not felt she was deserving of compassion, that her feelings and needs did not deserve to be heard. Through the process of connecting with her core pain and unmet needs, Jemma began to consider that she might deserve compassion. Unless it naturally arises earlier, self-compassion is directly addressed later in the therapeutic process of SPEAKS than in some other therapies. For this particular patient group, who demonstrate such strong coping modes of Compliant Surrenderer and Detached Protectors, these blocks to self-compassion must be at least partly overcome before the patient can truly begin to believe and 'feel' that they might deserve compassion. Once the patient has accessed a felt sense of the core pain of her Vulnerable Child, she is able to begin to show compassion to the pain, even if not ready to show it to herself more fully or in more general terms. Furthermore, self-compassion is directed from the HA; therefore, this part of self must be emerging in order for compassion to be authentically expressed in a way that connects in a 'felt sense' by the patient. Such explicit, connecting self-validation further strengthens the HA and consolidates the basis for new ways of navigating the self, relationships and the world.

Self-compassion work in this case was integrated into the empty-chair work with the parent described in Phase 3. The task was completed more than once. As soon as emotion was activated, the compassionate HA was introduced to comfort the grieving child in a two-chair task. Experience of this self-soothing and compassion deepened her connection with her emotional needs, as they felt validated and deserved. This gave further voice to, and thus strengthened, the HA.

Phase 5

By the end of therapy (around nine months from the start) Jemma was in a stable relationship with a new boyfriend. She had sought a change of location in her job to reduce her commute; something long desired, but not pursued for fear of what her manager might think. Jemma reported that she was able to show genuine compassion towards her mum, not an anxious compassion out of 'duty', which is how she reflected upon her previous feelings. This more balanced view also meant that she was able to take a step back and build her own needs and boundaries into the relationship.

This final phase of the SPEAKS therapy focuses on the therapeutic relationship coming to a close. Both therapist and patient talk about the feelings this brings, what has been gained via this nourishing connection, as well as the sadness and loss at the approaching close to the work . It is common for old ways of coping to resurface at this stage as the anxiety of separation is faced. This is normalised and the emotional pain underneath talked about, validated and met with compassion. Sometimes, the ending is tapered, or extended and sometimes patients come back for 'top-up' work. We may also give a transitional object or a reminder of the time spent together – as all relationships are different, all endings need to be managed on an individual basis, with flexibility, thought and care. A key task is letter writing, from therapist to patient and also from patient to therapist. These are read out to each other in session and offer a summary of the process from both perspectives. From the therapist's point of view, it is not a clinical letter, but one of the last ways that they can connect with their patient as from one human being to another. They are urged to reflect on their own emotional processes and express their own authentic healthy primary feelings in response to the ending, such as their sadness that they will no longer see the patient and/or their joy at having had this time and to have borne witness to the process and change.

Conclusion

In conclusion, SPEAKS is an integrative process-based model drawing on techniques from EFT and ST. The integration of EFT affords SPEAKS a core focus on emotion and in differentiating layers of emotions, from secondary to primary, to access core pain. Coping modes add to the conceptualisation of each case and the understanding of an individual's pattern of coping. Coping modes are viewed largely as 'blocks' to emotional experience, developing for understandable reasons, but ultimately denying the opportunity to resolve core pain. SPEAKS looks to collaboratively understand and gradually moderate these coping modes so that the patient's core pain can be felt and ultimately cared for by their HA. SPEAKS considers the HA not as a distinct mode, but, rather, a psychologically heathy sense of a core self, emerging during the therapy, which works to hear and understand all the other modes at play. Indeed, a core premise is that accessing core pain leads to a subsequent self-reorganisation of the individual such that an emergent sense of self can 'take in', be guided by, and act on, good emotional information and healthy associated needs.

Therapist tips

- Core to SPEAKS, drawn from both EFT and ST, is that therapists should 'follow the pain'. This means closely following emotional experience, guiding towards core pain. It is helpful to hold this in mind when watching and waiting for a session focus; also, try to land on the most emotionally salient work.
- In chair work, try to focus on the process and emotion, and not get overly caught up in the narrative content.
- Be aware of blocks to the emotions and progress in general. Consider that these may include therapist's own blocks relating to their emotional experience, schemas and modes as they struggle to follow their patient's core pain.
- The work requires an element of being 'brave', sometimes saying an intuitive guess or using therapist experienced emotion to suggest what a patient may be feeling. Done in a questioning and tentative way in the context of a strong therapeutic relationship, patients report that this is helpful. Even if the therapist is wrong, it can help the patient to remember to check in and 'land' on the actual feeling and create a sense of connection as therapist and patient learn to listen for, and sense, their core needs.

Note

1 The material presented is written so as to protect patient confidentiality, and session examples are composites of therapeutic dialogues with a number of patients

References

Aldao, A., Nolen-Hoeksema, S. & Schweizer, S. (2010). Emotion-regulation strategies across psychopathology: A meta-analytic review. *Clinical Psychology Review, 30*, 217–237.

American Psychological Association (APA). (2013). *Diagnostic and Statistical Manual of Mental Disorders*. Washington, DC: APA.

Angus, L.E. & Greenberg, L.S. (2011). *Working with Narrative in Emotion-Focused Therapy: Changing Stories, Healing Lives*. Washington, DC: American Psychological Association.

Elliott, R., Watson, J.C., Goldman, R.N. & Greenberg, L.S. (2004). *Learning Emotion-Focused Therapy: The Process-Experiential Approach to Change*. Washington, DC: American Psychological Association.

Freeman, D., Dunn, G., Startup, H., Pugh, K., Cordwell, J., Mander, H. ... Kingdon, D. (2015). Effects of cognitive behaviour therapy for worry on persecutory delusions in patients with psychosis (WIT): A parallel, single-blind, randomised controlled trial with a mediation analysis. *The Lancet Psychiatry, 2*(4), 305–313.

Herzog, D.B., Keller, M.B., Sacks, N.R., Yeh, C.J. & Lavori, P.W. (1992). Psychiatric comorbidity in treatment-seeking anorexics and bulimics. *Journal of the American Academy of Child & Adolescent Psychiatry, 31*(5), 810–818.

Lavender, A. & Startup, H. (2018). Personality disorders. In S. Moorey & A. Lavender Eds.. *The Therapeutic Relationship in Cognitive Behavioural Therapy*. London: SAGE.

Micali, N., Hagberg, K.W., Petersen, I. & Treasure, J.L. (2013). The incidence of eating disorders in the UK in 2000–2009: Findings from the General Practice Research Database. *British Medical Journal Open, 3*, e002646.

Miller, A.E., Racine, S.E. & Klonsky, E.D. (2019). Symptoms of anorexia nervosa and bulimia nervosa have differential relationships to borderline personality disorder symptoms. *Eating Disorders*, 1–14.

National Institute for Health, and Care Excellence [NICE]. (2017). *Eating Disorders: Recognition and Treatment: NICE Guideline [NG69]*. London: National Institute for Health and Care Excellence.

Oldershaw, A., Lavender, T., Sallis, H., Stahl, D. & Schmidt, U. (2015). Emotion generation and regulation in anorexia nervosa: A systematic review and metaanalysis of self-report data. *Clinical Psychology Review*, *39*, 83–95.

Oldershaw, A., Lavender, T. & Schmidt, U. (2018). Are socio-emotional and neuro-cognitive functioning predictors of therapeutic outcomes for adults with anorexia nervosa? *European Eating Disorders Review*, *26*, 346–359.

Oldershaw, A.V., Startup, H. & Lavender, T. (2019). Anorexia nervosa and a lost emotional self: A clinical conceptualisation of the development, maintenance and psychological treatment of anorexia nervosa. *Frontiers in Psychology*, *10*, 219.

Pos, A.E. & Greenberg, L.S. (2007). Emotion-focused therapy: The transforming power of affect. *Journal of Contemporary Psychotherapy*, *37*(1), 25–31.

Pugh, M. (2020). *Cognitive Behavioural Chairwork*. Abingdon: Routledge.

Sala, M., Heard, A. & Black, E.A. (2016). Emotion-focused treatments for anorexia nervosa: A systematic review of the literature. *Eating and Weight Disorders*, *21*, 147–164.

Smink, F.R., van Hoeken, D. & Hoek, H.W. (2013). Epidemiology, course, and outcome of eating disorders. *Current Opinion in Psychiatry*, *26*, 543–548.

Startup, H., Lavender, A., Oldershaw, A., Stott, R., Tchanturia, K., Treasure, J. & Schmidt, U. (2013). Worry and rumination in anorexia nervosa. *Behavioural and Cognitive Psychotherapy*, *41*(3), 301–316.

Startup, H., Mountford, V., Lavender, A. & Schmidt, U. (2015). Cognitive behavioural case formulation in complex eating disorders. In N.J. Tarrier Ed., *Case Formulation in Cognitive Behaviour Therapy: The Treatment of Challenging and Complex Cases*. Hove: Routledge), 239–264.

Talbot, D., Smith, E., Tomkins, A., Brockman, R. & Simpson, S. (2015). Schema modes in eating disorders compared to a community sample. *Journal of Eating Disorders*, *3*(1), 41.

Treasure, J. & Schmidt, U. (2013). The cognitive–interpersonal maintenance model of anorexia nervosa revisited: A summary of the evidence for cognitive, socio-emotional and interpersonal predisposing and perpetuating factors. *Journal of Eating Disorders*, *1*(1), 13.

Watson, H.J. & Bulik, C.M. (2013). Update on the treatment of anorexia nervosa: Review of clinical trials, practice guidelines and emerging interventions. *Psychological Medicine*, *43*, 2477–2500.

The SPEAKS intervention development and feasibility trial is independent research arising from an Integrated Clinical Academic Fellowship–Clinical Lectureship awarded to AO (ICA-CL-2015-01-005) supported by the National Institute for Health Research and Health Education England. The views expressed in this publication are those of the authors and not necessarily those of the NHS, the National Institute for Health Research, Health Education England or the Department of Health.

19 Brief work
Schema informed CBT

Stirling Moorey, Suzanne Byrne and Florian Ruths

Overview of chapter

This chapter is primarily aimed at Cognitive–Behavioural (CBT) therapists looking to integrate Schema Therapy ideas and techniques into their work to enhance treatment effectiveness. It first explores some ways in which Schema Therapy methods such as chair work using 'mode dialogue' can help to overcome roadblocks in standard CBT. It then considers how understanding the patient's unmet emotional needs can enrich the conceptualisation of chronic and treatment resistant cases, and guide therapy. A schema informed formulation can allow the therapist to introduce imagery rescripting, limited reparenting and empathic confrontation within the CBT framework. This approach is illustrated through a case description of therapy with a depressed patient. The last section of the chapter discusses the practicalities of applying Schema Therapy ideas in busy services geared towards short-term interventions.

Schemas in CBT and Schema Therapy

Schemas have been a central component of CBT theory since Beck first formulated his cognitive model of depression (Beck, 1963, 1964). In Beck's model, a schema is a hypothetical structure for making sense of the world, for 'screening, encoding and evaluating impinging stimuli' (Beck, 1964, p. 562). Schemas are often summarised as rules or beliefs (e.g., If I make a mistake, I am useless; I must always be loved). When these rules are applied in an inflexible and overgeneralised fashion, they predispose to psychological difficulties. Jeffrey Young worked with Beck but became dissatisfied with the applicability of cognitive therapy to personality disorders, in part because its strong emphasis on beliefs did not seem to do justice to the emotional complexity of the patients he was treating. His Early Maladaptive Schemas (EMS) differ from Beckian schemas in a number of ways. First, there is a more explicit developmental and aetiological description of what leads to an EMS: a maladaptive schema is formed when fundamental childhood emotional needs are not met. For instance, lack of validation and constant parental criticism lead to a *Defectiveness schema,* while enforced separation may affect attachment and lead to an *Abandonment schema*. Second, the EMS are seen to comprise not only cognitions, but also emotions, memories and body sensations. All of these typically come 'online' as a 'flood' of experience which explains the high levels of arousal often associated with schema activation. Young highlights some ways in which EMS can sabotage traditional CBT (Young et al., 2003, pp. 23–24).

1. A positive therapeutic alliance may be difficult to build if patients have schemas in the Disconnection and Rejection domain, for example, Abandonment, Mistrust/Abuse.
2. It may difficult to identify specific goals if patients have schemas in the Impaired Autonomy and Performance domain, for example, Dependence, Enmeshment/Undeveloped Self).
3. Patients may find it hard to access and verbalise cognitions and emotions if they have schemas in the Other Directedness domain, for example, Subjugation, Self-Sacrifice.
4. Patients may find it hard to comply with homework if they have schemas in the Impaired Limits domain, for example, Entitlement, Insufficient Control.

One might add to this list the commonly encountered head–heart disconnect, where patients can see the irrationality of their beliefs but cannot prevent themselves feeling bad, unlovable or helpless. Young's model would argue that this mismatch arises because the emotional, somatic and memory components of the schemas are not sufficiently addressed in traditional CBT. Schema Therapy techniques can be used to deal with some of these problems that lead to impasse or alliance rupture in CBT.

An important development in Schema Therapy has been the concept of schema modes. As has been described in the Introduction, a schema mode is an organising term for understanding the various schemas that may be active at a given time. In people with emotionally unstable personality disorder, certain schemas tend to coalesce into repeatedly occurring modes: the *Vulnerable Child, Angry Child, Punitive Parent* and *Detached Protector*. Individuals can flip between these self-states and this explains the rapid shifts in affect and behaviour towards the therapist within the session. People with personality disorder lack a well-developed *Healthy Adult* mode, which represents the internalisation of emotional regulation and soothing necessary to balance the other modes. The mode formulation adds a dynamic understanding to the more static cognitive conceptualisation of the Beck developmental model, which works better for Type C, rather than Type B, personality disorders. These separate self-states are just an extreme form of what we all experience: we all have a Vulnerable Child mode in which we feel inadequate, defective, abandoned, unlovable, etc., and we all employ coping modes where we overcompensate or avoid to protect our vulnerable self. Addressing these modes can help to unblock obstacles in therapy.

While long-term Schema Therapy has proved efficacy with personality disorders (see Jacob & Arntz, 2013), CBT remains the treatment of choice for anxiety disorders, depression and eating disorders (NICE, 2004a,b,c, 2005a,b, 2013). It is too early to say that a pure form of Schema Therapy for these disorders is as effective (see, for instance, the review by Taylor et al., 2017). However, some of the principles of Schema Therapy may augment CBT in cases that are not responding to standard treatment.

Applications of Schema Therapy principles in CBT

Overcoming roadblocks in CBT

The structure of therapy and collaboration in CBT go a long way to preventing schema activation in patients who do not have significant personality pathology. There is a clear agenda, clear goals and the patient is an active partner in the change process (Moorey, 2014 pp. 128–129). This reduces the chances of misinterpretation and allows therapy to be problem, rather than relationship, focused. For instance, the open collaborative stance of CBT can enhance trust in someone with a Mistrust/Abuse schema, where the focus on interpretation and free association by the psychodynamic therapist may increase suspicion. Despite this, schemas still get triggered and there may sometimes be resistance to the change techniques used in CBT. One common example is failure to comply with homework tasks. In anxiety disorders, this involves reluctance to engage in behavioural experiments to test fears and, in depression, a failure to carry out behavioural activation tasks.

There are various ways in which CBT negotiates these alliance ruptures (see Moorey & Lavender, 2018) but schema methods allow us to go beyond these to work at a more emotionally vivid level. Conceptualising this in terms of modes, for example, we can say that the failure to do the homework comes from the Detached Protector mode acting to protect the Vulnerable Child mode (which contains schemas such as defectiveness, failure, vulnerability to harm or dependence/incompetence). Through chair work, the therapist asks the patient to play the side of him or herself that is saying that change is too risky. The therapist then engages in dialogue with the Detached Protector mode, compassionately validating (acknowledging that the mode is doing its best to keep the Vulnerable Child safe) and asking the protector what the child fears. One of the assumptions here is that the Vulnerable Child is 'listening'. In the dialogue, the therapist utilises the material from the more cognitive cost-benefit analysis to dispel the fears and bolster the positive reasons for doing the homework. Through this more emotionally charged discussion, the therapist reassures the Vulnerable Child and counters the specific fears. A case example is outlined below.

Case example of a mode dialogue: Anna

Anna was a woman in her late 30s who presented with recurrent depression and difficulties in relationships. She had had past episodes of panic disorder and binge drinking. Her mother had been emotionally neglectful and her father had been the main caregiver, but he died when she was aged ten. Anna described herself as 'sabotaging' intimate relationships: she kept her feelings bottled up and did not express her needs, but this would lead to her feeling frustrated and resentful, and she would then explode angrily. She had some close friends but found any perceived criticism hard to manage. As a consequence, she would withdraw and ruminate. Therapy consisted of standard CBT for depression with activity scheduling and cognitive restructuring. As themes emerged in early therapy, the therapist made links to Anna's long-term compensatory strategies and past experiences (e.g., excessive standards, withdrawal in relationships, numbing via binge drinking).The concept of 'Healthy Anna' was introduced and served as an organising concept to promote healthy behaviours, such as exercising, drinking less and seeing friends.

Anna made some improvement but therapy became stuck and she struggled to evaluate negative automatic thoughts. Anna was able to view these thoughts from a rational perspective but not feel any emotional shift. Her key beliefs were 'I am stupid', 'I am worthless' and 'If others get close they'll hurt or reject me'. The therapist introduced the concept of modes and linked this to her formulation. The roadblock to progress in therapy seemed to be an Angry Protector mode which told her, 'Don't get too close because you'll get hurt (as you are unlovable and worthless)' and 'If others get close they'll hurt and reject you'. This protected her from external rejection, and also from her internal critical voice (Punitive Parent mode) which told her that 'This is all you deserve because you're stupid and worthless'. Chair work helped to illustrate the dominant modes and their effects. Anna moved from chair to chair as the modes talked. A key moment during this work was the dialogue with Anna's Angry Protector mode. The pros and cons of the Angry Protector mode were explored. Anna recognised its value to her as a child but began to question its place in her adult life. Her Healthy Adult looked at the pros and cons of change − the risks and benefits of being kinder to herself, taking risks in relationships by lowering her guard and expressing her needs. Anna began to experiment with reducing behaviours linked with her Angry Protector mode, using a schema (mode) flashcard to remind her that she didn't need this type of protection any more. She experimented with 'lowering the wall' by expressing her needs and there was significant improvement in many relationships. Anna remained fearful of closer intimacy and shortly after starting a new relationship came to a session upset as she could recognise 'old patterns of behaviour' and her 'default' mode being 'activated'. She reported feeling jealous of her new partner and being critical of him and withdrawing. Further chair work was used based on a recent incident. A dialogue between Anna's Healthy Adult and Angry Protector mode was set up and is outlined below. Anna decided to call her

Angry Protector mode an 'Old Woman' which seemed to help decentre the mode.

OLD WOMAN: You're stupid to trust him, you need to be on your guard, he'll only hurt you. You don't deserve happiness – it's best to get out now.

HEALTHY ANNA: You need to stop behaving this way towards me, telling me nothing lasts forever and to be on my guard. I understand why you're there but you're actually making things worse.

OLD WOMAN: [shocked at being questioned] You will get hurt and you are stupid not to see this. You don't deserve happiness and need to be on your guard.

HEALTHY ANNA: Look, I know you think you have my best interests at heart and you came out of the awful time we had at home. You tried to protect me when I was a little girl but I don't need your protection now. You're actually making things worse. You make me feel anxious and depressed and push people away. I am worth loving and have lots of good friends and am strong enough to take the risk of getting hurt. I want you to turn the volume down and let me enjoy my life.

OLD WOMAN: I'm worried that you'll get hurt.

HEALTHY ANNA: I may get hurt but that's okay. I've been hurt before and have survived. I'm strong enough to cope with it.

OLD WOMAN: [faded away].

Enhancing CBT for treatment resistant cases

There is evidence that people with chronic depression are more likely to have experienced significant childhood adversity, including poor parental bonding, than those with acute depression (Lizardi et al., 1995), more insecure attachment (Fonagy et al., 1996) and adverse early home environments (Durbin et al., 2000). This adversity may mean there is a lack of compelling evidence to counter the patient's core negative beliefs. For instance, someone with a Defectiveness schema may have been told over and over again that they were stupid and, because of their lack of confidence, they then went on to do badly at school. Someone who was taken into care at a young age may have an Abandonment schema based on many changes of foster parents. A patient with an Enmeshment schema may have had no experience of being allowed to function in an autonomous way. In these cases, important childhood needs have not been met. Cognitive techniques promote intellectual change, but the head–heart lag means that feelings of shame, abandonment or dependency have precedence over rational thinking.

In traditional CBT, the patient may become trapped in a ruminative cycle where the rational side is unsuccessfully debating with the emotional side. At other times, schema activation can overwhelm the rational self. When an Abandonment schema is activated it may feel as if you are six years old again, experiencing the death of your mother, or, when standing in front of your boss who is yelling at you triggers a Defectiveness schema, it may feel as if you're a little boy being told off by your father. The Healthy Adult is not strong enough to manage this 'schema attack'. The more experiential techniques of Schema Therapy have something to offer patients with chronic difficulties. In imagery work, the patient's Healthy Adult, or, if this is too underdeveloped, the therapist, comes into the image as a rescuer or soother. In chair work, the therapist models how to talk back to the punitive parent.

Imagery rescripting

Imagery work has long been used in standard CBT: for example, Beck et al. (1979) describes using imagery rehearsal in depression. Imagery rescripting is a key intervention in Schema Therapy, as has been described in Part II. This approach has been adapted for use in CBT for anxiety disorders – for example, to target early memories linked to negative self-images in social anxiety (Wild et al., 2008). How imagery rescripting is used will vary depending on the case and nature of presentation. Some examples are outlined below from our clinical practice:

1. Safe place imagery (Young et al., 2003 p. 113) was used at the start and end of imagery sessions with John, a 45-year-old man who experienced PTSD with dissociation in the context of childhood sexual abuse by his uncle. John used safe place imagery to manage high levels of emotion. This helped to develop his Healthy Adult mode and reduce reliance on his Detached Protector mode (which was associated with the use of drugs and alcohol). John made progress in therapy and his safe place imagery was adapted to help him to manage cravings to use cannabis and alcohol; when distressed he brought in a soothing voice which reminded him that he could cope, the feelings would dissipate in time and it wasn't his fault.

2. Ruth, aged 55, presented with chronic depression and a history of bulimia nervosa. Throughout her childhood, she and her siblings experienced physical abuse from her father. Her mother was complicit in this and told them this was 'what they deserved and should expect in their lives'. Ruth made progress in therapy but feelings of worthlessness and shame remained prominent, alongside a belief that she 'needed to be on guard all of the time or something bad would happen'. Bridging imagery was used from a recent upsetting event: the therapist asked Ruth to keep hold of the feelings but let the image go and see if an image from her childhood came into her mind (Arntz, 2012; Arntz & Weertman, 1999). Ruth's childhood image was of being aged eight, alone in the kitchen with her father, feeling scared and knowing from the look on his face that he was going to hit her. As Ruth had experienced protracted physical abuse and did not receive adequate parental care, the therapist assisted

her Healthy Adult. Adult Ruth felt too frightened to speak to her father but was able to be at the kitchen door giving instructions to the therapist. The therapist stood in front of little Ruth and her father and told him that he should not hit Ruth, that he should be ashamed of himself for hitting her, 'Ruth is only a child and needs to be protected and loved'. Little Ruth wanted to leave the kitchen and was told she was not to blame and that social services would not allow her Dad to hit her again. Little Ruth still felt scared and wanted to leave the house and go to the local park and sit in the sunshine on older Ruth's lap and have the therapist sit beside them. She wanted them to sit by the swings, where she felt safe and comforted and wanted to play on the swings.

Limited reparenting

A good CBT therapist will be adept at adjusting their style depending on the nature of the patient's presentation: for example, adjusting eye contact in early therapy with a socially anxious patient, modelling compassion to a self-critical patient, or imperfection to a perfectionistic patient. When working with more complex patients, the core relational qualities of warmth, empathy and positive regard are often not enough in themselves: for example, a patient with a Mistrust/Abuse schema as a result of parental abuse might expect and experience the therapist as letting them down, even when the therapist is reliable. Limited reparenting offers the CBT therapist some guiding principles for managing the relationship with complex cases in shorter-term CBT (see also, Lavender & Startup, 2018). The goal of limited reparenting is to help a patient develop and strengthen their Healthy Adult. The patient internalises their experiences of the therapist and the therapy relationship. Limited reparenting will be guided by an individual formulation of the patient's unmet needs; therapists are advised to think of what a good parent would do for each individual patient. Being flexible is key, with the aim 'to partially meet the child's unmet needs within the bounds of the therapeutic relationship' (Young et al., 2003 p. 183). The therapist needs to be reliable, dependable and to communicate to their patient that they are interested in, and care about and accept, them. Because CBT is usually shorter than Schema Therapy, it may be more appropriate to see this work as 'limited fostering' rather than limited reparenting (Nick Grey, personal communication): how would a good aunt or uncle respond to the child's needs?[1]

It is essential to formulate a patient's unmet needs so that limited reparenting can be tailored to specific needs at key points during therapy. Adaptations may include contact between sessions such as email or phone communication. Ruth valued the opportunity to contact the therapist between sessions; though she rarely did, she found this validating and containing. It is important to consider preparation for absences, particularly for patients with Abandonment schemas. Some therapists will give their patients a transitional object, such as a pen used in session, an audio recording with the therapist's voice, or an object which symbolises a key message. Ruth and her therapist had discussed how all children had the fundamental right to be protected and Ruth talked of how she admired the bravery, strength and dedication of a lioness protecting her cubs. In a subsequent session, just before a planned holiday, Ruth's therapist gave her a keyring with a toy lioness on it, which reminded Ruth she was 'safe now and could protect herself'. This helped Ruth develop her sense of self-efficacy and competence (the Healthy Adult mode).

Some standard CBT interventions can be understood as a form of limited reparenting in themselves, such as when therapists support patients to experiment with altering maladaptive beliefs and behaviours – for example, encouraging a depressed patient to push themselves to go for a walk when feeling low in mood, or make allowances for their symptoms when rating a sense of mastery and pleasure. Like a parent, the therapist provides a scaffolding where the patient practises something in the safety of therapy so that he or she can move on to doing it alone (similar to Vygotsky's Zone of Proximal Development: Vygotsky, 1978). CBT therapists encourage autonomy and so indirectly address dependence/incompetence schemas. With patients with more complex presentations, it can be helpful to identify specific unmet needs in this area, thus tailoring reparenting to encourage self-efficacy and competence.

Empathic confrontation

Empathic confrontation can also be adapted for use in CBT. Joan, aged 30, was numbing herself with Diazepam following being made redundant; she would forget to come to appointments. Her therapist showed empathy with the function of her behaviour, and linked this to her underlying beliefs originating from experiences of parental neglect. She encouraged Joan to experiment with more adaptive ways of managing her pain. In addition to chair work, Joan was encouraged to develop alternative strategies to recognise and manage her distress, including calling the therapist between appointments.

Schema informed CBT in action

We present a case example of a patient with recurrent depression and unmet core emotional childhood needs.

Jag was a 38-year-old British-Asian journalist. She was married with two daughters aged five and seven. Jag had been off work for six months due to severe depression. Her depression was characterised by significant guilt about letting her colleagues down, critical ruminations about being unable to work, anxiety about her future in journalism, and irritability with her children and husband. Jag was offered a course of 15 sessions of CBT for depression. Her mother had been highly critical and linked to her being a 'good girl', which set up a core belief: 'Deep down I am bad'. Her lovability was linked to pleasing mum. She developed the intermediate beliefs, 'If I am not giving my best, I will let others down', 'Others' needs are more important' and 'Whatever I do, I will never be good enough'. Her compensatory strategies prior to her breakdown included working excessive hours, and working on the computer during the night. Treatment included behavioural activation, sleep hygiene, testing her perfectionistic beliefs and collecting data from her life record to support the alternative core beliefs: 'I am good at what I do', 'Overall, I am a good person with good intentions' and 'I deserve to be loved by friends and family'. Jag returned to full-time work. and was discharged.

Jag returned 18 months later with depression and self-harm, using superficial cuts and head banging to help her manage a deep sense of guilt. Her negative beliefs were reactivated. She felt she should not be here and needed to be punished. After a psychiatric review, Quetiapine was added to augment the effect of the antidepressants. Her anxiety and agitation subsided and her self-harm stopped. The size of her unmet childhood needs were more significant than previously thought. Jag's mother's parenting had been at times cruel: she would go into unpredictable rages, and impulsively hit the children for offences they had not even committed. Jag remembered having to fix the buckle of her younger brother's seatbelt in the car. When she failed because it was fiddly, her mother ranted and raved and hit her in the face. If Jag cried, her mother told her to stop crying, otherwise she would hit her again for crying. Good marks and compliant behaviour would put mum into a good mood, with less hitting and shouting.

Introducing schema informed elements into CBT therapy

Jag agreed to engage in schema informed CBT. After the schema model had been shared, the Young Schema Questionnaire (YSQ) indicated schema beliefs in the mild–moderate range across 11 domains. The therapist decided that she would benefit from a mode model approach. Jag understood the concept of core emotional childhood needs, and identified unmet needs in all domains. For instance, in the Disconnection and Rejection domain, she missed out on safety, predictability, validation and trust, while in the Autonomy domain, guidance and a firm sense of identity were missing. She resonated strongly with the need to express valid emotions. Playfulness and spontaneity hardly existed in her childhood, and she struggled to bring up any memory from that domain. Jag remembered strong, if not excessive, limits from her parents, especially mum. A mode map was developed. She resonated strongly with the Demanding and Punitive Parent modes. In a chair exercise, she understood how the maladaptive coping modes 'People Pleaser' (Compliant Surrender), 'Cutter' (Avoidant Self-soother) and 'Hard Worker' (Overcompensator) manifested themselves constantly. She struggled to get close to her abused little lonely Jag. She got angry when taking the chair of the Punitive mode – 'This is me constantly, this damn chair never stops talking!' When back in her usual therapy chair, Jag had little sense of how a Healthy Adult could balance work needs, family needs and the need for relaxation and playfulness.

Imagery work

Session by session, the modes were explored and understood. When stronger emotions arose, when Jag noticed more intense sadness, fear or anger, this was connected back to her childhood memories. For example, when reporting a moment of fear while checking emails on her work computer, she was asked to do an imagery exercise with an 'affect bridge' to her childhood. Closing her eyes, and checking in with body sensations and emotional tone, Jag remembered her mum getting angry with Jag's little brother because he did not have his shoes on, ready for school. Mum was already late, and she hit both children on the head, blaming Jag for not helping her brother. The therapist asked Jag to describe mum's reactions vividly and in the first person tense 'as though it was happening now': the expression on mum's face, the noises she was making, etc. Just before mum was about to hit the children, the therapist asked Jag to freeze the image. The therapist then asked for permission to enter the image and placed herself in a position that protected both children. The core unmet need in the image was for safety and protection. In an act of partial reparenting, the therapist embodied the good parental figure and protected both children, limiting mum's anger and answering Jag's requests to keep her completely safe. When Jag said that she felt sorry for mum, the therapist told her mum would be sent to parenting classes to become a better and more loving parent. Until then, the therapist would protect the children, bringing in trusted figures, like the paternal grandmother, to take over until mum got better. The therapist reassured the child that mum would never be angry again, and would not be able to retaliate later. Once Jag felt completely safe and calm, the image was phased out. Alternate sessions were used for cognitive restructuring and behavioural pattern change. Cognitive restructuring focused on the demanding messages that came from the Punitive Critic mode. The therapist developed alternative, healthier messages. Jag learnt that this mode is a form of internal bully and was encouraged to get out of her Healthy Adult chair and fight the bully assertively, banishing her into the past and ridiculing her position.

Mode work

The coping modes were put on chairs that blocked the access of the Healthy Adult mode to the Vulnerable and Abused Child chair. The history and value of the coping modes during childhood was acknowledged: 'I know you were helpful when I was a child, but now you are not helping any more. You need to step aside!' The maladaptive coping was analysed in more detail: Jag understood self-harm as a form of self-punishment to comply with the punitive part. She realised that her overcompensation through working extra hard did not meet the need for praise, safety and empathy for her Vulnerable Child's distress. It needed to step aside. The Vulnerable Child chair was then brought close to her Healthy Adult chair. She could now soothe the Vulnerable Child directly and tell her: 'I am here to keep you safe. Nothing bad will happen any more, let me deal with the bully!' 'I am so proud of you for letting me be here with you, I can see your fear. It's okay that you are anxious!'

Jag gradually saw how her unmet childhood needs left emotional memories that drove her adult behaviour. The modes were still active, but Jag was reassured that the Healthy Adult mode was slowly growing in strength. The therapist modelled compassion by reassuring Jag and supporting her on her journey. Jag's social functioning improved; she returned to work and received good feedback from her manager. However, Jag found it hard to deal with conflict at work. The therapist played out tricky conflict-laden situations with her and both tested different ways of asserting Jag's preference, expressing her authentic feelings more clearly and avoiding the triggering of coping modes. Jag developed a behavioural routine for compassionately responding to, and containing, her Vulnerable Child: she listened to flashcards recorded in the therapist's voice, brought up an image of a safe place and would send a text to her husband, who sent her an emoticon back to remind her that he is present for her. Jag had a particular soft fleece that she would hold as a self-soothing sensory stimulus. This combination of techniques helped to heal the schemas and give Jag cognitive, behavioural and emotion-focused skills to manage her modes more effectively. Jag's anxiety and depression scores reduced further, she needed fewer days off-work and began lowering her Quetiapine after six months.

Sessions were then phased out: moving from weekly to two-weekly, and then to monthly to help Jag manage separation from her therapist over time, without feeling acutely dependent. Text messages between sessions amounted to about one per month. Jag began to recognise schemas in colleagues and friends and volunteered at Mind to help others with unmet childhood needs. The therapist and Jag stayed in touch and now meet on an 'if and when required' basis. Text messages are still occasionally exchanged.

Service considerations

In many countries, CBT is the main modality used within publicly funded mental health services, reflecting its strong evidence base across a range of disorders.

In England, most CBT is delivered within dedicated psychological therapy services with close links to primary care: the Improving Access to

Psychological Therapies (IAPT) services. These ostensibly treat the common mental health disorders of anxiety and depression, but the cases seen are often complex and there is considerable comorbidity. For instance, Hepgul et al. (2016) found that 72% of patients attending IAPT services met criteria for two or more psychiatric disorders, while 69% demonstrated personality disorder traits, and 16% met criteria for borderline personality disorder. Using the schema informed methods described in this chapter may help to overcome obstacles to short term CBT and enhance its effectiveness, but how might these techniques be applied in IAPT and similar CBT services in other countries? IAPT is used as an example here, but a similar approach could be taken with other time-limited CBT services.

IAPT services vary in the length of time available for a course of therapy, but 12 sessions seems to be the average time frame. It is certainly possible to use schema methods such as mode dialogue in a brief course of therapy when an impasse is reached, and these will often be sufficient to get therapy back on track. However, it may be difficult to apply the techniques we have described for more treatment resistant cases in much less than 20 sessions. In our experience, services should consider flexibility if offering therapy to more complex cases. Many IAPT services have a system for reviewing therapy when patients are not recovering in order to make an informed decision about whether to offer therapy beyond the usual contract. The IAPT therapist, together with their supervisor, might formulate the unmet emotional needs of the patient and then consider a trial of experientially based interventions, such as imagery rescripting, to address those needs. Between three and five sessions may sometimes be enough to move therapy along. Secondary care services usually have more flexibility than IAPT in the number of sessions they can deliver, and these may be the services where schema informed CBT for chronic treatment resistant cases has most to offer. An understanding of, and set of skills in, schema informed work can give therapists confidence in offering targeted help, rather than just more of the same. If therapists are using Schema Therapy interventions, including limited reparenting, the length of sessions offered needs to be considered and the ending of therapy needs careful consideration. This is more important than in long-term Schema Therapy because there is less time to prepare for the ending. Preparing by tapering/staggering sessions and having booster sessions, or some form of communication (e.g., email or text contact for a limited time, as with Jag above) after formal face-to-face therapy has ended, is important to consider.

Therapists should not undertake this work without some training: a number of courses are now becoming available both in formal Schema Therapy and in schema informed work. Clinical supervision is vital when treating complex cases because the interaction between the patient's and the therapist's schemas (i.e., transference and countertransference) can often have an impact on the collaborative relationship (Moorey & Byrne, 2018). Supervision provides a space in which therapist beliefs and schemas can be discussed. The availability of trained schema therapists to provide supervision is limited, so services might consider peer supervision between therapists who have received some schema training when complex cases are involved.

Summary

Schema methods offer an exciting addition to the CBT therapist's armamentarium. Schema ideas can be integrated in standard CBT without detracting from the power of the problem focused cognitive–behavioural formulation that is the great strength of the model. Two ways in which this integration can be achieved have been outlined here. Techniques can be used to overcome stumbling blocks in therapy, and techniques can be used to improve outcome in chronic cases. Understanding unmet childhood needs can enrich the CBT formulation and help therapists target more experientially based interventions, such as limited reparenting, chair work and imagery rescripting.

Therapist tips

1. A schema informed formulation can provide a whole-self conceptualization as part of a CBT framework.
2. Limited reparenting offers the CBT therapist some guiding principles for managing the relationship with complex cases in shorter-term CBT.
3. All standard Schema Therapy change techniques (imagery, chair work, empathic confrontation and limit setting) can be integrated into time limited CBT.
4. Clinical supervision is vital when treating complex cases because the interaction between the patient's and the therapist's schemas (i.e. transference and countertransference) can often have an impact on the collaborative relationship.

Note

1 Some encouraging pilot work in applying brief, 20-session group Schema Therapy in mixed personality disorders has been reported by Skewes et al. (2015).

Further reading

Boersen, J. & van Vreeswijg, M. (2015). *Schema therapy in groups: A short term CBT protocol*. In van Vreeswijk et al. (ed.) *The Wiley Blackwell Handbook of Schema Therapy. Theory, Research and Practice*. Wiley Blackwell.

References

Arntz, A. (2012). Imagery rescripting as a therapeutic technique: Review of clinical trials, basic studies, and research agenda. *Journal of Experimental Psychopathology*, *3*(2), 189–208.

Arntz, A. & Weertman, A. (1999). Treatment of childhood memories: Theory and practice. *Behaviour Research and Therapy, 37*(8), 715–740.

Beck, A.T. (1963). Thinking and depression: I. Idiosyncratic content and cognitive distortions. *Archives of General Psychiatry, 9*(4), 324–333.

Beck, A.T. (1964) Thinking and depression II: Theory and therapy. *Archives of General Psychiatry, 10*, 561–571.

Beck, A.T., Rush, A.J., Shaw, B.F. & Emery, G. (1979). *Cognitive Therapy of Depression.* New York: Guildford Press.

Durbin, C.E., Klein, D.N. & Schwartz, J.E. (2000). Predicting the 2½-year outcome of dysthymic disorder: The roles of childhood adversity and family history of psychopathology. *Journal of Consulting and Clinical Psychology, 68*(1), 57–63.

Fonagy, P., Leigh, T., Steele, M., Steele, H., Kennedy, R., Mattoon, G. … Gerber, A. (1996). The relation of attachment status, psychiatric classification, and response to psychotherapy. *Journal of Consulting and Clinical Psychology, 64*(1), 22–31.

Hepgul, N., King, S., Amarasinghe, M., Breen, G., Grant, N., Grey, N. … Wingrove, J. (2016). Clinical characteristics of patients assessed within an Improving Access to Psychological Therapies (IAPT) service: Results from a naturalistic cohort study (Predicting Outcome Following Psychological Therapy; PROMPT). *BMC Psychiatry, 16*(52). doi:10.1186/s12888-016-0736-6

Jacob, G.A. & Arntz, A. (2013). Schema therapy for personality disorders—A review. *International Journal of Cognitive Therapy, 6*(2), 171–185.

Lavender, A. & Startup, H. (2018). Personality disorders. In S. Moorey & A. Lavender (eds.) *The Therapeutic Relationship in CBT.* London: SAGE, pp. 174–188.

Lizardi, H., Klein, D.N., Ouimette, P.C., Riso, L.P., Anderson, R.L. & Donaldson, S. K. (1995). Reports of the childhood home environment in early-onset dysthymia and episodic major depression. *Journal of Abnormal Psychology, 104*(1), 132–139.

Moorey (2014). 'Is it them or is it me?' In A. Whittington & N. Grey (eds.). *How to Become a More Effective CBT Therapist: Mastering Metacompetence in Clinical Practice* (First edn. Chichester: John Wiley & Sons, pp. 132–143.

Moorey, S. & Lavender, A. (eds.) (2018). *The Therapeutic Relationship in CBT.* London: SAGE.

Moorey & Byrne. (2018) Supervision in S. Moorey & A. Lavender (eds.) *The Therapeutic Relationship in CBT.* London: SAGE, pp. 256–270.

NICE. (2004a). Anxiety: management of anxiety (panic disorder, with and without agoraphobia, and generalised anxiety disorder) in adults in primary, secondary and community care. *Clinical Guideline 22, National Institute for Clinical Excellence.*

NICE. (2004b). Depression: Management of depression in primary and secondary care. *Clinical Guideline 23, National Institute for Clinical Excellence.*

NICE. (2004c). Eating disorders: Recognition and treatment. *Clinical Guidelines 9. National Institute for Clinical Excellence.*

NICE. (2005a). Obsessive–compulsive disorder: Core interventions in the treatment of obsessive–compulsive disorder and body dysmorphic disorder. *Clinical Guideline 31, National Institute for Clinical Excellence.*

NICE. (2005b). Post-traumatic stress disorder (PTSD): The management of PTSD in adults and children in primary and secondary care. *Clinical Guideline 26, National Institute for Clinical Excellence.*

NICE. (2013). Social anxiety disorder: Recognition, assessment and treatment. *Clinical Guideline 159, National Institute for Clinical Excellence.*

Skewes, S.A., Samson, R.A., Simpson, S.G. & van Vreeswijk, M. (2015). Short term group schema therapy for mixed personality disorders: A pilot study. *Frontiers in Psychology, 5,* 1592.

Taylor, C.D.J., Bee, P. & Haddock, G. (2017). Does schema therapy change schemas and symptoms? A systematic review across mental health disorders. *Psychology and Psychotherapy, 90,* 456–479.

Vygotsky, L.S. (1978). *Mind in Society: The Development of Higher Psychological Processes.* Cambridge, MA: Harvard University Press.

Wild, J., Hackmann, A. & Clark, D.M. (2008). Rescripting early memories linked to negative images in social phobia: A pilot study. *Behavior Therapy, 39*(1), 47–56.

Young, J.E., Klosko, J.S. & Weishaar, M.E. (2003). *Schema Therapy: A Practitioner's Guide.* New York: Guilford Press.

20 Endings and the therapy relationship

Tünde Vanko and Dan Roberts

The therapy relationship forms the bedrock for change in Schema Therapy (ST) – it is the arena in which patient and therapist learn together about the schemas and modes that arise between them, it is where limited reparenting takes place and it is also where schemas and modes are empathically challenged and start to change. Patient and therapist grow (and often struggle) together in this process and the qualities and challenges of their therapeutic relationship take on extra significance as their work draws to a close. If you ask a patient about their experience of a previous therapy, they will more than likely speak to the relationship and it often appears central to what they internalised and took away from the work.

Ending reignites all of the key elements and material of ST: attachment patterns, core schema (Abandonment, Isolation), unmet needs (for presence, involvement, warmth and love) and core ways of coping (Avoidance, Surrender, Overcompensation), all of which play out in earnest as the separation approaches. Of course, the hope is that, after the end of face-to-face sessions, the therapeutic bond, in a sense, continues, as both therapist and patient hold each other and their relationship 'in mind'. However, the degree of childhood trauma and the strength of the patient's modes may affect their capacity to draw on this type of internalisation. The therapist's modes may also hinder or complicate the attachment. Thus, endings in the context of ST are likely to be a mixed bag; a rich source of further healing (with opportunities to work through poorly managed historical separations), as well as a time of old and less helpful ways of coping potentially resurfacing and painful feelings of loss intensifying.

The therapy relationship is also unique in the sense that patient and therapist have been working towards an ending from the outset. Up until this point, the patient and therapist have probably been focused on reasonably specific goals, usually with an agreed time frame in mind. Ideally, the ending phase occurs when patients have achieved these goals and made sufficient progress in terms of schema healing, a loosening of reliance on maladaptive coping modes and desired changes in key areas of their life, but this is not always the case. Endings can also arise in the context of therapy not working out, leading to feelings of disappointment and regret as hoped for changes did not come to fruition.

This chapter considers the ways in which the quality of the therapy relationship influences the end phase of therapy and what the patient takes with them after face-to-face sessions come to a close. It considers how attachment theory can inform our understanding of endings and how we can tailor our therapeutic stance to help foster growth and self-regulation, even after therapy ends. We also discuss ways of managing therapeutic ruptures and complicated endings. We share some practical ideas and personal experiences regarding endings with a variety of patients, including those with borderline personality disorder (BPD), who can present particular challenges when it comes to ending. Finally, we will explore how ST's limited reparenting and its 'result', the partial internalisation of aspects of the therapist's care, is indispensable to reaching the ultimate goals of ST – patient autonomy, individuation and self-regulation.

Attachment theory and the therapy relationship

Attachment theory helps the therapist understand and make predictions in regard to therapeutic endings. Bowlby (1969/1982) proposed that when a child is in distress, their 'attachment behavioural system' is activated, producing a set of strong impulses to seek out proximity to the main caregiver. If the caregiver is reliably and consistently available at times of need, and responds to the child in an attuned and soothing manner, they will become a 'secure base' for the child. Having experienced the repeated activation of their attachment behavioural system, the child forms a 'mental representation' of the caregiver's availability, including their own efficacy in terms of getting their needs met. Bowlby (1969/1982) called these mental representations 'internal working models' and he distinguished them from the 'model of others'. The two entities are complementary – if the attachment figure is available and caring, this will shape not only representations about the other, but also shapes the model of self. We all have an attachment behavioural system that comes 'online' when triggered. However, the difference between children and securely attached adults is that the physical presence of the attachment figure is not necessarily required for adults – it might be sufficient to activate a mental representation of the attachment figure(s) in order to promote self-soothing.

The ability to self-soothe and to reach maturational autonomy is based mainly on having developed these internalised positive experiences with attachment figures in childhood. When, early in life, consistent comfort was provided by nurturing caregivers, '... the models of self come to include introjected traits of the attachment figure' (Mikulincer & Shaver, 2007). When early experiences were not so positive, children form insecure working models.

Attachment and early maladaptive schemas

The notion of internal working models overlaps with the idea of Young's early maladaptive schemas (EMS). Both are formed through early life experiences with caregivers and significant others. Working models are, in a sense, relational EMS, reflecting what the child has come to expect from others in regard to getting their needs met. Once formed, working models, such as schemas, systematically bias our perception and '… direct attention and information processing' (Young, 2003). In the face of pervasive caregiver unavailability or mistreatment, internal working models become constrained and play a central role in mental health and relationship difficulties (Mikulincer & Shaver, 2007).

Bowlby (1988) argued that gaining insight into, and revising, insecure working models is the key to a successful therapeutic outcome. In ST, the core mechanism for achieving this corrective emotional experience is through limited reparenting, which begins from first contact with the patient and continues right up to the end of therapy. ST's core concept of limited reparenting incorporates the idea of Bowlby's secure base. This unique way of utilising the therapy relationship is the vehicle through which patients – sometimes for the first time in their lives – have the experience of their core needs being met. The therapist becomes an important attachment figure for patients. They can then turn to this secure base at times of distress and also explore and confront memories associated with earlier working models in a safe way.

While the parallel between Bowlby's child–mother relationship and patient–therapist relationship is clear, in the case of the latter, the reparenting is 'limited'. The therapist meets the Vulnerable Child's needs within the boundaries of the therapy relationship and also while considering her own needs.

The limited nature of this relationship can become especially salient at the end of therapy. So, for example, in ST – unlike in most other therapy approaches – it is considered appropriate to allow patients to occasionally stay in touch after finishing a course of therapy (for example, with an update of an important life event or with a request for a booster session). It is mainly patients whose core schemas are in the Disconnection and Rejection domain who benefit most from this and often deeply appreciate a continued sense of connection and care after the end of therapy. However, in many public health settings, this is not feasible and neither is it necessary to ensure a successful therapy ending. In these services (and to some degree for many patients) continuation of the relationship is more symbolic and internalised in terms of their attachment to the therapist and their journey together in therapy.

Case example (Amina): reparenting and the end of therapy

A course of therapy in the National Health Service (NHS) was coming to the end with a young female patient, Amina, who was in her 20s. In her earlier life, Amina had endured harsh and critical parenting from both her mother and father. As a result, her core schema was Defectiveness/Shame. Amina found it almost impossible to trust her own judgement within interpersonal situations where there was any sort of differing of opinion or conflict. Her Punitive Parent used these triggers to instigate an internal flood of self-attack, calling her stupid or difficult for thinking she 'might know better'. Typically, the onslaught of the Punitive Parent attacks would end in Amina getting lost in what she described as 'a pit of shame and guilt'. Both patient and therapist agreed that she would need tools to help her manage her Punitive Parent mode in ways that lessened the guilt and shame.

During the therapy, chair work was used to help Amina decentre from her Punitive Parent and practise standing up for herself. This was first modelled by her therapist and then encouraged from the position of her evolving Healthy Adult mode. Over time, she was able to find the words and conviction to validate her own opinions and viewpoints. Her Healthy Adult began to flourish, but, as is often the case, the ending was painful for Amina, who had dared to trust and connect with her therapist at an emotional level. As the ending approached there was a resurgence of 'core pain' (shame/guilt) and some increased self-attacks for being 'pathetic' for feeling so much loss. Her distress was validated in keeping with Amina's growing sense that she was entitled to have feelings and reactions. Her therapist also shared something of her own sense of loss at the ending of their face-to-face contact. In the penultimate session, the therapist gave Amina a small rock. The stone was far from perfect – its surface was not polished or smooth, but it had a unique beauty and strength. The therapist asked the patient to keep the stone in her pocket. Whenever she heard harsh criticism from her Punitive Parent, she could touch the stone and remember the therapist's words that she did not need to be perfect, that she was lovable just the way she was and that she, as her own wonderful person, was entitled to have her own views and opinions. This is a useful example of how the therapy relationship via the giving of a transitional object can endure way beyond the direct face-to-face contact.

Internalising the 'good enough' attachment to the therapist enables patients to form internal representations of the 'other' which they can call on at times of distress. Knox et al. (1999) argue that these internal representations combine auditory and visual information, as well as the 'felt presence' of the therapist. This memory of a corrective emotional experience via reparenting enables patients to continue their own self-nurturance long after the end of therapy.

Case example (Rebecca): summoning your therapist to mind

When a patient, Rebecca, with BPD, started therapy, her major presenting problem was that she could not hold down a job. She described feeling like a 'scared little girl' when she was at work. Rebecca revealed that she felt unable to speak up in meetings and constantly doubted her own competence. However, at the heart of her struggles was a history of abusive early relationships. She had few positive and safe role models to draw on. Over the course of therapy, Rebecca was initially resistant to her therapist's pulls for connection, but with time she relinquished reliance on a pronounced Detached Protector mode and allowed herself to be vulnerable with her therapist and to be comforted. However, whenever there was a break in therapy, Rebecca sunk back into feeling all alone and drew on self-harm through cutting to ground herself. Over time, her therapist used imagery techniques to help her learn to soothe herself via compassionate imagery. Rebecca started to respond with greater calmness to breaks in therapy. Whenever her Vulnerable Child mode emerged, she described being able to tune into the tone and comforting 'felt sense' she would experience in the presence of her therapist. The patient described how she not only heard the therapist's kind, reparenting words and reassuring voice, but she also felt the therapist's hand on her shoulder. She sensed a firm but loving pressure while the therapist offered concrete guidance about how to summon up her more compassionate Healthy Adult. This involved shifting posture so she felt stronger and more grounded. Towards the end of therapy, Rebecca and her therapist practised this skill in a range of potentially challenging situations to help her feel a continued sense of agency, connection and support.

Case example (Tony): returning to imagery rescripts

Another patient, Tony, towards the end of therapy, started to ruminate about the breakdown of his marriage, feeling lonely, abandoned and hopeless about the future. In order to contain his rumination, he remembered a particularly poignant imagery rescript where he was a ten-year-old child and his therapist provided kindness, company and someone to talk to in the face of a highly upsetting family conflict. As his marriage breakup had triggered his Abandonment schema and reminded him of being left alone as a child, remembering this healing experience with his therapist helped him feel less alone, and his rumination abated.

These are good examples of patients internalising the nurturing presence of their therapist, so they feel less alone and soothed in times of challenge or crisis, even after therapy has ended.

Attachment and the Healthy Adult

Internalising the attachment relationship with the therapist also helps build the patient's Healthy Adult mode. An ideal ending in ST is when we can see a well-established, sustainable Healthy Adult. The Healthy Adult serves an executive function in relation to the other modes (Arntz & van Genderen, 2009) and the therapist aims to encourage this side of the patient to nurture the Vulnerable Child, disempower the maladaptive parent modes and moderate the dysfunctional coping modes.

During the final stages of therapy, patients are encouraged to remain aware of their unmet needs and to learn to ask significant others for help and nurturance. The therapist continues to attune, and to offer care and validation, but also encourages the patient to check in with their Healthy Adult as to what they need to do to help the Vulnerable Child, moderate a coping mode, or meet a core need. At this stage of therapy, patients are growing in autonomy and are more in tune with their emotions and feel entitled to express vulnerability in their close, confiding relationships.

In some contexts, particularly where session numbers are very limited, this process is far from complete at the end of therapy. In such cases, the therapist needs to be open about the external constraints on their work and try to limit the most dysfunctional and damaging aspects of the patient's modes. Often, when the patient is aware the constraint is external and not because the therapist wants to end therapy, it is still feasible to have a good enough ending and for the patient to appreciate and value their progress. In other situations, the therapist may be handing over therapeutic work to another therapist or service, so there is a collective 'holding' and reparenting. This demonstrates that limited reparenting does not have to be carried out by a single caregiver, just as an extended family can all help raise a child.

Imagery rescripting and endings

Limited reparenting is interwoven throughout childhood imagery rescripting exercises, helping the patient 'feel' and internalise their therapist's attunement to, and care for, their Vulnerable Child. At the end of therapy, we might also want to employ imagery exercises to rehearse challenging future situations. For example, one patient embarked on an academic course which would continue after therapy ended. He found this very stressful, as it triggered his Defectiveness schema and reminded him of negative experiences during school. He did several imagery exercises with the therapist, where he imagined his Healthy Adult and the therapist sitting either side of him at his desk, reminding him to breathe, that he was perfectly capable of doing the work and that they would be there for him throughout the course. This helped him feel calmer and that he was not facing these challenges alone. These images stayed with him after therapy ended and helped him remain on the course, rather than dropping out.

Endings and therapist self-disclosure

A key part of limited reparenting is also the appropriate use of therapist self-disclosure. Novick (1997) argues that in order for endings to be constructive, the therapist should not refrain from expressing her own reactions, while skilfully holding in mind the patient's needs. The therapist can share genuine feelings about their journey together and express some of their feelings about the ending, potentially including harder topics, such as loss. There are creative ways of doing this. For example, with a long-term patient, Adam, in the final session both therapist and patient wrote a letter for each other in which they shared what they appreciated and learnt from each other – it was important that this was authentic on both sides, as the patient could then read this back and receive reparenting, both in terms of warmth and celebration and also honesty about areas that still needed work. This highlights the fact that good reparenting is not just about being validating and kind, but also about setting limits, maintaining boundaries and encouraging patients to do things they might need, but not want to do.

Ending therapy with BPD patients

In our experience, patients with insecure attachment styles, whose core schemas are in the Disconnection and Rejection domain, such as patients with BPD, seem to find endings particularly challenging. This may be due to their characteristically strong Abandonment schema and having had negative experiences of other endings or disruptions, either in therapy or their personal relationships. Therefore, ending therapy with this group of patients – especially if premature – might result in the hyperactivation of the attachment behaviour system; that is, wanting to be in constant contact with the therapist and feeling inconsolable about the loss (Mikulincer & Shaver, 2007). In such cases, it is helpful to explore feelings about the ending, validate the natural sense of loss and honour what therapist and patient have been through together. Furthermore, the internal representations of the therapy relationship may become a symbolic source of protection to the patient (Mikulincer & Shaver, 2007).

Critical to managing the ending with patients with BPD is holding in mind that you may have been one of a very small number of individuals the patient has dared to attach to. This has taken bravery and courage and it requires respectful management and a little 'going above and beyond' when distress is high. One sign is that, by the time of termination, the patient has internalised the therapist as a secure base (Bowlby, 1988) and has, one hopes, developed a small number of secure attachments with others outside of therapy. Another cue that might signal a readiness for ending therapy could be that their Abandonment schema has softened in intensity and readiness of activation and is more readily soothed by their Healthy Adult. Encouraging autonomy with this group of vulnerable patients is twofold: we gradually taper off or reduce the frequency of sessions and offer some contact after termination.

In this final phase of ST with BPD patients, we still need to pay attention to modes at play. The Punitive Parent mode might blame the patient for the ending for not being a 'good enough patient' and assuming the therapist is 'sick of seeing them'. The therapist can also empathise with the Vulnerable

Child's fears or sense of loss, but also empathically point out that he/she will not be able to meet all of the patient's needs, such as the need for day-to-day friendship or a partner.

A common pitfall with BPD patients is when therapists are not curious enough in investigating active modes related to ending. This may lead them to mistake a Detached Protector for a Healthy Adult; whereby, for example, the therapist might accept at face value the patient's statement that they are 'fine' about the ending, missing vital clues that the patient may be experiencing a range of other, more complex and painful reactions (e.g., abandonment, rejection, shame and anger). In particular, BPD patients might not offer these feelings because of their Subjugation schema, telling them they need to make their therapist feel all right about the ending. Indeed, many therapists do feel some guilt at finishing therapy, particularly if the patient is still struggling, making it tempting to collude with the Detached Protector by saying, 'It's fine – I'm okay.'

Case example (Christine): ending therapy with a BPD patient

The importance of attending to the relationship when someone has BPD was clear with a young female patient, Christine. Her main presenting problem at the beginning of therapy was a persistent difficulty in relationships, both with her boyfriend and close friends. She often felt that no one was paying her attention or that they were unjustifiably blaming her for things that were not her fault. In these cases, she became uncontrollably angry, breaking nearby objects or hitting the wall with her fist (in her Angry Child mode).

In the initial phase of therapy, Christine often commented to her therapist, 'I wish you were my mother. I never want to lose you.' Her therapist validated these feelings, as Little Christine never had anyone to nurture her. Their bond together was very strong from the beginning of therapy: Christine reached out to the therapist whenever she felt she couldn't cope. Although her therapist was not always able to respond immediately, she provided a transitional object (a small special box) and recorded audio flashcards containing limited reparenting messages that the patient could use to soothe herself. Christine was able to imagine how the therapist would comfort Little Christine, what words and tone she would use. She found this very comforting. Her mother had been an alcoholic, so she never experienced a consistent, nurturing caregiver as a child. This illustrates how the therapist becomes a secure base via the internalisation of them as a good attachment figure. Eventually, the patient started forming secure relationships outside the therapy, which broadened her secure base.

The patient was seen in private practice and her health insurance only covered 18 months of therapy, which felt to her like too short a time. For the last session, both therapist and patient wrote a farewell card and summarised all the techniques that she could use for tackling each mode.

This again helped the patient internalise the therapist as a secure attachment figure who would be 'there' for her well after therapy had ended.

A few months after discharge, the patient requested some top-up sessions – showing her proximity-seeking to the therapist during a crisis. She had become pregnant and was apprehensive that her Angry Child mode might hurt the baby. The therapist validated the patient's understandable request for support at this challenging time. Therapist and patient worked in a focused way over six sessions on the fear that she might harm her baby. Much of the work was not new; it involved supporting the patient to access the skills she had already learnt but to draw on them under this new condition of high anxiety related to her pregnancy. The therapist also worked with the patient to foster a 'positive parent' mode, in which the patient could be seen to creatively integrate aspects of the reparenting she received from her therapist to think about the type of mother she might like to be. Two years have passed since then. The patient still keeps in touch via text message and updates the therapist about her life, which is going well.

Difficult and premature endings

Bender and Messner (2003) distinguish between mature and premature endings. A mature ending involves reviewing one's goals and the personal development that has been achieved during therapy, and working through feelings related to the therapy relationship coming to an end (Vasquez et al., 2008). This process helps the patient integrate feelings of loss and abandonment, while allowing for shared joy and celebration.

However, not all endings are timely or in tune with the patient's needs. For example, we consider termination unhelpful in cases where there are clear indicators that the patient has been benefiting from therapy and would benefit from its continuation to reach their goals – that is, the work is incomplete, but the therapist, for whatever reason, does not or cannot enable the treatment to continue. This mistimed and misattuned ending could trigger intense feelings of abandonment, mistrust or failure depending on the patient's schemas, and trigger dysfunctional coping modes. This type of ending might also trigger understandable Healthy Adult anger in a patient who has made sufficient progress. There are many reasons why this type of unsatisfactory ending might occur and therapist blindness about their own schema triggers are usually a key ingredient.

We also consider an ending premature when the therapist has to finish treatment due to her own life circumstances having changed; when therapist and patient do not seem like a good fit; or when the patient commits suicide. It is important to note that, even in the first two situations, endings can still be handled healthily with limited reparenting and therapist authenticity.

Managing difficult and premature endings

Unfortunately, early on in our encounters with a patient, such as at the assessment stage, we may not be aware of the schema chemistry between us and our new patient and we may subconsciously act in ways that discourage the patient from engaging. For example, a therapist might reschedule the patient several times or delay contacting them. They might also find themselves being more formal/standoffish or inflexible, pushing the patient away and making it more likely that they will drop out.

Such reactions are understandable when the therapist feels out of their depth in some way, and supervision and personal therapy are invaluable in working on our schemas when we are triggered. In some cases, our reactions are driven by a genuine sense that we are unable to properly meet a patient's needs, so we may require some help in working out the best way of managing the referral.

Premature endings due to the therapist's life circumstances changing

Sometimes, despite their best intentions, the therapist needs to end therapy prematurely due to changes in life circumstances. This might happen due to maternity leave, illness or relocating. The therapist should share with the patient in good faith the reason for having to finish therapy. It is not necessary to go into detail about one's personal life, but it is important to give the patient an adequate explanation. This way, the patient will know that the therapist is not deliberately getting rid of them but has no other choice than to end therapy. Therapist authenticity can help manage the premature ending.

It is imperative to validate the patient's natural sense of loss and to work with modes manifesting in the remaining time. For example, the Punitive Parent mode might be activated, telling the patient that they will not be cared for by someone else because they are not good enough. The Angry Protector might say that they cannot trust anyone else again, so they do not want to be referred to another therapist or service. It also helps – if the therapist can resume sessions in the foreseeable future – to prepare a transitional object, such as a photo of the therapist or a card containing warm messages that they can hold on to during the pause in therapy.

During the assessment phase with a BPD patient, the therapist found out that she was pregnant. She shared the news of her pregnancy with the patient in her next session. She explained that as their relationship would be very important in the therapy it was not wise for them to continue, given her forthcoming maternity leave. She acknowledged this might be hard, given the patient's previous experiences of feeling let down and abandoned. The patient still became triggered, saying 'This is just my luck!' and 'I am being punished – nothing ever works out for me.' The therapist validated how hard this was for her and comforted the patient, taking care to refer the patient to a colleague she felt would be a good fit. It is important to remember that even a good parent cannot always keep promises, as life sometimes gets in the way.

Case example: therapist guilt

Three years after finishing therapy, the therapist discovered that a former patient had committed suicide. Although the patient had progressively withdrawn contact, so the therapist had no idea she was relapsing, her suicide triggered intense feelings of grief, shame and self-blame for the therapist, which took a great deal of work in supervision and support from his personal network to overcome. Eventually the therapist realised that the patient's death was not his fault, that he had done everything possible to help her, and that the risk of suicide was, sadly, an inevitable part of working with the highly complex patient population schema therapists take on. This helped Jose to process the tragedy and allowed him to refocus on his current caseload. It also enabled him to respond calmly and effectively when patients presented with suicidal ideation or impulses.

Summary

ST is, at its core, a relational model. We work with complex patients, many of whom have experienced few, if any, positive role models during their lives. Others will have endured significant abandonment, rejection, neglect or abuse. Ending with these patients is not something we 'do' – it is a process between two (or more) people that involves both of our attachment histories interacting, myriad complex emotions, as well as a range of coping patterns potentially resurfacing. If you, as the therapist, are suitably attuned and attached to your patient and if you experienced sufficient positive parenting in your earlier life (or personal therapy to support your Vulnerable Child), you will find a way through this process that has the potential to heal your patient and provide them with a new internal, healthy working model of interpersonal security and safety. The internalisation of a secure attachment to the therapist is, we believe, the key ingredient that will help the patient self-soothe and remain well even after therapy is over. Even in the face of complexity or challenge in therapy, the therapist can become a secure base for their patient, which means that the influence of ST continues even after face-to-face work has ended.

Therapist tips

- Therapists need to be aware of their attachment styles, schemas and modes to manage endings, whether mature or premature. Each of these factors will have an effect on the termination style.
- Exchange cards or ending letters where you both express your feelings about the work together and the ending of therapy.
- Record an audio flashcard containing reparenting messages.

- Invite updates about their life from time to time (if appropriate in your setting).
- Encourage them to summon you or another nurturing figure in their life, for example, in a mini-imagery at difficult times: 'What would my therapist say to me in this situation?'
- If faced with a patient who triggers our schemas, it may be an opportunity for us to take up the challenge and grow, with the help of our supervisor (Behary, 2018, personal communication)

References

Arntz, A. & van Genderen, H. (2009). *Schema Therapy for Borderline Personality Disorder.* Oxford: Wiley-Blackwell.

Bender, S. & Messner, E. (2003). *Becoming a Therapist: What Do I Say, and Why?* New York: Guildford Press.

Bowlby, J. (1969/1982). *Attachment and loss: Vol. 1. Attachment.* New York: Basic Books.

Bowlby, J. (1988). *A Secure Base: Clinical Applications of Attachment Theory.* Oxford: Routledge.

Knox, S., Goldberg, J.L., Woodhouse, S.S. & Hill, C.E. (1999). Clients' internal representations of their therapists. *Journal of Counseling Psychology, 46 (2),* 244–256.

Mikulincer, M. & Shaver, P.R. (2007). *Attachment in Adulthood: Structure, Dynamics and Change.* New York: Guilford Press.

Novick, J. (1997). Termination conceivable and inconceivable. *Psychoanalytic Psychology, 14 (2),* 145–162.

Vasquez, M.J.T., Bingham, R.P. & Barnett, J.E. (2008). Psychotherapy termination: Clinical and ethical responsibilities. *Journal of Clinical Psychology: In Session, 64 (5),* 653–665 doi:10.1002/jclp

Young, J.E., Klosko, J.S. & Weishaar, M.E. (2003). *Schema Therapy: A Practitioner's Guide.* New York: Guilford Press.

Index